BRITISH INSURANCE

Monographs on
British Economic Institutions

A series edited by
PROFESSOR E. VICTOR MORGAN

BRITISH INSURANCE

G. CLAYTON

ELEK BOOKS
All Saints Street London N1

ISBN 0 236 17618 8

Published by
ELEK BOOKS LIMITED
2 All Saints Street London N1

Printed in Great Britain by
Clarke, Doble & Brendon Limited
Plymouth

TO

RHIANNON

CONTENTS

PREFACE

IN WRITING this book I have been fortunate enough to have been able to call upon a large number of people for assistance. First, and foremost, I must acknowledge my great debt to my two research assistants, Mr. Derek G. Davies, formerly of the University College of Wales, Aberystwyth, and Mr. Malcolm Tink, formerly of the University of Sheffield. Such has been the scale of their help that, had either one of them been with me throughout the whole period involved in this study, I would have considered it appropriate to list him as a joint author. But, owing to my move from the University College of Wales, Aberystwyth, to the University of Sheffield, Mr. Derek Davies, who was closely involved in writing Chapters 1 to 8, ceased to be associated with the study. Mr. Malcolm Tink, on the other hand, undertook a great deal of the preparatory work for Chapters 11 to 17. In the circumstances I decided with regret that it was inappropriate to designate them as joint authors since in both cases they could not be held responsible for large sections of the book. Secondly, I have been able to consult closely with Professor E. Victor Morgan, the General Editor of the series, who has made many valuable suggestions and comments on the preliminary drafts.

Thirdly, I have been most fortunate in being able to draw upon the expert knowledge of many members of the industry who have been most generous with their time and advice. I hope that they will not take it as a sign of base ingratitude that I have not always been able to accept their interpretation of events and their views on the performance of the industry. Among this group I would like to make specific mention of Mr. A. Duval, Actuary of the Co-operative Insurance Society, Limited, and Mr. R. T. D. Wilmot, Secretary of the British Insurance Association. I have attempted at various points in the text to stress that I would have been less critical of many aspects of the industry's current operations had I been writing the book at any time other than the present. It is an unfortunate, but inevitable, fact that the industry is passing through one of the most difficult periods in its long, and mainly successful, history. The consequence is that any commentator on the contemporary state of the industry would be less than honest if he failed to refer to some of its more obvious shortcomings.

Fourthly, I am indebted to others who have studied in this field and whose work has been so generously and readily made available to me. In particular mention must be made of Dr. R. L. Carter of the University of Nottingham, whose unpublished thesis on 'Competition in the British Fire and Accident Insurance Market' provided much useful material for the chapters on the contemporary state of the industry. I would also like to thank Mr. Alan Parker of *The Economist* and Mr. Cunningham of Cunningham & Black for help with some of the difficult technical points involved in comparing the performance of individual companies.

In preparing the book for publication I am greatly indebted to Miss Catherine Bugden, Mrs. Mary Jones and above all to my present secretary, Mrs. Margaret Uttley, for their work in typing the manuscript and assembling the many statistical tables. Also my publishers, and in particular Miss Moira Johnston, have shown commendable patience in coping with last minute alterations to the text.

Finally, I must acknowledge the great debt I owe to my wife who has shown great forbearance and understanding on the many occasions when I have manifestly neglected my family responsibilities during the course of this study.

In spite of all this assistance I remain responsible for any misstatements of fact or errors of judgement that remain.

Part I

THE FORMATIVE PERIOD: BEFORE 1800

Chapter 1

THE ORIGINS OF INSURANCE

'Primitive peoples discovered no need for insurance, finding their needs fully protected by the family or tribe in which mutuality such as is established by insurance is a living reality. This was not true of the ancient civilisations of Egypt, Phoenicia, Greece and Rome in which the individual found himself exposed to numerous risks without recourse against the family community.' (Robert de Smet, *Trait Théorétique et Pratique des Assurances Maritimes*)

THE ORIGINS of insurance[1] are shrouded in obscurity, of that, and only that, can we be sure, for historical scholarship of the highest order has failed to provide irrefutable evidence of origin. Nor is it our duty to enter into the legal niceties of this esoteric subject, first because it would take up far more space than we are permitted and, secondly, because it would leave all but the most devoted reader totally confused. In this introductory chapter we propose to side-step the technicalities and merely examine the more salient historical facts.

The story begins with the Babylonians and their unique civilisation which flourished some 3,000 years B.C., and refers specifically to their recently[2] discovered Code of Hammurabi. This code, inscribed on a block of black diorite, consists of some 282 clauses and was compiled, as the name suggests, by Hammurabi, King of Babylon about 2250 B.C. This code reveals that the Babylonians had been excellent businessmen with a very clear idea of the nature of a contract and the value of money as a means of earning more by loans on usury involving simple and compound interest. This can be easily demonstrated by reference to the ease with which these ancient people evolved and practised a commercial contract later to be used and known the whole world over as the 'contract of bottomry'.[3] So important was this contract that it is well worth considering in some detail.

Bottomry is, or rather was, a commercial contract whereby money (or goods) was advanced for trade purposes either as true loans at a certain fixed rate of interest under which the lender had no right to any share in the proceeds of the trading venture, or as mixed loans and partnerships which, in addition to the payment of a fixed rate of interest to the lender irrespective of the result of the trading, entitled him to receive a share of the profits, if such profits exceeded a certain sum. This was on the understanding that the borrower should, in consideration of a high rate of interest,[4] be freed from liability in the event of certain accidents happening, e.g. failure of goods to arrive at their intended destination. Should the goods arrive, however, the borrower would then be liable for repayment of the loan, *plus interest*.[5]

The Babylonians were, of course, the great land traders of the times, but they were not the *only* great traders, for they had in proximity to them the Phoenicians, famous far and wide for their maritime commerce. It was therefore natural that the Babylonians, in their ceaseless search for new markets, should not only come into contact with the Phoenicians but also co-operate closely with them; and it follows that the Phoenicians should notice, adopt and adapt the peculiar commercial contract of the Babylonians and provide posterity with an evocative name into the bargain.[6]

The next stage in the evolution of bottomry was the adoption of the contract by the Greeks as a result of Phoenician trade expansion in the Greek littoral during the 10th and 9th centuries B.C., and the increasing domination of Greek traders in the Aegean Sea after 800 B.C. But the contract, as in the case of the Phoenicians, was not merely adopted—it was also adapted, even perfected, to such an extent that a number of very notable 19th-century maritime lawyers have claimed that Greek contracts of bottomry, similar to the one quoted by Demosthenes in a speech against Lacritus, were so nearly identical in nature with those in vogue in London in 1860 that *mutatis mutandis* they could have been used at that date.

The final stage in the evolution of bottomry in ancient times was the adoption of the custom by the Romans *circa* 300 B.C., and it is with the Romans that we enter the crucial, and highly controversial, stage of the procedure; for some writers forcefully argue that it was here, in Rome, that the principles embodied in the bottomry bond were translated into insurance as we understand it today.

Before we go on to examine the most persuasive of these arguments we ought to remind ourselves of the basic elements of an insurance contract. As we have seen, the contract is defined as one by which one party (i.e. the insurer) in consideration of a premium, undertakes to indemnify another (i.e. the insured) against loss. But for such a contract of insurance to be valid certain conditions must be satisfied:

(i) there must exist a risk to be insured against;
(ii) the property must possess value;
(iii) there can be no possibility of profit;

(iv) a premium must be paid;
(v) in the case of non-mutual insurance, the insured cannot act as an insurer of the person or persons with whom he is insured.

Now Professor C. F. Trenerry argues that these necessary elements were to be found in arrangements effected during the late classical times.[7] In support of his argument he cites three separate sources. The earliest documented reference to marine insurance occurs in Livy (XXIII, 48 and 49) in which he describes a guarantee given by the government in 215 B.C.; under the terms of this guarantee the government undertook in return for a premium (in this particular case the premium consisted of goods and supplies necessary for the Roman Army in Spain and supplied by the 'publicani') to insure the safe arrival of certain other shipments of supplies, shipped by the private trading companies who were the owners of these supplies. This arrangement, argues Trenerry, possessed all the necessary conditions of a genuine insurance contract, i.e. there existed a risk, the property was of value, and a premium was paid.

The second contract was referred to in a letter written by Cicero to Caninius Sallust, about 50 B.C., in which the former requested the latter to guarantee a sum of money that was to be transported from Laodicea to Rome. This, too, says Trenerry, possessed all the elements of a genuine insurance contract because:

(i) there existed a property to be insured—in this case the 'pecunia publica' which obviously did not belong to the guarantors;
(ii) the risk to be incurred in transit—the 'victurae periculum';
(iii) the premium which was paid to render the contract valid.

Now, since Cicero was referring to a genuine contract of insurance, it follows, Trenerry argues, that the custom of the shipper entering into a contract with the guarantors for the safe delivery of his shipment was commonly practised and generally understood; for had it been otherwise it is more probable that Cicero would have explained to Caninius in far greater detail (for the letter is very short) the nature of his proposed mode of action.

The third reference is one by Suetonius in his life of the Emperor Claudius. According to Suetonius, there was a severe famine in Rome in A.D. 58 which gave rise to popular demonstrations against the Emperor. (In fact he was pelted with dry crusts in the middle of the Forum.) This 'desperate conduct'[8] was due to the fact that no one expected any more food to be imported during the winter season. Claudius, therefore, in order to persuade the importers to render a vital service to the State, not only offered to pay a fixed bounty on all they imported, but also accepted personal responsibility for all losses arising from storms.[9] This definite offer, argues Trenerry, 'would have formed a contract, which it is contended is equivalent to that of marine insurance in its most modern form and restricted sense. The essentials of insurance namely (*a*) ownership of insured property, (*b*) risk, and (*c*) premium, are all present.'[10]

These specific references have, of course, been the subject of debate for centuries, and it must be observed that Trenerry's interpretation has had its critics. Marshall, for instance, in his 'Law of Insurance', argues that 'these instances only serve to show that the contractors were to transport the stores purchased of them to the places of their destination at the risk of the Republic. They have scarcely a resemblance in any one particular to the contract of insurance. . . .'[11] However, Marshall goes on to argue that ancient maritime commerce never attained the degree of importance which rendered its protection necessary, an assertion to which few informed people would today subscribe. Sir J. A. Park argues that the Livy reference 'seems to bear no resemblance to the contract of insurance for it is nothing more than every well-regulated state is bound to do by the ties of natural justice. . . .'[12]

Modern authorities, it seems, favour neither Trenerry's nor Park's attitude, but take their stand midway between the two. Dover, for example, argues that '. . . it is reasonable to suggest that a community which evolved so equitable a system as the Rhodian Law of General Average would have appreciated the benefits of a system of protecting merchants against fortuitous loss by marine perils, and the same contention may be advanced with equal force in support of the possible practice of marine insurance by the trading section of the Roman Empire. It is known that Rome was not unwilling to adapt to its own needs systems of law and of commercial practice the efficacy of which had been demonstrated by earlier civilisations.'[13]

Modern opinion is perhaps best summed up by Blackstock when he says 'the contract of insurance is a derivative of expedients that in one form or another have subserved in primitive fashion the purpose of insurance from ancient times. The doubtful question of the use of insurance in the transactions of antiquity has been the issue of prolonged classical and judicial controversy in which the authorities are sharply divided. There is, however, a general concurrence in the view that if the existence of insurance in the modern sense in the ancient world is doubtful and debatable, there is good and substantial evidence of the use of other forms of contract that in their essence and content resemble insurance, e.g. maritime loans. . . . Hendricks observed that the contract of nautical interest, or loan or bottomry or respondentia, was used from the very remote ages by the Greeks, Romans and other nations as their ordinary insurance contract, which end it perfectly answered: and that it eventually formed the tradition and groundwork on which rose the superstructure of the insurance system of modern Europe.'[14]

Life Assurance

Trenerry also argues that the Romans were cognisant of, and indeed practised, a form of non-mutual life assurance. Now the earliest extant life policy, as we shall see more fully in a subsequent chapter, is one dated 18 June 1583, so that Trenerry is unable to produce conclusive documentary evidence in support of his claim. However, it must be borne in mind that the type of contract Trenerry postulates is not the permanent contract at a level annual premium based upon the age at entry, requiring mortality statistics and sophisticated mathematical techniques, but rather a simple short-term contract covering the life of, for instance, a wealthy merchant intending to make a hazardous journey. For this type of contract, Trenerry argues, the Romans were fully equipped.

In the first place there is written evidence of the awareness of the problems of longevity and mortality. Indeed, such written evidence can be traced back to biblical times,[15] and subsequent ancient documents often alluded to the average life span of mankind. In Roman times, the observations on the Census of Vespasian by Pliny (A.D. 80) were particularly pertinent. Indeed, this interest in the facts of longevity and mortality is one which almost pervades Roman literature.

Then there is the knowledge of mathematics and finance, undoubtedly possessed by the Romans, which would have certainly been sufficient, Trenerry argues, for the sort of calculation required. For the Romans were, after all, well versed in arithmetic. For example, in A.D. 100, Nicomachus published a treatise on arithmetic which was followed in A.D. 300 by the Algebra of Diophantus. So highly regarded were these two works and so advanced were they, that they continued to retain their position as the standard works on the subject until the 13th and 16th centuries respectively. In addition, the Romans had the abacus, with the help of which they were able to work out quite intricate arithmetical calculations.

But this is not all, Trenerry argues. In addition to the aforementioned, the Romans also possessed a table of annuity values based upon actual mortality experience. This table, known as Ulpian's Table, was in constant use. In fact it continued to be used as the official annuity table in Northern Italy until the end of the 18th century.

Moreover, the Romans also possessed the knowledge and experience of several financial devices:

(i) interest, simple and compound, including discount and present values;
(ii) banking—current and deposit accounts, loans, securities, bills of exchange, repayments by instalments, foreign exchanges, etc.;
(iii) book-keeping.

In effect, then, this meant that the Romans were as well qualified to carry out life assurance business as were the Europeans of the 16th century. First, they possessed a sound financial and commercial infrastructure. Secondly, there is nothing in the early history of mathematics to suggest that the theory of probabilities was any better known in the 17th century than it was in the 1st. Thirdly, it is certain that they understood the concept of longevity and that they were in possession of a table of annuities based upon mortality experience. Therefore, despite the fact that the Romans cannot possibly have possessed the scientific knowledge of the modern actuary, they were certainly in a position to make *rough* calculations of the value of the risk incurred. That they *did* allow for such risks is conclusively proved by the numerous references to the excess, in the legal rate of interest on contracts of bottomry, over that of ordinary loans *precisely because of the risk involved*. That they did use this knowledge of risk in the field of life assurance is also conclusively proved by numerous references to such contracts in the literature of the times.[16]

Trenerry's argument is indeed persuasive, but one should not get swept away by its formidable logic. In the first place, documentary evidence is completely lacking; his conclusions are based almost entirely upon logical inferences, and the authorities he quotes are open to alternative interpretation. Moreover, the argument that the excess in the legal rate of interest on contracts of bottomry over that on ordinary loans arose because there was a risk involved, cannot be applied to life assurance problems, for marine risks are very different from those involving the probable mortality experience of different individuals.

Nevertheless, we should be equally wrong to conclude that non-mutual life assurance was unknown to the Romans. After all, it *was* known in 16th-century Britain at a time when, as Trenerry rightly points out, the theory of probability was no better understood than it had been in the 1st century. We can only conclude, rather lamely, in the absence of documentary evidence, that non-mutual assurance in Roman times was feasible.

Mutual Assurance in Roman Times

We now move from a possibility to a certainty, for when we tread the ground of mutual life assurance we can be sure of a firm foundation.

Mutual life assurance was, without doubt, the direct descendant of the ancient burial society.

The burial society, it seems, was a product of ancient Greece, but in its original form it fulfilled few, if any, of the functions one would normally associate with a burial society. The early Greek societies were in fact formed in order to worship a divinity; any funeral benefits that might accrue were peripheral—incidental to the main theme—and in the early days of the Republic they retained their essentially religious character. Roman burial clubs and societies were formed by persons, who, being either foreigners, freedmen, slaves or people expelled from their family, did not belong to any recognised 'gens'; they had the object of carrying on the worship of a particular divinity in honour of whom festivals were held, to whom sacrifices were made and for whom, in many cases, a temple or shrine was built and supported by the society.

Expenses for these functions were met by what came to be monthly subscriptions. But it was gradually appreciated that worship of the divinity necessitated the possession of a common burial place for the members of the society and that each member should receive the funeral rites prescribed in such worship. Consequently, the attention of the society was turned to the provision of such a burial ground and the funds of the society began to be shared between the two objects.

Subsequently, as the Romans drifted away from the religious beliefs of early days and became more or less indifferent to the performance of rites, these societies became pure burial societies. *Pari passu*, there was a widening of benefits to include the payment of a sum of money[17] to the relations of the deceased, instead of providing the deceased with a funeral. By the 4th century A.D., the great majority of societies made payment in this way. A refinement of this principle occurred when a number of societies began to vary the contribution, and hence the benefit, according to the individual members' means and desires for benefits. Clearly, at this stage, the very basis of modern mutual life assurance was emerging.

Medieval Developments in Insurance

When history comes to be written it is seldom, if ever, possible to write that history without recourse to arbitrary divisions according to vague, unsatisfactory chronological criteria. This is particularly true of that period of history unceremoniously sandwiched between the fall of the Roman Empire and the re-birth of classical antiquity known to posterity as the Renaissance. The Dark Ages it has been called—an unfortunate title implying a period of stagnation. Yet nothing, surely, could be more misleading,[18] not least when we consider the developments that took place in the evolution of insurance. For while it may be true that few new qualitative developments took place in marine insurance,[19] in mutual insurance, important, if tentative, strides were taken and new ground was undoubtedly covered.

These new developments centred on the gilds, those typically medieval institutions about which so much has been written but about which so little has been said. This is hardly surprising since the *origin* of the gilds in particular is peculiarly difficult to trace. Yet, despite the controversy, one thing is certain—that although there is an obvious discontinuity between the 'collegia' of the Roman Empire and the latter-day Anglo-Saxon gilds, and although there were obvious differences in their functions, in one fundamental respect they were identical, i.e. in their very *raison d'être*, for both owed their existence to the natural manifestation of the associative spirit inherent in mankind.

The earliest English gilds, as Walford,[20] the first chronicler of the English gilds, has pointed out, arose out of the family ideal; as indeed they did in the Low Countries and in Germany. As the primitive ideal of the family faded and its economic functions grew weaker, so the gild arose to fill a widely felt need. This was, in essence, the need for social security, and as Walford remarks 'they seem (i.e. the gilds) on the whole to have been Friendly Associations made for mutual aid and contribution to the pecuniary exigencies which were perpetually arising from burials, legal enactions, penal mulcts, and other payments and compensations'.[21] Note that burials head the list of pecuniary exigencies. This is important because, despite the fact that some of the earliest Anglo-Saxon gilds were religious in character, some were decidedly secular.[22] Yet it seems that all gilds had as one of their prior aims the proper burial of their members.

Yet this was not their only function. The first gilds of which we have any record, the 8th-century gilds of Flanders, had as their object the mutual insurance of their members against all sorts of risks, including loss of property through robbery.[23] The first English gilds of which we have any knowledge, the gilds of Cnihts, offered mutual aid for recovering stolen cattle and this was, as Walford remarked, 'very much in the nature of an insurance Association'.[24] Yet proper burial of dead, with its concomitant panoply of pomp and splendour, formed the cornerstone of these and later gilds and fraternities, as can be seen from the ordinances of the Fraternities of Cambridge, Abbotsbury and Exeter: 11th-century Fraternities whose ordinances are perhaps the oldest known in Europe. With reference to the Exeter gild, for instance, Brentano states that 'when any brother died every member was obliged to perform special devotions for the departed soul. The mutual care of the gild brothers was, moreover, shown by money contributions in the case of death.'[25]

This principle of mutual insurances carried forward and became, likewise, an integral feature of both merchant and craft gilds. It even survived the destruction of the gilds and came to reside instead in the 'box clubs' and Friendly Societies of the 17th and 18th centuries. 'In the Middle Ages the craftsmen's gild took care of the dependants and provided for the burial of their members; and when the gilds gradually passed out of existence or were abolished by sovereign command, other agencies sprang into existence which substantially fulfilled some of the essential functions of the former gilds. One of these was proper burial of the dead.'[26]

NOTES

1 An insurance contract may be defined as a contract by which one party (i.e. the insurer) in consideration of the premium, undertakes to indemnify another (i.e. the insured) against loss. Smith's *Mercantile Law*, 13th edition, edited by H. C. Gutteridge (1931), p. 406. For a more comprehensive definition see Steven's *Mercantile Law*, 13th edition, edited by J. Montgomerie (1960), pp. 318–320.

2 1902.

3 A Flemish term derived from the figurative use of the bottom or keel of a ship to express the whole ship.

4 Usually 100 per cent.

5 It must be borne in mind that the actual expression 'bottomry' refers only to marine contracts. However, the principle as evolved by the Babylonians and applied to land trading is, in other respects, identical, save for a few minor modifications.

6 This probably occurred during the great Phoenician expansion about 1600 B.C.

7 C. F. Trenerry, *The Origins and Early History of Insurance* (1926), pp. 107–124.

8 Trenerry, ibid., p. 119.

9 Suetonius: *De vita Caesarum*, v. 18: 'Nam et negotiatoribus certa lucra proposuit. suscepto in se damno, si cui quid per tempestates accidisset.'

10 Trenerry, ibid., p. 119.

11 Marshall, *Law of Insurance* (1802), I. i., p. 7.

12 J. A. Park, *System of the Law of Marine Insurance* (1842), p. lix.

13 V. Dover, *A Handbook to Marine Insurance*, 6th ed., 1962, p. 6.

14 Quoted by Dover, ibid., p. 7.

15 There are numerous references in the Old Testament to the average life span of 'three score years and ten', for instance.

16 Gaius, *Roman Civil Law* (A.D. 150) and the *Institutes* of Justinian (A.D. 533) are only two examples.

17 Known as the 'funeraticum'.

18 See Pirenne, H., *The Economic and Social History of Medieval Europe*.

19 The lack of progress in marine insurance, Trenerry argues, was a strict consequence of the degree of perfection already reached by the Romans in this branch of insurance. Be that as it may, it would be wrong to infer that no quantitative developments took place. It is possible that marine insurance

spread from Rome to other Italian cities, particularly Venice, Genoa and Pisa; for it is notable that during the period from the 7th century to the 11th century when the Western Mediterranean was completely bottled up by the Moslems, trade between these cities and the Eastern Empire flourished and expanded.

20 Cornelius Walford, *Guilds* (1888).

21 Walford, ibid., p. 5.

22 It must be borne in mind that these are *not* craft gilds to which we are referring. Craft gilds came later—in the 11th century.

23 These, the earliest of all known gilds, were first referred to in the Carolingian capitularies of 779 and 789.

24 Walford, ibid., p. 9.

25 L. Brentano, *History and Development of Gilds and the Origin of Trade Unions* (1870), pp. 1–2.

26 E. A. Woods, *The Sociology of Life Insurance* (1928), p. 99.

Chapter 2

THE EARLY DEVELOPMENT OF MARINE INSURANCE

> 'With regard to your saying that the ship had reached Barcelona safely you were no prophet, and if some harm had come to her you would have regretted sending without insurance. For you have your orders never to send any merchandise of ours without insurance, and let this be said to you once and for all.'
> (An extract from a letter written by Francesco di Marco Datini, a merchant of Prato, a town a few miles north of Florence, to one of his many agents, *circa* 1395)

IN THE first chapter we saw that an embryonic form of marine insurance originated in Rome and continued to be practised there, despite Moslem attempts to strangle trade in the Mediterranean throughout the early Middle Ages. It is the purpose of this chapter to continue the story. We must now see through what channels the marine insurance principle became a widespread practice, and what form early marine insurance contracts took.

This is not an easy task, for the place of origin of the earliest contract of marine insurance is still a matter of much debate. However, the present writer favours the argument that the principle of marine insurance was conceived and born in Italy (i.e. Rome) and that here, too, it attained its adolescence. Medieval marine insurance was both son and daughter of the Italian city states.

The argument is, after all, quite persuasive. First, we have an obvious geographical connection between the classical quasi-insurance of Roman times and the medieval insurance of the Italian city states. Secondly, the uninterrupted commercial history of the Italian states (they were almost entirely free from the inhibiting forces of the Moslem empire) gave rise to a tradition that was to cause the Italian cities to attain commercial preeminence in the early years of the 14th century. Thirdly, we have the very fact of this commercial supremacy itself to invoke. After all, Rome was the hub of the wheel of Christendom and in this capacity drew papal taxes and dues from throughout Western Europe. This system, as we shall see more fully later, involved a complex organisation of papal agents and Italian financiers both outside and within Italy. There was thus in existence a commercial infrastructure which could be, and in fact was, fully utilised. But this involved the use of certain essential commercial practices—and marine insurance certainly ranked amongst the most essential. It was simply impossible to ship valuable merchandise from England and elsewhere to Italy without such a system of insurance. Finally, it must be remembered that the earliest extant policies are *written in Italian* and that Italian policies became the model upon which others, notably Lloyd's as we shall see later, were developed. Therefore, in the absence of persuasive evidence to the contrary, it is contended that the Italian city states fostered the development of marine insurance.

The first trace of marine insurance in Italy dates from the early 14th century. Pegalotti, for instance, in a treatise dated 1350 refers to the insurance contract as a 'rischio de mere e di genti', while in an earlier work he says that Florentine bills on England contained one or other of the phrases 'rendu sauf en terre' or 'en aventure de mer et des gens',[1] and the excess charge made when the first phrase was substituted for the second represented in effect a premium for insurance. But the whole issue of early contracts is a difficult one, and is complicated by the usury laws of the time.

Usurious practice was not merely a moral crime contravening the laws of the church—it was also a civil crime. This double element is clearly illustrated in a letter written by Luca del Sera to Francesco Datini in January 1394. 'I think you have already heard from our men in Genoa that the King has brought the usurers to trial, and has had leave from the Pope to do so. They consider those who sell with deferred payment to be usurers, and they intend to follow this rule, they will ruin the city.'[2] But whilst it was illegal to charge interest, it was not illegal to share in the projects of a venture financed by a loan, providing the venture involved a certain degree of risk. Therefore, because the incorporation of a premium in an insurance policy was redolent of usury, the policies were disguised in many different forms, amongst which the bottomry bond was very popular. It was very often quite impossible to separate the loan element from the premium. It was not until the last quarter of the 14th century, during a period of relative relaxation in the State's attitude to usury, that a separate contract of marine insurance came into widespread use. Bensa,[3] for instance, quotes the case of a notary of Genoa who, in the year 1393, drew up not less than eighty contracts of insurance. But it was in Florence, rather than Genoa, that most progress was being made, as the documents left by a merchant of the times show us.

This merchant, Francesco di Marco Datini, was a remarkable man[4] and his life's work, too, was remarkable. Francesco was born in Tuscany about 1335; at the age of 15 he travelled to Avignon where he embarked upon what was to be a brilliant commercial career. But later in life, not satisfied with his success at Avignon he moved to Prato, a town a few miles north of Florence. Here his business interests widened and intensified and he became in turn merchant, financier and underwriter. In 1365, he ordered his agents to preserve all correspondence and documents, and himself did the same. The result was a unique collection of correspondence, account books, ledgers, etc., which has provided posterity with a remarkable account of commerce at the time; for amongst the collection were over 500 bills of exchange and some 400 insurance policies. The very fact that there were so many insurance policies clearly reflects the extent to which insurance was practised but it is also significant, as the opening quotation shows, that the habit had not bitten deeply enough. Further selections from Francesco's correspondence reveal this. In a letter to his wife in 1395 for instance, he says:

'I dreamed last night of a house which had fallen to pieces and all my household were inside it. . . . And the meaning of this dream gives me much to ponder on, for there are no tidings of a galley that left Venice more than two months ago bound for Catalonia, and I had insured it for three hundred (300) florins, as I did the other ship for Domenica and Cambia which perished the next day. . . . I am so vexed by many matters it is a wonder I am not out of my mind, for the more I seek, the less I find. And God knows what will befall me.'[5]

But why should Francesco have been 'out of his mind' when his goods were insured? He provides the answer himself in another letter to his wife in which he tells her of a galley containing goods worth 3,000 florins sailing from Venice to Catalonia. If it goes down, he says, he will lose 500 florins 'for when they insure it is sweet to them to take the monies; but when disaster comes it is otherwise and each man draws his rump back and strives not to pay'.[6]

In short, underwriters were not always prepared to meet their contractual obligations. Sometimes they merely stalled for a period, at other times they repaid only part of the sum, and occasionally they defaulted. But why? First, risks were exceptionally heavy and innumerable contingencies had to be accounted for. In a policy dated 1385 and drawn up in the form then customary in Florence and Pisa, these risks are enumerated: 'from Act of God, of the sea, of man, of fire, of jettison, of confiscation by princes or cities or any other person, of reprisal, mishap, or any other impediment';[7] and in another drawn in Florence in 1397 similar perils are mentioned: 'of God, the sea, of nations, fire, jettisons, restraint by lords or peoples or any other person, of lettres of marque, of arrest, and of every other case, peril, chance, impediment which in any way could occur, excepted only what concerns custom dues and ballast'.[8]

Quite clearly, these conditions were virtually all-embracing but it is important to note that loss caused by piracy was included. Piracy was perhaps the most important single source of loss. Yet premiums could have been sufficiently high to take account of this.

Here, in fact, we have the second, and more important, reason for underwriter's defaults. The lack of statistical knowledge meant that premiums were only very roughly calculated and as a result were often set too low. Francesco Datini, himself, was guilty of this mistake. In one of his account books[9] is preserved many of his insurance transactions. The cover reads: 'This is the Book of Francesco of Prato and his partners, living in Pisa, and we shall write in it all insurances we make on behalf of others. May God grant us profit and protect us from dangers.' The goods insured included wool from Catalonia and Minorca, to Porto Pisano and Tunis, Palermo and Naples; silk and fustian from Porto Pisano to Barcelona, and malmsey to Sluy and Southampton. The premiums varied from $3\frac{1}{2}$ to 5 per cent except for malmsey which was 8 per cent! Yet according to Giovanni da Uzzano, premiums of 12 and 15 per cent were usual. Little wonder that Francesco was a light sleeper!

It should be fairly clear from the foregoing, then, that though marine insurance was practised in northern Italy, and though a large variety of risks were insurable, the insurance habit was not ingrained and the system was by no means perfect. Many merchants were still prepared to risk their merchandise at sea without insurance cover and many more merchants were not prepared to insure the full value of their merchandise. Moreover, often through lack of knowledge, premiums were not set sufficiently high and this resulted in failure to meet part or all of some claims, whilst some underwriters were not averse to deliberate fraud. Nevertheless, despite these obvious imperfections, the progress made by the merchants of northern Italy was remarkable. The next task is to examine the channels through which the Italian's knowledge of marine insurance was disseminated, and the effect of this dissemination upon the development of the insurance contract itself.

We have already referred to the networks of papal and Florentine and other city agents that were spread throughout Europe. The papal agent's function was the *collection* of papal taxes and dues. It was the function of the Florentine agents to help *remit* those taxes by arranging carriage or shipment of the merchandise that was almost always offered in payment of those taxes and dues. England's main form of payment, for instance, was wool. Thus, the Florentine agent would ensure that the wool reached the port, that it was the correct quality, quantity, etc., and that it was properly stowed and insured. The last point was rarely difficult because the agent was usually the underwriter. The wool would then be shipped to Florence where it would be made into fine cloth; and from the sale of the cloth the taxes and dues would be paid. This was a common procedure.

It follows, therefore, that there was already in existence an established widespread commercial network. It was this network that facilitated the dissemination of marine insurance. Raynes has put it this way: 'Already there was a general body of business practice among merchants in connection with their trading with one another. Custom and use brought these commercial practices into some measure of uniformity, and insurance in its practices was no exception to that tendency to uniformity which marked the custom of merchants—their relations with one another on such matters as charter parties, bills of lading and bills of exchange.'[10] The first countries to benefit from this tendency towards uniformity in commercial practices were the Low Countries, Spain and England.

Bruges, as an important centre of the wool trade, must certainly have been one of the earliest cities to practise marine insurance. Indeed, some writers[11] argue that a Chamber of Insurance was established there as early as 1310, and in support of their argument cite a statement from the 'Chronyke van Vlanderm' which says: 'At the request of the inhabitants of Bruges, in the year 1310, he (Count Robert of Flanders) sanctioned the establishment in this town of a Chamber of Insurance wherein merchants might be able to insure their merchandise against risks, marine or otherwise, at a cost of a few deniers per cent, as is the practice today.'[12] However, other writers refute the statement[13] on the grounds that it is uncorroborated by other contemporary writers and not made until 400 years after the alleged event. Certainly no evidence has come to light, up to the present time, which would support the statement. The earliest piece of authentic evidence resides in a judgement given by the College of Echevins, recorded in the Ouden Wittenbouc and dated 12 April 1377. This entry in the city records sets out the judgement given by the échevins on an action brought by the insured under a charter ('van zecggerscepe') to recover the value of certain parcels of silk and stuffs, ('Van diverse parcele van ziden, van flourschen gaerne ende van witten ende blaewen lynwade')[14] which had been lost and were covered by the policy referred to. Under the judgement the insurer was forced to pay the insured an indemnity for the loss of the articles. Trenerry argues that because there was a marked absence of explanatory phrases accompanying the judgement, the practice of insurance must have been already well understood by all parties. In short, marine insurance must have been a practice of some standing. All this is highly conjectural but it is quite clear that Bruges was *one* of the first centres of marine insurance. In the 15th century it was similarly to become one of the most important centres.

There seems little doubt that as soon as insurance became a practice in northern Italy and Bruges, it also became a practice in Spain, so close were the trade connections between Barcelona, Pisa and Florence. It would be superfluous at this point to draw attention, therefore, to early Spanish policies. Suffice to say that Spain deserves special mention rather because Barcelona was the first city to attempt to regulate the practice of marine insurance by ordinance. The basic object of the ordinance of 1453, as Raynes points out, was to 'prevent fraudulent abuses and to give a preference in treatment to their (i.e. Barcelonian) own ship owners'.[15]

When we come home to England it is, once more, difficult to be precise about the earliest marine insurance contracts. Insurance, it seems, came to England later than to either Spain or Belgium, for in commerce the London merchants lagged seriously behind their Continental counterparts, both in the volume of trade conducted and in mercantile practices. It is not until the 16th century that we find records of insurances being made by them. That is not to say that no insurance was conducted in England before the 16th century. It was, but by Lombard rather than English merchants. The Lombards had come early to England and soon established strong commercial roots, but they were forced to share common ground with the Jews for many years. However, after the expulsion of the Jews from England by Edward I in 1290, the Lombards were left in sole possession of the field of finance for at least fifty years, and it was not until financial difficulties beset such great houses of Florence as Bardi in 1345[16] that their influence began to wane (even so they were still an important element as late as the mid-16th century). Thereafter, English merchants began to assert their position, yet they still had to fight the privileges enjoyed by the Flemish and Hanse merchants; old privileges which dated back to Ethelred II. It was not until the final withdrawal of the 'valiant steelyard'[17] merchant's privileges by Cecil and Gresham in 1578, that the English merchant could call his home his own. Yet if he could now call his home more or less his own, the same could not be said of his currency: when the Lombards left they gave their name to one of London's oldest and most famous streets; when the Easterlings[18] left, it was the coin of the realm that continued to remind us all of their once much-needed but much-envied presence.

But the Italian merchants and financiers left more than the name of a London street. They also left behind a strong deeply-rooted commercial tradition, of which insurance formed an integral part. Witness the fact that the word insurance or, as it was formerly called, assurance, is of Italian origin and so too is the word policy, derived from the word 'polizza', a promise. If the Lombard contribution to the development of marine insurance in England is immeasurable, it seems also to be almost infinitely durable, as the following sentence from a present-day Lloyd's policy shows: 'And it is agreed by us, the Insurers, that this Writing or Policy of Assurance shall be of as much Force and Effect as the surest Writing made in Lombard Street or in the Royal Exchange or elsewhere in London.'

Although, as we have seen, the date of the origin of the English contract is almost impossible to ascertain, the preamble to the famous Elizabethan Act of 1601 proclaims insurance to have been 'tyme out of mynde an usage amongste the merchantes, both of this realme and of Forraine nacyons'. Of 'forraine nacyons' we have already heard. What, then, of 'this realme'? When Frederick Martin wrote his famous history of Lloyd's, the earliest known policy was one dated 15 February 1613.[19] But the diligent research of R. G. Marsden has revealed policies of a much earlier date. His source—the records of the Court of Admiralty[20]—is one which can be traced back to the year 1524, and it is from the records of these cases that our earliest knowledge of insurance in this country is derived. The earliest policy on the Admiralty files is one dated 20 September 1547,[21] and though the bulk of the policy is written in Italian, there is attached a contemporary English translation which runs. 'John Broke causeth himself to be assured from Cadiz into this town (London) upon Malvaises in the Island of Candia in the ship called the *Santa Maria* of Venice of which the captain is Francis Fidely, the adventure beginneth from the day and hour that the said ship with the said Malvaises set sail to the port of Cadiz and that it may dure until the time that they be discharged or unladen in this city of London, on land at good safety: as to the adventure that the assurers shall stand at it is to be understood that this present writing hath as much force as the best mode or dicted bill of surance which is used to be made in this Lombard Street of London.' Then there follows the contributions of the underwriters:

'I William Maynard Mercer am content to assure upon the good ship in manner and form above written for twenty-five pounds: written this twenty-second day of September 1547.'

'I Thomas Lodge am content to assure upon this good ship the sum of twenty-five sterling the twenty-second day of September 1547. I say £25.'[22]

A second policy on the files covers a cargo of English cloth. It runs: 'In the name of God, Amen. The twenty-sixth day of November 1548. Tomaso Cavolcanti and Giovanni Girale and Company of London make themselves to be assured by the order and account of Paule Ciceny of Messina upon the ship called the *Santa Maria* of Porto Salvo, captain Matutyno de Maryny upon a hundred pieces of carseys and fryseys to be laden in Hampton until they be arrived in Messina and discharged on land in good safety and the assurers to be content that this writing be of as much force and strength as the best that ever was made or might be made in the Lombard Street according to the order and custom whereof everyone that assureth as they that cause themselves to be assured, are content to be bound: and God send the good ship in safety.' Once again came the underwriters' subscriptions of which there are this time nine. Maynard is again amongst them.

An essentially similar though rather longer policy was one dated 22 November 1563, which concluded: 'Be it further understood that merchants which hereunder have written do by this present warrant and assure the aforesaid fruit raisins and merchandise and every other part and parcel of the same during the time and times aforesaid from the danger of the sea (etc.) . . . and if any mischance do happen to the said fruit raisins or merchandise . . . in a manner and form as in like case is accustomed to be done by the Course called Lombard Street in London and further they are content that this bill to all intents be taken to be as much force and effect is in like case is the best bill which as touching assurance is accustomed to be done in this Course called Lombard Street in London aforesaid. And as God will so be it.'[23]

Thus, from these and the many other contracts that have been preserved amongst the Admiralty files, a very clear picture of the state of marine insurance in London in the 16th century can be built up. For instance, one is immediately struck by the pre-eminence and customary force of Lombard Street itself. In the three policies we have seen pointed reference to the custom, tradition and binding force of insurance underwriting in that street. This is important, for the development of insurance underwriting depended upon mutual confidence in underwriters in the same way that joint stock banking in the 19th century depended upon mutual confidence in the note issue. That this confidence existed and continued to exist is plainly evidenced by further reference to the form of the present day Lloyd's policy, one clause of which, as we have already seen, reads: 'And it is agreed by us, the Insurers, that this Writing or Policy of Assurance, shall be of as much Force and Effect as the surest Writing or Policy of Assurance heretofore made in Lombard Street, or in the Royal Exchange, or elsewhere in London.'

Because this sense of custom did so strongly exist, it follows that policies were really very short. Conventions had been established and merchants and underwriters were morally bound by those conventions. Hence the brevity of the policy.

In addition, although one may regard Lombard Street as the centre of the insurance market, it would be incorrect to impute from this any degree of uniformity or organisation in that market. On the contrary, marine insurance in the 16th century is notably characterised by a complete absence of corporate character. There was no body of men specialising solely in insurance underwriting and occupying the same premises, as was later to be the case at Lloyd's, for instance. The great bulk of underwriters were themselves merchants—division of labour had not yet reached its logical conclusion. Furthermore, as it was the custom of shipowners of the time never to own one single ship but rather to own small fractions of many ships,[24] so too was it the custom of merchants to underwrite not one large cargo but rather many smaller cargoes. £25 was a normal undertaking and amounts less than £25 were not unusual. Few merchants or financiers were prepared to underwrite to an extent exceeding £100.

Defoe was quick to recognise this fundamental weakness 'for I believe anyone will grant me this; it is not the smallness of the premiums (that) ruins the insurer but it is the smallness of the quantity he insures'.[25] In other words, the underwriters of the time were carrying on their business with insufficient capital; their operations were casual and often extremely speculative. The business called for organisation on a larger scale, for adequate information and for greater technical precision in the estimation of risks and the fixing of premiums, so that insurer and insured might both be more fully protected. Many of these requirements were completely lacking in the 16th century, and it was not until the formation of Lloyd's that they began to appear.

But signs of an increasing awareness of the need for improved organisation in the insurance market were beginning to emerge towards the end of the 16th century, not the least important of which was the establishment, first of the Royal Exchange in 1570, and then the Office or Chamber of Assurances in 1576. The Royal Exchange was the result of the work of Sir Thomas Gresham, who, following a proposal initially put forward by his father, Sir John Gresham, suggested that a bourse very similar to the famous one in Antwerp be erected in London. The result was the erection of a building on Cornhill which was opened by Queen Elizabeth on 23 July 1570 and henceforth known as the Royal Exchange. Here, merchants who had previously met twice daily in the open air of Lombard Street, were able to congregate to discuss their business. This important development undoubtedly constituted the first step on the road towards an organised uniformity in marine insurance business.

The second step was the establishment of the Chamber of Assurances within the Royal Exchange in the year 1576. It had long been felt by the Privy Council, for they took an interest, not unnaturally, in all mercantile affairs, that certain malpractices were prevalent to the obvious detriment of the insurance market generally. Notable amongst these was the practice of double or over-insurance, so that in the event of loss or damage profit would accrue. The preamble to the patent that was eventually granted put it this way: '. . . the trade of merchandise have been and yet be often times greatly abused by evil disposed people who for their private gain and advantage have assured one thing in sundry places thereby intending any loss should happen, to recover in all said places, and so often times have done to the great loss and hindrance of divers such honest merchants as did assure the same.' The establishment of an office at the Chamber of Assurances in which all policies would have to be registered, it was felt, would eradicate these malpractices.

A patent, a part of the preamble of which we have already quoted, was duly granted to one Richard Candler on 21 February 1575, and in addition commissioners were appointed under the nomination of the Lord Mayor to settle fees and disputes which might arise from time to time. Perhaps not surprisingly, the former task proved more difficult than the latter, but despite fervent opposition from notaries and brokers of the City, Candler's patent stood firm. The results of the establishment of the Chamber of Assurances were two-fold. In the first place, the burden placed upon the Admiralty Court was significantly reduced, and more importantly, as a result of the policies being drawn in one office, there was a marked tendency towards standardisation of the form of the policy itself. This was an important consequence.

A third step on the road towards organised uniformity was taken in 1601 with the enactment of the 'Act touching Policies Assurances used among merchants',[26] the very first piece of English legislation concerned with marine insurance. This statute established a court 'for the hearinge and determynynge of causes arisinge from pollicies of assurance'. The court consisted of fourteen commissioners, six of them professional lawyers, i.e. 'the judge of the Admiraltie for the time beinge, the Recorder of London for the time beinge, two Doctors of Civial Lawe, and two common Lawyers', and eight other commissioners who should be 'grave and discrete merchantes'. It was intended that a court should meet once a week. Unfortunately, the new court found no favour with the mercantile community for whose benefit it was established and, after existing nominally for a generation or two, fell into complete disuse. Nevertheless, the Act of 1601 in retrospect was important, not for the work it accomplished, but rather for what it represented: the first legislative attempt to regulate the practice of marine insurance. This Act was to set a precedent and for that it deserves to be remembered.

NOTES

1 'Pratica della Mercatura' (1335–1343). Quoted by E. Bensa, *Il Contratto di Assicurazione*, p. 9.
2 Quoted by Iris Origo, *The Merchant of Prato*, p. 154.
3 Quoted by W. Mitchell, *The Early History of the Law Merchant*, p. 151.
4 For an account of the man and his times see Iris Origo's fascinating study, ibid.
5 Quoted by Iris Origo, ibid., p. 137.
6 I. Origo, ibid., p. 139.
7 I. Origo, ibid., pp. 139–140.
8 Quoted by W. Mitchell, *The Early History of Law Merchant*, p. 150.
9 Dated 1384.
10 H. E. Raynes, *A History of British Insurance*, 1st edition (1948), p. 10.
11 Notably C. F. Trenerry, ibid., pp. 265–269.
12 Quoted by Trenerry, ibid., p. 265.
13 Notably Pardessus, *Lois Maritimes*, Vol. 1, p. 356.
14 Quoted by Trenerry, ibid., p. 264.
15 Raynes, ibid., p. 10.
16 The financial collapse of the Florentine banks in that year was the direct result of Edward III's repudiation of his debts to those banks.
17 F. Martin, *A History of Lloyd's*, p. 10.
18 From 'Easterlings' as the Hanse merchants of the Baltic were known, came, of course, our term sterling. See H. A. L. Fisher, *A History of Europe*, Vol. I (Fontana edition, pp. 270–272).
19 The Tanner manuscript collection No. 74, 32, Bodleian Library, Oxford.
20 The Admiralty Court dates from about the middle of the 14th century, when two Admirals of the King's ships were given judicial functions to deal with maritime cases which could not be settled in Common Law Courts, and in 1540 Henry VIII extended the powers of the Admiralty Court so they could try matters concerning freight, cargo, etc. It is from this date that a great increase in business took place.
21 R. G. Marsden, *Select Pleas in the Court of Admiralty*, 1547–1602, Selden Society Publications, Vol. II, pp. 47–49.
22 Marsden, ibid., Vol. II, pp. 47–49.
23 Marsden, ibid., p. 53.
24 See Violet Barbour, Marine risks and insurance in the 17th century, *Journal of Economic and Business History*, Vol. I, 1928–29. She cites the example of one Sir Henry Johnson of Stepney who owned shares in thirty-eight ships, the largest fraction being 18/32nd and the smallest 1/56th. In all he possessed 96/32nd and 1/56th of ships, his total investment of this kind amounting to £18,488 8s. 6d. This desire for risk-spreading was common in other countries at the time.
25 Daniel Defoe, *Essay on Projects*, p. 163.
26 43 Eliz., C.12.

Chapter 3

THE BIRTH OF FIRE INSURANCE

'Class one for private dwelling house
For household goods and shops allows;
Provided these are built of brick
Or stone, and tiled and slated thick.

'Thatched dwellings and their whole contents,
We deal with—also with their rent,
Oh, glorious Phoenix look and see
These are dealt with in class three.'
(E. Nesbit, *The Phoenix and the Carpet*)

ALTHOUGH THE exact geographical origin of marine insurance may still be in some doubt, there can be no doubt about the origin of insurance against 'the terrible Fury of that devouring Element, Fire'.[1] Insurance against loss by fire was conceived and born in one city, namely London, which in the first half of the 17th century had doubled its population, and in so doing had immeasurably increased the risk of fire. For the voracious demand for housing which accompanied the commercial growth of London during the first half of the 17th century had been met largely by a band of commercial adventurers known by the rather derogatory title of 'speculative builders'. Consequently, houses were constructed almost exclusively of timber, the cheapest building material then available, and were so tightly packed together that anyone living under such conditions, having been fortunate enough to survive such everyday hazards as smallpox, bubonic plague or venereal disease, had only to resist the obvious temptation of insanity through claustrophia in order to live out the rest of his life in comparative calm! For roof-top bent over backwards in its desire to form a closer association with opposite roof-top, or so it must have seemed; and under such conditions, a small, apparently minor local fire could soon become a raging inferno involving thousands of dwellings.

On 2 September 1666 it happened. That night a fire broke out at the house of 'one Faryner, the King's Baker' in Pudding Lane which soon engulfed the larger part of the City of London; it burned for four days and laid waste 400 streets, 13,200 houses and 89 churches, the damage being estimated in Stowe's survey at £10,689,000.[2] London had seen nothing like it before and the people were stunned.

Yet fire was no new phenomenon in London; for as early as the 12th century, one author commented that 'the only pests in London are the immoderate drinking fools and the frequency of fires'. Certainly there had been serious fires at frequent intervals—in the years 798, 893, 982, 1077, 1086, 1087, 1135 and 1212, culminating in the Great Fire of 1666. That these fires were no small affairs may be gathered from a record which states that the fire of 1086 'beginning at Oldgate burnt down Houses and Churches all the way to Sudgate, together with the stately fabric of St. Paul's and the strong castle called the Palatine Tower which stood in the West part of the city'.

The inquiring reader might well ask, in view of the frequency of fires in the city, whether no precautions were taken against this very real risk. The short answer is that these were practically non-existent. It is true that certain fundamental precautions had been laid down at a very early date. For instance, in 1189 Henry Fitz-Aylin, the first Lord Mayor of London, stipulated that houses in London should be built of stone with slate or burnt tile roofs[3] and that party walls three feet thick should be placed at intervals to arrest the spread of fire.[4] But these regulations soon fell into abeyance and, despite attempts to revive such basic regulations in 1607, 1608 and 1615 and 1620,[5] few, if any, positive precautions ever seem to have been taken, save for the provision of such crude fire-fighting equipment as ladders, crooks and buckets. The truth is that fire was regarded as an act of God over which no mortal could possibly exert control.

But there were some people who wanted to change this fact of life and who furthermore appreciated that a reduction in the risk of loss through fire was possible. Thus, in 1638, Charles I was petitioned for a Royal Grant, the 'owners of houses within the City and Suburbs of London, Westminster and Southwark, paying 12 pence per annum per house yielding £20 rent, and pro-rata, shall have his house re-edified and set in as good or better state than before'. The patent was granted; but the political troubles of the day crushed the enterprise, for England was now on the verge of Civil War. Renewed efforts were made in 1661, but these, too, came to naught through sheer lack of support from householders, for, strange as it may seem, the risk of fire was now considered too remote to necessitate insurance. The Great Fire, however, transformed people's attitudes.

Although the Fire brought untold personal suffering and hardship, in some senses it proved a blessing in disguise. It certainly purged the City after the terrible plague of the previous year. More significant for the future development of insurance was the fortunate fact that no real progress had been made in fire insurance prior to the Fire. Such a calamity arising a few years after the establishment of fire insurance offices would surely have strangled the business at birth, for such a colossal claims experience before the era of accumulated funds would have completely extinguished the hopes, ambitions and enthusiasm of any Board of Directors.

The most important result of the Fire, however, was the Rebuilding Act of the following year. Under the terms of this Act, only 9,000 houses were to be erected in place of the 13,000 which had been destroyed; these houses were to be built of brick or stone, the thickness of walls was to vary with height and position relative to other buildings, timber was not to be used in proximity to flues, and wrought-iron doors were to be fitted to certain openings in party walls. Shortly afterwards, a further Act[6] was passed under the terms of which the City and Liberties were divided into four quarters. Each quarter was obliged to provide 800 leather buckets, 50 ladders, 2 hand-squirts for every parish, 24 'pickaxe-sledges' and 40 'shod-shovels'. Moreover, each of the 12 City livery companies was obliged to provide 30 buckets, 1 engine, 6 pickaxe-sledges, 3 ladders and 2 hand-squirts. These regulations were, of course, rudimentary and totally inadequate, but they represented the *first systematic attempt to reduce the risk of fire*—an essential prerequisite for the development of fire insurance. It is quite clear, therefore, that at that very time when the demand for fire insurance was increasing rapidly, the insurance business was in the process of being rendered less risky than it had previously been. The combined effect of these two influences was sufficient to call into being the country's first tangible fire insurance schemes.

In 1674, Mr. Newbold, a London Merchant and Deputy, drew up a scheme for fire insurance which he presented to the Lord Mayor of London that same year. As was almost always the case, a matter of greater moment was occupying the City at the time, and though the scheme seems to have received a fair measure of support it was temporarily shelved. But Newbold was not deterred and in 1679 published a pamphlet entitled 'London's Improvement and the Builders' Security Asserted' in which he set forth the advantages that might accrue to the City from the raising of a Joint Stock as security for his proposed fire insurance undertaking.

The scheme itself was a mutual one. Newbold estimated that there were approximately 12,000 brick houses in the City of London. These he valued at £250 each. If only one-third of these householders contributed 5 per cent of the value of their houses, i.e. £12 10s. this would yield a fund of some £50,000 out of which all houses burned would be rebuilt. In November 1680 a committee was appointed 'to peruse and consider' the 'sertaine proposalls humbly offerred to this Court by Mr. Deputy Newbold'. Twelve months later, on 16 November 1681, the Committee agreed 'to ye Generall proposals annexed, which we conceive will not only Invite Cittyzens and others into this Insurance, but will alsoe be certaine to raise a good Revenue to the Chamber'. Yet, though the City as they said themselves agreed 'to ye General proposalls' the scheme which resulted was not identical with the original scheme suggested by Mr. Newbold. It differed in two important respects—the enterprise should be carried on by the Corporation rather than by individuals and lands and ground rents of a capital value of £100,000 should be settled on trustees for the security of the insured.[7]

The date of publication of this scheme is highly significant, for only two months earlier, i.e. September 1681, an almost identical scheme had been launched by a speculative builder-cum-physician by the name of Nicholas Barbon. Barbon was in many respects a remarkable character. The son of Praise-God Barbon, the Fifth Monarchy man who had given his name to the 'Barebones Parliament', he initially studied medicine, first at Leiyden and later at Utrecht. In 1664 he became an Honorary Fellow of the Royal College of Physicians, but it seems that the Plague of London in 1665 'failed him' for he gave up medicine in favour of building.[8] The Fire of London proved more profitable than the Plague and in the years that followed Barbon was busily engaged in helping to restore London to its former glory. But he was a restless man, ever conscious of the desire to find new ways of making money, and fire insurance was one of the many avenues that he explored. In September 1681, Barbon, together with eleven associates, founded the 'Insurance Office for Houses' behind the Royal Exchange.[9]

The first official notice of what came to be known as the Fire Office appeared in the 'True Protestant Domestick Intelligence' of 7 May 1680 but, as Barbon explained in September 1681, 'much Labour, much Time, hath been spent in Settling the Affair' so that some delay was unavoidable. Broadsheets published in 1681 set forth the terms: 'These are to give notice insuring houses from fire after the rate of 6d. per £ for brick houses and 1s. for timber is now perfected and settled and persons concerned in the security will attend every day at their office on the backside of the Royal Exchange from the hours 9 till 12 in the forenoon and from 3 to 6 in afternoon to subscribe policies for all persons desirous to insure their house as far as the number of 3,000 houses.'[10] Ground rents in London to the value of £2,106 were settled on trustees in order to provide a fund for the payment of claims.

The similarities between this plan and that of the City of London are outwardly remarkable. They become considerably less remarkable when it is appreciated that both were based on the original scheme submitted by Deputy Newbold in 1674. The City's scheme, however, enjoyed the advantage of being published two months later than Barbon's and it certainly used every ounce of that advantage. The City were evidently intent on driving 'Damned Nicholson Barbon' out of business, for not only did they offer insurance for terms longer than the Fire Office's maximum of 31 years, but they also undercut every premium quoted by the Fire Office by a substantial amount, as Table 1 shows.[11]

Table 1

COMPARISON OF FIRE INSURANCE RATES OFFERED BY THE FIRE OFFICE AND THE CORPORATION OF LONDON

	Fire Office per £100 value			*Corporation of London per £100 value*		
Term	£	*s.*	*d.*	£	*s.*	*d.*
Perpetuity		—		3	6	8
100 years		—		3	2	5
51 years		—		2	17	6
31 years	2	15	0	2	8	7
21 years	2	10	0	2	0	11
11 years	1	15	0	1	8	4
7 years	1	5	0	1	0	9
1 year		5	0		3	9

Source: H. E. Raynes, ibid., p. 85.

Barbon, a polished, unscrupulous business man, immediately retaliated in print, accusing the City of plagiarism and of putting forward a scheme which was economically unsound. The main plank in his platform of attack was the low level of premiums quoted by the City, though the City probably suffered greatest damage from the 'impropriety of those citizens that managed the revenue of the city . . . stewards of the rest through rashness and want of knowledge, venturing the public revenue of the City on a project that brings loss and thereby prejudices the whole body of citizens'. Barbon concluded his attack with these words: 'the Gentlemen on the Committee did not well Understand the Design they were about; for which they are not to be Blamed; for it is not reasonable to expect that they should so well (on a suddain) understand a Design as the Inventor of it, who had spent much Time and study in the Contrivance.'[12]

The City, of course, replied to this vitriolic, patronising diatribe with much the same mixture. Barbon, they said, was a person 'whose chamber door daily suffers an Assault and Battery, from a whole posse of Bricklayers, Carpenters, Masons. etc. and who, if one may judge by the several actions of the Debt that every Term are brought against him is in fair way to Retire for Refuge into one of his own Chambers that he hath built in the Temple'.[13] In another letter, speaking of the ground rents of the Fire Office, the City claimed that 'a great part of them lying in Marine Square, near Ratcliffe, would hardly yield 24 years' Purchase'. The City's ability in polemics was not matched by its soundness as an economic institution, and faced with a reduction in the Fire Office's premium rates, it bowed gracefully off the insurance stage. But the Fire Office had little time to bask in the sun of its hard fought monopoly, for the City's withdrawal from the insurance market only made room for a far more efficient and determined rival.

The Friendly Society for Securing Houses from loss by Fire (commonly known as the 'Friendly'), the brain child of William Hale, of King's Walden, Herts., and Henry Spelman of London, was founded in August, 1684. Unlike the Fire Office, the Friendly was a mutual society in the sense that members could be called upon for contributions in the event of loss (30s. for each £100 insured), although they do not appear to have had any share in the profits or the Management of the Society. Each member was obliged to deposit a proportion of the amount insured as security (6s. 8d. per £100) which was returned when the contract was terminated. Finally, each member paid an annual premium (1s. 4d. per £100). These rates were for brick buildings—a double rate applied to timber buildings. Insurances were for terms of seven years and lands valued at £16,000 were settled on trustees for the security of the insured. But this fund differed in concept from that of the Fire Office since it was not regarded as one out of which claims could be met, being merely a guarantee of the 'Undertaker's good faith'.

This last point provided Barbon with a sharp weapon of attack. 'There can be no insurance unless there be a fund settled that is both certain and able to make good the loss,' he claimed.[14] But the Friendly's reply was both prompt and telling. 'If the money insured on any house burnt down, blown up or demolished be not paid by the insurers within fifty days after the rate is set, the trustees by mortgage or sale of lands or rents are empowered to pay the same.'[15] It was clear to Barbon and his associates that this was no City of London and that the stage was set for an arduous battle. The opening parry was a cautious but logical one—competition, fair competition; so for the next three years the respective protagonists tested each other out. But Barbon was ill-equipped for this type of battle and, on 8 April 1687, he and his partners presented a petition for a monopoly of fire insurance within the London Bills of Mortality.

The opposition quickly retaliated, filing a counter-petition on 29 April of the same year. There followed a period of devious machinations, of claims and counter-claims, pressures and counter-pressures until a solution finally emerged. The Fire Office should have a monopoly for one year, after which business was to alternate quarterly between the Fire Office and the Friendly. Here, indeed, was a 'Gilbertian solution'! It is pleasing to record that this preposterous compromise was never effected and in the ensuing years fire insurance increasingly became not the prerogative of one or two companies but rather a rapidly expanding business in which any company prepared to offer security and attractive, sometimes specialised, terms, combined with a sound financial backing, might well prosper.

There is little doubt that the 'Amicable Contributorship' founded in 1696, and subsequently known as the Hand-in-Hand after the emblem on its fire-mark, fulfilled all these conditions despite the expected attempts of the two existing companies to establish otherwise. Of course, foundation of the Amicable was followed by the usual verbal battle, though this proved not merely ineffective but essentially irrelevant, for there was sufficient business available to justify the existence of all three companies.

But growth was unquestionably slow. The Fire Office, for example, according to Benjamin De Laune, had 7,300 houses on its books in 1690 and by 1700 had reached only 10,000. According to Relton, the Office issued only 1,800 new policies during its first ten years of existence. Both these estimates seem to be erroneous and grossly underestimate the progress that this office made. It seems probable that during the period 1681–7 the Fire Office issued 5,650 new policies and that thereafter the rate of growth stabilised itself at roughly 1,000 new policies per annum. This is probably true of the other offices. For instance, in 1687 the Friendly was said to have accepted 3,400 new houses in the previous two and a half years and it actually claimed to have issued 1,000 policies in its first year of business. During the first 8 years the Hand-in-Hand issued 7,313 policies.

There were many reasons for this comfortable, if unspectacular, rate of growth. The most obvious was the geographical limitation imposed by operating solely in London. Provincial cities were beginning to emerge from their embryonic stage of development and would soon be entering that brief adolescence of quasi-industrialism. It was to these that the fire offices would have to turn in order to realise a more spectacular rate of growth.

An allied problem was the constraint imposed by the restriction of insurance cover solely to dwelling houses, which necessarily implied that the average sum insured was small. For instance, during the first 8 years of the existence of the Hand-in-Hand, the average sum insured was only

£192. Larger sums were clearly required and these could be obtained only by extending cover to business premises, factories, warehouses and goods. Both the needs of the society and the offices' desire for greater profits rendered this diversification a fundamental pre-requisite for economic growth in general and the growth of fire insurance in particular. For both were, and indeed always will be, inescapably related.

Fire insurance also suffered from being new; for whereas in marine insurance risks were already capable of classification and premiums were accordingly calculated in relation to the degree of risk involved, the same was not true of fire insurance. Early premiums were probably set too low. Support for this thesis is provided by a statement of Barbon's. He estimated that half the premiums he received had already been paid out in claims despite the fact that only one quarter of the policies had expired. In 1700 for instance, the actual premiums received by the office totalled £18,000 and claims paid amounted to £7,000 'besides charges'. This is undoubtedly a high claims experience judged by modern standards. It is not surprising therefore to find in 1712 a statement that the office had sustained losses 'to above £50,000 by several fires'. And there is evidence that the other companies were faced with the same sort of dilemma in the early years of their existence, for none of the offices had yet developed the idea of an annual income from premiums sufficiently large to meet all claims.

It was with the intention of eliminating some, if not all, of these inhibiting factors that Charles Povey embarked upon a brief, but in retrospect historic, career in fire insurance. Povey, like Barbon, was a restless man, constantly seeking new outlets for his dynamic financial acumen, and like Barbon he possessed great talents as a 'projector'. Unlike Barbon, however, he possessed none of the perseverance and adaptability so necessary for success in business and these weaknesses were sufficient to bring him down.

Povey's earliest known venture was a wholesale coal business, but the modest profit that accrued failed to satisfy him. In 1705, he leased a house in Hatton Garden which he named the Traders' Exchange House. At first he used the premises for advertising purposes, as a centre where business could be conducted either by personal contact or through advertisements in newspapers, but it was not long before his attention was turned to the prospect of insurance. In May 1706 he announced that he was opening subscription books for a life assurance society, but this venture soon proved as transitory as the others, for no sooner had he established his life assurance office than he was won over by the prospect of fire insurance. Povey was fully aware of the need to abandon the restrictive conditions which continued to operate in the fire insurance business. Therefore, in 1708 he offered to insure at the Traders' Exchange House 'Moveable goods, Merchandises and wares from loss of Fire', throughout Great Britain, and in November 1708 he decided to bring in twenty 'Governors and Directors' to help him.[16]

On the face of it, Povey's willingness to insure goods as well as houses, without as well as within London, constituted a radical and significant departure. But the road to Hell is paved with good intentions. During the first year business was confined solely to London and insurance taken out on 'moveables, goods . . .' etc. was minimal. It appeared that Povey's manifesto was false and that the Exchange House Fire Office, as Povey's business was known, would tread the same secure paths as its rivals. But the 'doubting Thomases' had apparently failed to reckon with this financial philanderer, for on 9 May, in order to carry out his plan for the acceptance of country risks and also to implement a plan involving the carriage of small parcels from London into the provinces, Povey formed the Company of London Insurers, and on 26 May he 'proposed to unite the Stocks of the Exchange House Fire Office in London and the Exchange House Fire Office in the Countrey and that Writings should be drawn reciprocally between Mr. Povey and the Company of London Insurers'.[17] By this device Povey hoped that the single company thus formed would pay him a capital sum for his rights and that he would retain his interest as a Director. His hopes appeared to have been realised when in January 1710 a six-man committee was appointed to finalise the necessary arrangements. Povey was to receive a capital sum of £960 and an annuity of £400 for life. But no sooner had these terms been settled than the Company contracted a severe dose of 'cold feet', for by now it was felt that Povey was a man who could not be fully trusted.[18] Povey's capital payment was consequently reduced to £480 and his annuity to a sum not to exceed £200 in any one year. On 24 March 1710, Povey transferred all his rights to the 'Exchange House alias Sun Fire Office now kept in Hatton Garden', and on 7 April the Company entered into a deed of mutual co-partnership. Thus the Sun Fire Office was born.

One might well imagine that the way was now open for the extension of the scope of fire insurance in the manner Povey had originally envisaged, but nothing could be further from the truth. Until the reorganisation of the Sun's management in 1720, the office's activities proved to be characterised by the very same conservatism which Povey had hoped to destroy. In the first place, insurances were limited in amount; until 1719, £1,000 was the maximum value insurable and this was divided equally between house and goods. More significantly, policies were still confined to London. Efforts appear to have been made to open country agencies, but they were half-hearted and came to nought. Growth was consequently slow, premium income during the first year amounting to little more than £200. Although by 1713 it had risen to nearly £1,000, the cash balance was pitifully low. In 1715 and 1716 losses were so heavy that the managers were forced to dip into their own pockets to meet further claims, and it was not until 1718 that a healthy balance was achieved. Thereafter, the rate of growth quickened and the future began to look bright for the Sun.

Yet one should not be surprised at its slow rate of growth during these difficult early years. After all, insurance was very much a 'parvenu' and, like all innovations, deeply mistrusted in some quarters. Outside London it was almost totally unknown and in an age of appalling communications this state of affairs could not be quickly remedied. Moreover, the Sun had to face the prospect of added competition, for in 1714 the Union Office 'for insuring of goods and merchandises from loss by fire' was established and the deed of settlement was enrolled on 3 January 1715. Like the Sun, the Union Office confined its activities to London, but in 1716 the scope of its operations was extended to cover the surrounding districts. The Union also, like the Sun, placed an upper limit on the amount insurable but this stood substantially higher at £1,000. The Sun at first continued to enforce its limit of £500, but in 1719, with the prospects looking very much brighter, it, too, raised its limit to £1,000.[19]

In 1717, further competition presented itself in the form of the Westminster, a fire office which owed its origin to the 'great inconvenience put upon them by removing the Hand-in-Hand office from the liberty of Westminster to Snow Hill. . . .' The constitution expressly laid down, therefore, that 'it shall not be in the power of the directors or general meetings to remove the office from the liberties of Westminster'. The office, quite clearly, was modelled on the Hand-in-Hand. A fund was established by the provision of '12s. for every £100 insured . . . on brick buildings, and double for timber', 10s. of which was returned on the expiry of the policy. The period of insurance was for a minimum of 7 years. The small initial success of the office can be gauged from the fact that levies of 11d. and 1s. 10d. per £100 on brick and timber respectively were raised on members to cover losses. However, it was not long before the Westminster, like most other offices, began to enjoy more prosperous times and in 1721 it was able to declare a substantial dividend.

Thus, by 1720 there were six fire companies established in London,[20] all operating within London on fairly competitive terms and all of them enjoying only very moderate success. The factors making for this modest rate of growth have been noted but they are worth reiterating at this point.

First, insurances were confined almost exclusively to London and its immediate environs. Secondly, buildings other than dwelling houses were almost entirely excluded. Thirdly, the classification of risks was inadequate; insufficient distinction was made between relatively hazardous and relatively safe insurances, and premiums were often inadequate to cover losses. Finally, insurances were usually for a term of years (generally seven) and none of the offices had yet developed the idea of an *annual* income from premiums sufficiently large to meet all claims.

Clearly, then, if the profit motive was to be fully exploited, these fundamental deficiencies in the scope, structure and organisation of the insurance market would have to be repaired. We must now examine the extent to which the market faced up to these problems, and the success, if any, that it achieved.

The extension of activities beyond London was clearly an objective of utmost priority. We have already noted that the Sun was quick to recognise this fact and made tentative steps towards the establishment of country agencies shortly after its establishment in 1710, but that these efforts proved abortive. However, with the reorganisation of the office management in 1720 came fresh impetus and renewed efforts (this time successful) for the establishment of country agencies.

In 1721, following the decision of December 1720 'to Appoint Persons of Reputation and Substance in the chief Towns and Cities to Distribute Policies and receive all Quarterages, and to Allow such Persons One Shilling in the Pound as an Equivalent for their Trouble Exclusive of the Policies', agencies were established at Oxford, Cambridge, Winchester and Buckingham. These were followed in 1722 by agencies at Portsmouth and Exeter and in 1726 at Canterbury, Bath and Norwich. Strangely enough, Bristol, then the second largest city in England did not acquire an agency until 1737, though it is doubtful whether one would have been necessary for, as noted above, an independent company, The Bristol Crown, had been established in that city in 1718. It is interesting to note that, with the exception of Newcastle, all the agency appointments were in the South of England, but this is not really surprising, for the South was unquestionably the focal point of economic life. Northern and Midland factory industrialism was still very much in the embryonic stage. Birmingham acquired its first agent in 1744, Wolverhampton in 1772 and Liverpool in 1783, though Manchester had acquired its first agent as early as 1729. It was not until the rapid upsurge in economic activity which took place in the 1790s that 'Country' fire insurance really took root in the North, and even then there were many gaps which would obviously have to be filled if factory development was to continue.

The most fundamental condition which had to be met was the extension of fire insurance to cover factories, warehouses and mills. Fire insurance was initially confined to dwelling houses, though business premises and small warehouses were soon included. Goods and moveables were particularly well covered by the Union Office which, of course, specialised in this field. But larger business premises, warehouses, factories and mills were a difficult problem for the insurance offices, largely because of their size. Financial organisation was nothing short of rudimentary in all the offices and accumulated funds were not yet sufficient to meet the needs of these larger would-be insurers; and, because fire offices were new, there existed the very real, and related, problem of classification of risks according to the degree of risk involved. The earliest, and crudest, classification was that of brick and timber buildings where the premium on timber buildings was double that on brick; but in May 1721, the Managers of the Sun, obviously dissatisfied with this classification, singled out sixteen 'hazardous' trades on which 14s. per £500 rather than 10s. per £500 would in future be charged.[21]

In 1727 a more comprehensive system of classification was adopted, according to Article IV of the proposals of that year. Insurances were divided into three categories, i.e. Common Insurances, Hazardous Insurances and Doubly Hazardous Insurances. Common Insurances were defined as 'any Buildings covered with Slate, Tile or Lead and having the Front, Rear and Side Walls of Brick or Stone and wherein none of the Hazardous Goods or Trades hereby specify'd are carry'd on'.[22] Hazardous Insurances were defined as 'Timber and Plaster Buildings and Goods and Merchandises therein, not Hazardous, or Brick or Stone Buildings wherein Hazardous Goods or Trades are deposited or carry'd on'. Finally, Doubly-Hazardous Insurances were defined as 'all Thatch'd Buildings, all Timber or Plaster Buildings wherein Hazardous Goods or Trades are deposited or carry'd on and also the following Trades and Buildings as Sugar Bakers, and Distillers in Brick or Stone Buildings, any China, Glass or Earthenwares, Houses on London Bridge, and Mills'.

This classification proved so effective that, in fact, it endured in roughly the same form for well over a century, though, of course, with the passage of time and the concomitant accumulation of experience, many additions, subtractions, and transfers were made. For instance, though the houses on London Bridge had been classified as Doubly Hazardous in 1724, in 1734 it was decided that expiring policies should not be renewed at all. However, in 1746 it was decided that in fact they could be reinsured at the very high rate of 10s. per cent. Again, by the proposals of 1727 mills of all types were expressly excluded but this condition was gradually relaxed during the 1750s. Similarly, it had been decided in 1727 that no sugar houses should in future be insured, but in July 1729 the decision was reversed; in future, they could be insured at a rate of 10s. per cent up to £1,000 value, 15s. per cent for the next £1,000, and 20s. per cent for the next £1,000, above which no insurance would be accepted. However, this limit was raised, first to £5,000 in 1777 and in particular approved instances, to £7,000 in 1785.

In this way, i.e. by adapting old classifications to meet new needs, by varying premiums according to the degree of risk within any given classification, and by manipulating the upper insurable limit, the scope of fire insurance was adapted to meet the needs of an ever-changing society. This contention is supported by empirical evidence. A sample of the Sun policies analysed by Mr. P. G. M. Dickson,[23] reveals the changing emphasis in the type of property insured during the 18th century. For instance, in 1716, 67 per cent of the policies and premiums were in respect of houses and shops, 10 per cent were insurances on inns, 9 per cent were on warehouses, 5 per cent on farms, barns, etc., and 10 per cent on mills, factories and workshops. By 1790, though houses and shops still accounted for 67 per cent of the *number* of policies, they now only accounted for 43 per cent of the *premiums*; inns now accounted for 4 per cent and farms 10 per cent of total premiums, while warehouses comprised 33 per cent, and mills, workshops and factories a further 8 per cent. The two significant features of these figures are, first, the large increase in the proportion of total premiums given over to warehouses, which by this time formed the most rapidly expanding category of insurance business and, secondly, the relatively insignificant role of mills, workshops and factories.

Yet this is not a surprising result. After all, although the Sun had first fixed its rates for water mills, timber mills, metal mills, oil mills and windmills in 1752, the significant expansion in this category lay some way in the future. It was not until the cessation of the American War of Independence in 1783 that the Lancashire cotton textile industry began to undergo the remarkable metamorphosis which has led certain writers to detect a causal connection between the take-off of this leading sector and the consequent growth of the British economy in general. The problem of determining premiums for these highly hazardous insurances was therefore borne largely by those managers who were fortunate, or unfortunate, enough to be 'in the van' of fire insurance during the last decade of the 18th century and the early decades of the 19th century. But by this time the major problems of the earlier period of fire insurance history to which this chapter has been largely devoted had been successfully worked out.

NOTES

1 Ambrose Godfrey, *An Account of the New Method of Extinguishing Fires by Explosion* (1724). Quoted by P. G. M. Dickson, *The Sun Insurance Office,* 1710–1960 (1960), p. 1.

2 This figure is said to have represented a quarter of the nation's income at the time.

3 This promulgation was known as the 'Assize of Buildings'.

4 Oxford adopted similar stipulations in 1190.

5 The proclamation of 1020 was quite the most comprehensive ever issued. It affected not only the City but the whole of districts within five miles of the City gates. In addition to the instructions concerning buildings of brick and stone, minute regulations were given as to the number and height of storeys, thickness of walls, size of windows and so on. It further required that walls should be straight, 'without a jutties, or jutting or cant windows'.

6 Entitled 'An Act for Preventing and Suppressing of Fires within the City of London and Liberties thereof', November 1667.

7 It was also laid down in the scheme that 'a further additional fund' should be accumulated by the 'Praemium which shall be received'. This represents the first application of the modern term premium in insurance business.

8 Actually it is for his economic treatises, notably his Discourse on Trade (1690), that he ought really to be remembered. In this work he reveals himself as an original thinker. He certainly anticipated Ricardo's theory of rent.

9 Walford states that Barbon's Office was first established in 1667, and this statement has been copied by both Delton and Scott. However, this contention, based upon a statement in Haydn's Dictionary of Dates appears to be unsupported by any evidence.

10 British Museum, 816m. 10/68.

11 The table of rates refers to brick-built houses. Timber-built houses were charged double the rate.

12 British Museum, 816m. 10/66.

13 Quoted by P. G. M. Dickson, *The Sun Insurance Office,* 1710–1960, p. 9.

14 British Museum, 816m. 10/74.

15 British Museum, 816m. 10/75.

16 These 'Governors and Directors' did not provide any capital. Their function was to ensure that the business ran smoothly, mainly by attention to administrative detail.

17 Quoted by P. G. M. Dickson, ibid., p. 28.

18 The seeds of dissatisfaction had undoubtedly been sown by Povey's abortive attempt to collect and deliver letters within the London Bills of Mortality at a halfpenny a letter. This plan had been projected largely because his earlier plan for the carriage of small parcels did not seem to come within the 'Tenor of the Act of Parliament for Maintaining the General Post'. This new project apparently infringed the royal monopoly of postal services and Povey was consequently sued in the Court of Exchequer.

19 It is important to remember that the period following the failure of the Jacobite Rebellion of 1715 was a prosperous one which culminated in the speculative South Sea Bubble scandal of 1720.

20 The first provincial fire company was opened in Bristol in 1718. This office, the Bristol Crown, was a partnership concern with an authorised joint stock of £40,000. It was shortly followed by the Friendly Society (1719), the first fire office established in Scotland.

21 These trades were apothecaries, bread-bakers, brewers, chemists, colourmen, distillers, dyers, flax-warehousemen, hemp-warehousemen, oilmen, pastry cooks, roasting cooks, ships' chandlers, soap-boilers and tallow-chandlers.

22 The hazardous trades and goods were defined as apothecaries, chymists, bread and bisket bakers, ship and tallow chandlers, stable keepers, inn-holders, and malt-houses; hemp, flax, tallow, pitch, tar, turpentine, hay, straw, fodders of all kinds, and unthrashed corn.

23 See *Sun Insurance Office*, 1710–1960, p. 97. Mr. Dickson takes a random sample of 250 policies for the year 1716 and 350 policies for the year 1790.

Chapter 4

LLOYD'S AND MARINE INSURANCE IN THE 18th CENTURY

'Each for himself and not one for another.'
(The Gospel of 19th-century Lloyd's according to Wright and Fayle)

IN CHAPTER 2 we saw, first, how marine insurance evolved and secondly, the process by which it became an integral feature of English commercial life. We saw, for instance, that its early development was characterised by a singular lack of organisation and that this lack of organisation really sprang from the market's unspecialised structure. There were no underwriters in the modern sense of the term; underwriting was the prerogative of anyone and everyone, though the great bulk of it was performed by merchants and financiers. There was, in effect, a mutual taking of risks. But the heterogeneity of the market meant that sums insured were usually small and often inadequate and that, owing to the imperfect calculation of risks, heavy losses were sustained so frequently that bankruptcy was common. We also noticed that towards the end of the 16th century some of these deficiencies were being recognised and measures, albeit tentative, were being taken to rectify them. Thus we had the establishment of the Royal Exchange in 1570 and the Chamber of Assurances in 1576, with which all policies were required to be registered, and in 1601 we had the first legislation pertaining to marine insurance. It is true that this Act proved largely ineffective while the former requirement gained only a modicum of success. Sometime during the 17th century (we are not sure exactly when), the registration of policies ceased to be compulsory.[1] Yet, though the Royal Exchange was burnt down in the Great Fire of 1666, a new Exchange was quickly built and a new Chamber of Assurances opened in it.

The continuation of the Chamber of Assurances is therefore significant, so significant, in fact, that one highly respected authority has asserted that the Chamber 'was instrumental in moulding marine insurance in this country during its formative period', and was 'from some points of view the forerunner of the later organised market for individual underwriting'.[2] In this Raynes is unquestionably correct, but he is correct in an additional sense, for the congregation of merchants, brokers, bankers, and financiers at the Royal Exchange was instrumental in fostering the establishment of institutions which, unwittingly, were to play an indispensable part in the development of that 'organised market for individual underwriting'. We mean, of course, the coffee-houses, and it is to the coffee-houses, in particular those of one Edward Lloyd, and to their impact upon the development of marine insurance underwriting that this chapter is wholly devoted.

From early times it had been the habit of merchants, money-lenders (and others of less repute) to meet at lunch-time or later in the day at the many inns and taverns dotted around the City of London, in order to discuss the affairs of the day in as relaxed and convivial a manner as these rather dubious establishments allowed, and perhaps initiate or complete important business. There can be little doubt that this custom originated in the provision by the inns and taverns of alcoholic refreshment, but it is also true that their success sprang partly from the fact that they were usually the only places where men could meet in comfort in London at that time. In short they almost monopolised the market in social intercourse.

This monopoly was rudely, and in retrospect, auspiciously broken when one Pasqua Rosee opened an establishment 'To sell the new drink generally known as Kauphy, the berries of which he was one of the first to import, and he did his best to make popular'.[3] The date was 1652 and the place St. Michael's Alley, Cornhill; and this was the first coffee-house London had seen. But it was the first of many, for so popular was 'the new drink generally known as Kauphy' that in a short time London was bristling with them.[4] A small number became very famous very quickly, for each seemed to cater for, and attract, a particular type of customer. Amongst the most famous of these early houses were 'Hain's' coffee-house in Birchin Lane, 'Elford's' in George Yard, Lombard Street, 'Paynter's' described as being 'over against St. Michale's Church' and, further West, 'Farr's' coffee-house in Fleet Street.[5]

The reason for the success of these early coffee-houses was really quite simple. They were more strictly conducted, more peaceful and naturally more sober than the inns and taverns, and here respectable business men could be free from the 'vexatious interruptions from sots and roisters'.[6] There is no doubt that the taverns of London were often (though not always) fearful places where drunkenness walked hand in hand with prostitution and crime and where one was never free from the attentions of the press gangs. The landlord of the 'Spread Eagle' in the Strand, for example, once remarked that 'his was a very uncommon set of customers, for what with hangings, drownings and sudden deaths, he had a change every six months'.[7] We can be sure that there was nothing unique about this particular set of customers!

It is only natural for people who share the same interests to share the same clubs, inns, or in this case, coffee-houses, and it was not at all surprising that the commercial classes of the city should choose those coffee-houses where they could be sure to meet their friends. One must remember that there was no single centre where everyone could meet. The commonest rendezvous was, of course, the Royal Exchange, but this was only a place of business and so the coffee-houses dotted around the courts and alleys of the Exchange became natural meeting places. The most famous of these was probably 'Garraway's' coffee-house, immortalised by the poet Swift, but there were many others, notably 'Hain's' and 'Thomas Good's'. In these the mercantile community began to congregate and with the passage of time they increasingly became the accepted addresses for many merchants, underwriters, brokers and financiers. Notices even appeared in newspapers giving names of these coffee-houses as business addresses and it was not long before mercantile transactions were being made in them. The most important transactions usually involved the sale of ships and their cargoes and these soon formed an integral feature of life in the city coffee-houses. The first notice of such a transaction appeared in the *City Mercury* No. 12, dated January 1675, which stated that a vessel named the *Society Ketch* would be 'exposed to sale by the Candle at Mr. Hain's Coffee-house in Birchin Lane on Thursday, 3 February next at three of the clock in the afternoon'. It was not long before such sales were a common occurrence.

Under these circumstances it was not surprising that coffee-houses holding regular auction sales should attract, amongst others, those merchants who also took on the function of insurance underwriters, though it must be emphasised at the outset that we have no evidence of any underwriting business being done. Neither have we any evidence to show that the proprietors of the chief coffee-houses made any extra effort to further this part of the business—except one man and he, in doing so, quite unintentionally laid the foundation stone of what is today the world's greatest insurance institution. His name was Edward Lloyd.

The first evidence we have of a coffee-house in the name of Edward Lloyd occurs in the *London Gazette* No. 2429 dated February 1688, from which it is clear that the house was in Tower Street, 'a spacious street, well built and inhabited by able Tradesmen, and the rather so as being so great a Thorough-faire to and from Wapping, the Tower, St. Katherine's and those Parts bordering upon the Thames, replenished with Sea-faring persons'.[8] Here clearly was an excellent site, for the Custom House, Trinity House and the Navy Office were all in close proximity. But Edward Lloyd did not remain long in Tower Street. In 1691 he moved to a new site at 16 Lombard Street. This move, claims Martin, was 'a decidedly progressive step, calculated to make his establishment, more than could otherwise have been the case, the meeting place of merchants of the highest class'.[9] 'Calculated' is the right word for there was clearly a decided advantage to be had by moving closer to 'divers eminent coffee-houses, Garraway's, Jonathan's, Baker's, Elmer's, chiefly frequented by Brokers, Stockjobbers, Frenchmen, Jews, as well as other Merchants and Gentlemen'.[10] Edward Lloyd was not long in establishing a shipping clientele, for in the *London Gazette* No. 2817, dated October 1692, was placed an advertisement which read: 'On Tuesday the 8th of November next at Bennet's Coffee-house in Plimouth, will be exposed to sale by Inch of Candle,[11] 3 ships with all their furniture, the names whereof are the *Teresa*, the *St. Thomas*, and the *Palm*, two of 400 tuns, the other of 200 tuns. The Inventories thereof are to be seen at Lloyd's Coffee-house in Lombard Street, London.' This advertisement is highly significant for 'it constitutes the first evidence of that specialisation in shipping business which was ultimately to make Lloyd's Coffee-house the centre of the marine insurance world and the direct ancestor both of the Corporation of Lloyd's and Lloyd's Register'.[12]

From this it was but a short step to the actual sale of ships and their cargoes at Lloyd's, the first of which occurred in February 1700. From this date auction sales became an increasingly common occurrence at Lloyd's, so much so, in fact, that Addison in the *Spectator*, dated 23 April 1711, calls it the place 'where auctions are usually kept', and goes on to relate at some length an amusing incident which had occurred at Lloyd's a week earlier. Frederick Martin in his *History of Lloyd's* gives a detailed, though incomplete, list of sales at Lloyd's Coffee-house from 1698 to 1712.[13] This reveals that a multiplicity of items were auctioned, ranging from shares of the Lustring Company to wine, clarets and brandies, but that an increasing number of ships were auctioned during the period.

By 1710 Lloyd's Coffee-house had become 'the chief commercial sale-room in London'.[14] It had also become the chief *mercantile* sale-room in London, outstripping even the famous 'John's' Coffee-house in Birchin Lane. *But*, it had not yet emerged as a centre of marine underwriting. Indeed, we have no reason to believe that any underwriting was conducted at Lloyd's Coffee-house prior to 1710, while any business done prior to 1720 must have been insignificant; for during the long debate over the proposals for the establishment of the country's first marine insurance companies, from 1717 to 1720, not one mention was made of Lloyd's Coffee-house. Had Lloyd's been an underwriting centre of any repute, there is no doubt that its name would have cropped up. The fact is that marine insurance underwriting had still not evolved into a *specialised business*; people prepared to accept marine risks were to be found throughout the City of London—in their private offices, at the Royal Exchange and at the many coffee-houses in the City. Brokers were forced to waste their time 'picking up the Insurers here and there'. It was not until the need for a recognised centre was appreciated that Lloyd's became in turn a centre and then *the* centre of insurance underwriting in this country. Ironically enough, it was the establishment of two companies with monopoly rights over insurance underwriting in company form which provided for this need and, in so doing, played a vital part in the formation of an association of individual underwriters which was eventually to blossom into the marine insurance colossus 'par excellence'.

The idea of a Chartered, joint-stock insurance corporation was not a new one, since such a project had been considered as early as 1629 in Holland. But the idea only gained currency in this country after the disastrous sinking of the Smyrna Fleet by Admiral Tourville in the Bay of Lagos. This was indeed a catastrophe for 'an incredible number of the best merchants in the kingdom sunk under the load',[15] so much so, in fact, that a bill to force composition upon creditors was hastily drawn up and placed before the House of Commons. This, the Merchants' Insurers Bill, duly received its three readings in that House; but the Lords proved far less amenable and rejected it on 9 March 1693. Here the matter rested and with the passage of time the feeling of need for a joint stock corporation seemed to be slowly declining.

Before long, however, the matter was once again in the limelight: the occasion a wave of speculation which expressed itself in Europe in an orgy of gambling, in France in the Mississippi swindle, and in England in the South Sea Bubble. During a few short but turbulent years some two thousand schemes involving a nominal capital of £600 million (said to be about five times as much as the current cash of all Europe) were floated, the majority in the shape of joint-stock undertakings. Approximately a hundred of these ostensibly concerned insurance in one form or another, but it is hard to imagine how many of them could be taken seriously.

At the Brown Tavern in Smithfield, for instance, a subscription book was opened for 'an insurance office for horses dying natural deaths, stolen, or disabled', while an enterprising gentleman by the name of William Helmes set up a well patronised 'Assurance of Female Chastity'. Needless to say such amusing but irreverent projects did not endure long but two much more serious-minded projects did. These were the Royal Exchange Assurance Corporation and the London Assurance Corporation, both incorporated under the terms of the Bubble Act which received Royal

Assent on 10 June 1720. (Charters were formally granted on 22 June of the same year.)[16]

The Bubble Act itself, of course, was not concerned merely with suppression of speculative insurance ventures; its avowed function was to prohibit all undertakings which might prejudice trade, and all corporate undertakings with the exception of the East India Company, the South Sea Company, and those 'settled' before 24 June 1718. But its title gives some indication of the chief pre-occupation, for it was 'an Act for the better security of certain powers and privileges intended to be granted by his Majesty for the Charters for Assurance of ships and Merchandise at sea, and for lending money upon bottomry, and for restraining several extravagant and unwarranted practices therein maintained'. The vital part was clause 12 whereby 'All other Corporations or Bodies Politick, before this Time erected or established, or hereafter to be erected or established . . . and all such societies and Partnerships as now are, or hereafter shall or may be entered into by any Person or Persons for assuring Ships or Merchandise at Sea or for lending Money upon bottomry' were expressly prohibited. In short, corporate marine underwriting was now the sole prerogative of two companies, the Royal Exchange and the London Assurance and any other corporations, societies, or partnerships found fulfilling the function of marine insurance underwriting would be sued.

The significant feature of the Act was the exclusion of 'private or particular persons' from its terms. Individual underwriters and brokers were quite free to continue their marine insurance businesses since the Act did not touch them. These people, therefore, suffered not one iota from the establishment of the two corporations; on the contrary, the Act freed them from the danger and worry of competition in company form, and in so doing ensured their continued prosperity and growth.

But in terms of the subsequent history of Lloyd's, the Act was vitally significant in another sense, for, in order to make headway against the competition of the Royal Exchange and London Assurance, private insurers would clearly have to offer at least equal facilities. The new corporations had one clear advantage over the underwriters and brokers—they had centrally situated offices which subscribers could easily locate. The brokers, on the other hand, had to 'pick up the Insurers here and there'. The significance of the Bubble Act really resided in the fact that it made underwriters and brokers aware, for the first time, of the need for a similarly central position. This was the first step on the road to modern-day Lloyd's.

By this time, of course, Lloyd's Coffee-house had acquired an extensive shipping and mercantile connection and had for many years been frequented by merchants-cum-underwriters. There is no doubt that

Edward Lloyd himself was responsible for this for apart from the auction sales, he had also tried his hand at quasi-commercial journalism. It had always been taken for granted that the coffee-house was a source of news, both of world-wide and local interest, and it was for this reason that many people visited the coffee-houses. The mercantile community, for instance, attended certain coffee-houses in the hope of picking up news of special interest to them and their business, and with this very much in mind Edward Lloyd established, in September 1696, a newspaper containing the sort of news that he thought would appeal to his customers. A facsimile of a copy of this paper, *Lloyd's News*, is reproduced in Wright and Fayle's *History of Lloyd's*.[17]

It reveals *Lloyd's News* to have been a newspaper of a general trade type, providing information of war, of other foreign events, of domestic events such as parliamentary proceedings, and of shipping intelligence. The shipping intelligence was derived from *Portletters*, of which other newspapers such as the *Post Boy* and *Flying Post* also made use. The paper cannot therefore be regarded as a direct antecedent of its more illustrious successor *Lloyd's List* (about which we will have more to say in a moment). Nevertheless, the brief career of *Lloyd's News* (it lasted only four months) was a minor landmark; for it succeeded in establishing Lloyd's Coffee-house more firmly than ever as a centre of general mercantile interest.

We have seen that a more important factor had been an exogenous one, i.e. the effect of the Bubble Act of 1720. To this, and to the influence of *Lloyd's News*, must now be added an endogenous factor to which it is almost impossible to ascribe too much importance, namely the desire of the underwriters for a cheaper and more efficient delivery of shipping intelligence. With the eclipse of *Lloyd's News*, underwriters and brokers had reverted to a more costly method of acquiring shipping intelligence. This involved the transmission of the required intelligence by port correspondents at extremely expensive postal rates. For instance, one ounce of news cost 1s. 4d. for any distance over 80 miles while letters from Edinburgh or Dublin bore a 50 per cent surcharge. Since information was probably required daily from twenty or thirty English and foreign ports, the cost was clearly heavy—too heavy for the likes of Lloyd's underwriters.

The solution to the problem was really very simple, but nonetheless ingenious. After what must have been protracted negotiations, the Master of Lloyd's and the Postmaster-General agreed that, in future, the port correspondents should send their shipping intelligence direct to the Postmaster-General marked 'Lloyd's'. On arrival the letters would be opened and handed to a messenger sent by the Master of Lloyd's. The Master would consequently receive the news hours before the ordinary delivery of letters. Not only was the arrangement quicker, it was also much cheaper because all letters sent to the Postmaster-General were sent *free of charge*. For this exclusive privilege payment of £200 was expected and indeed received. Unfortunately we are not sure of the precise date of the successful negotiation of the arrangement because no record of it exists. The first record the Post Office has is dated 1788. However, it is highly probable that the arrangement was made at a much earlier date, probably during the last year of Thomas Jemson's life, i.e. 1734.[18]

The next step was the publication of a newspaper containing the shipping news acquired by the above-mentioned process. This newspaper, *Lloyd's List* was initially published weekly, beginning in 1734, but the paper proved so popular that some time in 1737 it was decided to publish twice weekly, on Tuesdays and Fridays (because on these nights the foreign mails were despatched). Unfortunately, the earliest copies of *Lloyd's List* have not survived, and so its first date of publication has been deduced from the dates of subsequent copies. The earliest extant copy of *Lloyd's List* is dated Friday, 2 January 1740, a facsimile of which is to be found in Wright and Fayle's book.[19] This shows the List to have consisted of a single leaf, 12 inches by 7½ inches, on the front of which was published: (*a*) the rate of exchange at London on Dublin and fourteen continental centres; (*b*) aids in the Exchequer given and paid off; (*c*) the price of gold per ounce in coin, pieces of eight, and gold and silver bullion; (*d*) the price of annuities; (*e*) the price of cochineal per pound; (*f*) announcements of State lottery prizes; (*g*) Stock Exchange quotations. On the back is the Marine List of arrivals, sailings, destinations of ships touching at a port of call, and finally the winds at Deal. For this information, which remained materially unchanged throughout the 18th century, Lloyd's subscribers paid the modest fee of 12s. per annum. So successful was the paper that it did not long remain the sole prerogative of Lloyd's clientele. 'I need not remind your Lordships,' wrote the Secretary to the Post Office in 1792, 'that *Lloyd's List* is universally received all over the country as the Gazette of ship news', and by 1808 it was so popular on the Continent that in view of the fact that England was at this time at war, the paper had to be carefully censored.[20]

There is no doubt that the publication of *Lloyd's List* constituted a landmark in the history of Lloyd's for, whereas we cannot say with certainty in the absence of written evidence that *any* marine insurance was being underwritten at Lloyd's in 1720, the very fact that a newspaper in the nature of *Lloyd's List* was so much in demand in 1734 in itself indicates the probability that marine insurance underwriting was increasingly becoming an accepted part of the daily life of Lloyd's. We in fact know that by 1740 Lloyd's Coffee-house had become pre-eminent amongst the coffee-houses of London as an underwriting centre, and every year that passed witnessed an increase in its already impressive stature. The chartered companies were really pygmies by comparison: underwriters were drawn to Lloyd's as by a magnet;[21] and, as the need for closer association arose, Lloyd's seems to have been more and more used for that purpose, not all at once or even exclusively, but with a steady persistence which finally led to the complete concentration of the business.[22]

We have already noted some of the reasons for this success—Edward Lloyd's deliberate policy of attracting members of the mercantile community by such devices as the publication of *Lloyd's News*, auction sales, the establishment of the two chartered companies which left individual underwriters free to continue their activities, the improved delivery of shipping intelligence, and finally the publication of *Lloyd's List*. But two factors remain to be discussed, the first of which is fundamental not only to the history of marine insurance but to every aspect of commercial life during the first half of the 18th century, i.e. the brilliantly enlightened foreign policy of Robert Walpole, the 'first and most successful of our Peace Ministers'.[23]

Robert Walpole assumed office at a time when the economic future of this country looked distinctly black. We had just emerged from the long war with France; the blockades, counter blockades, and the demands made upon our physical resources had left us virtually exhausted. On top of this there were serious political difficulties arising out of the Hanoverian succession, which manifested themselves in 1715 in the famous Jacobite Rebellion, virtually a civil war. Its legacy was a festering sore on the body politic which refused to heal up. Then there were serious financial problems arising out of the speculative financial orgy commonly known as the South Sea Bubble. The bursting of this Bubble in 1720, the same year that Walpole assumed office, brought financial chaos and despair of the deepest kind throughout the country to many small, innocently-minded people who were caught up in it.

Walpole's problem was essentially this: how to restore the nation's economic solvency and at the same time maintain political equilibrium at home. His solution was a policy of peace abroad[24] combined with freer trade between England, the Colonies and Europe. Thus, in one session alone, he abolished the export duty on 106 articles and the import duty on 38 raw materials. The consequent increase in trade was almost instantaneous. Wages rose, prices remained stable, the price of land rose, and population increased. Above all exports expanded, and, since the demand for British goods was primarily a Colonial demand, there was a rapid explosion of urban growth in response to it. Birmingham and Manchester doubled their size in only thirty years, while ports such as Liverpool underwent what can only be described as a metamorphosis.

Given this rapidly changing environment, the growth of Lloyd's is more easily explained. Freer trade meant greater trade, greater trade required a greater number of ships, and a greater number of ships involved a large increase in insurance cover. It was really as simple as that.

Then in 1739, the second factor emerged. This was a war, a needless war which began over a sea-captain's ear and broadened out into the protracted struggle of Austrian succession with France and Spain fighting against us side by side. Like all wars involving England in the 18th century it was a predominantly sea-war. The sea-war required more ships, and these required more, much more, insurance. But this time the rates were considerably higher, for underwriters ran dreadful risks in times of war. It was a period of risky, heavy but often lucrative business and Lloyd's took the lion's share.[25]

Then came the Seven Years War (1756–1763) and with it an influx of new underwriters anxious to cash in on the rich harvest which was so obviously to be reaped. With the return of peace in 1763 the inflated war-time rates collapsed, and underwriters who had grown fat on the rich harvest were forced to slim. The result was an outbreak of gambling which bore little or no relationship to genuine underwriting. Wager policies on ships and cargoes had been prohibited since 1746 as indeed had policies of re-insurance.[26] However, wager policies on lives and events had not been included within the framework of the Act, and these consequently became the subject of incredible gambles. Wagers on lives of famous people were particularly popular with the gambling element which had arisen within Lloyd's, but such policies did not meet with unanimous approval. Mr. Thomas Mortimer, in 1782, published a vitriolic attack upon the habit, and those who practised it. 'A practice likewise prevailed,' and here Mr. Mortimer is referring to the years immediately following the Seven Years War, 'of insuring the lives of well-known personages, as soon as a paragraph appeared in the newspapers announcing them to be dangerously ill. The insurance rose in proportion as intelligence could be procured from the servants, or from any of the faculty attending, that the patient was in great danger. This inhuman sport affected the minds of men depressed by long sickness; for when such persons, casting an eye over a newspaper for amusement, saw that their lives had been insured in the Alley at 90 per cent, they despaired of all hopes, and thus their dissolution was hastened.'[27] This 'pernicious habit' seems to have been the work of a band of degenerate Scotsmen, for a contemporary attack upon Lloyd's in the *London Chronicle* of 1778 stated that 'when policies come to be opened on two of the first Peers in Britain losing their heads, within a year at 10s. 6d. per cent and on the dissolution of the present Parliament within one year, at 5 guineas per cent, which are now actually doing, and underwrote chiefly by Scotsmen at the above Coffee-house [Lloyd's] it is surely high time for the administration to interfere, and by exerting the rigour of the laws against the authors and encouragers of such insurances (which must be done for some bad purpose) effectually put a stop to it'.[28]

If, in fact, a group of our cousins north of the border *were* responsible for wagers on lives and the like, there is no doubt that our Sassenach ancestors followed quick on their heels, for in a very short space of time the habit was widely practised. Unfortunately, reputable underwriters were unavoidably associated with these underwriting charlatans and were understandably annoyed about it. So annoyed were they, in fact, that they decided to seek separate accommodation and to establish a society of underwriters and brokers, held together by fixed rules, under which none but persons of good repute could be admitted. To that end the following advertisement appeared in the *Public Advertiser* on Monday, 20 March 1769:

> To the Merchants in general, Owners and Freighters of Ships, Insurance Brokers, etc. etc. Thomas Fielding, Waiter from Lloyd's Coffee-house begs acquaint them that his House in Pope's Head Alley, Lombard Street is now genteelly fitted up and will open for the reception of Gentlemen, Merchants, etc. Tomorrow the 21st instant by the name of New Lloyd's Coffee-house, where he hopes to receive their favours which shall be gratefully acknowledged by.
>
> Their most obliged servant,
> Tho. Fielding.

The move to Pope's Head Alley was duly made and New Lloyd's Coffee-house was born, but the battle was by no means over. The old Lloyd's continued to publish *Lloyd's List* and it continued to attract a sufficiently large clientele to enable it to continue. But this clientele was of the worst kind, consisting mainly of gamblers whose interest in assurance underwriting was nothing more than superficial, and the old Lloyd's slowly sank into oblivion. By 1785 the old premises had been vacated and old Lloyd's Coffee-house, the former retreat of many a mercantile man, was quite appropriately sunk without trace.

On moving to their new premises the underwriters and merchants quickly came to an agreement with the General Post Office to receive the vital shipping intelligence, and soon a *New Lloyd's List* was in print. (The old Lloyd's continued to publish its *Lloyd's List* first under the title of *Old Lloyd's List* and later merely *Lloyd's List*. But the cost of maintaining the paper in the face of declining trade proved too great and it finally succumbed with the House. *New Lloyd's List* ceased to be 'New' from 1 January 1789.)

However, within a short space of time the new premises proved inadequate and in 1771, only two years after the establishment of New Lloyd's, 79 merchants, underwriters and brokers signed an agreement 'to pay our several subscriptions into the Bank of England in the names of a Committee to be chosen by ballot for the building of a New Lloyd's Coffee-house'.[29] This document was indeed an historic one, for it constituted the first formal association between underwriters and brokers and Wright and Fayle go as far as to say that this agreement was 'the most important document in the history of Lloyd's'.[30]

This document really marks the foundation of modern Lloyd's. In 1772 the Committee of Lloyd's was set up to manage its affairs and in 1774 Lloyd's finally moved to its new premises in the Royal Exchange, a site which it was to occupy right up until its removal to the new premises at Leadenhall Street in 1928. The lease, though negotiated by John Julius Augerstein, a figure of immense stature in the history of Lloyd's, was in fact taken in the name of the Committee men, who then installed the two old Lloyd's waiters, Thomas Fielding and Thomas Tayler, as tenants-at-will and joint Masters. (It is interesting to note that the attendants at Lloyd's are to this day known as 'waiters', a term which readily evokes those early days at Tower Street and Lombard Street.) A levy of £20 per member was initially raised, but this proved to be more than sufficient and the levy was subsequently reduced by £5.[31]

Success, it seems, was almost instantaneous. By April 1774 the original 79 subscribers had increased to 179 and thereafter new members joined steadily every year. So heavy was the congestion that, in 1791, two additional rooms had to be taken.

The reason for Lloyd's success really resided in its superior efficiency. Apart from its efficient receipt of shipping intelligence, which by itself would have been sufficient to guarantee its pre-eminence, it also began to record ships lost or safely arrived in a green vellum book not surprisingly known as 'The Book'. This gave Lloyd's a clear advantage, an advantage which it continued to build upon in the years to come. The progress Lloyd's had made in only a few short years can be gauged from the fact that as early as 1779 the subscribers evolved a printed policy, which as we have already seen in an earlier chapter, differed in only a few minor particulars from that in use today. This in itself is sufficient testimony to the superiority of that institution whose origins were humble enough.

NOTES

1 For instance, Charles Molloy, in his *De Jure Maritimo* (1676), distinguishes between 'public' and 'private' insurances. 'Private' insurances he defines as those 'which the assured keeps . . . secret not deeming it fit that any should see or know their cargo or adventure or what premio they have given or assurance they have made and the same being never entered in the office. . . .' Quoted by Raynes, ibid., 1st ed., p. 57.

2 H. E. Raynes, *History of British Insurance*, 1st edition, p. 63.

3 Frederick Martin, *A History of Lloyd's and Marine Insurance* (1876), p. 55.

4 E. Hatton in his *New View of London* (1708) estimated that at that date there were 'near 3,000 nuisances'; though this is undoubtedly an exaggeration there were numerous coffee-houses, probably running into hundreds by this time. There were probably about 100 during the period 1674–88.

5 There is an interesting story attached to the last-named house, for in 1657 the proprietor of Farr's was prosecuted for 'making and selling a sort of liquor called Kauffee, being a great nuisance and prejudice to the neighbourhood'. Other prosecutions followed which culminated in an extraordinary ordinance of Charles II which ordered 'the shutting and suppressing of all coffee-houses', for though 'the retailing of coffee might be an innocent trade . . . it was used to nourish sedition, spread lies, and scandalise great men. . . .' So great was the furore which followed that the courts were forced to qualify the edict. In future, coffee-houses could be kept open provided the Masters agree to 'prevent all scandalous papers, books and libels from being read in them, and hinder every person from declaring, uttering or divulging all manner of false and scandalous reports against the government or the Ministers thereof'. (F. Martin, *History of Lloyd's and of Marine Insurance*, p. 47.) Needless to say, this incredible anti-coffee act soon fell into complete disuse.

6 C. Wright and C. E. Fayle, *A History of Lloyd's* (1927), p. 35.

7 Quoted by M. Dorothy George, *London Life in the XVIII Century*, p. 275.

8 Strype's edition of Stowe's, *The Survey of London*.

9 F. Martin, ibid., p. 63.

10 From Stowe's *Survey of London* (Strype's edition) quoted by Raynes, ibid., 1st edition, p. 110.

11 Sale by 'inch of candle' was a common method of auction and seems to have been particularly popular in coffee-houses. At the commencement of the sale an inch of candle was lighted and bidding continued until the candle was extinguished. The final bid made before the flame actually expired took possession of the property. One such sale is brilliantly described by Pepys in his Diary, dated 3 September 1662. 'After dinner by water to the office and there we met and sold the Weymouth, Successe, and Fellowship hulkes; t'were pleasant to see how backward Men are at first bid; and yet when the candle is going out how they bawl and dispute afterwards who bid the most first. And I observed one man cunninger than the rest that was sure to bid the last man, and to carry it; and enquiring the reason he told me that just as the flame goes out the smoke descends, which is a thing I never observed before, and by that does he know the instant when to bid last, which is very pretty.' Quoted by Wright and Fayle, ibid., pp. 19–20.

12 Wright and Fayle, *A History of Lloyd's*, p. 19.

13 F. Martin, ibid., pp. 81–85.

14 Wright and Fayle, ibid., p. 26.

15 Daniel Defoe, *Essay on Projects* (1692, reprint 1887, p. 77).

16 The petitions, counter petitions, machinations and subterfuges which preceded the incorporation of these two companies make fascinating reading. Unfortunately we cannot go into it here. Those interested might consult Wright and Fayle's official *History of Lloyd's*, pp. 44–60, for a highly readable account of this entangled affair.

17 Wright and Fayle, ibid., p. 23.

18 Thomas Jemson was Master of Lloyd's Coffee-house from 1727–1734. Edward Lloyd had died in 1713. He was succeeded by William Newtown, the old head waiter at Lloyd's, who himself died in 1714. Newtown's widow then married Samuel Sheppard who consequently became Master. When he died in February 1727, Thomas Jemson, his brother-in-law took control.

19 Wright and Fayle, op. cit., p. 77.

20 Ibid., p. 77.

21 The Parliamentary Committee on Marine Insurance (1810) stated that during the earlier part of their existence, the chartered companies had only 10 per cent of the marine business in London. The remainder was in the hands of the private underwriter.

22 Though it must be emphasised that no official relationship existed between Lloyd's Coffee-house and the underwriters and brokers. This was merely a voluntary association completely devoid of any legal status and herein lay its strength.

23 J. R. Green, *A Short History of the English People*, Vol. IV, p. 1593.

24 It was his proud boast that 'There are fifty thousand men slain this year in Europe and not one Englishman', a truly immortal sentence.

25 This war was particularly popular with the mercantile classes for it was hoped that it would result in the opening up of the Spanish Colonies in America to the British. When Porto Bello on the Spanish Main was captured it appeared that the result would shortly be achieved, and that all the bells in England would soon be ringing out in celebration. This premature exuberance brought forth from Walpole the prophetic remark: 'They are ringing the bells now; soon they will be wringing their hands.'

26 19 Geo. II, c. 31.

27 *Every Man his own Broker*, 13th ed., 1801, pp. 111–112.

28 Quoted by Wright and Fayle, ibid., p. 96.

29 Quoted by Wright and Fayle, ibid., p. 110.

30 Wright and Fayle, ibid., p. 110.

31 The subscription of £15 gave life membership, admission to the subscribers' room, and a right to vote at the General Meetings. In addition to the £15, however, an annual subscription was also paid.

Chapter 5

THE EQUITABLE AND THE EMERGENCE OF LIFE INSURANCE

> 'The history of the Equitable is the history of life assurance in this country. If that be not strictly true, it is yet much nearer the truth than the uninformed could imagine.'
>
> (Cornelius Walford, *History of the Equitable*)

We now turn our attention to the early history of a branch of insurance which, for the great majority of us, is perhaps the most familiar for it plays an important part in our day-to-day lives. This is, life insurance, or as it is generally known in this country, life *assurance*.[1] In Chapter 1 we noticed that a form of life assurance was practised by the members of the Roman 'collegia' and refined to include variable payments and benefits according to individual members' means and needs. Here is an ancestor of what is known today as industrial life assurance about which we shall have more to say in a subsequent chapter. For the moment we must consider the history of life assurance proper, emphasising as we go its early rudimentary origins and its subsequent development into a scientific discipline based upon representative mortality statistics and sound actuarial principles.[2]

In its earliest form, life assurance was linked with the development of maritime commerce, for those merchants and financiers who were prepared to underwrite marine risks were frequently prepared to insure also the life of the captain of the vessel for the duration of the voyage. It is not unlikely that life cover was also provided for the more important members of the crew, although unfortunately we have no records of such contracts. The earliest extant contract we have is one dated 18 June 1583, when Richard Martin, a citizen and alderman of London, agreed to pay a group of merchants the sum of £30 13s. 4d. in consideration of which it was stipulated that if a certain William Gibbons (also spelt Gybbons) should die, within twelve months of the date of the contract, £383 6s. 8d. was to be paid to Richard Martin. In the event, Gibbons did die within the year—345 days after the contract had been effected—but the underwriters tried to avoid payment on the grounds that he had not died within 'the full twelve months accounting 28 days to every month'. However, the Court ruled that 'the month is to be accounted according to the course of the Kalendar and not after 28 days to the month', and the defendants were thus ordered to pay 'the several sums of money specified'. Strangely enough, this earliest extant life assurance contract was *not* associated with a sea venture, but the association may readily be appreciated by reference to a work entitled *Le Guidon* by an unknown author of the period. 'Another kind of insurance is made by other nations upon the life of men in case of their decease upon their voyage to pay certain sums to their heirs or creditors. Creditors may even insure their debts if their debtor removed from one country to another; the same can be done by those having rents or pensions so as in a case of their decease to continue to their heirs such pension or rent as may be due to them.'[3]

The common feature of these early life policies was the brevity of their duration. Few, if any, were for periods of longer than a year while the great bulk were for very much shorter periods, say, a few months. The brevity of such policies in fact constituted a natural barrier to the development of life assurance and, had life assurance remained of that character, it would certainly not have developed on the grand scale which it has done. However, towards the end of the 17th century attention was drawn to the possibility of establishing funds which would undertake to pay annuities with benefit of survivorship.[4] One such scheme was placed before the City Authorities by a Mr. Wagstaffe in 1674 under the terms of which subscribers who had contributed £20 or multiples of £20 were to receive an annuity of £6 per cent which would increase as members of the fund died off. The scheme did not in fact materialise but it was an interesting forerunner of later contracts for it was a permanent contract in which members were to be classified according to age.

A scheme which did materialise, however, was one established in 1698 by the Mercers' Company which guaranteed reversionary annuities at 30 per cent of the purchase price.[5] These terms proved to be over generous and were reduced by one-third in 1738; but even then the scheme ran into difficulty and, in 1750, Parliamentary relief had to be obtained.

A similarly unsuccessful scheme known as the Society for Assurance of Widows and Orphans was launched in the following year, i.e. 1699. This was a scheme of mutual benefaction involving 2,000 subscribers whereby on the death of any one of them the survivors paid 5s. each so that the widow might receive £500. The society's existence proved ephemeral, however, for it lasted only 14 years.

From this abortive scheme of mutual benefaction it was but a short step to the mutual society in which premiums contributed by its members would be shared amongst the descendants of those who died, the total sum available depending upon the actual number of deaths per annum. This step was in fact taken when the Amicable Society for a Perpetual Assurance Office was established by charter in 1706. The Amicable offered 2,000 shares for which subscribers paid £6 4s. per annum on the understanding that £10,000 (i.e. £5 per annum per subscriber) would be shared between the nominees of those subscribers who died during the year. Only those between the ages of 12 and 45 were eligible and each person was entitled to no more than three shares. The subsequent history of the Amicable was one of moderate success. In 1770 membership reached its limit of 2,000 shares, by which time the Society had a fund of £33,000 in 3 per cent stock, and claimed that during its existence it had paid out a total of £378,184 to 3,643 claimants.[6]

In contra-distinction to the schemes which we have outlined so far, the Amicable's success proved enduring and it was in fact taken over by the Norwich Union Life Insurance Society in 1866, but that is not to say that it survived without criticism. As knowledge of scientific life assurance principles evolved, the Amicable was increasingly attacked on the grounds that its original scheme was 'exceedingly defective, absurd, and inequitable'.[7] But Raynes is correct when he says that this attack was too severe, for 'the society did provide a very real benefit to its members, and its long history is testimony to this'.[8]

Nevertheless, the fact remains that the Amicable and the other life assurance schemes launched during this early period[9] were extremely rudimentary for they all lacked a firm scientific foundation. Scientific life assurance is characterised by the permanent contract with a level annual premium based upon the age at entry. A level annual premium is necessary because the insurer must plan his policy according to his future income and expenditure pattern. This requirement necessitates first, comprehensive and representative mortality statistics and, secondly, a fairly sophisticated mathematical apparatus consisting of compound interest and probability theory. In 1720 these fundamental pre-requisites did not exist, but the outlook for the future was distinctly brighter. In the first place there was developing rapidly a widespread consciousness of the need for, and the usefulness of, a quantification of English commerce based upon comprehensive statistical information. This need was, quite clearly, a function of the contemporary economic thought which successive generations have chosen to call Mercantilism.[10] According to the central doctrine of Mercantilism, economic welfare should be measured in terms of the magnitude of the nation's export surplus—the larger the export surplus, the wealthier the country. This dubious index of economic welfare required adequate statistical information, and the need for commercial statistics provided the governing classes with a knowledge of simple arithmetic which they had hitherto lacked. It was against this background that the new science of 'political arithmetic' naturally evolved.[11]

A second encouraging feature was the gradually emerging interest in the interpretation of mortality statistics. Bills of mortality were first used to produce a very rudimentary life table by John Gaunt, a friend of Sir William Petty; but according to Edmund Halley, the astronomer, 'the deduction from these bills of mortality seemed . . . to be defective: first in that the number of people was wanting; secondly, that the ages of the people dying was not to be had; and lastly that both London and Dublin, by reason of the great and casual accession of strangers who die therein (as appeared in both by the great mass of funerals above births) rendered them incapable of being standards for this purpose which requires, if it were possible, that the people we treat of should not at all be changed, but die where they were born, without any adventitious increase from abroad or decay by migration elsewhere.'[12] Halley then proceeded to construct a superior mortality table based upon the bills of mortality of Breslau. Taking a five year period from 1687 to 1691 he found that 6,193 people were born but only 5,869 buried. This gave a per annum natural increase of 65. From these figures he was able to calculate the total population of Breslau (34,000), the numbers living and dying in each age group, and consequently the values of annuities over the whole age range. His table of annuity values at 6 per cent interest for quinquennial ages revealed that the value of £1 per annum at age ten was 13·44 years' purchase price but at seventy only 5·32 years' purchase.

Halley's calculations constituted the vital breakthrough, in that they provided the basis for an elementary theory of probability, 'it being 100 to 1 that a man of 20 dies not in a year and but 38 to 1 for a man of 50 years of age'. The knowledge of the theory of probability was not new. Indeed the Romans, who were inveterate gamblers, particularly with dice, were fully aware of the frequency of certain combinations turning up, but they were unable to apply this knowledge or to express it mathematically. Halley was really the first to apply the theory, but his mathematics was crude by comparison with the mathematical theory originally developed by Pierre de Fermat (1601–65), Blaise Pascal (1623–1662) and Christiaan Huygens (1629–1693), the last of whom systematised the theory in a treatise published in 1657. The first systematic treatment in English was accomplished by Abraham de Moivre (1667–1754), a Huguenot friend of Sir Isaac Newton. De Moivre soon became recognised as an expert on the doctrine of chance, the value of annuities, and reversionary interests, for he published numerous papers on the subjects between 1718 and 1727. It was partly as a result of these publications that the mathematical and actuarial basis of life assurance was generally and firmly established.[13] The way was now clear for the genesis of scientific life assurance.

On 28 February 1756, James Dodson, Master of the Royal Mathematical School at Christ's Hospital, placed an advertisement in the *Daily Advertiser* to the effect that anyone interested in the formation of a mutual life assurance company should meet him at the Queen's Head, Paternoster Row, on 2 March. On 8 March a second advertisement appeared, this time in the *Public Advertiser*, which read: 'The gentlemen who have assisted at two former meetings at the Queen's Head in Paternoster Row will meet again tomorrow the 9th March at six in the evening precisely to make further progress therein. Note: it is proposed to insure lives either for a single year or for a number of years certain or for the whole life on premiums proportionate to the several years of the insured (provided the same be not less than eight nor greater than 67) which premiums will be in most cases much cheaper than usually paid, in some cases not a half of them and the risk is proposed to be bourne by the whole body as in the Hand-in-Hand and Union Fire Offices.' Here we have notice of the first attempt to establish a company offering whole life assurance at a level premium based upon age at entry.[14]

Unfortunately, James Dodson died before his brain-child was born but the force of his initial impetus was sufficiently strong to sustain the project, and on 20 April 1757 a petition for the incorporation of the Society for Equitable Assurances on Lives and Survivorships was presented to the Privy Council. Naturally enough the petition was opposed by the three offices already conducting life assurance business, i.e. the Amicable, the Royal Exchange and the London Assurance, with the result that it was referred to the Attorney General and Solicitor General. Deliberations proved to be lengthy, and it was not until 14 July 1761, that the report was issued.

Unfortunately, the report was adverse to the petitioners. In the first place it was criticised 'because it appears to us altogether uncertain whether this project will or can succeed in the manner in which it is proposed; and if the success is uncertain the fund for supporting it, which is to arise from the profits of the undertaking, will be precarious . . .';[15] secondly, the law officers objected on the grounds that 'the success of this scheme must depend upon the truth of certain calculations taken upon tables of life and death whereby the chance of mortality is attempted to be reduced to a certain standard: this is mere speculation, never yet tried in practice and consequently subject, like all other experiments, to various chances in the execution. . . . We are more apt to doubt the event (i.e. the success of the venture) because it has been represented to us by the affidavit of Mr. Savage, that all the profit which has been received by the Royal Exchange Assurance from the time of its commencement to the present time amounts only to a sum of £2,651 4s. 6d., the difference between £10,915 2s. 6d. paid in premiums and the sum of £8,263 17s. 8d. disbursed in losses, which small profit must have been near exhausted in the charges of management. . . . If the petitioners, then, are so sure of success there is an easy method of making the experiments by entering into a voluntary partnership of which there are several instances now subsisting in this business of insuring; and if upon trial these calculations are found to stand the test of practical experiment, the petitioners will then apply with a much better grace than they can at present, whilst the scheme is built upon speculative calculations.'[16] Their third objection was that 'Parliament, in erecting two great companies already mentioned, have sufficiently declared their opinion that such charters ought not to be granted without some benefit accruing to the public . . .; and, as the two great companies paid a very large sum to the public for the privilege of their charters, we cannot advise the Crown to entrench upon their rights on the bare request of any set of men without a clearer and more certain prospect of public good. . . .'[17] By hindsight it is all too easy to show our exasperation at the narrow interpretation placed upon the petition by the lawyers, but it is as well to remember that they possessed no hindsight and could judge the merits and demerits of the project only against the background of contemporary knowledge and experience of commercial life assurance, which, as we have already shown was, to say the least, thin. We must, therefore, not be premature in our judgement for on balance the decision was a reasonable one. On receipt of this adverse report, a number of the original subscribers withdrew, but a hard enthusiastic core, headed by Edward Rowe Mores, remained.[18] As a result of these men's efforts, a deed of settlement was drawn up, largely by Mores, and executed on Tuesday, 7 September 1762, though it was not enrolled in the Court of King's Bench until Hilary Term, 5 George III, 1765. Nevertheless, the former date, 7 September 1762, may be regarded as the birthday of the Society for Equitable Assurances on Lives and Survivorships, hitherto known as the Equitable.

The Society was, of course, a mutual one—in other words, it was owned by the policyholders, not the shareholders as is the case of a proprietary organisation—and assurances were taken out, as the original advertisement promised, (*a*) on a whole life basis, (*b*) on a term basis (i.e. a stipulated number of years) and (*c*) on a single year basis. Initially, premium calculations were made by Edward Mores, but the Society was not long in procuring a table drawn up by James Dodson, for which payment was made to his children. However, in 1764, Dodson's son, also named James Dodson, was appointed Actuary on the death of the Society's first Actuary, William Mosdell. For a short time he computed the premiums, but he resigned in 1767, and was succeeded first by John Edwards and then by John Pocock. Unfortunately, this rapid turnover of actuaries did little to stabilise the Society nor did it help to put it on a scientific footing. Actuarial ideas consequently remained rudimentary and John Edwards was the first to lend the Society a degree of scientific respectability. Until his appointment there had not even been a statement of accounts and the preparation of such a statement became his immediate preoccupation. It is from this statement showing the financial position of the Society on 1 December 1766 and subsequent years that we are able to judge the Equitable's performance during this time.

Table 2

THE STATE OF THE SOCIETY ON DECEMBER 1st OF EACH YEAR FROM 1766–1772[19]

	Assurances in Force			*Accumulated Funds*		
Year	*Number*	*Amount*	*Premium Income* £	*Nominal amount of 3% stocks* £	*Cash* £	*Outstanding claims*
1766	450	119,404	3,021	8,000	515	?
	14	556*				
1767	556	145,060	5,807	10,000	1,190	3,660
	19	478*				
1768	538	144,228	6,358	12,000	956	1,840
	26	1,127*				
1769	506	140,496	6,147	17,500	660	2,050
		530*				
1770	471	126,210	5,720	17,500	865	920
	19	510*				
1771	522	151,208	7,037	23,875	763	3,220
	20	620*				
1772	567	174,282	7,558	29,875	313	2,910
	20	694*				

* Annuities

Although the figures in Table 2 reveal a fairly healthy trend in premium income and invested funds, they are by no means spectacular. Given that a large proportion of the assurances were temporary and there were many lapsed policies, the blunt truth was that the Equitable was still not operating on sufficiently sound principles. Fortunately at this point a new character set foot upon the stage of life assurance in the person of Richard Price.[20]

Richard Price was born at Tynton, near Bridgend, Glamorgan, on

23 February 1723, the son of Rees Price, a Calvinist dissenter. He was brought up in the true dissenting tradition, receiving his education at a dissenting academy at Talgarth, Breconshire, and from 1740–1744 at Mr. Coward's dissenting academy in Tenter Alley, Moorfields. Here he was taught by John Eames, F.R.S., a man once described by Isaac Watts as 'the most learned man I know'. Eames was primarily a mathematician, a great friend of Sir Isaac Newton, and it was as a result of Eames' excellent tutoring that Richard Price acquired a first-class grounding in mathematics. For the next twelve years Price was family chaplain to a Mr. Streatfield of Stoke Newington, a position which allowed him plenty of time to pursue and develop his interest in mathematics. When Streatfield died in 1756, he left Price a handsome legacy which allowed him to move to Newington Green, Stoke Newington, where he became morning and afternoon preacher at the meeting house.

It was here that he became friendly with Benjamin Franklin and Joseph Priestley, and it was here also that he became interested, and subsequently involved intimately in, the mathematics of probability theory and of life contingencies. For his work on probability he was elected Fellow of the Royal Society in 1765 and in 1769 he gained public recognition for his 'Observations on the Expectations of Lives'. This success was followed in 1770 by an essay entitled 'Observations on the proper method of calculating the values of Reversions depending upon Survivorships', a study which led him to consider the problems of annuities. The culmination of this activity was his 'Observations on Reversionary Payments', a publication which went through seven editions in forty years. It proved to be a classic and Benjamin Franklin went so far as to describe it as 'the foremost production of human understanding that this century has afforded us'. So immense was its stature that it remained a standard text in actuarial science for a century, a true testimony to its greatness.

Three years prior to the publication of this work, contact had been established between Richard Price and the Equitable. In 1768, John Edwards, the Equitable's actuary, had been given a proposed insurance involving complicated survivorships on three lives. He was not able to perform the calculations and Richard Price, already renowned, was consulted. He duly provided the calculations, and in a letter to the Equitable said that 'I have more on the same subject. . . . I have considered the printed account of your Society, which you were so good as to give me, and I cannot help thinking that it is a Society that may be of great service if proper care is taken.'[21] In retrospect, this conversation was an historic one for it marked the beginning of a dialogue between Price and the Equitable which was to last for fifteen years, during which time the very guidelines of scientific life assurance were laid down.

In his official capacity as Consultant, Price's brief excluded nothing that was of importance for the Equitable's future but he was nevertheless preoccupied with two problems in particular. The first was the organisation of the Company's accounts and the direction of its investment policy. Price had been particularly scathing about the accounts at a meeting at the President's home on 27 January 1775, when he remarked that 'nothing can be rightly inferred from the present method of stating the accounts of the Society', and in addition he emphasised the need for continually accumulating funds in order to meet future claims 'It becomes the Society, therefore,' he said, 'to be very cautious: and if its number is kept up, its capital (i.e. the funds of the Society) ought to go on increasing for at least sixty to seventy years; nor will it be proper to divide any of the Stock. . . . For should it appear the annual payments added to the interest of its growing stock are more than sufficient to support the growing annual claims . . . the right measure will be either to increase the claims or sink the payments (i.e. reduce the premiums), and not to enter upon the Stock.'[22]

His second problem was the improvement of the existing mortality tables which were, by now, recognised as imperfect, for he was sure that the Society, 'furnished with a set of tables . . . more correct and elegant that it now uses . . . tables founded on observations . . . might well be capable of being made an object of great consequence not only to this, but to other kingdoms. . . .' As a result, Price constructed a new table based upon the bills of mortality of Northampton, for he felt that this town represented the mean between mortality in cities and country districts. He took the parish of All Saints, Northampton, from 1735 to 1770 and used his calculations to effect a close comparison with the results of a parish census made in 1746. In addition he calculated a new table which included a further ten years' deaths. Thus he constructed a table based upon 46 years of mortality. So accurate was the table that it 'made a profound impression on the general mass of intelligent persons' and 'remained for a century by far the most important table of mortality, employed as the basis of calculation by leading companies in Great Britain, and adopted by the Courts as practically part of the Common Law. Parliament, followed by some legislatures and many Courts in America, even made it the authorised standard for valuing annuity charges and reversionary interests.'[23]

The early history of scientific life assurance was very much a family affair, for in 1774 Richard Price's nephew, William Morgan, had been appointed Assistant Actuary on the death of John Edwards. The story goes that when the vacancy occurred the young man was staying with his uncle at Newington Green. Price suddenly thought of his nephew and said, 'Billy, do you know anything of mathematics?' 'No, uncle,' he replied, 'but I can learn.'[24] The following year he was appointed Actuary, an office he was to hold with rare distinction for over fifty years. On his resignation in December 1830, the Equitable ranked amongst the largest and wealthiest corporations in the world—a position which was in no small measure due to William Morgan's ability to learn.

At this point it is apposite to break off from the main stream of the narrative in order to make brief mention of a very important piece of insurance legislation, promulgated in 1774. In the previous chapter we saw that during the latter part of the 1760s, a wave of speculative gambling forced a group of marine underwriters to break away from Lloyd's Coffee-house. The object of the 'pernicious habit' of gambling was, as we have seen, the lives of great men. A passage from John Francis' *Annals of Life Assurance* will serve to remind us of the practice. 'Policies,' he says, 'were opened on the lives of public men with a recklessness at once disgraceful and injurious to the morals of the country. That of Sir Robert Walpole was assured for many thousands and at particular periods of his career, when his person seemed endangered by popular tumults, as at the Excise Bill, or by party hate, as at the time of his threatened impeachment, the premium was proportionately enlarged. When George II fought at Dettingen, 25 per cent was paid against his return. The rebellion of 1745, as soon as the terror which it excited had passed away, was productive of an infamous amount of business. The members of Garraway's, the assurers of Lloyd's, the merchants of the Royal Exchange, being unable to raise or lower the price of stocks any more by reports of the Pretender's movements, made sporting assurances on his adventures and opened policies on his life. . . . The seat of a Prime Minister or the life of a highwayman, assured equally to the purpose of the policy mongers; and India or Minorca, Warren Hastings or Admiral Byng were alike to them if they could put money in their purses. There was absolutely nothing on which a policy could be opened that was not employed as the opportunity of gambling.'[25]

The danger inherent in these speculative ventures sprang from the absence of what is known as 'insurable interest', by which we mean that the assured must derive some benefit from the existence of the person (or thing) insured, and will be prejudiced by death (or loss). It is clear that in the cases just quoted no such interest, apart from the wager itself, or prejudice in the event of death existed and it was to stamp out such wagers that the Life Assurance Act, commonly known as the Gambling Act, was passed in 1774.[26]

Section I sets the tone of the Act: 'No insurance shall be made by any person or persons, bodies politick or corporate, on the life or lives of any person or persons or on any other event or events whatsoever, wherein the persons or person for whose use, benefit, or on whose account such policy or policies shall be made, shall have no interest, or by way of gaming or wagering; and every assurance made contrary to the true intent and meaning hereof shall be null and void to all intents and purposes whatsoever', while Section II of the Act states that 'it shall not be lawful to make any policy or policies on the life or lives of any person or persons, or either event or events, without inserting in such a policy or policies, the person or persons' name or names inserted therein, or for whose use, benefit or on whose account such policy is so worded or underwrote'. There is no doubt that the Gambling Act achieved to a great extent its desired effect, for it is still on the Statute Book.

And so the century gradually drew to a close with the Equitable firmly established as the pre-eminent life assurance company. From its early rudimentary origins it had developed strong scientific roots—level premiums or whole life assurances based upon age at entry, careful selection of lives, limitations on the amounts insured, periodical valuations and distributions of profits, and equitable surrender values. The results speak for themselves.

Table 3

ASSURANCES IN FORCE ON 31st DECEMBER
OF YEARS INDICATED

Year	*Number*	*Amount in Thousands of £*
1771	542	151
1776	978	357
1781	1,268	552
1786	2,311	1,090
1791	4,344	2,652
1796	5,008	3,606

Source: M. E. Ogborn, ibid., p. 117.

The crucial years were clearly 1781 and 1786. In 1781 the Northampton table and reversionary payments were adopted and premiums were reduced, while a further reduction was made in 1786. Consequently, we need look no further for an explanation of the Society's spectacular growth after 1786.

The very fact that by the end of the 18th century the Equitable was pre-eminent implies that it was not without competitors. We have seen that the Royal Exchange had been conducting life assurance since 1721 but it offered only annual contracts which had such little appeal that the volume of business was very small. During the period 1721–83 total life premiums amounted to only £33,840, of which £18,263 was paid out in claims. However, in 1783, the Royal Exchange adopted whole life terms with level premiums based upon age at entry, premium levels being equivalent to those used by the Equitable before the introduction of the Northampton Table. Its subsequent history proved to be one of success not only in life, but also in other classes of business. Even so, it has never been able to shake the Equitable's impregnable position.[27]

In 1792 a fifth life assurance organisation was formed, under a deed of settlement and a capital of £150,000 (of which £50,000 was paid up). This, the Westminster Society for Insurance of Lives and Survivorships, in fact proved ephemeral as an individual entity, for it was amalgamated with the Guardian Assurance Company in 1863. Little is known about its early history but it is unlikely that it ever conducted business on anything but a very modest scale, though it has earned a place in the history books of life assurance by virtue of the fact that it was the first proprietary life office.

The Equitable's final 18th-century competitor was the Pelican Life Insurance office, an offshoot of the Phoenix, established in 1797, along similar lines to the Westminster, i.e. it was a proprietary company established by deed of settlement. The position of this office, and indeed of every other office, *vis-à-vis* the Equitable, may be gauged by reference to an article succinctly entitled 'Assurances' by Charles Hutton in *A Mathematical and Philosophical Dictionary.* In this article he mentions five principal offices i.e. the Royal Exchange, the London Assurance, the Amicable, the Westminster and the Equitable, but completely ignores the Pelican. However, the Equitable commands the bulk of the article and is most highly praised, for 'the Society (i.e. the Equitable) follows the rules which have been given by the best mathematical writers on the doctrines of life annuities and reversions'. Here, indeed, is the heart of the matter, explaining as it does why one should look no further than the opening quotation of this chapter for a very fitting conclusion.

NOTES

1 The distinction between insurance and assurance is a subtle, but unimportant one. Nevertheless, to avoid confusion, the difference is this: an *in*surance contract provides against loss in the event of something happening, i.e. there is an element of *uncertainty*. In the case of an *as*surance contract, the provision is made against the effect of a *certain* event, i.e. death.

2 The reader should perhaps be aware of the difference between life assurance and industrial life assurance at this stage. Life assurance simply involves the

receipt of certain financial benefits in return for smaller annual premiums (they may in fact be paid quarterly or monthly although payment by this means will be slightly more expensive). Industrial life assurance involves similar benefits but the method of payment is rather different. Collectors are employed by the industrial life offices to collect premiums directly at frequent intervals. The Industrial Life Assurance Act of 1923 specifies that collection should be made at no more than two monthly intervals. Industrial life assurance was the product of the 19th century urban masses' abhorrence of the 'pauper funeral', a desperately degrading affair involving mass burials in huge pits some 20 ft. deep. The great bulk of poor people in the 19th century lived in constant fear of such a fate, but the industrial life assurance movement helped to alleviate this fear by the frequent collection of small contributions from those people who desired a decent burial.

3 Quoted by F. Hendricks in the Journal of the Institute of Actuaries, Vol. II, p. 228, from *Les Us et Coutumes de la Mer,* by E. Cleirac, 1661.

4 The term 'annuity' is derived from the Latin 'annus' meaning a year, and is a series of payments made at uniform intervals during a given status or a definite period. The fundamental and consistent feature of an annuity is the relation

$$\frac{1}{a} = \frac{1}{s} + i$$

which means that the annuity which a unit of principal will purchase is of two parts, i, the interest on the amount invested and $\frac{1}{s}$, the sinking fund or sum to be set aside to be accumulated so as to replace the invested unit by the time the annuity ceases. Survivorship benefit means that, as some of the subscribers to the fund die off, the survivors obtain proportionally increased annuities.

5 A reversionary annuity is one which is entered upon only on the death of another life.

6 Richard Price, *Observations on Reversionary Payments,* 3rd edition, pp. 151–152.

7 Francis Bailey, *Doctrines of Life Annuities* (1813), p. 479.

8 H. E. Raynes, ibid., 1st ed., p. 123.

9 In 1721, the two chartered companies, the Royal Exchange and the London Assurance were granted supplemental charters to conduct life assurance. However, they only granted yearly contracts and, as a result, were never forces to be reckoned with in life assurance business.

10 Mercantilism is often regarded as the universal manifestation of a specific body of economic thought, bound together by immutable dogma. In fact, Mercantilism is really the product of successive generations' attempts to rationalise an essentially 'ad hoc' process involving often diametrically opposed ends and means, but in which several recurrent doctrinal threads constantly emerge. For a refreshingly balanced synopsis of the 'Mercantilist Controversy', see M. Blaug, *Economic Theory in Retrospect,* ch. 1.

11 Perhaps the leading exponent of this new subject was Sir William Petty (1623–1687), one of the founders of demographic and economic statistics. His various *Essays in Political Arithmetick* and his *Political Survey or Anatomy of Ireland* presented population estimates and calculations of social income, but he is best remembered for his 'Treatise on Taxes and Contributions' (1662),

in which he expounded what he thought to be the main economic function of the state.

12 Edmund Halley, *Philosophical Transactions*, Vol. XVII, p. 579.

13 The noun 'actuary' with its adjectival form 'actuarial' is derived from the Latin word 'actuarius' denoting the legal writer or recorder responsible for the official records of the Senate. The man who chose the title, Edward Rowe Mores, about whom we shall have more to say in a moment, envisaged the actuary's function as that of a recorder of contracts. The title now describes anyone 'who is qualified to deal with all questions affecting insurance, and particularly life insurance, from the mathematical, statistical, financial, legal, medical and economic points of view'. (Definition according to Pitman's *Dictionary of Life Assurance*, edited by S. W. Richmond and F. H. Sheriff.)

14 The story runs that Dodson had been refused terms by the Amicable because of his age—he was 46 at the time of application and the Amicable's upper age limit was 45. It was this rejection that led him to try to establish a new life assurance company.

15 Quoted by M. Ogborn in *Equitable Assurances, The Story of Life Assurance in the Experience of the Equitable Life Assurance Society* (1962), p. 35.

16 M. Ogborn, ibid., p. 35.

17 M. Ogborn, ibid., p. 35.

18 We have already referred to Mores in a previous footnote. Born in 1731, he proved to be a very intelligent child and was educated at Merchant Taylor's and Queen's College, Oxford. His early intellectual pre-occupation seems to have been with genealogy and heraldry but his reading interests were wide. He seems to have been especially interested in mathematics, for included amongst his immense collection of books were Dodson's *Calculator* and *The Mathematical Repository*, de Moivre's *Doctrine of Chances* and *Annuities upon Lives*, Price's treatise on reversionary payments and West's *Symbolography*. It was this background that prepared him for the important part that he was subsequently to play in the genesis of scientific life assurance. He died on 28 November 1778.

19 Reproduced from M. Ogborn, ibid., p. 83.

20 For a biography of Richard Price see Roland Thomas, *Richard Price, Philosopher and Apostle of Liberty* (1924).

21 Quoted by M. Ogborn, ibid., p. 90.

22 M. Ogborn, ibid., p. 103.

23 W. Cow, *Encyclopaedia Britannica*, 11th edition, an article on life assurance, p. 665–666.

24 Roland Thomas, ibid., p. 57.

25 John Francis, *Annals of Life Assurance*, p. 141.

26 19, Geo. III, c. 37.

27 The other chartered company, the London Assurance, also offered life assurance on yearly terms, but its working profit during the greater part of the 18th century was little more than a couple of hundred pounds per annum.

Part II

THE PERIOD OF ASCENDANCY

1800-1914

Chapter 6

THE ECONOMIC BACKGROUND

> 'There are today on the plains of India and China men and women, plague-ridden and hungry, living lives little better, to outward appearance, than those of the cattle that toil with them by day and share their places of sleep by night. Such Asiatic standards, and such unmechanised horrors are the lot of those who increase their numbers without passing through an industrial revolution.'
>
> (T. S. Ashton, *The Industrial Revolution*, 1760–1830)

WITH THE history of life assurance from early times to its emergence as a scientific discipline we conclude the Formative Period. We now move on to our second period, the Period of Ascendancy, which, roughly speaking, dates from the end of the 18th century to the outbreak of the First World War. During this long period of over one hundred years, the firm foundations laid down in previous years, and described in previous chapters, were quickly built upon and Great Britain emerged as the 'patron' of the insurance movement. We hope that in the course of this section some of the explanations of this pre-eminence will emerge naturally. However, the general course of the narrative requires for its further appreciation some elementary understanding of the general course of the main late 18th- and 19th-century macro-economic trends. In this chapter, therefore, we must stop and take stock of the flows.

If we pause for a moment and reflect upon the growth of insurance up to the end of the 18th century we are struck, or at least ought to be struck, by its essentially limited geographical development. We have noticed, for instance, that marine insurance developed, not unnaturally, in response to the growing needs of the mercantile classes for protection against the ever-present risk of loss through storms, fire, seizure, war, etc., and that this demand found tangible expression in the evolution of the now world-famous Lloyd's. But, following the title of a recent book dealing with the history of Lloyd's, it was very much 'Lloyd's of London',[1] for the metropolis was the focal point of British foreign trade. That is not to say that the business of foreign trade was confined solely to London. There were a number of smaller ports of long standing, the largest of which, Bristol, had enjoyed a particularly prosperous history, while a smaller number were quickly growing in status. Liverpool, of course, is the outstanding example in this category, increasing its population almost tenfold during the course of the 19th century. But by virtue of London's complete commercial domination, the marine insurance market was orientated towards the metropolis and, although comprehensive figures for 18th-century marine insurance do not exist, it seems highly likely that a far greater proportion of ships sailed from the provincial ports without any, or at least without adequate, insurance cover than was the case at London. This, at least, is the impression given by correspondence between Bruce Fawcett and Co. of London and the same firm's Bombay House during April and May, 1801 concerning the insurance of a ship known as the *Scaleby Castel*. In the first letter, dated 26 April, the London insurers state that:

> 'We have insured on the *Scaleby Castel* £109,000 viz: £93,000 here, £10,000 at Manchester and £6,000 at Hull, and in consequence of your directions shall proceed as far as possible. We have great doubts that it will be practicable to do above £25,000 more. We have all the responsible London underwriters on our London policy, and we must now apply to the public offices. We expect only one of them will take any risk and that will not be more than £10,000 with advanced premium. We shall write to Bristol immediately and perhaps to Glasgow for insurance at these places.'

But on 10 May a second letter was despatched which ran:

> 'After all our endeavours it will not be possible to complete your order for insurance on the *Scaleby Castel*, and we have done to the following extent. . . .

		£
London	Private underwriters	92,000
	Royal Exchange	10,000
		102,000
Manchester		10,000
Hull		6,000
Glasgow		4,700
Greenock		3,400
Bristol		11,400
Liverpool		10,000
		£148,000[2]

Of course, there is no doubt that the full cover could have been effected had there been recourse to less experienced or perhaps less reputable underwriters, but the *Scaleby Castel* was a particularly difficult risk and only first-class underwriters were approached. Nevertheless, the degree to which the first-class provincial underwriters were able to repond was undoubtedly small, and the figure for Glasgow is surprisingly low.

What was true of marine insurance was equally true of fire insurance. Provincial expansion, we have seen, was slow in coming and, when it did, it was by no means adequate. Admittedly, extra-metropolitan expansion involved hitherto unexperienced hazards but the London underwriters were nevertheless slow to face up to their responsibilities. For some considerable time London had offered an adequate market and its continued expansion fostered the inertia and the smugness of its underwriters. But competition was beginning to become more intense and the need for fresh markets was increasingly felt. In some senses the London underwriters were fortunate in that the relative 'drying up' of opportunities in London coincided with the rapid expansion of population and industry in the North of England, and the prospective profits from these new markets finally enticed them out of their metropolitan shell.

In the development of early life assurance the extent to which this branch of business suffered from the constraints imposed on it by the excessive domination of London was altogether less but nevertheless recognisable. As we have seen, life assurance developed rather later than either marine or fire insurance, largely because the scientific basis did not exist before 1760, but in its early stages it was similarly confined to London. However, it is probably true to say that the greatest constraint upon its development resided in the general level of real income which was far too low to enable the great bulk of the population to save anything at all. Clearly, taking the long-term view, what was required—and this was true not merely of life assurance but all branches of insurance—was a substantial rise in per capita real income (such that contractual saving would become a distinct possibility for the great bulk of the population) allied to a considerable increase in the size of the total population; the expansion accruing largely outside London, so that the relative importance of the capital would decline. That such a revolution did occur is, of course, well known. Nevertheless the main trends must be noted.

(1) *Population Trends*

Though we are primarily interested in the 19th-century trends, to some extent they cannot be separated from earlier developments, and we have therefore included a brief reference to 18th-century population movements. Having said this we must emphasise the paucity and imperfection of 18th-century population statistics. The first population census was not taken until 1801 and before that date only two contemporary estimates are accepted as reasonably reliable—those of Gregory King for England and Wales in 1695 and Alexander Webster for Scotland in 1755. All other estimates depend upon adjustments of the statistics of baptisms, burials, and marriages collected by John Rickman at the time of the first Census from the parish registers of England and Wales. The statistics used in this section are those estimated by John Brownlee,[3] although the other estimates reveal similar orders of magnitude (which is hardly surprising since they are all derived from the same source) for the years before 1801, and the Registrar General's estimates for the middle of each year from 1801 onwards.[4] The results are to be found in Table 4. These reveal that during the first five decades of the 18th century population growth was extremely slow (in fact, only approximately 1 per cent per decade) but that during the second half of the century the pace of growth quickened considerably (49 per cent for

Table 4[5]

TOTAL POPULATION BY AREA 1901–1911

(in millions)

Year	*England and Wales*	*Scotland*	*Great Britain*	*Ireland*	*U.K.*
1701–	5·826	1·040	6·866	2·540	9·406
1711–	5·981	—	—	2·765	—
1721–	6·001	—	—	—	—
1731–	5·947	—	—	3·015	—
1741–	5·926	—	—	—	—
1751–	6·140	1·250	7·390	3·125	10·515
1761–	6·569	—	—	—	—
1771–	7·052	—	—	3·530	—
1781–	7·531	1·369	8·900	4·048	12·948
1791–	8·247	1·500	9·747	4·753	14·500
1801–	9·156	1·599	10·755	5·216	15·972
1811–	—	—	12·147	5·956	18·103
1821–	—	—	14·206	6·802	21·007
1831	—	—	16·368	7·767	24·135
1841	—	—	18·551	8·200	26·751
1851–	—	—	20·879	6·514	27·393
1861–	—	—	23·189	5·788	28·977
1871–	—	—	26·158	5·398	31·556
1881–	—	—	29·789	5·146	34·934
1891–	—	—	33·122	4·680	37·802
1901–	—	—	37·093	4·446	41·538
1911–	—	—	40·918	4·381	45·299

the second half compared with 5 per cent for the first half). This was almost entirely due to a sharp acceleration from the 1780s onwards. Between 1781 and 1801 the population of Great Britain increased by 20·8 per cent, an increase which was more than sustained during the first two decades of the 19th century. Thereafter, though the *rate of growth* of population declined somewhat, *total population* continued to expand. If we take the 19th century as a whole, the total population in fact increased by some 245 per cent. Looking at it another way, the upsurge that began in the 1780s led to a doubling of the population of the United Kingdom by 1841. By 1911, population had increased almost four-fold.

We have included the population history of Ireland in Table 4 in order to illustrate that country's essentially divergent experience. It is true that Ireland's population expanded *pari passu* with the rest of the home countries throughout the whole of the 18th century and the early part of the 19th century. However, the potato famine of 1841 truly decimated the population and a reversal of the earlier trend set in—a reversal which continued without interruption right down to the First World War. In 1911, the total population of Ireland stood at little more than its 1781 level. For this reason one must always consider Irish economic history of the 19th century on a distinct and separate basis. For perhaps a closer understanding of the magnitudes of the trends implicit in Table 4, the figures in that Table are expressed on a percentage basis in Table 5.

Associated with this remarkable increase in total population was a significant rise in the proportion of the population living in urban areas. For instance, at the beginning of the 18th century, London's population amounted to just over half a million, but only three other towns had populations in excess of 20,000—Bristol, Edinburgh and Norwich—and with the exception of Birmingham and Glasgow, no other town in Great Britain had a population in excess of 10,000. However, as the century progressed there was a marked increase in the size of provincial towns. During the first half of the century, Liverpool, the centre for the West Indies trade and Birmingham, the centre of the metal industry, were subject to steady population expansion. Liverpool, in fact, trebled its population during the first four decades of the 18th century,[6] whilst Birmingham is estimated to have increased its population 45 per cent between 1675 and 1760.[7] During the second half of the 18th century, Manchester grew faster than any other English town, and between 1773 and 1801 its population is estimated to have more than trebled.[8]

These 18th-century examples are not spectacular because they involve expansion from a very limited base. In fact, it was the 19th century that provided the most spectacular increases in population as we can see

Table 5

RATES OF GROWTH OF POPULATION 1701–1911
(Percentage increase per decade)

Decade	*England and Wales*	*Great Britain*	*United Kingdom*
1701–11	+ 2·7	—	—
1711–21	+ 0·3	—	—
1721–31	− 0·9	—	—
1731–41	− 0·3	—	—
1741–51	+ 3·6	—	—
1751–61	+ 7·0	—	—
1761–71	+ 7·3	—	—
1771–81	+ 6·8	—	—
1781–91	+ 9·5	+ 9·8	—
1791–1801	+11·0	+10·2	—
1801–11	—	+13·7	+13·8
1811–21	—	+16·9	+16·0
1821–31	—	+15·2	+14·9
1831–41	—	+13·4	+10·8
1841–51	—	+12·5	+ 2·4
1851–61	—	+11·1	+ 5·8
1861–71	—	+12·7	+ 8·9
1871–81	—	+13·9	+10·7
1881–91	—	+11·2	+ 8·2
1891–1901	—	+12·0	+ 9·9
1901–1911	—	+10·3	+ 9·1

Source: Deane and Cole, ibid., 2nd ed., p. 288.

from Table 6. The statistics were provided by Thomas Walton in a paper read before the Royal Statistical Society on 20 November 1900.[9] This Table takes the twenty-four largest towns in England and Wales in 1891 and compares their total populations at that date with their populations in the year 1801. Once again the figures speak largely for themselves. However, a few comments are appropriate.

The percentage increase in the population of a number of the towns is, of course, dramatic to say the least. The total population of Cardiff for instance increased by some 5,000 per cent between 1801 and 1891, but then Cardiff was nothing more than a village in 1801. More significant were the increases in towns like Manchester, Liverpool and Birmingham, for these were already large towns at that early date. And so to a lesser extent were Leeds, Sheffield and Newcastle. Perhaps the most striking feature of the figures, however, is the extent to which Northern and Midland towns dominate the Table.[10] With the exception of Cardiff, Bristol, Portsmouth, Plymouth, Brighton and Norwich, all the towns are situated either in the North or the Midlands. Now it is true that urbanisation and industrialisation are by no means always synonymous but it is significant that, almost without exception, the growth of these towns was linked directly with their industrial development. The growth of Manchester, Liverpool, Oldham, Blackburn, Preston and Bolton was clearly associated with the phenomenal growth of the cotton industry after 1780, whilst one need look no further than expansion of the iron and steel industry for the concomitant expansion of Birmingham,

Table 6

POPULATION OF SELECTED TOWNS 1801–1891

Town	*Population* *1801*	*1891*	*% Increase 1801–1891*
Manchester	121,141	881,622	728
Liverpool	89,127	872,999	979
Birmingham	79,196	602,618	761
Leeds	53,162	367,059	690
Sheffield	47,179	334,538	709
Newcastle	46,215	310,318	672
Bristol	70,419	304,866	433
The Potteries	35,612	246,674	684
Nottingham	41,644	238,242	572
Bradford	15,498	210,964	1,361
Hull	31,892	205,085	643
Portsmouth	44,521	184,703	415
Leicester	19,696	176,909	898
Plymouth	42,286	157,716	364
Brighton	7,662	142,129	1,855
Sunderland	24,998	141,693	567
Cardiff	2,664	141,339	5,306
Oldham	12,024	131,463	1,093
Blackburn	15,375	125,193	814
Preston	17,148	122,983	717
Bolton	20,374	121,634	597
Halifax	23,772	101,823	428
Norwich	36,854	100,970	274
Derby	12,472	98,410	789

Sheffield, Derby, Newcastle and Sunderland. Of course, it is impossible to isolate any one factor in explanation of this rapid industrial development, and it would be wrong in fact to try, but if we were to, there can be no doubt that the application of rotary motion to Watt's steam engine would be high on the list. Indeed there is one writer on the subject who goes so far as to say that 'the application of rotary motion to the blast furnace, to textile machinery and to other forms of industrial production was the true beginning of the new industrial era'.[11]

(2) *Real Income*

Any attempt to calculate 18th- and 19th-century *per capita* real income is so heavily circumscribed by the inadequacies of wage and price statistics that the attempt is hardly worth the effort, so great would be the resultant margin of error. So instead we have followed the line taken by Deane and Cole[12] and taken *per capita* real output. The results are shown in Tables 7 and 8.

Table 7 reveals an upward trend in the average real output in the 1740s which was followed by a much sharper upward trend in the last two decades of the century. There is a remarkable similarity here with the course of total population, which, if the reader turns back to Tables 4 and 5, he will see took an upward turn in the '40s and in the '80s. This

Table 7

ESTIMATED ANNUAL RATES OF GROWTH OF 18th-CENTURY AVERAGE REAL OUTPUT

Decade	*i*	*ii*	*iii*
	%	%	%
1695/1715–1725/1745	0·3	0·4	0·1
1725/1745–1745/1765	0·6	0·8	0·5
1745/1765–1765/1785	0·0	0·1	0·0
1765/1785–1785/1805	0·9%	1·1	0·6

(*i*) denotes 1700 base including home industries
(*ii*) denotes 1700 base excluding home industries
(*iii*) denotes 1800 base including home industries

Source: Deane and Cole, ibid., p. 80.

acceleration in the rate of growth of total and average real output (and hence income) in the 1870s is, in fact, in accordance with the Rostovian thesis of the 'take-off into self sustained growth'.

Table 8 continues the history of real output through the 19th century and we can see clearly that the acceleration of the last two decades of the 18th century was continued well into the first half of the 19th, in fact, *circa* 1830. However, after this date the rate of growth of real output began to slacken (exactly why we are not sure, though Deane and

Table 8

19th-CENTURY RATES OF GROWTH IN BRITAIN: REAL PRODUCT
(Compound Rates per Cent per Annum)

Decade	*Total growth of National Product* %	*Growth of National Product per head of Occupied Population* %	*Growth of National Product per head of Total Population* %
1801/1811–1831/1841	2·9	1·5	1·5
1811/1821–1841/1851	2·9	1·4	1·5
1821/1831–1851/1861	2·3	0·9	1·1
1831/1841–1861/1871	2·2	0·9	1·0
1841/1851–1871/1881	2·5	1·4	1·3
1851/1861–1881/1891	3·2	2·0	1·9
1861/1871–1891/1901	3·3	2·2	1·7

Source: Deane and Cole, ibid., p. 283.

Cole believe that an important contributory factor must have been the Irish potato famine, the result of which was to flood Britain with unskilled labour). *Circa* 1860 the rate of growth resumed its upward path and did not turn down again until the century drew to a close. (Again it is difficult to explain the downturn, though it has become fashionable lately to explain it in terms of a 'climacteric' following the 'massive' application of steam and steel).[13]

(3) *Foreign Trade and the Balance of Payments*

Foreign trade, of course, is and always has been the life-blood of the British economy and no survey of the 19th-century British economic history would be complete without its inclusion. In this particular context it has even greater relevance, for the history of foreign trade is inevitably and inextricably linked with the history of marine insurance underwriting in particular.

During the 18th century, British exports, valued at constant prices, increased approximately five-fold, while national income during the same period increased slightly less than three-fold. According to Gregory King, domestic exports from England and Wales were between 5 per cent and 6 per cent of national income in 1688,[14] but by the end of the 18th century the proportion had risen to 14 per cent.[15] This figure was sustained for the first two decades of the 19th century, but thereafter the proportion declined. On balance the average proportion during the first half of the 19th century was probably around 9 per cent. During the 1860s domestic exports resumed their upward path, reaching a peak in the 1870s of 23 per cent of national income. In the 1880s the first challenge to our international trading supremacy was experienced and during the period known as the 'Great Depression' the proportion of domestic exports to national income fell. During the half-century before the First World War, the figure ranged between 15 per cent and 21 per cent. Table 9 summarises the 19th-century trade and national income growth trends.

Table 9

GROWTH IN THE VOLUME OF INTERNATIONAL TRADE AND NATIONAL INCOME IN THE 19th-CENTURY

(Compound Rates per cent per annum)

Year	*Volume of Exports*	*Volume of Exports and Imports*	*Real National Income*
1801–31	2·9	2·6	2·7
1811–41	4·0	4·0	3·1
1821–51	4·7	4·4	2·8
1831–61	4·5	4·5	2·0
1841–70	4·9	4·6	2·3
1851–80	3·8	4·1	2·6
1861–90	3·1	3·5	3·5
1871–1901	2·3	2·9	3·1
1881–1911	2·7	2·5	2·4

Source: Deane and Cole, ibid., p. 311.

The trade figures are for the U.K. and the National Income figures are for Great Britain.

This Table shows clearly the tendency for the volume of trade to outstrip the growth in real income during the first three-quarters of the century. But notice the close correlation between the decline in the growth of trade in the last quarter and the decline in the growth of real income. Indeed, throughout the course of statistically documented British economic history there has been this close (though sometimes lagged) correlation, which is an indication of the paramount importance of international trade for the fortunes of the British economy.

Table 10 provides a breakdown of Britain's 19th-century trading structure. The immediate and most striking feature of the Table is the contrast

Table 10

U.K. BALANCE OF PAYMENTS 1816–1913

(Annual Averages in £m. All Figures have been Rounded)

Year	*Balance of Visible Trade (1)*	*Net Shipping Earnings (2)*	*Profits, Interest and Dividends (3)*	*Insurance Brokerage Commission (4)*	*Emigrants, Tourists, Smugglers Govt. etc. (5)*	*Balance of Invisible Trade (6)*	*Net Balance (7)*
1816–20	− 11	+ 10	+ 8	+ 3	− 3	+ 18	+ 7
1821–25	− 8	+ 9	+ 9	+ 2	− 2	+ 18	+ 10
1826–30	− 15	+ 8	+ 9	+ 2	− 3	+ 17	+ 3
1831–35	− 13	+ 5	+ 11	+ 3	− 4	+ 19	+ 6
1836–40	− 23	+ 11	+ 15	+ 4	− 4	+ 26	+ 3
1841–45	− 19	+ 12	+ 15	+ 4	− 5	+ 25	+ 6
1846–50	− 26	+ 14	+ 18	+ 4	− 6	+ 30	+ 5
1851–55	− 33	+ 19	+ 24	+ 6	− 8	+ 41	+ 8
1856–60	− 34	+ 26	+ 33	+ 8	− 8	+ 60	+ 26
1861–65	− 59	+ 34	+ 34	+11	− 8	+ 81	+ 22
1866–70	− 65	+ 45	+ 57	+13	− 9	+106	+ 44
1871–75	− 64	+ 51	+ 83	+16	−12	+139	+ 75
1876–80	−124	+ 54	+ 88	+16	− 9	+149	+ 25
1881–85	− 99	+ 60	+ 96	+16	−11	+177	+ 88
1886–90	− 89	+ 57	+115	+15	−11	+161	+ 61
1891–95	−134	+ 57	+124	+15	−10	+186	+ 52
1896–1900	−159	+ 62	+132	+16	−11	+199	+ 40
1901–05	−177	+ 71	+149	+18	−13	+226	+ 49
1906–10	−144	+ 89	+196	+22	−18	+290	+146
1911–13	−140	+100	+241	+27	−22	+346	+206

Source: Deane and Cole, ibid., p. 36.

between the merchandise trade account and the invisible trade account. The merchandise account was passive throughout the century (indeed, it seems that this passivity has been characteristic of British trade for more than 250 years) and progressively worsened as the years went on. The balance of invisible trade, on the other hand, was always active, particularly so after 1850. Indeed, the rapid rise in the balance of invisible trade is perhaps the most striking feature of the figures. Also interesting is the steady increase in the totals in columns (2) and (4), for these serve to some extent as an index of the volume of marine business and underwriting during the 19th century. The most pleasing feature, and this is especially true of column (4), is this unspectacular, yet solid, progress, which is, save for a few exceptions, a reflection of the general course of insurance history during the 19th century. However, this is a subject about which we shall have more to say in subsequent chapters.

Before we leave the subject of marine insurance we might well make note of one more index of growth, namely the increase in the size of the United Kingdom Shipping industry. The figures are provided in Table 11. Since Britannia, according to the popular song, is said to have wanted

Table 11

GROWTH OF THE U.K. SHIPPING INDUSTRY 1795–1908

(Annual Averages in £m.)

Year	*Value of tonnage built and registered in the U.K.*	*Value of tonnage built in the U.K.*	*Net shipping earnings from the rest of the world*
1795–1804	2·0	2·1	—
1800–1809	2·2	2·3	—
1805–1814	2·5	2·6	—
1810–1819	2·7	2·9	—
1815–1824	1·9	2·0	9·7
1820–1829	1·7	1·8	9·3
1825–1834	1·9	2·0	9·9
1830–1839	2·1	2·2	11·2
1835–1847	2·5	2·6	12·9
1840–1849	2·5	2·7	14·6
1845–1854	3·2	3·5	16·5
1850–1859	4·7	5·2	20·6
1855–1864	6·8	7·9	28·6
1860–1869	8·8	9·9	37·5
1865–1874	11·6	14·6	46·6
1870–1879	13·0	16·3	51·1
1875–1884	14·9	17·9	56·6
1880–1889	13·8	17·1	58·7
1885–1894	11·6	14·5	57·3
1890–1899	12·4	16·0	59·1
1895–1904	14·0	18·7	64·1
1900–1908	16·7	22·6	75·7

Source: Deane and Cole, ibid., p. 234.

to rule the waves during this period, it is not surprising to find that the 19th century witnessed an eleven-fold increase in this country's shipbuilding capacity. Throughout the century the great bulk of ship production was domestically orientated although there was an increasing trend towards production for foreign markets. By the end of the period some

26 per cent of British production was destined for foreign markets compared with only 5 per cent during the years 1815–1825 (this was the first post-war period).

This concludes our brief and admittedly superficial survey of British economic development during the 18th and 19th centuries. In selecting our indices of growth we have been motivated by the need to highlight the conditions which might favour the growth of insurance in particular, but this should not detract from the essential characteristics of those years which fall within the compass of the Industrial Revolution. We have seen that the last decades of the 18th century were a watershed in our economic history for it was during this period that we 'took off' into self-sustained growth. All available indices point to such a take-off and the case cannot lightly be dismissed. We have seen that population began its expansion around this date and continued to grow throughout the 19th century, while the upturns in real income, real output, and foreign trade all had their origins during these critical years. The way was now clearly open for those with initiative, enterprise, and a little capital. The time was ripe to stage a revolution.

NOTES

1 D. E. W. Gibb, *Lloyd's of London—A Study in Individualism,* (1957).

2 Quoted by Raynes; see 2nd ed., pp. 171–172.

3 John Brownlee, 'History of the Birth and Death Rates in England and Wales taken as a whole from 1570 to the present time', *Public Health,* June and July, 1916.

4 It ought to be added, however, that this whole subject has recently become a matter of academic dispute. For a fuller discussion of the inadequacies of these statistics see P. Deane and N. Cole, *British Economic Growth, 1688–1959,* 2nd edition, 1967, pp. 99–104.

5 Reproduced from Deane and Cole, ibid., 1st ed., 1962, p. 6.

6 James Wheeler, *Manchester, its Political, Social and Commercial History* (1836), p. 146.

7 Conrad Gill, *History of Birmingham* (1951), Vol. I., p. 56.

8 Wheeler, op. cit., p. 146.

9 The paper was entitled *On the Distribution of Population in England and Wales, and its Progress in the Period of Ninety Years from 1801 to 1891.*

10 According to E. C. K. Gonner, 'Population of England in the 18th Century', *Journal of the Royal Statistical Society,* 1912–1913—the density of population in 1700 (excl. the counties in the London area) ranged from 141 per sq. mile in Worcestershire to 54 per sq. mile in Westmorland. A century later the population density of Westmorland was almost unchanged, but others had more than doubled, Lancs. heading the list with 353 per sq. mile. Taking the counties located to the N. of a line from the Severn to the Wash, we find that their share of the total population rose from 43½ per cent in 1701 to 50 per

cent in 1831, most of this advance apparently being achieved in the second half of the 18th century.

11 M. W. Flinn, *Origins of the Industrial Revolution* (1966), p. 15.

12 Deane and Cole, ibid.

13 See F. H. Phelps and S. J. Handfield-Jones, *The Climacteric of the 1890s: A Study in the Expanding Economy,* Oxford Economic Papers, 1952. For a rather different view see D. J. Coppock, *The Climacteric of the 1890s: A Critical Note,* Manchester School of Economics and Social Studies, 1956.

14 Gregory King, *On the Naval Trade of England anno 1688,* p. 65.

15 Deane and Cole, ibid., pp. 28–29.

Chapter 7

THE DEVELOPMENT OF JOINT-STOCK COMPANIES IN INSURANCE 1800-1850

'The gods help them that help themselves.'
(Aesop—Hercules and the Waggoner)

DURING THE course of the narrative we have drawn attention to the many pitfalls implicit in the process of awarding succinct titles to long, and usually heterogeneous, periods of history. The warning once more has to be served, for one must not be misled into the automatic assumption that *circa* 1800 British insurance emerged suddenly from its adolescence to stride the world 'like a Colossus'. On the contrary, the process was a gradual one, involving set-backs as well as advances, and consequently the path was not always smooth. Nevertheless, the fact that around the turn of the century a number of important economic indices took an upward trend, allied to a significant increase in the volume of business underwritten, to some extent justifies the observation that a new era was at hand.

This had, in fact, become evident even before the turn of the century, for these closing years witnessed two movements which, during the first two decades of the 19th century, were to gain immensely in momentum—first, the increasing number of new companies engaged in fire and life business and, secondly, the movement for the abolition of those clauses of the Bubble Act which rendered corporate joint-stock marine underwriting a legal impossibility. Then, to confirm the impression, followed a period of foreign expansion, albeit tentative, but nevertheless significant. We shall deal with these three movements in turn.

We have already noted that the last quarter of the 18th century was one of rapid economic progress, so much so that the three leading London offices soon found it impossible to cope with the expansion. Some indication of the demand for new offices may be gained from the assertion of Adam Smith that, in 1776, not one house in a hundred was insured against fire. This figure would appear to be something of an exaggeration but the paucity of reliable statistics unfortunately precludes any attempt at refutation. It is obvious, however, that a vast market did exist, for twenty years later, in 1802, it was fairly reliably estimated that only a third of the insurable property of the United Kingdom, i.e. £600 million, was in fact insured against fire.

The first challenge to the comfortable position of the three London offices came in 1782 with the establishment of the Phoenix Fire Office. This office was the direct product of the existing offices' consistent refusal to insure the premises of sugar refineries at reasonable rates:[1] in 1781 an association of sugar refiners was formed and in January 1782 its first policy was issued. In 1783 a charter was applied for and refused; and so instead the company was established by a deed, dated 19 August 1783. The company was originally known as the New Fire Office, but it was not long before it became known as the Phoenix after the symbol on its fire-mark.[2]

By virtue of the quantity of untapped business available the new company quickly became an established concern—so much so, in fact, that the older offices readily built up a friendly liaison with it. So successful was the company that in 1797 it extended its scope to life assurance by the establishment of a separate company known as the Pelican, to which we have already referred.[3] Though the Pelican remained a separate company throughout the 19th century, it continued to be very much a sister company of the Phoenix, and was in fact absorbed by the Phoenix on 1 January 1908.

Another London company, the British Fire Office, opened for business on 25 March 1799 and it, too, quickly became an accepted member of the 'establishment' for in that year, in a petition against the application for a charter by the Globe, the British Fire Office claimed that 'in every considerable town throughout the United Kingdom there are offices under the direction of your petitioners (i.e. the British Fire Office) for making fire insurances'.[4]

Of far greater consequence, however, was the Globe itself for not only did it rapidly become one of the most prominent fire and life companies but, as we shall see in a moment, it was this company which led the attack against the monopoly of corporate marine underwriting held, since 1720, by the Royal Exchange and the London Assurance. An application for a charter was presented in 1799 but, despite the presence on the petition of such famous names as Sir Ralph Eden (plus twelve members of parliament), it was rejected. A fresh application was made in 1801 but in 1803 a Committee of the House once more rejected it. As a result, the promoters established themselves under a deed of settlement, dated 2 June 1803. The initial success of the company was such that, only two years later in 1805, it ranked sixth in terms of the amount of stamp duty paid.[5]

Between 1804 and 1810, the pace of formation of new companies quickened. In 1804, the Imperial Fire Office was established and this was followed, in 1805, by the Albion Fire and Life Insurance Company and the Caledonian, an Edinburgh company. In 1806 came the Provident Life Office, the Rock Life Office and the London Life Office; in 1807 the County Fire Office and the Eagle Insurance Company, in 1808 the Atlas Assurance Company; in 1809 the North British Insurance Company (also an Edinburgh company) and finally, in 1810, the Sun Life Assurance Society.

With the exception of the Caledonian and the North British, all the companies mentioned were, of course, London companies. However, at the same time, and indeed preceding the period 1804–1810, considerable provincial expansion was taking place, which, though obviously not as significant in terms of the *volume* of business effected, nevertheless constituted a major educative force. The first provincial office, the Bristol Crown (to which we have already referred), was established as early as 1718 but the reluctance of others to follow indicates its essentially pioneering function. However, in 1767, the Bath Fire Office was formed and two years later Bristol acquired its second office, not unnaturally named the Bristol Fire Office. In 1771, Ireland acquired its first fire company when the Hibernian opened in Dublin whilst the Manchester Fire Office also saw the light of day that year. Bath acquired a second office—the Bath Sun—in 1776 and Liverpool did so a year later in 1777; in 1780, the Salop Fire Office was formed and in 1783 two more companies, the Leeds Fire Office and the Newcastle Fire Office were established. In 1783, the first of a number of Norwich offices was established, the Norwich Fire Office, and in 1790 came the Worcester Fire Office and the Wiltshire and Western Fire Office. In 1792 a second Norwich Office, the Norwich General, was formed and in 1797 came the Norwich Union Fire Office. In 1802 the Kent Fire and Life Insurance Company arrived on the scene and two years later, in 1804, the southern counties of Hampshire, Sussex and Dorset were provided with their first company. In 1807 two more companies, the West of England Fire and Life Insurance Company and the Essex and Suffolk Equitable Insurance Society were established, and 1808 witnessed the birth of the Norwich Union Life Insurance Society.

Clearly, then, during the early years of the 19th century fire and life assurance received a shot in the arm especially in the 'country' where a new industrial life-blood was begining to flow. It would be wrong, however, to exaggerate the magnitude of this provincial expansion for, although it possessed a very wide geographical basis, companies were, by and large, very small and tended to handle only relatively safe business.

Unfortunately, we do not have figures for early life assurance but we do have the figures for the total fire insurance transacted during the year ending 5 January 1806.[6] These are provided in the tables below.

Table 12

LONDON OFFICES

Duty Paid for the Financial Year ending 5th January 1806

		£
1.	Sun	92,845
2.	Phoenix	59,162
3.	Royal Exchange	44,096
4.	Imperial	23,141
5.	British	18,744
6.	Globe	17,249
7.	Westminster	12,278
8.	Hand-in-Hand	12,121
9.	London Assurance	6,210
10.	Union	4,783
11.	Albion	3,568
	Total	£294,197

Table 13

COUNTRY OFFICES

Duty Paid for the Financial Year ending 5th January 1806

		£
1.	Kent	4,752
2.	Newcastle-on-Tyne	3,759
3.	Bristol Town	3,321
4.	Norwich	3,064
5.	Salamander	2,829
6.	Liverpool	2,790
7.	Bath (old)	1,599
8.	Worcester	1,427
9.	Norwich Union	1,347
10.	Hants, Sussex and Dorset	1,313
11.	Bristol Crown	1,258
12.	Bath Sun	1,137
13.	Essex Equitable	1,036
14.	Birmingham	925
15.	Finching Field	52
16.	Woolder	43
	Total	£30,652

Table 14

SCOTTISH AND IRISH OFFICES

Duty Paid for the Financial Year ending 5th January 1806

		£
1.	Friendly	2,948
2.	Glasgow	1,956
3.	Dundee	1,521
4.	Aberdeen	971
5.	Caledonian	663
6.	Dublin	4,197
7.	'In the Country'	218
	Total	£12,474

Source: H. E. Raynes, Op. cit., p. 210.

While the duty was levied at 2s. 6d. or 3s. on every £100 insured, the premium income could not differ very substantially from the duty paid.

These figures quite clearly reflect the inverse relationship between the number of offices and the *value of business* transacted, *vis-à-vis* the metropolis and the provinces. Despite fairly rapid provincial expansion, in 1806 a far smaller number of London offices dealt with a far greater volume of business than their provincial counterparts. Obviously, provincial development was still very much in its infancy.

However, around 1810 the rate of growth of new offices slackened considerably and a hectic first decade was followed by a quiescent second decade. The reasons are not altogether clear but a number do suggest themselves. First, England and France were embroiled in a protracted war of economic as well as military attrition, producing, as it did, an uncertain environment for new commercial endeavours. Moreover, after 1809 there was a brief period of falling prices which may have induced caution and constituted an added disincentive to effort. Thirdly, loss ratios had been rising gradually since the 1770s largely because of the increasing complexity of industrial and mercantile risks and these losses reached a peak around 1810. Fourthly, the burden of government taxation on fire insurances, in the form of the much maligned stamp duty, was by this time exceedingly heavy to bear. And finally, the effect of the new competition during the early years had been to force down the premium rates below a truly acceptable level. It was at this juncture, however, that the second movement, to which we have already alluded, namely the movement to repeal those clauses of the Bubble Act forbidding the establishment of any new joint-stock marine insurance companies, became once more a living issue.

We say 'once more', because several earlier attempts had been made, all without success. We have already referred to the Globe's attempts to secure a charter for the conduct of fire and life business in 1801 and its subsequent failure in 1803. However, Sir Frederick Eden and his associates were not discouraged by the adverse decision and, in 1806, made another attempt, but this time they included in the petition a request to conduct marine insurance also. Unfortunately, the Bill did not get beyond its Second Reading and one might well imagine that that would have been the end of the matter. But this was not so, for towards the end of 1809 a powerful organisation of wealthy merchants, ever eager to lay their hands on a larger portion of the fat marine underwriting profits—the spoils of war—decided to establish a giant new company with a nominal capital of £5 million. Such was the strength of the organisation that a number of Lloyd's underwriters, 'looking upon themselves as passengers in a vessel about to be wrecked by collision, and deeming it best for their safety to jump on board the ship that was looming in the distance, bearing upon their doomed craft',[8] weighed in with their personal reserves. On 8 February 1810,[9] the petition was laid before the House and on the 14 February there followed a request by Sir William Manning, M.P. for the City of London 'that a Select Committee be appointed to consider the Act of the 6th of George the First, concerning marine insurances, together with our present means of affecting marine insurances'. This request was brilliantly opposed in the House by Joseph Marryat, M.P. for Sandwich, an underwriter of the highest character and father of the more famous naval novelist, Captain Frederick Marryat. So instructive was his speech that it deserves fairly lengthy quotation. He began by saying :

'If I am asked why I object to . . . the appointment of a Committee to consider our present means of effecting marine insurances in Great Britain, I answer, because the subject was completely investigated so lately as July 1806, by the Committee appointed on the Globe Insurance Company's Bill; before whom it was so satisfactorily proved, that our means, both in point of extent and solidity were completely adequate to every possible occasion, that the parties abandoned their application to Parliament.'[10] He then went on to draw an illuminating picture of the way in which business was carried on at Lloyd's.

'Exclusive of the two chartered companies,' he said 'there are about one thousand five hundred subscribers to Lloyd's, the greater number of whom daily attend there for the purpose of transacting insurance business. The merchant, when he receives an order to effect insurances from his correspondents abroad, or has the occasion to cover property shipped by himself at home, he applies to an insurance broker, who transacts the business either with the public companies, or with individual underwriters, according as he finds it to the most advantage of his employer. The House will see the extent to which competition is carried by this mode of effecting insurances. The merchant is well aware that his credit with his foreign correspondents depends upon his executing their orders on the best terms possible. The broker is equally aware that his credit with his employer, the merchant, depends upon the same circumstance. The underwriter is also aware that, unless he writes at the very lowest current premium, the brokers who are in the habit of showing him their policies, will transfer their accounts to other underwriters, and from this consideration he frequently accepts a premium which, in his best judgement, he considers inadequate to the risk, rather than lose his connections. Thus competition is carried to the highest possible pitch; and thus has the reputation of his country for effecting marine insurances on the most reasonable terms been so universally established, that orders from every part of the globe are sent here, the property annually insured in this country amounting to nearly two hundred millions, as is proved by the duty paid for stamps upon policies.'[11]

Marryat then attacked the oft-levied assertion that insurances made with a corporate organisation might well be safer than insurances made with private individuals. 'I maintain,' he said, 'that Lloyd's offers better security to the assured than can be given by any chartered company. I say so for this plain reason, that every man at Lloyd's is responsible for his engagements to the last shilling of his fortune, while the members of an incorporated company are responsible only for the amount of the capital originally invested; and the capital of the underwriters at Lloyd's infinitely exceeds that of any chartered company whatever. For instance, the capital of this new company is intended to be five million, of which one million, I understand, is to be actually advanced. In point of fact, the one million so advanced is the whole extent of the security offered to the public; for though the original subscribers to this undertaking are men of fortune and able to pay the other four millions in case of need, yet they, from various motives may be induced to sell out, and may sell to men of straw, mere speculators who would not be able to pay the other four millions. But giving them the whole advantage of this argument, and taking their capital at five millions, that sum bears no proportion to the aggregate capital of the underwriters at Lloyd's; for I could name fifty out of the 1,500 subscribers to that house, who could pay down these five millions at any time, without the smallest inconvenience, leaving the capital of the other 1,450 subscribers wholly untouched. Events have occurred within these few years that would have more than swallowed up the capital of this company, and yet have scarcely occasioned the failure of a single individual at Lloyd's; for every prudent underwriter regularly classes all his risks, and propositions the amount he hazards on those of each particular description to his means of payment in case of loss; a precaution which could not possibly be observed in the vast mass of business that would be undertaken by this new company.'[12]

Marryat's eloquent address met with prolonged applause but, following Mr. Alexander Baring's cogent reply in favour of the petition, the ardour of the House cooled to such an extent that the motion to appoint a Select Committee was in fact carried by a small majority. The members of the Committee were duly appointed on 20 February and amongst them were Marryat and Baring. Manning, the chief proponent of the petition was made chairman. Needless to say, the bias represented by this appointment was sufficient to carry the day for the proponents of the petition, despite persuasive and impressive evidence to the contrary. As a result, on 24 May, Mr. Baring laid a Bill before the House to repeal 'so much of the Act of 6 George I as gives to certain companies the right of underwriting policies of Marine Insurance to the exclusion of all others'. However, after a protracted struggle in the Commons the division on the motion to commit the Bill found twenty-six 'no's' against twenty-five 'yeas'. Thus it 'passed in the Negative' by the narrowest of all possible margins.

And there the matter rested, for the ensuing years were pregnant with uncertainty.[13] In fact, the matter rested for some fourteen years until one day, quite unexpectedly, the old bone of contention was uncovered, and the fight was renewed. But at the centre of the new struggle there was a new and truly remarkable character by the name of Nathan Meyer Rothschild.[14]

The story goes that one day, in the spring of 1824, Rothschild was 'leaning . . . against his favourite pillar in the Royal Exchange when his cousin ran up to him in a high state of excitement. 'Vat ish de matter?' queried Nathan. Thereupon the other recounted, in gasps, how he had been applying for the vacant actuaryship of a large insurance company, and had been beaten in the competition, though being admittedly the best candidate, on account of his religion, the Directors saying that they would have no Jew. Now Nathan, too, got excited. 'Vat,' he cried, disengaging his hands from his pockets and laying hold of his cousin by the shoulder; 'not take you because of your religion! Mine Gott! Den I vil make a bigger office for you den any of dem.'[15]

And Rothschild was true to his word. Gathering around him his most trusted friends such as John Irving, Francis Baring, Samuel Gurney and

Sir Moses Montefiore, he quickly formed the 'Alliance British and Foreign Fire and Life Assurance Company' with a nominal capital of £5 million. Immediately following the issue of the prospectus, an application was made to Parliament for the repeal of the Act of 6 George I so that the Directors of the Alliance might add marine insurance underwriting to their advertised activities. The leadership of this attack in Parliament was entrusted to Thomas Fowell Buxton, a personal friend of Rothschild who knew next to nothing about marine insurance but whose prowess as a leader of the anti-slavery party had won him considerable parliamentary respect and influence. Moreover, he had been appointed auditor of the new company. So, not unnaturally 'he threw himself into the fight with all the zest and venom of a practised advocate'.[16]

Lloyd's, of course, were prepared to fight the petition 'tooth and nail', as they had done in 1810. Unfortunately, from their point of view, the economic climate had changed radically during the intervening years, and with Huskisson now President of the Board of Trade, a free-trade bias was inevitable. On 17 May, Buxton was given leave to bring in a Bill to repeal the Act of 6 George I in so far as it imposed restrictions on marine insurance. The die was immutably cast.

Marryat, in the meantime, had died and the fight on behalf of Lloyd's was carried in the Commons by Alderman William Thompson, M.P., for Sunderland. Thompson, though not a subscriber to Lloyd's, had extensive business connections in the Rooms and was well suited to conduct the campaign in the House. In fact, he performed with great panache and was surprisingly supported by William Manning, the proponent of repeal during the 1810 debate. But the House was in no mood to listen. On 15 June, after an all night sitting, a tired House refused an appeal for adjournment and passed the Bill. On 24 June 1824, it received the Royal Assent.

The star of *laissez-faire* was now clearly in the ascendant, for in the following year the remaining provisions of the Bubble Act were swept away.[17] It will be remembered that the Bubble Act had two objectives; the first was the establishment by incorporation of two monopolistic marine insurance companies; the second was the legal condemnation of all undertakings acting to the prejudice of trade; the subscriptions, assignments, transfers and other devices for the furtherance of such undertakings; the acting or presuming to act as a corporate body; the raising of a transferable stock or the assigning of such stock without authority either by Act of Parliament or by Charter. There was now no confusion between a corporate and a non-corporate commercial society. Henceforth, the privilege of possessing a transferable stock which brokers or jobbers could manipulate was to belong only to a corporate society. We have seen that the first object had finally been defeated by the repeal of the first 17 clauses of the Act in 1824, whilst fire insurance companies had been recognised as early as 1782 by the Act of 22 George III C. 48, which stated: 'licences . . . shall be granted to . . . two or more . . . partners as and for the whole company or partnership and in every case the licence shall continue in force until the end of the year.' The remaining constraints upon joint-stock enterprises with transferable shares were now finally removed by the Act of 1825. However, as Raynes rightly points out, although the Bubble Act had now been repealed, joint-stock companies still had no status in the eyes of the law, and in this sense, the Chartered Companies Act 'in effect did nothing of constructive value for insurance companies',[18] for instead of applying for charters they continued to act under their deeds of settlement but with the added right to sue and be sued in the name of an officer. This deficiency was to some extent rectified by the Chartered Companies Act of 1837,[19] which empowered the Crown to grant, by letters patent to the unincorporated joint-stock company, the 'privileges which, according to Common Law could be granted to a Company by Charter on Incorporation'.

Yet even now all was not well because unregulated and often fraudulent companies requiring no returns of their purpose or purposes, deed of settlement, shareholders or capital, could continue to conduct business. This deficiency was finally rectified by the Act for the Registration, Incorporation, and Regulation of Joint-Stock Companies[20] under the terms of which a Registrar of Joint-Stock Companies was empowered to demand half-yearly returns of all changes of membership.

The adoption of a more enlightened attitude towards the legal status of the joint-stock company with freely transferable shares was clearly conducive to the expansion of the insurance business, and the joint-stock structure rapidly became the most popular form of financial organisation amongst insurance companies. But the *laissez-faire* creed favourably affected the fortunes of the insurance companies in other ways through the direct stimulation of trade and the consequent increase in business confidence inherent in the application of the doctrine.

We have seen that the period 1793–1815 had been one of continuous war during which business confidence was severely shaken. There is no doubt that a number of marine underwriters profited greatly by the inflated wartime rates, but such a war also involved the very real risk of heavy losses and a number of less experienced underwriters were faced with ruin. The position was not improved by the decline in prices which started in 1815. The return of peace did not immediately restore business confidence, for the normal post-war problems had to be faced, but it was not long before the old rosiness returned to the entrepreneurial cheeks.

In 1819, a Bank Committee under the chairmanship of Peel and intellectual guidance of Huskisson was appointed to consider the vexed question of currency reform, and in 1820 cash payments were resumed. Gold thus became the sole standard of value, the currency was settled on a firm and lasting basis, and the greatest cause of business insecurity was, at one fell swoop, removed.

The next step was the reformation of taxes and tariffs. During the war taxes had been imposed haphazardly on almost every consumable article, with the object of raising revenue for war purposes. Huskisson now proceeded to abolish many of the unproductive taxes and to revise and reduce others. In addition, important inroads were made into the tariff barrier that had slowly but inexorably been building up over the years of the preceding century. Acting on the principle that English manufacturers should have only a very slight protection and that raw materials should be allowed in as freely as possible, duties on foreign manufactures (which had previously varied between 40 per cent and 18 per cent) were reduced to between 15 per cent and 30 per cent, whilst import duties on raw materials were either drastically reduced or abolished altogether.

Huskisson also initiated the vital reform of the complex and, by now old-fashioned, Navigation Laws, the first of which required that the produce of Europe should come to England either in Bristish ships or in the ships of the country producing the goods, and the second of which required that the goods of Asia, Africa and America should be imported only in British ships. With the successful secession of the United States similar laws were enacted on the other side of the Atlantic, which meant that the ships of both nations were now required to accomplish half of each journey without a cargo. This preposterous state of affairs was to some extent ameliorated during 1820–1821, when Wallace, the Vice-President of the Board of Trade, did something to relax the Laws. Huskisson took this relaxation policy a little further in 1823, and on 21 March 1825, in a famous policy speech, further measures were outlined. In the following year the Navigation Act was repealed and replaced by a more liberal set of requirements based upon the principle of reciprocity.

The effects of these diverse measures were indeed startling. Whereas in 1820, the official valuation of our exports was £38 million, by 1824 the valuation had reached nearly £49 million. Business confidence was once again buoyant. The continents of America and Europe were now open markets and Britain, situated between the two, with the finest merchant marine in the world, was admirably situated to exploit its unique position and 'the great industrial revolution, which had enabled England to endure the strain of the Napoleonic struggle, was succeeded and consummated by an equally great commercial revolution, which enabled her to pay the cost of it'.[21]

This judgement is confirmed by the events of 1824–25, for during that year, the factors already outlined above coalesced to create a period of business speculation, not unlike the more famous (or should it be infamous?) period immediately preceding the Bubble Act of 1720. Once again insurance promotions featured heavily in the speculations, as Table 15 reveals. The figures were compiled by a solicitor, Joseph Parkes for

Table 15

FORMATION OF NEW COMPANIES 1824–1825

Type of Company	*Nominal Capital* £	*Amount Paid Up* £
Fire and Life Assurance	32,040,700	2,242,800
Foreign Loans	26,950,000	19,000,000
Loans, Pawn Broking, Investment, Annuity and Banking	22,160,000	2,216,000
Railroads	21,942,500	219,425
S. American Mining	14,475,000	1,447,500
Canals and Docks	14,134,000	282,680
Mining Corporations (G.B.)	10,400,000	520,000
Gas	7,370,000	737,000
Steam, Navigation, etc.	3,680,000	368,000
Provisions, Milk, Flour	3,160,000	158,000
Water Works	2,680,000	26,500
Colonial Companies	2,000,000	200,000
Total	£160,992,200	£27,417,905

Source: Raynes, ibid., p. 240.

the Select Committee on Joint-Stock Companies, before whom Parkes gave evidence in 1841. The Table shows that, in terms of nominal capital, fire and life assurance companies constituted the largest single class of speculative enterprise, whilst, in terms of capital actually paid up, they constituted the second largest class.

Needless to say, a great number of companies floated during this period of speculation were utterly fraudulent and soon collapsed, once more taking with them the savings of unsuspecting and often ingenuous investors. Others proved slightly more enduring, surviving until the Select Committee of 1841 exposed them for the fraudulent conspiracies which they undoubtedly were. But others again were based on the soundest insurance principles, so much so that a number of them formed during this rather unsavoury period have survived, in one form or another, down to the present day. One such company, to which we have already referred, i.e. the Alliance, was instrumental in breaking the long-standing monopoly of the two chartered companies and, having succeeded, quickly established a reputation which was, and of course still is, beyond reproach.

A similarly irreproachable company, although established slightly before the mania reached its peak, was the Guardian Assurance Company, established in 1821. This company, too, was based upon the soundest principles and is especially noteworthy in this context because, under Article 69 of its deed of settlement, it provided for the separation of the fire, life and annuity accounts, and under Article 70, the losses and expenses of each department were to be met out of the funds of that department. This condition, which the Guardian pioneered, was subsequently enforced by statute.[22] Other famous companies formed during this period include the Yorkshire Insurance Company (1824), the Scottish Union and National Insurance Company (1824), the Clerical, Medical and General Life Assurance Society (1824), the Standard Life Assurance Company (1825), and the Scottish Amicable Life Assurance Society (1826).

Nine years later, according to Parkes, there followed a second period of speculation. 'I should say that . . . in the spring of 1834 there appeared to set in a similar mania in speculations—I should say its height was in the year 1834 to the beginning of 1835.' According to Parkes, this speculation of 1835 'was nearly equal in sterling amount and number of companies to the bubbles of 1824–25 and that many more were ridiculous'.[23]

He calculated that during the period 1834–36, 310 joint stock companies with a total nominal capital of £135,248,700, were floated, and of this total amount there were 11 insurance companies with a nominal capital of 7,600,000. Although we do not have the number of insurance companies floated during the earlier period. in terms of nominal capital the second period bore no resemblance to the first, the figures being £7 million and £32 million respectively. In point of fact, although a number of dubious organisations were conceived during the period they would appear to be outweighed by the number of excellent companies which were floated. Amongst these we may mention the National Provident Institution (1835), the Metropolitan Life Assurance Society (1835), the North of Scotland Fire and Life Assurance Company (1836), the Legal and General Assurance Society (1836) and the Liverpool and London and Globe Insurance Office (1836). The last named is especially worthy of inclusion for it subsequently emerged as the leading British insurance office operating in the huge and vitally significant North American market. We shall, however, have more to say about this company in the suceeding chapter.

In many ways the 1830s proved to be more significant than the preceding decade particularly in the fields of marine and fire insurance where the 1820s were not always kind. In particular, Lloyd's was dealt a severe blow by the repeal of the 1720 Act, and many of its subscribers were forced (or chose) to take up appointments with the Alliance and the other marine companies which were springing up. A particularly notable example was Mr. John Staniforth, an ex-member of the House Committee of Lloyd's who, in 1824, left to promote the Indemnity Mutual Marine Assurance Company, a company which had no less than 22 of its 26 directors from the Subscription Room of Lloyd's. This company was quickly followed by the establishment of other marine companies including the South Devon, the Sunderland, the Tyne, the Unanimous of South Shields, the General Maritime, the Liverpool Marine, the Ocean Marine, the Scotch Commercial and a number of Irish companies. Many, if not all, of these new competitors had what Wright and Fayle call 'renegade' subscribers amongst their agents and officials but the expertise and know-how thus acquired was wholly insufficient to support many of these highly doubtful companies and a number of them duly crashed.[24]

Even Lloyd's was stretched more than a little, for the financial crisis of 1825, allied to a falling market in marine business, combined to create a serious dearth of new business. The Alliance was similarly placed and it was not until 1829 that it was able to declare its first dividend. Thereafter, its fortunes revived and a steady dividend declaration was made possible. Lloyd's, however, was not so readily amenable to revival and the dark clouds of depression did not begin to lift until 1834. But in the case of Lloyd's there was the added difficulty imposed by a malignant internal dissension. The ostensible cause of the trouble was the remuneration of the Committee provided for under the by-laws of Lloyd's, but it seems that this was only the visible expression of a much deeper dissatisfaction with the way in which Lloyd's was managed generally. Fortunately, commonsense prevailed and a compromise satisfactory to all parties was reached in 1834. (The reader will find the details of the compromise in Wright and Fayle's *History of Lloyd's.*) This, combined with a reduction in the onerous Stamp Duty in that year, the establishment of Lloyd's register of British and Foreign Shipping on a formal basis in the same year, and a general increase in the volume of business was sufficient to blow away the clouds of depression. For the first time in ten years the sun shone on Lloyd's of London.

In 1837 another important landmark in the history of Lloyd's was reached when *Lloyd's List*, hitherto a twice weekly paper, became a daily paper. As a result circulation increased and such was the demand for the paper that in 1854 it was doubled in size. If this fact serves as an index of the fortunes of the subscribers, one may also note that not even the destruction by fire of the premises they had occupied since 1774 could shake their solidarity and when, on 26 December 1844, a new, third Royal Exchange was opened, an even more magnificent phase in proper keeping with their sumptuous new surroundings was ushered in.

The history of fire insurance during the 1820s reveals the same depression which affected Lloyd's and the marine companies; and the nature of this depression is well illustrated by the fortunes of the Sun, still by far the largest first office. We have seen that the early history of the Sun was one involving spectacular growth but that, *circa* 1790, this rate of growth began to decline. By 1815 it had become painfully slow and the resumption of peaceful conditions did nothing to ameliorate the position for competition had driven premium rates below the accepted level. During the period 1825–27 premium income actually fell below £100,000 for the first time since 1807 and it was not until 1833 that the 1817 level was once more attained.[25] By this date, the office, and indeed the other offices too, according to available figures, were forced to insure a far greater amount of property in order to maintain a stable premium income.

It was at this point that the tide of fortune began to turn in favour of the Sun, as annual premium income began once more to rise. By 1840, domestic premium income had reached £170,000 p.a., whilst the office also received a small income from foreign insurances and by 1850 domestic premium had grown to £192,000, almost double the 1825 figure.

The principal cause of this reversal of the declining trend in premium income was a significant increase in provincial business from 1830 onwards. Before that date the provinces' share of total business effected fluctuated between 40 per cent and 48 per cent but thereafter the proportion steadily increased. By 1840 the provincial share had risen to 60 per cent and this trend was maintained after 1840. (By 1882, in terms of sums covered, the share had increased to 71 per cent and in terms of premium income this figure was only marginally less.)

Precisely *why* this trend became apparent after 1830 is explained by the rapidly changing structure and organisation of the economy consequential upon the equally rapid industrialisation of the country. In Chapter 3 we examined the structure of the Sun's insurances *circa* 1770, i.e. on the eve of the industrial 'take-off'. Now let us compare those results with a sample of 500 policies taken out in 1840, at a date when the process of industrialisation had reached a fairly advanced stage.[26]

Table 16 shows quite clearly the tendency which we have implied; namely, that despite the fact that, in 1840, policies on dwelling houses and shops were still *numerically* preponderant, policies on mercantile and industrial property provided the *largest proportion of the premiums.*

Table 16

STRUCTURE OF THE SUN'S INSURANCES—1840

Type of Property	*Proportion of Total Policies* %	*Proportion of Total Premiums* %
Dwelling Houses plus contents	56	25
Shops	6	3
Farms and Stock	12	6
Mercantile Warehouses	12	34
Cotton Mills	1	9
Miscellaneous	13	23

Additional evidence is provided in Table 17, which gives the occupational breakdown of the 500 insured. Notice the disproportionate influence of the merchant category—although forming only 12 per cent of the policy holders, they held 33 per cent of the total premiums. In fact, it was this increasing tendency towards the concentration of business in the hands of the industrial and commercial classes which really paved the

Table 17

OCCUPATION OR STATUS OF THOSE INSURED WITH THE SUN—1840

Occupation or Status	*Proportion of Total Policies* %	*Proportion of Total Premiums* %
Shopkeepers, Tradesmen, and Craftsmen	30	23
Merchants	12	33
'Esquires'	6	6
Gentlemen	13	5
Professional Men	9	6
Farmers	9	3
Miscellaneous	21	24

way for the permanent and increasing prosperity of the Sun and its competitors during the years that followed. That, and of course the excursion into foreign markets.

It is almost impossible to state with certainty the date of the first foreign insurance, but we do know that it must have been a fire policy, for Relton, in his 'Account of the Fire Insurance Companies' states that fire insurance on property in the West Indies had been effected at Lloyd's Coffee-house from a very early date. Certainly, we have evidence that the Albion Mills in the West Indies were covered by Lloyd's underwriters for they in fact paid out £20,000 following a fire at the Mills in 1791. This, and similar insurances, were effected merely by post, and this simple, but risky, procedure seems to have become increasingly popular during the years that followed, so much so, in fact, that in 1810 an act extending the conditions of the 1781 Stamp Act to foreign policies effected in London was placed upon the Statute Book.[27]

However, a far more convenient and certainly less risky method of effecting foreign insurances proved to be the appointment of a foreign agent with the power of attorney. It appears that the first foreign agency was established by the Phoenix at Hamburg in 1786.[28] In 1805, the same company established another agency in New York (although it was withdrawn in 1815) and this was quickly followed by agencies in a number of the principal cities of the United States. However, the outbreak of war between Britain and the United States virtually terminated this type of business and it was not resumed on a really large scale until the end of the American Civil War in 1865. It was from this date that the massive development of the North American market by British companies, a phenomenon about which we shall have more to say in the following chapter, really began.

This does not mean that the underwriting of United States risks was non-existent between the two wars. The Phoenix, for instance, continued to receive proposals from the United States during the whole of this period, whilst in the 1840s and 1850s, a number of offices were established in the principal cities.[29]

There can be no doubt that the Phoenix, established in 1782, pioneered the extremely hazardous but, ultimately, lucrative business of foreign insurances and it became the model upon which other companies based their foreign *modus operandi.* The Sun, for example, immediately following its decision in July 1836 to appoint European agents, wrote to the Phoenix asking details of the rates which that company charged for foreign risks. However, the Sun, it should be mentioned, was laggardly in this respect but certain other offices were by no means as conservative.

The Alliance certainly was not, for early in April 1824, it was resolved that 'foreign assurance, both Fire and Life, should be taken in the capitals and principal towns of Europe, in the British Colonies of America, the West Indies and British settlements in India', and a statement in French and German was prepared so that it might be 'transmitted by the friends of the company to their Foreign Correspondents in such a manner as shall appear most expedient to the Foreign Assurance Committee to which the Management of this business is referred'.[30] The Alliance even ventured into North America, but the New York Agency closed down after only a year although it was not until 1851 that the company 'resolved that the prosecution of Fire Assurance business by the Company in Canada should be abandoned'.[31]

But during these early days it was the relative proximity of the European market which constituted the most magnetic attraction for British companies and it was here that the greatest activity was to be found. Germany proved especially attractive, particularly the old Hansa towns of Hamburg, Bremen and Lubeck, but other agencies were soon established in such towns as Berlin and Hanover. Other continental cities quickly acquired the services of British insurers, notably Stockholm, Copenhagen, Amsterdam, Rotterdam, Lisbon, Oporto, Gibraltar and even the island of Madeira. The Russian market proved almost impossible to penetrate by virtue of the fact that Russian companies had a monopoly of insurance in that country. However, these companies were small and were often unable to cover large risks: re-insurance contracts with British and German companies were therefore common. In 1842, for example, the Sun had 89 Russian policies in force, including one on Prince Boratinski's mansion and seven on large breweries.[32]

Elsewhere, particularly in the British colonies and in the Far East, the influence of British insurance companies was strongly felt and the Colonies especially proved to be an exploitable market. Profitable liaison was quickly established between the insurance companies and the great merchant houses of the day with the result that the agency network of fire offices in particular proceeded apace.

Thus, by 1850, British pre-eminence in the now vitally important sphere of insurance had become an established fact. At home, powered by the vast engine of industrial progress, the vehicle of insurance had been driven, not always sensibly, but at least without serious accident, to a high peak from which it was possible to look back down the valley at the panorama with some satisfaction, in the full knowledge that even higher peaks lay in the distance. Abroad, the road had been less smooth and the journey shorter but it was already clear that an exciting, and eventually profitable, adventure lay ahead.

By this time no less than 236 insurance companies had been promoted of which by far the greatest number, 157, transacted life assurance either on its own or in combination with other classes of business; 64 companies were underwriting fire insurance and 46 dealt in marine business and that growing body of miscellaneous hazards thrown up by the advancing complications of society which was later to be known as accident insurance. As Table 18 shows, few of these enterprises lasted long and one hundred years later only 37 had survived.[33]

Table 18

FORMATION OF COMPANY UNITS UP TO 1850 AND THEIR SUBSEQUENT HISTORY UP TO 1950

Date of Formation	*Total*	*Amalgamated or Absorbed*	*Wound Up*	*Existing in 1950*
Formed before 1800	29	12	7	10
Formed between 1801 and 1820	24	17	—	7
Formed between 1811 and 1820	9	5	3	1
Formed between 1821 and 1830	42	31	3	8
Formed between 1831 and 1840	53	37	10	6
Formed between 1841 and 1850	110	81	24	5
Total	267	183	47	37

Note: There were in fact 236 companies but, since several of them undertook more than one class of business, the table shows a total of 267 units.

Source: A. F. Noyes, ibid.

NOTES

1 These sugar refineries or 'sugar houses' had always proved a difficult problem for the established offices because of the highly inflammable nature of the product. In 1727, for instance, the managers of the Sun decided that no such premises should be insured at all, but in 1729, they agreed that they could henceforth be insured at the rate of 10s. per £1,000, 15s. for the second thousand pounds, 20s. for the third thousand, above which no more insurance would be accepted. During the 1730s premium rates ranged between 18s. and 30s. In 1771, maximum cover was raised to £5,000 even though 'the buildings alone cost £1,000 to £10,000 and the fixtures and stock in trade were seldom valued at less than £5,000 and in some cases exceeded £20,000'. (Phoenix Insurance, 1782–1915.)

2 This company should not be confused with the Phenix Fire Office of Nicholas Barbon, for there seems to be no traceable connection between the two. The Phenix, it seems, had disappeared by 1720.

3 The name refers to the 'Pelican in her piety, sacrificing her life blood for the benefit of her nestling brood'. (Pitman's *Dictionary of Life Assurance*, p. 390.)

4 Sir Frederick Eden, *Insurance Charters*, Appendix I, p. 13.

5 The stamp duty was a compulsory *ad valorem* duty first imposed in 1782, at a time when the Treasury was at its wits' end to finance the closing years of the War of American Independence. The duty was initially 1s. 6d. per £100 of

property insured against fire, but it was raised to 2s. in 1797, and to 2s. 6d. in 1804. In 1815 it was again raised, this time to 3s., but this figure was reduced to the original 1s. 6d. in 1865. It was finally abolished, after having caused much ill-feeling, in 1869.

6 These statistics were obtained by Sir Frederick Eden, Chairman of the Globe, from the Inland Revenue, and are taken from Raynes, 1st ed., ibid., p. 210.

7 Except for the fact that the Irish figures are for 1801.

8 Frederick Martin, ibid., p. 231.

9 On the same day, the Globe's application was renewed but 'nobody seems to have troubled one way or another about the Globe; but the petition of the London Merchants was another matter'.

10 *Hansard,* Vol. XV, p. 405.

11 *Hansard,* ibid., p. 407. This duty is not the duty levied on fire policies. This was a very nominal duty payable on all policies. The *ad valorem* duty on fire policies was an additional, and far heavier, one.

12 *Hansard,* ibid., pp. 408–409.

13 As a matter of fact, a half-hearted attempt to renew the struggle was made in 1812, but the victory of the anti-petitioners was too recent. The application therefore fell quietly into abeyance.

14 Nathan Rothschild was born on 16 September 1777, third son of the founder of the great banking house of Anselm Rothschild. At the age of 21 he came to England with only £80 in his pocket, but within five years this small sum had made him a fortune of £200,000, almost entirely in Manchester. He then ventured south to London where his incredible financial wizardry was seen to even greater advantage. He was quickly taken into the confidence of the Government and the knowledge thus acquired served only to multiply his already vast fortune. All his speculations depended upon the acquisition at the earliest possible moment of both domestic and foreign news and one example indicates the ends to which he was prepared to go in order to get the information. In the full knowledge that millions of pounds, largely in the form of wages, were staked on the outcome of the Battle of Waterloo, Rothschild witnessed the battle himself; then, on a day when no ships could leave the French harbours because of the severe gales that were blowing up in the Channel, he crossed in an open rowing boat! For some twenty-four hours he was the only man in England who knew the result of the great conflict at La Belle Alliance, during which time a million pounds sterling was added to the fortune of this incredible man.

15 Frederick Martin, ibid., p. 291.

16 Wright and Fayle, ibid., p. 309.

17 6 George IV, C. 91.

18 Raynes, ibid., 1st ed., p. 250.

19 7 William IV and I Victoria, C. 73.

20 7 and 8 Victoria, C. 110.

21 H. W. V. Temperley, Article in the *Cambridge Modern History,* Vol. X, 1907, p. 589.

22 First, under the Life Assurance Companies Act of 1870 and, more importantly, under the Assurance Companies Act of 1909.

23 *Report of the Select Committee on Joint Stock Companies,* 1841. Question 2343 *et seq.*

24 Frederick Martin in his *History of Lloyd's and Marine Insurance*, p. 307, lists the dates of expiry of some of these companies.
25 P. G. M. Dickson, ibid., p. 137.
26 Both tables are based upon statistics provided by Mr. P. G. M. Dickson, ibid., p. 140.
27 50 Geo. III c. 35.
28 Walford, ibid., Vol. III, p. 486.
29 For example, the Liverpool and London and Globe established an agency at New York in 1848, whilst the Royal took the decision to enter the U.S.A. in 1881. Although the Colonial Life Assurance Company was not established until 1846, by 1851 it had a total of £351,404 assured in North America.
30 Sir William Schooling, *Alliance Assurance*, 1824–1924, p. 37.
31 Loc. cit., p. 47.
32 P. G. M. Dickson, ibid., p. 185.
33 A. F. Noyes, 'British Insurance and World Economy', *Journal of Chartered Insurance Institute*, Vol. L (1953), p. 261.

Chapter 8

THE GOLDEN AGE OF BRITISH INSURANCE 1850-1914

' 'Tis not in mortals to command success,
But we'll do more, Sempronius, we'll deserve it.'
(Joseph Addison (1672–1719); Cato I, ii, 43)

THE YEARS from the middle of the 19th century to the outbreak of the First World War mark the summit to which we have already referred and in this chapter we attempt to survey that summit. The task is of no small order within the confines of one chapter for few periods in history can match this one in terms of political, social and economic eventfulness. Indeed, so eventful was the period that a mere catalogue of the more salient incidents would require more space than we are permitted. It would also prove an unsound approach because, as one writer has aptly put it, 'minute attention to the crowded and animated canvas diverts attention from the main emphasis of the picture as a whole'.[1] It is trends rather than events that we should be interested in and this chapter seeks to outline the main trends. The interested reader may fill in the details by reference to the rather richer literature of these years.

We begin with a review of domestic developments, and in particular with a class of insurance which, though something of a novelty at the beginning of the period, rapidly took on the mantle of its more illustrious predecessors. This was accident insurance or, as it is known in the United States, casualty insurance. But accident insurance as understood today differs slightly from the original meaning of the word for it originally involved protection against *personal* accidents only. Today the expression is something of a portmanteau for related types of insurance, notably steam-boiler, plate-glass, burglary, motor, aviation and fidelity guarantee and we shall give brief attention to all these categories of accident insurance in turn.

Personal accident insurance was a product of the railway age which first saw the light of day with the construction of the Stockton-Darlington line in 1825 and which by 1843 had spawned some 1,800 miles of finished line.[2] In 1845, two companies, the Railway and British and Foreign Life and Property Insurance Company and the Railway Steam Vessel Life and Casualty Company were registered for the specific purpose of providing insurance against accidents incurred on, or in connection with, railway travel. Strangely enough, neither of these companies ever issued a policy, for reasons which still remain obscure. The pioneer work in the field of personal accident insurance was therefore left to the Railway Passengers Assurance Company founded in 1849, the Railway Assurance Company founded a year later in 1850, and the Accidental Death Insurance Company No. 1, also founded in 1850.[3] The former company proved especially successful and is today a subsidiary of the North British and Mercantile Insurance Company, now combined with the Commercial Union. The success of the company may be gauged from the fact that during the first year of business its accident premium income amounted to £4,618 2s. 3d. and that some twenty years later this figure had risen to over £1 million.

The early method of effecting insurance is interesting and deserves brief mention. A traveller merely purchased a separate insurance ticket at the ticket office of the railway station, for which he paid either 1d., 2d. or 3d. according to the class of his rail ticket. In return, the relatives of the insured, in the event of his death consequent upon, or incidental to, railway conveyance received compensation of £1,000 (1st class), £500 (2nd class) or £200 (3rd class), and in cases where injuries sustained were not fatal 'liberal' and 'immediate' compensation was paid. The discrimination in benefits arose primarily because third and second class carriages were roofless and therefore exposed the travellers to greater risk.[4]

The success of this scheme is well illustrated by a letter which appeared in the *Morning Chronicle* on 1 December 1849 (a copy of which is now in the British Museum). It reads:

Dunstable,
28 November 1849

I was travelling by Railway from Penrith to Preston on the night of the 1st instant, and having occasion to go out of the train at the latter station, by the carelessness of the porter I was led over the edge of the turntable and seriously injured on the head and ribs, and three of my teeth forced out, which laid me up for several days. I had previously effected an insurance against railway accidents with the Railway Passengers Assurance Company, and when sufficiently able to get up to London, I at once gave notice to the officers of that company, in Old Broad Street, that I had met with an accident. They immediately sent their medical officer to Mullin's Hotel where I was staying, and in the course of a few days I was well enough to make my claim in person at the offices of the above company.

I adduced evidence of my costs, both for medical attention in the country and London, and my hotel expenses, and within three weeks after the day of the accident received the compensation which I thought fit to demand without demur or at the loss of an hour's time.

(Signed) William Good,
Late of Lymington, Hampshire.

It is not clear from this letter whether Mr. Good purchased a single ticket or periodical (for periodicals were also available) but only three years later the company issued another form of insurance, policy insurance, whereby insurance could be obtained by payment of a single premium for the whole of life or for a term of years. A further innovation was introduced in 1855, when the company widened its scope to include accidents which were not consequent upon or incidental to railway conveyance. In this respect it was following lines initially laid down by the Accidental Death Indemnity Company (i.e. the Accidental Death Insurance Company No. 1) which had been founded with the object of providing cover against accidents whatever the cause. The premium charged was £1 per £1,000 at death, and for an additional £2 10s. compensation for non-fatal injury at £5 per week during total disablement, plus a sum not exceeding £10 for medical attendance during the injury was provided.

In the same year (i.e. 1855) the General Accident and Compensation Company introduced a scheme of compensation for 'complete disability or total loss of health from any cause', and also introduced 'Family Insurance', whereby a family of parents and not more than eight children under 21 might insure to receive £1,000 in case of death of any one of them by paying £18 p.a. In 1866, the Accident Insurance Company undertook 'specific compensation' insurance for defined injuries, e.g. £100 for the loss of one eye, £250 for the loss of two eyes, the same for the loss of legs or arms, £50 for the loss of one hand, and £25 for the loss of one or more fingers.

A further extension of accident insurance was made with the introduction in 1885 by the Sickness and Accident Assurance Association (later known as the Century Insurance Company) of protection against disablement through sickness and this new scheme rapidly became popular. It was primarily directed towards the middle class professional people and two types of cover were offered—temporary sick benefit, for which allowances were paid during the first six months of illness in any one year, and permanent sick benefit under which allowances were paid for the entire duration of the illness. There was an upper age limit of 65. In 1893 specified diseases were added to the annual accident insurance contract by the Law Accident Society, including infectious diseases as defined by the Infectious Diseases (Notification) Act of 1889. The first fully comprehensive accident and sickness policy was issued by the Preferred Accident Insurance Company of New York, when it opened an office in Great Britain in 1900, and the first British office to offer such a policy was the Sun Life in May 1903.

Personal accident insurance evolved, as we have seen, in response to the needs of the rapidly industrialising society and so too did another branch of accident insurance, now known as engineering insurance but originally known as steam-boiler insurance. Ever since it was first realised that the by-product of boiling water could be utilised to provide motive power, accidents had been frequent and very often fatal. Thus, in 1854, the Manchester Steam Users' Association was formed and this was followed in 1858 by the formation of the Steam Boiler Assurance Society. Within a short space of time, a number of similar companies had come into existence, whilst many existing companies had opened departments to deal with this new type of business. The first step in steam-boiler insurance was, of course, the insurance of the boiler itself 'against loss from damage occasioned by explosion or collapse'. In the early policies there was no mention of third party cover. By 1876, most policies included damage to adjacent buildings and plant. In the modern policy it is possible to ensure against injury or death to a third party.

A vitally important adjunct to the actual insurance process was, of course, the inspection and proper maintenance of the boilers themselves, and this principle had been recognised at an early stage. The Manchester Steam Users' Association had been formed solely for that very purpose, although there was a strong school of thought which maintained that the function of an insurance company was to insure and not to inspect or maintain. However, in December 1872, the Boiler Insurance and Steam Power Company (now known as the Vulcan) led the way with inspection and other companies soon followed with the result that inspection of boilers is now an integral feature of steam-boiler insurance. Indeed, this class of insurance is much more than mere insurance—it is now a first-class service involving expert advice 'perhaps more important than the insurance itself'.[5]

An important influence on its growth and development has been parliamentary legislation of which the first example was the Boiler Explosions Act of 1882. This made it obligatory for every boiler explosion to be reported to the Board of Trade, which was given powers of investigation. Should the responsibility for such an accident be established, the guilty party can be ordered to bear part or whole of the costs of the enquiry. Hence most owners of boiler equipment have found it cheaper to avoid the risk of such an eventuality by having their boilers inspected regularly by representatives of the insurance companies. In 1890 the provisions of the 1882 Act were extended to any explosion occurring aboard a British ship and in 1901 official control and supervision was intensified by the Factory and Workshops Act which laid down that inspections should occur once every fourteen months. The scope of the legislation is now even wider and the broader term, engineering insurance, covers not only such additional items of plant as hoists, lifts, cranes and other lifting appliances but also oil, gas and electrical installations. Naturally, this progressive legislation has resulted in an enormous increase in business for engineering insurance companies which before the 1914–18 War were a select band of specialists. The leaders included the Steam Boiler Assurance Company,[6] the National Boiler Insurance Company,[7] the Engine and Boiler Insurance Company,[8] the Scottish Boiler Insurance and Engine Inspection Company,[9] and the Ocean Accident and Guarantee Corporation.[10] Although technically we are straying beyond our chosen period, it is convenient to mention here that these companies formed the nucleus of the Engineering Offices Association which was established in 1920. After the 1914–18 War old prejudices largely disappeared and there was a much more general appreciation of the expert services rendered to the owners of plant by highly-trained independent engineers. Consequently, since then most of the composite offices have written engineering insurance either directly or through working arrangements with other offices.

Another branch of accident insurance, with which the general reader may perhaps be more familiar, is (rather misleadingly) known as 'plate-glass' insurance.[11] Certainly, there are more companies engaged in this class of business than the other. Plate-glass, like personal accident insurance, arose during the middle of the 19th century when the need for protection against loss through damage to expensive shop fronts first arose. To meet this new demand the Plate Glass Insurance Company was founded in 1852 and was initially solely concerned with plate-glass insurance but it soon extended its scope to cover all types of glass and was immediately successful. Two years later, in 1854, the National Provincial Plate Glass Insurance Company was formed and in that same year the first mutual company, the Huddersfield Mutual Plate Glass Insurance Company was established. Thereafter companies mushroomed but unfortunately many were fraudulently founded. Between 1900 and 1909 no less than 55 new companies were founded[12] but even so the Assurance Companies Act of 1909 excluded plate-glass companies from the need to deposit a capital sum as security before beginning operations.

Burglary insurance forms another important element within the general framework of accident insurance, but it is of much more recent origin than those mentioned to date. It is true that many early attempts were made to initiate a scheme for protection against loss by theft, attempts which date back to the South Sea Bubble era, but not one of them met with success largely because the demand was insufficient to justify their existence. For instance, in 1864 the Property Protection Insurance Company was established but the Company seems to have transacted no business and was, in fact, wound up in 1867. Similar projects, it seems, enjoyed the same abortive fate and it was not until 1887 that the first successful scheme was launched. Strangely enough it was a Lloyd's underwriter who, on the suggestion of a broker, took the initiative 'more in fun than in earnest'.[13] It happened that at this time Jack the Ripper was performing his macabre acts in the streets of Whitechapel and there was an associated increase in burglaries and housebreaking during the same period. Consequently, the timing was propitious and the initiative of the Lloyd's underwriter was quickly followed by the establishment of the Mercantile Accident and Guarantee Insurance Company of Glasgow in 1889. The policy provided by this company was superior in many respects to the Lloyd's policy in that it was a fully-fledged burglary policy, renewable annually on payment of a renewal premium, with a full statement of risks covered. Other companies soon followed the lead provided by the Guarantee and even fire companies were keen to underwrite this new class of business. By 1910, all fire offices had burglary departments.

The business of motor vehicle insurance is, of course, essentially a post First World War phenomenon, but its origins go back to 1896 when the first public motor vehicle trial-run between London and Brighton was successfully completed. The first known policy was in fact issued on that day by the Scottish Employer's Liability and Accident Company, the terms of which ran as follows:

INDEMNITY INSURANCE

For the day of 14 November 1896 (Journey to Brighton).

To include accidents to passengers 20s. p.c. on the sum assured, plus 5s. per car.

To assure injury to the cars themselves £5 0s. 0d. per cent on the value of each car.

ANNUAL RATES

Cars running in London:

£2 p.c. on sum assured plus £2 per car.

The above rates will not cover accidents etc. caused by frightened horses.

But the real pioneer of motor insurance was the Law Accident Insurance Society which had produced a sophisticated comprehensive policy by 1901. In 1903, the first specialist motor insurance office, the Car and General Insurance Company, was established and in the same year the Motor Car Act was passed. Thereafter, increasing interest was taken in the new business—interest which was not always healthy. For example, in 1906 two companies were formed with the sole intention, it seems, of expanding premium income but they did not prosper. One was wound up, in 1910, and the other was amalgamated with the Liverpool Victoria Insurance Corporation.

Lloyd's, too, took an early interest in motor insurance and in 1906 the fire offices entered the field. Competition was severe largely because motor companies, like plate-glass companies, were not required to deposit the £20,000 which was demanded from other insurance companies and premium rates were severely depressed. It was not until the private car tariff (1913–1914) the commercial vehicle tariff (1915) and the motor cycle tariff (1921) were introduced that the market stabilised itself. Nevertheless, motor insurance companies were not required to make a deposit until 1934.

Aviation insurance, to an even greater extent than motor insurance, was largely a phenomenon of the years following the First World War although some aviation policies were issued before 1914. It is true to say that, prior to the flights made by Orville Wright in France in 1908, the flying machine had never been taken seriously; but Wright's pioneer work did much to change that attitude—so much so, in fact that by 1910 there were 578 certified aeroplane pilots (353 French, 57 British and 26 Americans) almost all of whom used the new mode of transport merely for sporting purposes. Insurance in Britain was effected almost entirely through the Union of Canton and a number of Lloyd's syndicates but, quite obviously, the volume of business was insignificant compared even with motor insurance. It was the impetus provided by the rapid development of aviation during the 1914–18 War which gave aviation insurance a more general appeal.

We conclude our treatment of accident insurance with a brief reference to a type of insurance known as Fidelity Guarantee which, in the insurance sense, means an indemnity to an employer against loss through the dishonesty of an employee. Attempts to provide this type of cover had been made as early as 1720 but the first company to transact such business was not formed until 1840. This company, the Guarantee Society undertook 'on the payment of a small premium . . . to make good, in case of default by fraud or dishonesty, any loss which may be sustained to an amount specifically named and agreed upon in their policy, and by such means obviate the necessity for private sureties'. Subsequently, this class of business grew considerably and by 1890 there were almost thirty companies issuing fidelity guarantee policies.[14]

This list is by no means complete, however, for accident insurance now embraces a whole host of miscellaneous risks from baggage insurance to weather insurance. The great bulk of these fall outside the context of our immediate period and therefore require no treatment here, but for a fuller list and description the interested reader might consult Pitman's *Dictionary of Accident Insurance* (edited by J. B. Welson).

A second notable feature of the period of ascendancy was the rapid rise to prominence of a class of insurance which we have already mentioned in passing. This is industrial life assurance, which may be defined simply as life assurance adapted to the needs of the weekly wage-earner. Its growth was associated with another feature which was to have increasing impact on the development of the insurance industry, namely state intervention and supervision. In an earlier chapter we saw that industrial life assurance originated from the poorer classes' intense abhorrence of the pauper funeral, and found an early manifestation in the 'box' club and friendly society. The friendly society, involving frequent small contributions by a group of people for the alleviation of financial embarrassment caused by the death of a relative, filled a great gap and gradually acquired a national rather than a merely local status. But the friendly societies, despite their obvious usefulness, were in many respects inadequate. Their inadequacy arose chiefly out of their financial instability which in turn derived from inadequate premiums and mismanagement of funds. Moreover, they were subject to no legal control in their early days. In 1828 this deficiency was to some extent rectified by the appointment of a barrister to keep a register of friendly societies; and in the following year he was, in addition, empowered to examine and certify their rules. In 1846 the Treasury took over his appointment from the National Debt Commissioners and gave him the title of Registrar of Friendly Societies. This in 1875 was made even more imposing by the addition of the prefix 'Chief'.

Although this appointment to some extent met the criticisms levied against the friendly societies, it was not in itself sufficient to rectify the fundamental weakness in their system—i.e. the inherent inability to concentrate their energies solely upon the collection of premiums and the distribution of benefits (because of their wider social brief). Fortunately, towards the middle of the century there evolved a type of society which had as its sole object these two vital functions. Amongst the earliest of these were the Blackburn Collecting Society (1839), the Wesleyan and General Assurance Society (1841), the Liverpool and Victoria Friendly

Society (1843), the Royal Liver Friendly Society (1850), the Scottish Legal Life Assurance Society (1852) and the British Industry Life Assurance Company (1852).

In 1853, the House of Commons, mistrustful of the solvency of insurance business in a period of considerable speculation, appointed a Select Committee on Assurance Associations to conduct an enquiry. The Registrar of Friendly Societies, who was summoned to give evidence, left the Committee in no doubt that these societies were now providing the same services for their members as assurance companies provided for their policyholders, although obviously there were differences in the average size of sums assured by the two organisations. There was, however, a growing feeling that the friendly societies when they ventured beyond their original field of funeral benefits were amateurs in a field in which the assurance companies were the professionals. Thus, while the friendly societies enjoyed continued support, more and more people were turning to the companies with requests to them to undertake small-scale life assurance. It was not surprising, therefore, that the Select Committee reported favourably on the benefits to be derived from the greater involvement of insurance companies in this type of business.

But the vital breakthrough did not come until two years later (i.e. 1854) when a small assurance and loan association, struggling hard for its very existence, took the plunge which far larger and financially sounder organisations had been curiously reluctant to take and dived into the pool of industrial life assurance. This company was called the Prudential, and such was the order of its early success that it was able, only six years later, to take over the pioneer British Industry Life Assurance Company.[15]

The reason for its success fundamentally resided in the nature of the class of business which it was conducting. Ordinary life assurance was very much the exclusive privilege of the wealthier classes for only they could afford the large annual, half-yearly or quarterly premiums. But frequent collections of small contributions were ideally suited to the wage earning system. Dermot Morrah puts it this way: 'A household to which wages are brought home weekly frames its budget accordingly; it seldom has a reserve of income from which to make large payments at frequent intervals, and still more seldom a bank account on which cheques can be drawn. If systematic contributions to assurance are to be kept up in these conditions, they must be related to the weekly or monthly pay envelope and collected when the money is in hand. Failing this the odds are that the money will be used in other ways. The surplus remaining after provision for such essentials as rent, food and clothes, is generally small and the temptation to spend it on entertainment, luxuries, or immediate pleasures is often too strong to be resisted without the moral support of the industrial assurance collector.'[16]

The Prudential soon established itself as the market leader by rapidly acquiring a larger premium income than any of its competitors such as the Refuge Friendly Society (1858), the City of Glasgow (1862) or the Pearl Assurance Company (1864). At the time of the establishment of the Pearl the Prudential was already writing between 1,500 and 1,800 new policies every week and by 1887 it had cornered three-quarters of the companies' share of the business with an annual premium income of £3,058,500 and a life assurance fund of £4,937,000. Assurances in force at the end of 1886 amounted to 7,111,828, and the total sum assured stood at a gigantic £66,689,111.[17]

The dominance of the Prudential did not end there but continued down to the First World War and beyond—so much so in fact that Lord Passfield was able to remark in 1915 that the Prudential '. . . has . . . become absolutely the highest shareholder in the Bank of England, as it was in the River Company; the most extensive owner of railway securities as well as of freehold ground rents; the most considerable holder of Indian and Colonial Government Bonds and Stocks; one of the greatest London ground landlords owning more than half of a square mile of the Metropolis, and probably the greatest owner of freehold property in the United Kingdom'. In recent years, with over £2 million per week to be invested, it has become one of the most important sources of capital not only for the Government and the local authorities but also industry and the property market.

But, although the growth and the development of the Prudential since 1854 is a success story, a considerable number of societies and companies tried their hands at the business without success and failure was not uncommon. Thus there developed a growing feeling that the whole business of industrial life assurance was a thinly disguised swindle organised at the expense of the poor. Such was the extent of public unease that the malcontents managed to gain the ear of Gladstone who, as Chancellor of the Exchequer, delivered a harsh attack on the business in a speech to the House of Commons in 1864.[18] In particular he concentrated on two criticisms which were to be heard time and time again, namely, the high rate of lapse and high expense ratios. His remedy was for the State to set up shop in competition with the companies in the hope that by selling insurance on better terms than they, to the working classes, the State would force the companies to fall into line with its supposedly higher standards or drive them out of business.

As a result the Government Annuities Act of 1865 was passed whereby the Postmaster-General was empowered to conduct life assurance business on behalf of the Commissioners of the National Debt. The main features of the scheme were, first, that policies could be issued on the life of any person between sixteen and sixty years for sums between £20 and £100 and, secondly, that it replaced the agency system by placing the obligation on the insured to pay in premiums at stated intervals to a Post Office of his own choice. In the first sixteen years of its existence a total of only 6,500 contracts were issued and in 1882 a Select Committee was appointed to examine the weaknesses of the scheme and to find a cure for its lack of success. As a result the Government Annuities Act of 1882 was passed which, although it embodied certain minor changes in the administration of the scheme, did not grapple with its basic deficiency: its attempt to dispense with collectors who, with all their faults, at least encouraged policyholders to maintain their payments. The Act had some immediate impact but despite extensive publicity the effects soon wore off. In 1896 another attempt was made to breathe life into the corpse by reducing premium rates but after an initial improvement the decline was soon resumed and continued, notwithstanding another official report in 1907, until 1914. In the event the scheme lingered on until the end of 1928 when the number of contracts in force was 9,956 for total sums assured of about £494,000.[19]

The failure of this attempt at state intervention, however, did little to stifle criticism of industrial life assurance and a long succession of legislative measures and public enquiries kept the industry under continual and persistent scrutiny. In the late 1860s the Earl of Lichfield introduced a Bill and urged the establishment of a Royal Commission to investigate the current state of the business. The Bill's purpose was to restrict the insurance of children, to give security against lapse and prevent transfer between companies (as a result of amalgamation or the sale of books to another society) without the policyholder's consent. Nor surprisingly, it was strongly opposed by the companies and was withdrawn when Disraeli promised to establish a Royal Commission.

Although the Societies, led by the Royal Liver and the Victoria Legal (now the Liverpool Victoria), had made no secret of their dislike of Lord Lichfield's Bill, they were not averse to the idea of legislation for the improvement of practice in industrial assurance. At the same time the public was greatly shocked by the failure in 1869 of the Albert Life Assurance Company, mainly due to an over-ambitious policy of takeovers of other companies; the parent company had been founded in 1838 and had absorbed twenty-six other offices during the ensuing thirty years.[20]

In the same year of 1869 investigations were initiated into the operations of the European Life Assurance Company which finally collapsed in 1872. The demand for some form of legislative control became irresistible and in 1870 the first piece of legislation designed specifically to regulate insurance companies, namely the Life Assurance Companies Act of 1870, reached the Statute Book. Although its first concern was life business, composite companies in so far as they transacted life business were also affected.

The first important provision was that every company established in the United Kingdom after the passing of the Act, and any new company commencing business, had to deposit a sum of £20,000 with the Accountant-General of the Court of Chancery. This could be refunded when the life assurance fund reached £40,000. Secondly, every company transacting life and other business was compelled to keep a separate account for the life and annuity business and all receipts emanating from this class of business had to be assigned to a distinct 'life assurance fund'. Thirdly, specialist life offices had to furnish revenue accounts and balance sheets in a form prescribed by the Act and composite companies transacting life business had to present separate revenue accounts for life, fire, marine and other classes of business, if any. Finally, a company was obliged to submit its financial condition to investigation by an actuary—once every five years if established after the Act was passed and at least once in every ten years if established earlier. An abstract of the actuary's report, which must contain details concerning the date of valuation, the proportion of premiums reserved for future expenses, etc. was to be deposited, along with the other information enumerated above, at the Board of Trade.

Despite this legislation Disraeli's promise to establish a Royal Commission to enquire into the working of friendly and building societies was not forgotten by the new administration under Mr. Gladstone, who invited Sir Stafford Northcote to undertake this task. The investigations of the Northcote Commission lasted from 1871 to 1874 and resulted in the publication of four substantial reports. In particular the members of the Commission were suspicious of the commercial motive in the provision of industrial assurance, and attempted to encourage the Government to intensify official competition through the ill-starred Post Office scheme; they further criticised the number of lapses and deplored the ease with which new societies could be formed and the absence of adequate safeguards of their bona fides.

However, a considerable time elapsed before legislation was introduced to give effect to some of the Northcote Commission's recommendations. When a Bill was eventually published in 1875, the provisions fell short of the Commission's proposals, most notably by ignoring the suggestion that the State should enter into competition with the societies and companies by adopting their methods of house to house collection. Had it not been for this omission, the subsequent history of industrial life assurance might well have been dramatically changed. The Bill had a comparatively easy passage through Parliament and became the Friendly Societies Act of 1875. It provided facilities for the formation of friendly societies and laid down rules for their conduct, the basic intention being to protect the members from management abuses, whether in the form of improvident handling of funds or unfair conduct towards individuals. Furthermore, for the first time it recognised industrial assurance as a single entity and endeavoured to place both the societies and the companies transacting such business as nearly as possible on a common footing. New societies of adults were debarred from accepting members under sixteen years of age but those which had established the practice of admitting them before the beginning of 1876 were allowed to continue. The purpose of this provision was to allay the suspicions surrounding the high level of infantile mortality and the demand for infantile assurance, particularly the fear that a parent, who knew that he stood to gain financially from the death of his sick child, might neglect to take adequate steps to save his life. However, the Act permitted the creation of new societies of infants under special regulations provided that they consisted entirely of members between the ages of three and sixteen. Of this provision, Morrah says, it 'recognised the valuable work that was being done by juvenile societies which recruited members in childhood, inculcated early habits of thrift and passed them over at the age of sixteen to full membership of the appropriate parent societies'.[21]

At the same time an attempt was made to ensure that no one should benefit from the death of a young person, by the stipulation that the aggregate sum payable on death, whether by one or more societies, should not exceed £6 if the child died under the age of five, or £10 for children between five and ten years. Payments could be made only to the child's parent or his personal representative and then only on the prior production of a special death certificate.

In order that no policyholder of a registered collecting society or industrial assurance company should unwittingly lose the benefits of his insurance through failure to pay premiums for the first time, it was enacted that no forfeiture should be incurred though defaulting on payment of contributions until written notice of liability to forfeiture had been delivered to him. Such notice had to give a policyholder at least 14 days in which to clear any arrears. Also, in order to protect policyholders from possible loss of benefits through transfer from one office to another, the Act required that no such transfers should be made without the policyholders' written consent.

This Act, amended in detail from time to time, provided the legal framework within which individual assurance was conducted for the next twenty years. But many of the earlier problems which beset the industry remained unsolved. For example, the question of lapses was still troublesome. 'The opulence of the eighties had not yet gone far to transform the conditions of the poor, who remained little better off than they had been half a century before.'[22] In consequence premiums continually fell into arrears and many policies lapsed. The business also was not lacking in unscrupulous agents who would persuade policyholders to drop their existing insurances and reinsure through them. The general effect was, on balance, bound to be detrimental to the individual policyholder's interests inasmuch as the new assurance was begun at a later age and hence paid for at a higher rate of premium. An attempt by the offices to eradicate this evil led to the setting up of the Industrial Life Offices Association but it did not come into formal existence until 1901 and 'in the late eighties "transfers" had already become an object of public censure'.[23]

Further criticism arose over attempts by new companies to evade the legal requirements under the 1870 Act to deposit £20,000 with the Board of Trade. There were cases of businessmen acquiring control of derelict insurance companies the registrations of which under the Companies Act had never been cancelled. Thus they could enter the insurance market as 'old' companies and avoid the need to make a deposit. By 1889 the time was ripe for yet another inquiry—this time a Select Committee of the House of Commons. The evidence collected tended to suggest that lapses were still too frequent and management expenses too high—the familiar strictures. There was also evidence that the Board of Trade and the Registrar of Friendly Societies lacked sufficient powers to enforce the law. The Act of 1875, the Committee thought, had been proved weak through the lack of facilities for official inspection of societies, the obstacles in the way of summoning special meetings of members and the inadequate provisions for dissolution. The Committee recommended that the Chief Registrar be given full discretion with regard to the number of signatures which he should require on a petition asking him to act in such matters, and that he should even have authority to act on his own initiative if satisfied that it would be in the interests of members.[24]

The Committee also gave considerable attention to the problem of administrative costs but found it difficult to make definite proposals and, although they considered it, they shrank from laying down any standard ratio of management expenses to benefits. At the end of their labours they made a long list of recommendations for closer supervision of the business, many of which became important in later years even though they did not result in immediate legislative action.[25] Mention should be made of their deep concern over infantile assurance which, as we have seen already, was a recurring source of public anxiety. Their conclusion was that no safe deductions about the danger and extent of abuses in the insurance of children's lives could be founded upon the evidence they had heard and they hinted that a further inquiry should be undertaken. This was precipitated by a philanthropic campaign for the protection of children against pecuniary exploitation through insurance which resulted in 1890 in the appointment of a Select Committee of the House of Lords under Lord Peterborough. Its main task was to consider the proposal that any sums payable on the deaths of young children should be handed over to the undertaker and not to the parent or guardian who had paid the premiums. The suggestion was overwhelmingly rejected on the grounds that it would constitute an unwarranted usurpation of parental rights and the controversy over the principle of assurance on children's lives can be regarded as settled after 1890. By the Friendly Societies Act of 1896 the collecting societies were allowed to admit minors to membership from one year of age and the Act of 1898 allowed acceptance from birth.

We have sought to illustrate that one of the outstanding features of the period of ascendancy, the rapid growth of industrial life assurance, itself gave rise to an equally notable feature, the growth of state intervention and supervision which was to be a matter of controversial debate up to the present day. Although the insurance companies and friendly societies tended to view this as a threat to their activities, theirs was too hasty a reaction and there are vivid illustrations of the way in which legislative action gave a fillip to a particular branch of insurance as we have already seen in the case of engineering insurance. An even more striking example is employers' liability insurance which is designed to provide an indemnity to employers in respect of liability for accidents and industrial diseases sustained by their employees.

This type of business is entirely a creation of the law. The Employers Liability Act of 1880 imposed a liability on employers for accidents to their employees and during the many discussions which accompanied its progress to the Statute Book the possibility of using insurance as a safeguard against such a liability was frequently canvassed. It is not surprising, therefore, that a scheme was soon drafted and an insurance company launched in the person of the Employers Liability Insurance Co. Ltd. which saw a tremendous potential market in this field. Its prospectus stated:

> 'The primary object of this corporation is to enable employers to protect themselves by means of insurance against the liability imposed

upon them by the Employers Liability Act, 1880, and its necessity is already amply proved by the numerous applications for rates received since its registration from some of the largest and most influential firms in the United Kingdom.'[26]

The Act had a number of shortcomings of which the most significant was that it applied to comparatively few types of industrial accident. Nevertheless, the company found that during the years immediately after the passing of the Act underwriting was not as profitable as it had anticipated because the number of claims lodged by employees was unexpectedly large. At first it was thought that the explanation was to be found in the newly discovered recognition by employees of their more advantageous position under the law. But later it became apparent that they were being encouraged to take up litigation by unscrupulous solicitors who took up doubtful cases in the hope of being able to arrange out-of-court settlements, the benefits of which would mostly accrue to them in the form of 'costs'.

'There is a large number of solicitors in different parts of the United Kingdom who are always ready to take up what I call flimsy cases, on which they hope to bring us into court or at all events, if they do not bring us into court, to frighten us with the expense which may be incurred so as to compel us to make a settlement. In the majority of these settlements the larger portion of the money paid does not go into the pockets of the claimants.'[27]

Unfortunately, even in cases where such claims failed and costs were awarded to the company, the latter would usually be unable to collect them. The overall consequence was that litigation absorbed an unduly large proportion of premiums paid.

In 1897 after a number of abortive attempts to change the law relating to employers' liability the Workmen's Compensation Act was passed. The Act applied to the more hazardous occupations only[28] but was pathmaking in the sense that it provided for compensation for occupational accidents to be paid by employers without proof of negligence. The Workmen's Compensation Act 1900 extended cover to agricultural workers and that of 1906 applied to workmen in general, including non-manual workmen earning not more than £250 per annum, and for the first time benefits from compensation were made available to sufferers from some industrial diseases.

In the early years of this century it became evident that, if employers generally were to adopt the practice of offsetting their liability through insurance, it was essential that the resultant insurance business should be controlled. Since employers' payments to employees were often of long duration, it was, therefore, essential that the employee (and the employer) should be protected against the risk of the failure of insurance companies conducting employers' liability business. For this reason in 1907 legislative control was introduced in the guise of the Employers Liability Insurance Companies Act which sought to apply the principles of the 1870 Life Assurance Company Act to this sector of the industry. The first important provision was that new companies transacting this business must deposit £20,000 with the Board of Trade; such a deposit was refundable once the employers liability insurance fund amounted to £40,000 provided the company maintained a deposit for another class of business. Secondly, companies had to make a revenue statement to the Board of Trade in respect of employers liability insurance and, thirdly, special reports on annual claims experience were required so that the authorities could judge whether or not adequate resources were available to cover outstanding claims. In practice legal interventions did nothing to inhibit, and much to enhance, the profitable growth of this type of insurance.

Shortly afterwards the logic of extending the type of legislation embodied in the 1870 Act to other branches of the business as well as employers liability insurance became irresistible. In 1909 a Bill was introduced into Parliament and in the course of the ensuing debate frequent mention was made of the abuses which could, and did, arise in companies not covered by the 1870 Act. It reached the Statute Book as the Assurance Companies Act, 1909, which brought within its scope life, fire, accident, employers liability and bond investment insurance.

There were three main provisions. In the first place, every insurer had to deposit the sum of £20,000 with the Postmaster-General which in the case of life business was not returnable when the life fund attained £40,000; furthermore, when a company carried on more than one of the classes of business enumerated above, a separate deposit was required for each of them. Secondly, the separation of funds was carried a stage further than under the 1870 Act; a distinct fund had to be maintained for each class of business, although in the parts of the Act relating to fire and accident business it was conceded that separate funds were not necessary. Thirdly, separate revenue accounts were required for each class of business; furthermore, if marine, sinking fund or capital redemption business were undertaken, then the accounts had to be further subdivided. The main significance of the Act for the practice of industrial assurance was that it brought it within the ambit of the doctrine of 'insurable interest' which had been a part of the general law of insurance for a century and a half. It empowered both the companies and the collecting societies to issue policies covering the funeral expenses of a parent, grandparent, grandchild, brother or sister of the person taking out the policy; and it further provided that no policy effected with a collecting society or an individual assurance company before 3 December 1909, should be void for want of insurable interest if the person effecting it had at the time a bona fide expectation that he would incur expenses in connection with the death or funeral of the person whose life was insured.

The end of this period witnessed the most ambitious attempt by the State to participate directly in the insurance industry when the Liberal Government turned its attention to the enactment of its plan for compulsory health insurance for practically the whole population. The National Insurance Act, 1911, gave legal expression to two strands of contemporary political thought. The first was the philanthropic radical impulse to improve the economic condition of the poor whether they were conscious of their need or not. The second was the traditional liberal impulse to avoid the direct intervention of the State in economic affairs unless it was absolutely necessary. 'The result was a compromise; Mr. Lloyd George invited the industrial offices to co-operate and become agents for the administration of the statutory scheme. There would be no formal overlap between the two kinds of business, for health and life assurance are clearly distinguishable financial processes; but there was an evident economy in conducting the two in some sort of association, apart from the advantage of introducing the working classes to State insurance through a machinery of thrift to which so many of them were already accustomed.'[29] The violent opposition of the friendly societies and the insurance companies during the Bill's passage through Parliament was to some extent blunted by the device whereby the scheme could be administered through 'approved societies' sponsored by them. The Act, as passed, laid down three conditions concerning the establishment of such approved societies. In the first place they must not be conducted for profit; secondly, they must be controlled by a majority vote of insured members; and, thirdly, they must not be societies which periodically divided their funds. All kinds of friendly societies, especially the collecting burial social societies, could satisfy these conditions but it was also possible for an industrial assurance company to set up an approved society, provided that the fund from which the statutory benefits were paid was entirely distinct from the life assurance funds of the company itself. In the event the compulsorily insured population came to divide itself almost equally between the two main types until, as we shall see, the scheme was superceded by a scheme directly administered by the State.[30]

Having completed our survey of the growing impact of State supervision and intervention, we turn to the fourth great feature of this period. This was the process of amalgamation and absorption of smaller offices which within the short space of some twenty-five years provided the United Kingdom with a small, but extremely powerful, group of large composite companies dealing in all classes of insurance rather than in one or perhaps two classes, as had been the case hitherto. Strictly speaking much of this process falls outside the immediate confines of our period but to separate our accounts of events for the sake of chronological neatness would be unnecessarily pedantic. For our purposes the first quarter of the 20th century should be treated as a whole.

If the death of Queen Victoria, in January 1901, 'marked the end of an era in British life',[31] it also marked the birth of an era in the development of British insurance, a birth whose conception really dates back to the foundation of the Railway Passengers' Assurance Company in 1849, for the intervening years saw the rapid growth of accident insurance, and it was to these new, vital, expanding companies that the established offices turned their attention at the turn of the century.

The first significant absorption occurred a year prior to the death of Queen Victoria when the Commercial Union, founded in 1861 as a direct consequence of the great Tooley Street fire, and for many years, with the exception of the two chartered companies, the only existing composite company, absorbed the Palatine Insurance Company, a Lancashire business which, although founded in 1886 originally as an accident company, had built up an extremely healthy fire business.[32] With this absorption the Commercial Union became the first truly composite British insurance office for it now dealt in all four classes of insurance. The Commercial Union was to enjoy this exclusive privilege for several more years.

Other absorptions soon followed. In 1901, the same company acquired the Globe Accident Insurance Company, a specialist in plate-glass insurance, and the Vehicular and General; whilst in that year, too, the London and Lancashire, a colossal fire company also born of the Tooley Street conflagration, absorbed the Equitable Fire and Accident Office, a Manchester concern with a £50,000 accident business. In 1903, the Commercial Union absorbed that part of the Vulcan Boiler and General Insurance Company's business which related to workmen's compensation, general accident and fidelity guarantee, and in 1906 it absorbed the Accident Insurance Company. In 1910 the Commercial Union acquired the Ocean Accident and Guarantee Corporation, the largest British independent accident office.

These transactions were typical of the early absorptions for they involved the take-over of relatively recently established accident offices by larger, and primarily fire-orientated companies, of rather greater longevity. Thus, of the twenty-four first-class independent accident companies in existence at the turn of the century, none survived twenty-five years later, twenty-one having fallen within the orbit of the larger fire (and other) companies and the remaining three having themselves become the dominant partners of composite groups. (See Table 19.)

Table 19

AMALGAMATIONS INVOLVING THE LARGER COMPANIES, 1900–1920

Name of Company	*Established*	*Premiums (for 1898)* £	*Purchasing Company*	*Year*
Accident Insurance Co.	1849	77,882	Commercial Union	1906
Engine Boiler & Employers' Liability	1878	42,133	Royal	1912
Globe Accident	1890	45,233	Commercial Union	1901
Horse Carriage & General	1875	34,021	Royal	1913
Imperial Livestock	1878	24,593	Commercial Union	1912
Lancashire & Yorkshire	1877	46,025	Scottish Union & National	1906
Law Accident & Contingency	1892	110,521	London & Lancs. Fire	1907
Law Guarantee & Trust	1888	75,099	Guardian (on liquidation of Law Guarantee)	1909
London Guarantee & Accident	1869	206,666	Phoenix	1922
National Boiler & General	1864	32,352	Alliance	1923
Northern Accident	1882	38,713	Royal	1906
Norwich & London	1856	137,262	Norwich Union	1908
Ocean Accident	1871	706,614	Commercial Union	1910
Palatine	1886	47,337	Commercial Union (with large fire income as well	1900
Provident Clerks' Guarantee	1865	25,857	Northern	1917
Railway Passengers	1849	240,205	North British	1910
Scottish Accident	1877	47,487	Scottish Amicable Life	1919
Sickness Accident & Life	1885	40,944	Friends Provident	1919
Scottish Employers	1881	124,012	London & Lancs. Fire	1904
Scottish Metropolitan	1876	31,249	Northern	1923
Vulcan Boiler	1859	139,464	London Assurance	1920

Source: H. E. Raynes, ibid., p. 374.

But *pari-passu* with the absorption of accident companies by older fire companies there proceeded a similar absorption of marine companies. The London and Lancashire was one of the first in the field, taking over the Standard Marine Insurance Company of Liverpool in 1907. In 1909, the Royal entered the marine business for the first time by absorbing the British and Foreign Marine Insurance Company, whilst two more marine companies came within the orbit of fire offices when the Thames and Merseyside and Union Marine were transferred to the Liverpool and London and Globe and the Phoenix respectively, in 1911. And so the process continued. At the turn of the century there had existed some sixteen independent companies engaged in purely marine underwriting; by 1927 all but one of the sixteen had been absorbed. (See Table 20.)

Table 20

MARINE INSURANCE COMPANIES TRANSACTING BUSINESS IN 1899 (OTHER THAN THE THREE COMPOSITE COMPANIES)

Name of Company	*Established*	*Capital Subscribed* £	*Transferred to, or Shares purchased by*	*Year*
Alliance Marine & General	1824	1,000,000	Alliance Assurance	1905
British & Foreign	1863	1,340,000	Royal	1909
Hull Underwriters	1893	170,000	Provincial	1927
Indemnity Marine	1824	1,005,000	Northern	1916
London & Provincial	1860	1,000,000	Yorkshire	1913
Marine	1836	1,000,000	London & Lancashire	1917
Maritime	1864	500,000	Scottish Union & National	1914
Merchants Marine	1871	500,000	Employers' Liability	1919
Northern Maritime	1863	50,000	Union Marine & General (already controlled by Phoenix)	1917
Ocean Marine	1859	1,000,000	North British	1907
Reliance Marine	1885	500,000	Guardian	1916
Sea	1870	500,000	Still independent	
Standard Marine	1871	500,000	London & Lancashire	1907
Thames & Mersey	1860	2,000,000	Liverpool & London & Globe	1911
Ulster Marine	1887	100,000	Yorkshire	1918
Union Marine	1863	1,308,000	Phoenix	1911

Source: H. E. Raynes, ibid., p. 375.

To a somewhat lesser extent proprietary life offices also proved vulnerable to the acquisitive attentions of the fire offices and the process of amalgamation took place during a similar time span.[33] On this occasion the Alliance was first on the scene, absorbing the Imperial Life in 1902 and the Provident Life in 1906. But, once more, other companies followed the lead, so that by 1925, 22 of the 29 proprietary offices conducting life business only at the turn of the century had been absorbed into larger organisations. Another, the Gresham Life was absorbed by the Legal and General in 1933. (See Table 21.)

Furthermore there were some amalgamations between fire offices. While there were thirty companies which in 1898 collected fire premiums in

Table 21

PROPRIETARY ASSURANCE COMPANIES
DOING ONLY ORDINARY LIFE BUSINESS, 1899

Name	*Established*	*Subscribed Capital* £	*Now Associated With*	*Since*
British Equitable	1854	250,000	Royal Exchange	1924
City of Glasgow	1838	600,000	Scottish Union & National	1913
Clerical Medical & General	1824	500,000	Employers' Liability	1920
Eagle	1807	1,678,675	Eagle Star	1917
Edinburgh	1823	500,000	Commercial Union	1918
English & Scottish Law	1839	1,000,000	Eagle Star	1918
Equity & Law	1844	1,000,000	Still independent	
General Life	1837	1,000,000	General Accident, Fire & Life	1924
Gresham Life	1848	100,000	Legal & General	1933
Imperial Life	1820	750,000	Alliance	1902
Law Life	1823	1,000,000	Phoenix	1909
Legal & General	1836	1,000,000	Now transacting all classes other than marine	1919
Life Association of Scotland	1838	400,000	Still independent	
London, Edinburgh & Glasgow	1881	445,113	Pearl	1910
London & Lancashire	1862	100,000	Northern	1923
Pelican	1797	1,000,000	Phoenix	1907
Provident	1806	250,000	Alliance	1906
Provident Free Homes	1889	25,000	Still independent as the Provident Association of London	
Rock	1806	1,000,000	Law Union (now in association with the London & Lancs).	1909
Sceptre	1864	45,425	Eagle Star	1917
Scottish Life	1881	250,000	Still independent	
Scottish Imperial	1865	500,000	Norwich Union	1906
Scottish Metropolitan	1876	150,000	Northern	1923
Scottish Temperance	1883	100,000	Still independent	
Standard	1825	500,000	Converted to mutual office	1925
Star	1843	100,000	Eagle Star	1917
Sun Life	1810	480,000	Still independent	
University	1825	598,000	Equitable Life	1919
Westminster & General	1836	100,000	Guardian	1906

Source: H. E. Raynes, ibid., p. 376.

excess of £100,000 per annum, half were absorbed or became associated with other offices during the first quarter of this century. (See Table 22.) It is also worth noting at this stage that two important industrial assurance companies, which transacted ordinary life business as well, entered general business in 1920 and expanded successfully in this new sphere—the Prudential and the Pearl.

Table 22

AMALGAMATIONS 1900–1925

Office	*Premiums* £	*Absorbed or Allied with*	*In*
County Fire	283,545	Alliance	1906
Equitable Fire & Accident	214,459	London & Lancs.	1901
Hand-in-Hand	109,150	Commercial Union	1905
Imperial	612,545	Alliance	1902
Lancashire	705,788	Royal	1901
Law Fire	151,816	Alliance	1907
Law Union & Crown	137,909	London & Lancashire	1919
Lion	190,333	Yorkshire	1902
Liverpool & London & Globe	1,500,793	Royal	1919
Manchester	831,218	Atlas (fire business)	1904
Norwich Union Fire	941,011	Norwich Union Life	1925
Palatine	663,465	Commercial Union	1900
Scottish Alliance	155,463	Union in 1903 and thence to Commercial Union in	1907
Union	456,808	Commercial Union	1907
Westminster Fire	105,663	Alliance	1906

Source: H. E. Raynes, ibid., p. 376.

Thus, within a very short space of some twenty-five years, the structure and organisation of the British insurance market underwent what can only be described as a metamorphosis, as a small but extremely powerful group of composite companies emerged from the bewildering patchwork of local, regional and national marine, fire, life and accident companies which had been the norm until the turn of the century.[34] More often than not, as we have seen, the fire offices were responsible for this process, for it was they who had not only the necessary financial reserves built up over the years of careful trading, but also vision and general business acumen, although there were outstanding examples of alternative types of growth such as the General Accident, Fire and Life which was originally an accident company only and the Eagle Star, a composite company from the outset. It should be stressed that the companies were not induced to amalgamate through financial weaknesses for, in general, the purchasing company had to pay for the shares of the company acquired at a price well above that quoted in the market. A major motive was the need to maintain and improve market penetration by offering a wide range of insurance services. A second important inducement arose out of the fact that the fire and marine underwriting accounts intermittently experienced periods of high loss ratios 'due to causes not common to both and, therefore, not generally coincident'.[35] An office with underwriting accounts in both branches, therefore, tended to stabilise profit results as compared with an office transacting only one category of business. As accident accounts grew in importance, this branch provided another potential profit stabilising factor. Hence, in order to secure a well-balanced business, some companies were prepared to pay a high price for an experienced organisation in any class of insurance in which the company had not previously participated. That the companies had, in general, taken the opportunity of strengthening their financial position proved in the light of subsequent events propitious, for it is doubtful whether the great bulk of the smaller fire offices, or indeed some of the larger ones, could have withstood the series of disasters which were to befall them during the years between the turn of the century and the outbreak of the First World War, had not the process of amalgamation and absorption proceeded at the pace it did. We shall, however, have more to say about the Chicago, Boston, Baltimore, San Francisco, Valparaiso and Jamaica disasters in a moment.

First we must turn our attention to the most outstanding feature of the period, and the one which invests the period with the stamp of ascendancy, namely the remarkable expansion of British insurance, notably fire and accident business, in overseas markets. However, so incredibly complex was the chain of events abroad that a simple catalogue would be impossible. At the outset, therefore, we should recognise the fact of this brilliant expansion and then 'seek in the main currents of politico-economic thought and action an explanation of the manifold events. . . .',[36] through which this overseas expansion was expressed. The factors governing the course of events may be conveniently divided into general and specific. We look first at the *general* factors.

A crucial one was the failure of the European continent during the whole of the 19th century to establish political, economic and social stability. The root of the trouble can be effectively traced back to the Vienna Settlement of 1815, a settlement whose 'reactionary basis and disregard of racial aspirations sowed the seeds that kept Europe in a ferment of social and international unrest for most of the 19th century.'[37] The explosive uprisings of 1848 were only one example of the social unrest which prevailed throughout Europe, whilst the Franco-Prussian War of 1871, was only one example of the prevailing international unrest.

It is to Britain's eternal credit that she succeeded in avoiding these running sores, and, in the comparative immunity of her insularity, political, social and economic emancipation was allowed to develop. Particularly significant was the degree to which she was able to implement the practical aspects of the 'new' economic philosophy known as *laissez-faire* whose basic tenets had been propounded as far back as 1776. Nowhere was this more clearly brought out than in Britain's policy of enlightened self-interest towards her rapidly expanding Empire. Political pragmatism was really the order of the day and it reaped handsome dividends. One has to look no further than Canada for an ample demonstration of the truth of this statement, but British policy in Australia, New Zealand and India brought equally telling results. British insurance owes as much to the 'liberalising genius of the Manchester School' as it does to those intrepid characters who pioneered the way in the new lands with nothing but a unique product to sell.

But of inestimable assistance was the complementary pattern of 19th-century world trade. On the one hand, the new lands producing primary products and needing manufactured goods and, on the other, Britain producing the manufactured goods but requiring primary produce, assured a continued and expanding volume upon which a sophisticated commercial infra-structure was easily grafted. The basic instruments of commerce were, of course, already at hand, none more so than the bill of exchange, a device the almost universal acceptability of which had already established London as the centre of the world's payment system. Now was added the total acceptability of the pound sterling and that other 19th-century financial monument, the international gold standard. The development of the third part of the financial trinity, the mechanism for the issue and exchange of indebtedness, i.e. the capital market, completed the edifice. London was now truly the home of international trade.

It is against this background of commercial and financial pre-eminence that we must view the spectacular progress made by British insurance, and, in particular, the *specific* advantages which consequently accrued. High on this list ranks the experience British insurance derived from its domestic evolution and in particular the experience derived from the practice which gradually evolved of sharing facilities and pooling knowledge. Raynes has put it this way: 'The insurance community is not one of such extreme individualism that the competitors take pleasure in defeating their neighbours. . . . There is competition in the market but it is an ordered competition with rules and conventions to which members feel themselves bound to conform.'[38] One such 'convention' and one which developed at a fairly early date was the practice of reinsurance, a mechanism whereby risks too large for individual companies to bear were, and indeed still are,[39] redistributed in much the same way as a book-maker 'lays off' a large bet. The reinsurance treaty was perhaps the earliest form, originating on the Continent, particularly in Germany[40] where the patchwork of small states made treaty arrangements inevitable, but its practice was by no means confined to the Continent. On the contrary its spread was rapid and reinsurance is now a highly specialised branch of general insurance.[41]

The gradual evolution of a tariff system culminating in the formation of the Fire Offices Committee constitutes a further example of this desire for conformity and solidarity. The first tentative moves towards the formation of such a system were made by Jenkin Jones of the Phoenix and Sutherland Mackenzie of the Scottish at a meeting at the Waterloo Tavern, Edinburgh, on 18 July 1829, and this was followed by a succession of such meetings involving other offices' representatives. The Scottish offices, in particular, proved extremely enthusiastic in their desire to establish a uniform tariff for each risk. The tariff agreements of the rating committees of the Fire Offices Committee represent yet another instance of the way in which Scottish initiative and enterprise in the world of business and industry has acted as a catalytic agent on their rather more tardy southern cousins.[42]

Another factor contributing to the success of British insurers overseas was their very readiness in the face of unknown hazards to underwrite such business at all and then, having taken the plunge, to continue to do so. We may sum this factor up in two words—enterprise and adaptability. It was enterprise of the highest order which led essentially cautious men into unknown territories and allowed them not merely to stay but to expand and diversify. The Royal, for instance, did not enter foreign markets until 1845 but by 1861 it was firmly established in sixteen widely distributed countries. And the Royal was fairly typical of British offices. Thus by 1913, there were 75 British offices in the U.S.A. and 40 in Canada.

Finally, we may also note the policy adopted by British offices of retaining a portion of their assets in the currencies in which liabilities were expressed. These assets, usually government securities, 'formed a stable nucleus of investment of real importance to the respective economies' and also constituted a 'source of steady support in territories where public credit was not too high and stock markets were narrow and immature'.[43] In the North American market of course such a policy was a legal prerequisite for existence but this was by no means a general rule elsewhere. It is therefore to the credit of British insurers that this policy was maintained irrespective of individual countries' legal requirements.

Not only did the insurance companies display initiative and enterprise in developing their own overseas business, they also used their flair for innovation to pioneer new types of insurance, such as credit insurance, to aid and abet the expansion of overseas trade. We have already noted the contribution of the bill of exchange to London's position as the centre of the world's payments mechanism. In the 1890s there was serious financial trouble in Australia which led British merchants who were accustomed to drawing bills of exchange on Australian buyers to try and protect themselves against loss. Consequently, a few small companies came into existence by offering credit insurance to traders but their life span was comparatively brief. It was not long before the major part of this new business was acquired by the National Provincial Trustees and Assets Company but this concern also soon found itself in financial difficulties, which, as it happens, were *not* a result of its involvement in credit insurance, and in 1896 it went into liquidation. A group of insurance men, who believed that credit insurance had a bright future and that the goodwill created by the National Provincial Trustees and Assets Company with respect to this part of its business should not be dissipated, decided to form a syndicate to take over its existing portfolio of credit insurance by means of reinsurance. This syndicate, which was named the Trade Acceptances Guarantee Syndicate (1896), was in turn bought out by the Commercial Union in 1901. However, one of the Directors of the Commercial Union was also a director of the National Discount Company and he was apprehensive over the possible prejudicial effects which credit insurance might have on his interests in bill discounting. Hence in the middle of 1903 the business, or what was left of it, was transferred from the Commercial Union to the Excess Insurance Co. Limited which had been founded by the man who is usually regarded as the 'father' of credit insurance in Great Britain, Cuthbert Heath, a member of Lloyd's. His importance as a pioneer may be judged by the following quotation from a speech by Sir Frank Nixon, former head of the Exports Credit Guarantee Department in 1956.

> 'The supremacy of the bill of exchange which lasted over a hundred years has been a little diminished. War, nationalism and the general feeling of insecurity have made it difficult for the bill of exchange in the 20th century to fulfil the same role that it did in the 19th. Just as it took a genius to invent a bill of exchange, so it required another genius to devise and launch the instrument which might not supplant but supplement the bill in this brave, new and insecure age. I believe that that instrument is the credit insurance policy. I believe that the genius who launched it was Cuthbert Heath.'[44]

It took some time for the credit insurance business to recover lost ground but, under the aegis of Heath and the Excess Insurance, business progressed steadily until 1914 and in the process made an important contribution to the growth of Britain's overseas trade.

To return to the main theme, British insurers, armed with a background of solid, uncompromising attitudes based upon years of trial and error in the domestic market, prospered abroad despite the series of disasters which befell them in their early years of expansion. The catastrophes of Yokohama, Chicago, Boston, Baltimore, San Francisco, Valparaiso and Jamaica involved British companies in enormous losses. They were able to survive these setbacks only because of the large reserves they had built up over the years. The fire at Yokohama, for instance, which started on 26 November 1866, blazed for three days and caused damage valued at £1 million. Compared with subsequent disasters, individual losses amongst British offices were not great (for instance, the London and Lancashire sustained a £20,000 loss), but these were early days and any loss, no matter how small, was quite likely to discourage further effort. The fire, which broke out on 9 October 1871 at Chicago, was a much larger affair altogether and on this occasion British companies were heavily involved. The cause of the fire is still unknown (though it is often attributed to the overturning of an oil lamp by Mrs. O'Leary's cow), but what is known is that twelve thousand buildings covering an area of nearly five square miles were destroyed. Total damage amounted to £33 million, adjusted losses to £20 million, and British losses to £1,200,000. As if this were not enough, in the following year a fire at Boston caused £15 million worth of damage, and this time British offices had to meet claims amounting to nearly £1 million. This fire, following so quickly upon the heels of the Chicago fire, proved too much for many U.S. offices and bankruptcies proved rife. Every British office, however, honoured its debts in full with a promptness which drew nothing but admiration from the American public. Despite these disasters of the early 1870s, therefore, British offices went from strength to strength and premium income from the American market alone quickly rivalled domestic premium income.

But British offices were by no means immune from the shattering effects of massive fires and other disasters as events following the turn of the century were to demonstrate. In February 1904, the great 'Baltimore Conflagration' resulted in British offices meeting claims amounting to £1,150,000, and this was followed two years later by the San Francisco disaster, a disaster so terrible that it was commonly regarded at the time as 'the greatest devastation that had visited a city since the burning of Rome in the reign of Nero'.[45] The first tremors were felt at dawn on Wednesday, 18 April 1906, and three hours later the city was engulfed in flames. The fire raged for three days, devastated four square miles of city, destroyed 25,000 buildings and caused damage totalling £60 million. It has been estimated that total underwriting losses amounted to £45 million, of which British offices were liable for £10 million. The largest individual loss, £1·75 million, fell upon the London and Lancashire but other British offices were also heavily involved. The San Francisco disaster was quite the most stupendous disaster the British insurance market had ever been forced to withstand.

This was not all. Only a few months later, Valparaiso was visited by earthquake and fire and damage was estimated at £20 million. However, only £2·25 million was held attributable to fire and British losses were, therefore, relatively small. The London and Lancashire, for example, paid out £50,000. But then, on 14 January 1907, earthquake and fire struck Kingston, Jamaica. Once again, British offices refused to pay in full on the grounds that the great bulk of the damage was the result of fire occasioned through earthquake, for which, they claimed, they were not liable. After a protracted legal battle British offices paid out claims totalling £800,000.

Despite these successive disasters British offices continued to expand[46] and to build up a reputation throughout the world for honesty, integrity, and above all unimpeachable financial security. It was a reputation fully deserved for British offices had all these qualities in full measure. That they did so is not so easily explained within so brief a compass but we have tried, in this chapter, to offer some of the reasons for their success.

NOTES

1 A. F. Noyes, 'British Insurance and the World Economy', *Journal of the Chartered Insurance Institute*, Vol. LIV, p. 264.

2 In that year, i.e. 1843, the Board of Trade calculated that 24,000,000 passengers had travelled on the railways in that year, an average of 15 miles per traveller. By 1849, this figure had almost trebled to nearly 64,000,000. During that year accidents totalled 96 persons killed and 75 injured.

3 In 1852 the last two companies amalgamated.

4 W. A. Dinsdale, *History of Accident Insurance in Great Britain*, p. 55.

5 H. E. Raynes, ibid., 1st ed., p. 292.

6 Now known as the Vulcan and merged with London Assurance in 1920.

7 Later called the National Boiler and General Insurance Company and merged with the Alliance in 1923.

8 Allied with the Royal in 1912.

9 Later named the Scottish Boiler and General Insurance Company and allied with the Yorkshire Insurance Company in 1913.

10 Allied with the Commercial Union in 1910.

11 We say 'rather misleadingly' because plate-glass actually embraces all types of fixed glass.

12 W. A. Dinsdale, ibid., p. 251.

13 W. A. Dinsdale, ibid., p. 263.

14 H. E. Raynes, ibid., p. 289.

15 This company was a pioneer in as much as it was the first of the limited companies in this field.

16 Dermot Morrah, *A History of Industrial Life Assurance*, p. 25.

17 D. Morrah, ibid., p. 53. In 1913 total premium income stood at £17,292,000.

18 D. Morrah quotes from his speech as follows: 'Has the House the smallest idea of the number of these lapsed policies? Had I not had it in the positive figures, I could not have believed it. It will appear a strange revelation to those who hear me when I state that the number of these lapsed policies in the Friend in Need Society during the five years was 18,000 out of 86,000 policies made . . . 18,000 men who had insured their lives and paid for a certain time, lost the whole benefit of their money.' Ibid., p. 29.

19 The extent of the scheme's failure may be judged by comparison with the position of the industrial assurance companies and collecting societies on the date of its final demise. They had over 74,000,000 policies in being and were assuring a total sum of almost £1,150 million. Morrah, ibid., p. 34.

20 See William T. Thomson, *Present Position of Life Assurance Interests of Great Britain*, Edinburgh, 1852.

21 Ibid., p. 50.

22 D. Morrah, ibid., p. 56.

23 D. Morrah, ibid., p. 57.

24 These powers over the societies which the Committee wished to see strengthened did not extend to the industrial assurance companies, for the interests of shareholders were left to the protection afforded by the Companies Act. Only a cautionary note was added on the possibility that the policyholders might suffer at the hands of unskilful or unscrupulous promoters.

25 The interested reader may consult the details in Morrah, ibid., pp. 62–64.

26 W. A. Dinsdale, *History of Accident Insurance in Great Britain*, p. 149.

27 Lord Claud Harrison's speech at a shareholders' meeting of the Employers Liability Insurance Company, Ltd., quoted by H. E. Raynes in *History of British Insurance*, p. 305.

28 It applied to employment on railways and in factories, mines, quarries, engineering and certain building work.

29 D. Morrah, ibid., pp. 76, 77.

30 'On the eve of the Second World War there were about eight million each insured in approved societies connected with industrial life offices and with friendly societies respectively.' D. Morrah, ibid., p. 77.

31 E. V. Francis, *London and Lancashire History*, p. 53.

32 By 'composite' company we mean that the Commercial Union was the only company conducting marine insurance in association with fire and life business. A number of offices, of course, were engaged in fire and life.

33 We say 'proprietary' life offices because, of course, mutual life offices by virtue of their constitution were not amenable to takeovers.

34 This does not mean that small companies were excluded for, as we shall see,

there are still many small companies surviving even today in the insurance market. What was new was the dominance of a relatively small group.

35 H. E. Raynes, ibid., p. 378.

36 A. F. Noyes, 'British Insurance and the World Economy', *Journal of the Chartered Insurance Institute*, Vol. L, p. 204.

37 A. F. Noyes, ibid., p. 264.

38 Raynes, ibid., 2nd edition, 1964, p. 325.

39 Reinsurance is nowadays a vast business. For instance in 1964 American companies alone re-insured $242 million in the London market compared with $57 million in all the other international markets.

40 The first recorded treaty was made in 1820.

41 For a fuller account of reinsurance see H. E. Raynes, *Principles of British Insurance*, Chapter 6; or C. E. Golding, *History of Reinsurance.*

42 At this time the introduction of such cartel agreements was probably on balance beneficial in that it gave the market much needed stability. This does not mean that in recent years tariff agreements have necessarily been in the public interest as we shall see in later chapters.

43 A. F. Noyes, ibid., p. 278.

44 D. E. G. Gibb, ibid., p. 287.

45 E. Liveing, *A Century of Insurance—The Commercial Union Assurance Group, 1861–1961*, p. 99.

46 In 1913, premium income from the North American market alone, totalled over $100 million.

Part III

THE PERIOD OF CHALLENGE 1914-1970

Chapter 9

THE CHALLENGES OF WAR AND DEPRESSION 1914-1939

> 'It has been a tradition among economists that recovery from war is usually more rapid than had been expected. There is the solid economic fact that, although one may borrow money and leave behind a National Debt, one cannot mobilise the "real" resources of the future. One has to pay as one goes. Interest incurred on a debt at home is a mere transfer of income from one side of the balance to another. Thus, at the end of the war labour and resources are available to supply current needs, and so recovery comes quickly. Even the existing situation cannot be rightly judged unless the effects of the war are borne in mind.'
>
> (Sir Roy Harrod, *The British Economy*)

AUGUST 4 1914 marks the beginning of the end of the period of ascendancy, for on that day the British people embarked with enthusiasm, engendered by a wave of jingoism, on a war with Germany and the Austro-Hungarian Empire which was to prove the first of the bloody and protracted struggles that have been such a disquieting feature of the 20th century. Four years later the United Kingdom emerged victorious but irreparably damaged, still a great power but no longer pre-eminent. Her reign as the world's industrial, commercial and political monarch had come to an end.

Many observers, viewing Britain's changing role in the world economy from the vantage point of the late 1920s, perceived in this situation little more than the extension or strengthening of tendencies already perceptible in the pre-1914 economy. Admittedly, they argued, the war served to accelerate the processes of adjustment which would have taken place, albeit more gradually, had there been no war. The diminishing reliance of the primary producing countries on British manufactured goods, the industrialisation of Japan, India and Russia and, more significant still, the meteoric rise to industrial stardom of Germany and the U.S.A., all supported their argument. Between 1900 and 1913 the quantum of world trade in manufactured goods doubled while industrial production during the same period increased by two-thirds. Britain's trade and production, of course, showed an absolute increase during these years but her relative shares declined appreciably. The United States, on the other hand, succeeded not only in doubling her industrial output but also in almost doubling her share of world trade in manufactured products. The lesson to be learnt, the critics argued, was that Britain's continued concentration on the production and export of her historically staple products, i.e. coal, textiles, iron and steel, had left her unable to compete in the markets for new products which offered the promise of rapid expansion such as chemicals, electrical engineering, automobiles and their by-products, etc.

By 1913 the United States, by virtue of her concentration on these expanding branches of world trade, had forged ahead so rapidly that she was producing one-third of the world's manufactured output—a figure not far short of the combined shares of the United Kingdom, France and Germany.[1] The writing, it seemed, was on the wall for all to see. The 1914–1918 War simply served to accelerate these trends and with the return of peace the United Kingdom's industrial pre-eminence was lost in the face of an increasing challenge from the technological superiority of the United States.

But from the vantage point of the 1960s this view stands in need of modification if we are to appreciate not merely the picture of the world economy and the United Kingdom's place in it but, more specifically, the changed position of her insurance industry following the 1914–18 War and the re-adjustment which the industry was consequently forced to make. We now recognise more clearly that the First World War was a powerful catalyst the impact of which was nothing short of metamorphic. For the pre-war commercial superstructure required for its smooth running an efficient international payments mechanism, stable capital movements and unfettered opportunities for the development of multi-lateral trade. The First World War, in effect, sounded the death-knell of these three pre-requisites and in the process sowed the seeds of the neo-mercantilism and economic nationalism which were such stifling aspects of the 1930s.

The pre-war payments mechanism, as we have seen, was based on London from which the market in bills of exchange and the international gold standard were controlled. Here international debts were set off, one against the other, and temporary balance of payments disequilibria were relieved. But the 1914–18 War changed all that. The resumption of peaceful conditions brought in its train a crippled Europe, ravaged by inflation, and a vanished international gold standard; so that a return to pre-war financial stability was seen to be not merely a desirable end in itself but also a fundamental pre-requisite for European, and even world, recovery. To serve this overriding objective the British Government saw as an essential policy the restoration of the link between sterling and gold at the earliest possible moment although it was not until 1925 that conditions were considered normal enough to return to gold at the pre-war dollar parity. The United Kingdom's initiative was soon followed by a number of other major countries and by 1928 the pilgrimage to the shrine of gold was completed.

Viewed retrospectively, the decision to return at the pre-war parity proved to be an albatross around Britain's neck, for it effectively priced her traditional exports out of world markets. Had she returned to the gold standard at 20 per cent below the dollar parity, full employment, expanding production and expanding exports might at least have been attainable objectives. This is at least the view of Professor W. Arthur Lewis who also argues that a more rational decision about the chosen parity might well have avoided the economic and social disasters of the General Strike and the financial crisis of 1931. This argument contains more than a germ of intelligent conjecture but he is certainly right when he avers that 'for the prestige of the pound, regained for only six years, an exorbitant price was paid'.[2]

London, of course, had also been the origin of the major international capital movements. In 1914, for instance, her outstanding foreign investments are estimated to have been in the region of $18,000 million (at the 1914 exchange rate) whilst the United States, on the other hand, had a net debit on capital account of $3,000 million. But the onset of peace found Britain's foreign investments reduced by one-quarter and the United States elevated to the role of the world's most important capital exporter. Furthermore, and more significantly for the future, the fabric of lending had become a complicated tapestry. Germany had now become the recipient of the great bulk of U.S. lending (mainly short-term), whilst the old European lenders, notably France, succeeded in lending short to Eastern European countries, which were in urgent need of funds for rehabilitation, only by borrowing long from the United States. The situation was aggravated in the first place by the fact that U.S. lending was extremely volatile. While the total funds lent by private investors amounted to $5,000 million in 1927, they declined sharply to $1,000 million in 1928 and $233 million in 1929 as the feverish attraction of the boom on Wall Street became irresistible. Secondly, a great deal of the capital funds were used for consumption rather than productive investment. Thirdly, the rise of New York as one of the world's financial centres, in addition to London, resulted in a diffusion of the decision-making function and a failure to coordinate policies in times of crisis.

The consequences were brought home with awesome force in October, 1929, when the collapse of Wall Street ushered in what quickly, and justifiably, became known as the Great Depression. Throughout the world prices, output and trade declined. The Hawley-Smoot Tariff, 'one of the most ill-judged pieces of legislation in history'[3] was instrumental in fostering the spirit of protection which, so far as Britain and the Commonwealth were concerned, culminated in the Ottawa Agreement. Under these conditions world trade collapsed. By the third quarter of 1932 the volume of world trade was only two-thirds of the quarterly average in 1929, whilst by 1933 the value of world trade had fallen from its previous peak by more than two-thirds. British exports fell dramatically, so much so that in 1932 they amounted to only 63 per cent of the 1929 figure. Equivalent figures for the U.S.A., France and Germany were 53 per cent, 59 per cent and 59 per cent respectively.

The floor of the depression was reached in 1933 and thereafter in varying degrees recovery took place. Industrial production gradually improved and the fall in prices was arrested and gradually reversed. However, recovery in world production was not matched by a corresponding recovery in world trade for even as late as 1937 the volume of trade barely equalled the 1929 level. In the U.K. a 24 per cent increase in the volume of industrial production between 1929 and 1937 was accompanied by a 16 per cent reduction in the volume of her exports during the same period. It is against this sort of background of prolonged economic malaise that we must appraise the performance of British industry during the inter-war period.

But, first, we must consider the impact of the War itself. What effect did such a fundamental disruption exert upon the insurance market? Let us begin by putting the War into some sort of perspective. While it involved all the world's major powers and its economic cost was staggering, physical destruction of property was mainly confined to a relatively small geographical area comprising Belgium and Northern France and was relatively light in comparison with that inflicted by the Second World War. Since, so far as Britain was concerned, the greatest losses occurred at sea rather than on land, it is the effects on the marine branch which we consider first.

The outbreak of hostilities in 1914 found Lloyd's and the marine market generally carrying a heavy load of war risk at peacetime premiums and on a number of occasions total losses were incurred where the underwriter had only received a nominal premium of 6d. or 1s. per cent. However, the State was quick to appreciate its responsibility to insurance underwriters in times of war and, in August 1914, the Government, with the support of the three War Risk Associations, formed a Committee to fix premium rates. In addition, the Committee agreed to re-insure 80 per cent of each risk, leaving the remaining 20 per cent to the Associations.

At the same time, the State Insurance Office was established to cover war cargo risks which the underwriters preferred not to accept. These two major interventions by the Government at one operation removed the bulk of uncertainty from war-time marine underwriting and thus left the companies and Lloyd's free to operate in the remaining expanses of ocean where merchant ships still sailed free from the belligerent attentions of the German U-boat fleet. Although, with the intensification of the War. these expanses of ocean shrank rather frighteningly, particularly during the 1917 blockade, underwriters were amply compensated by massive U.S. convoy assistance. Thus, despite grave risks, marine underwriting proved profitable, and though no comprehensive statistics are available to illustrate the profitability, we may be sure of the fact, for 'between 1914 and 1918 the Government lost on cargo insurance seven million five hundred thousand pounds. On hulls and in other branches of its war insurance it made a gross profit of thirty-two million pounds.'[4] As a typical example of company fortunes we may cite the case of the London and Lancashire, whose premium income increased five-fold between 1914 and 1918 to close on £3 million.

Fire business was affected by the War, for Europe, and Germany in particular, had always been an important market for British fire underwriters. The Commercial Union, in particular, had extensive fire insurance interests in Germany which, with the war, were naturally surrendered. Business was also severely curtailed in the Austro-Hungarian and Ottoman Empires whilst, with the prosecution of the War, links with Belgium and Rumania were also lost. British insurers were fortunate in that these continental losses were more than offset by gains made in the North American market. These gains came largely with the entry of the U.S.A. into the war in 1917, for this event resulted in the cessation of enemy insurance activities in the U.S., thus clearing the way for British hegemony there, but also of importance was the increase in the value of buildings, plant and machinery engaged in the production of armaments and other war-time requirements. A similar rise in values was recorded in the U.K. too. The figures in Table 23 indicate the success of British fire underwriters during the war years.

For very obvious reasons the war had a considerable impact upon the life departments but, quite apart from the plethora of claims arising out of the war (these reached their peak in 1916, the year of the ghastly battle of the Somme), other factors held back their progress. For instance, the introduction of conscription in 1916 served to dry up even further the stream of new proposals, as young men everywhere joined the colours. A second inhibiting factor was the increase in domestic mortality arising out of the Spanish influenza epidemic of 1918.[5] Thirdly,

Table 23

TOTAL ANNUAL EARNINGS AND RESERVES OF BRITISH FIRE DEPARTMENTS, 1914–1918

(to nearest £1,000)

Year	*Premium Income*	*Reserves at end of Year*
1914	28,899,000	27,989,000
1915	29,971,000	29,175,000
1916	31,895,000	30,574,000
1917	36,019,000	32,687,000
1918	41,721,000	36,164,000

Source: Insurance Directory and Year Book.

companies were adversely affected by the increase in the rate of income tax effected in 1916. Yet despite these adverse influences at work healthy, if unspectacular, gains in premium income and reserves were made during the war period, as Tables 24 and 25 show.

The worst war-time performance was put up by the personal accident and sickness branch; premium income showed a slight downward ten-

Table 24

ORDINARY LIFE ASSURANCE, 1914–1918

(to nearest £1,000)

	Premium Income			*Life Assurance Fund*
Year	*for U.K.*	*from outside U.K.*	*Total*	*at end of Year*
1914	28,999,000	3,285,000	32,204,000	390,054,000
1915	29,452,000	2,950,000	32,402,000	390,477,000
1916	30,226,000	2,839,000	33,065,000	395,194,000
1917	30,477,000	2,814,000	33,291,000	396,373,000
1918	33,805,000	3,236,000	37,041,000	411,004,000

Source: Insurance Directory and Year Book.

dency until 1917 but thereafter the pre-war trend was resumed.[6] But other branches of accident insurance, particularly motor vehicle insurance, revealed promise. As we have already noted, the motor insurance market was very unstable in its early period of development but the introduction of the private motor car tariff in 1914 and that for commercial vehicles in 1915 produced some order out of chaos. In its immediate impact the 1914–18 War had adverse effects. First, many private motor vehicles were requisitioned by the Government and private motoring was greatly curbed by the introduction of petrol rationing. Secondly, the

Table 25

INDUSTRIAL LIFE ASSURANCE, 1914–1918

(to nearest £1,000)

Year	*Premium Income*	*Life Assurance Fund at end of Year*
1914	17,983,000	58,701,000
1915	18,565,000	61,382,000
1916	19,573,000	64,992,000
1917	20,959,000	69,435,000
1918	22,398,000	74,028,000

Source: *Insurance Directory and Year Book.*

cost of repairs rose sharply and there were delays in effecting them through the shortage of experienced motor engineers. Thirdly, many competent drivers joined the armed forces and their places were taken by women who were often entrusted with driving heavy lorries of which they had had very little previous experience. On the other hand there were favourable effects. In the first place the transport of war supplies necessitated a considerable increase in the number of petrol-driven trucks and vans. Secondly, the values of private cars rose sharply because new production virtually ceased. Although we have no statistics to reveal the outcome of these conflicting forces, there are grounds for believing that premium income from motor vehicle insurance increased perceptibly during the later years of the War.

Thus, despite the fears and apprehensions generated by the War, the insurance companies, by and large, emerged from it in a stronger financial position than when they had entered. We say 'by and large' because, not surprisingly, there were exceptions which arose almost exclusively from companies which had an undue concentration in one line of business. The composite companies with their large reserves, greater flexibility and widespread diffusion of interests were able to offset losses in one branch or in one part of the world, with compensatory gains elsewhere. Little wonder then that the process of amalgamation continued apace for the pursuit of size and a balanced underwriting portfolio were very desirable objectives.

An added impetus was provided by the post-war boom. This hectic upsurge in production followed quickly on the heels of the Armistice, for depleted stocks, particularly of consumption goods, had now to be replaced. Prices, money wages and interest rates, therefore, rose under the pressure of consumer demand. But by 1920, when prices, money wages and interest rates had soared to new heights, consumer demand was temporarily satisfied; thereafter consumption declined, prices fell and widespread unemployment followed.

This cyclical swing was clearly reflected in the fortunes of the fire underwriters, for it is true to say that fire insurance is a fine barometer of economic pressure as Table 26 shows.

Table 26

FIRE INSURANCE, 1915–1921

Year	*Premium Income*	*Reserves*
1918	41,721,000	36,164,000
1919	49,526,000	41,489,000
1920	58,507,000	46,053,000
1921	54,216,000	42,898,000

Source: Insurance Directory and Year Book.

An important element in the reduced premium income figure for 1921, quite apart from the reduction in domestic values, was the high claims experience of British companies in the North American market. British fire wastage in the United States was nearly £75 million in that year, the highest total since the disastrous San Francisco earthquake. But, here again, not all companies were hit equally hard. The London and Lancashire seems to have escaped lightly, but other large composite companies fared badly. Fire losses of the Liverpool, London and Globe, traditionally the most important British office operating in the U.S., reached record proportions, whilst the Commercial Union experienced a loss ratio of 57 per cent, equal to that experienced during the San Francisco earthquake.

Marine insurance, too, went through difficulties during this period for in 1921, as a result of the world-wide depression, world tonnage of shipping and the insured value of vessels still employed shrank dramatically. The Liverpool, London and Globe proved particularly susceptible to the trend and premium income fell from over £800,000 in 1920 to well under £400,000 in 1921; losses during this year totalled nearly £550,000. Marine income of the London and Lancashire was halved during the year to £1·4 million 'and barely recovered beyond that level even at the height of the subsequent peak of 1929'.[7] The Commercial Union suffered a similar experience and by 1929 net premium income was less than six-sevenths of the 1919 figure.

Accident insurance, however, prospered, partly through growth in the more traditional types of accident insurance, e.g. personal accident, but more importantly because of the rapid rise after the war of new classes of accident insurance. Motor insurance and aviation insurance were two such classes. Both, as we have already noted, had been effected before the War but underwriters, not unnaturally, were generally sceptical of the new fangled machines. The War changed all that and the return of peace heralded in a new era both for the traveller and the underwriter. The most profitable market soon proved to be the United States for it was here that the incredible mechanical revolution had its home. By 1927, there were some 27 million vehicles on the roads of America. No wonder they called these years the 'Roaring Twenties'. By 1931, the first year for which we have separate motor insurance statistics, British companies' premium income from motor insurance totalled over £32 million.

Immediately after the 1914–18 War there was considerable activity in the world of aviation due to the rapid development of the aeroplane as an effective fighting machine and the foreseeable future for it in a peace-time commercial and sporting role. Generally, the activities of insurers at this time tended towards group underwriting with companies and Lloyd's syndicates combining to write aviation insurance under the name of the White Cross Aviation Insurance Association. In 1922 there was formed the British Aviation Insurance Group out of the White Cross Insurance Association and the Union Society of Canton, the latter company having commenced underwriting aviation insurance in 1919. A further company was formed in the same year—the Aviation and General Insurance Company—but it was wound up in 1927. With the development of commercial flights the aviation insurance market was presented with the problems of the insurance of larger, more valuable aircraft and heavier personal accident losses. Whilst there appeared to be no demand by airlines to insure their legal liabilities to passengers on scheduled flights, the passengers themselves, not surprisingly in view of the risks involved, effected cover for personal accident insurance. Because of the type of passenger using air transport it followed that the personal accident cover was usually for large capital sums assured in the region of £5,000 or £10,000 and sometimes as much as £100,000. The rate for a passenger travelling between London and the Continent was fairly stable at £1 per thousand, i.e. ten times the present rate.

With the advent of large passenger aircraft more space became available to carry cargo but this form of commercial transport was not used to any great extent, although insurance was available in the aviation insurance market. Later on, however, most of this class of business was underwritten in the marine market due, it is thought, to the ease with which the marine policy could be extended, or amended, to cover cargo whilst being carried by air.

Thus, despite Britain's changing role in the world economy and despite the manifold difficulties that the decade following the war threw up, insurance on aggregate showed remarkable growth, as Table 27 shows.

But that growth was seriously tested when, in 1929, the capitalist world was visited by quite the worst economic depression it had ever

Table 27

PREMIUM INCOME OF SELECTED BRANCHES, 1918–1928

(to nearest £1,000)

Year	*Life Premiums (Ord.)*	*Fire Premiums*	*Personal Accident Premiums*
1918	37,041,000	41,721,000	2,247,000
1928	72,788,000	50,017,000	3,902,000

Source: Insurance Directory and Year Book.

experienced. It was also the most prolonged and, although recovery in some sectors was obvious by 1934, in others the dreadful malaise persisted, even until 1939. Under these conditions underwriting was a difficult business and much effort had to be put into securing new business as Table 28 indicates.

Life premiums, it will be seen, continued to expand despite the depression and even during the trough of the depression exceeded the postwar peak of 1928. There are two main reasons for this. In the first place, as we have already noted, life assurance is contractual and therefore constitutes a prior claim on income. Secondly, although there is no scientific basis for this assertion, it is probably true that in bad times people's pessimism deepens and fears concerning the future multiply and assurances therefore increase. The continual accretion of new policies during the bleakest years of the depression certainly points to such a conclusion.

Table 28

PREMIUM INCOME, 1928–1939

(to nearest £1,000)

Year	*Life Premiums (Ordinary)*	*Fire Premiums*	*Personal Accident Premiums*	*Marine Premiums*
1928	72,788,000	59,017,000	3,902,000	—
1937	76,831,000	48,352,000	3,607,000	11,387,000
1939	91,666,000	49,609,000	4,548,000	14,797,000

Source: Insurance Directory and Year Book.

The fire branch enjoyed no such success and recovery from the trough was extremely slow, so much so that even in 1939 premium income was only marginally greater than in 1933. But the fire branch is always susceptible to changes in the economic climate and these years were no exception. The fire departments were hit especially hard by the severity of the depression in the United States where nearly every British fire company had a stake. With the gradual recovery of that country's economy fire premium income improved but the wars in Spain and China, in 1936 and 1937 respectively, plus European currency depreciations in 1937 arrested the progress. It was to take another major war on a world-wide scale to revive the flagging spirits of the fire underwriters.

Personal accident premium income followed a similar path and no general comments are called for. It was the newer forms of accident insurance, notably motor insurance, which put up an encouraging performance. During the 1920s there had been considerable criticism of the working of the motor insurance market with regard to the ease with which disreputable and unstable companies could enter the market. Increasing concern was also felt for the plight of innocent victims of road accidents who were unable to get compensation from the drivers responsible and hence arose the demand for compulsory third-party motor insurance. Against this background the Road Traffic Act of 1930 was passed, although strangely enough this piece of legislation was not welcomed by motor underwriters mainly because at the time they were pre-occupied with the unremunerative nature of motorcycle insurance. The major requirements of the Act were that motor insurers had to make a deposit of £15,000 irrespective of any other legal deposits already made, and third party risk insurance was made compulsory. In the event Sir James Leigh-Wood's observation in 1932 that 'motorcycles are a frequent source of accidents'[8] was borne out and this class of insurance proved to be unprofitable throughout the period. Nevertheless, by 1939 compulsory third-party motor insurance had risen, along with workmen's compensation, to a place of pre-eminence within the accident insurance branch with a premium income of £36,500,000 in that year. Despite the growth in premium income the motor insurance branch continued to have problems some of which, as we shall see later, prompted future legislation. The Accident Offices Association was constantly preoccupied with the problem of rate-cutting by new entrants some of whom deluded the public by giving inadequate protection. In 1928 it introduced standard proposal and policy forms the use of which was made obligatory for all members; in 1932 the tariff offices adopted the policy of offering cumulative no-claims bonuses, thereby following the lead of some of the non-tariff companies; and in 1935 they introduced zonal rating for private cars with differential charges based on three geographical areas. These were just three of the responses to the changing conditions of the 1920s and 1930s.

In aviation insurance the most significant event of the period was the Warsaw Convention of 1929 which was originally signed by twenty-three countries. Its main purpose was to provide for international uniformity by establishing certain rules relating to the liability of air carriers in respect of passengers, baggage and goods and, as it turned out, the British aviation insurance market was able to make profitable use of these standard terms and conditions. 1931 saw the formation of the British Aviation Insurance Company Limited, the first of the major aviation insurance companies as we know them today. The British aviation insurance group, having previously become incorporated in an agency for aviation insurance business, was considerably enlarged by additional capital subscribed by a number of leading insurance companies and a prominent firm of insurance brokers; at the same time its objectives were altered in order to enable it to underwrite aviation insurance risks on its own account. This was the first important step taken by composite offices to establish a specialised aviation underwriting concern. In 1935 there appeared on the scene another aviation insurance company, the Aviation and General Insurance Company which was formed in a similar manner by a group of insurance companies and broking firms. By that year Lloyd's were playing an increasingly important part in the aviation insurance market with the emergence of several specialist aviation underwriters. At the suggestion of the Committee of Lloyd's the Lloyd's Aviation Underwriters' Association was formed in October 1935, in order that some organisation which represented the Lloyd's aviation market should be available to deal with various matters then being referred to Lloyd's by the Air Ministry, the International Air Traffic Association and other bodies. Membership was at first confined to underwriters of specialist aviation syndicates but was later made available to the underwriters of any Lloyd's syndicate underwriting insurance business. With these structural and organisational changes the aviation market by the end of the 1930s was well established as an important, if subsidiary, part of accident insurance.

Despite the massive reduction in world shipping caused by the depression the marine insurance branch of the industry rode out the storm surprisingly well, mainly because the reduction in merchant shipping was partially compensated for by the construction of a number of enormous passenger liners. The *Queen Mary*, for instance, launched in 1936, with a gross registered tonnage of 80,774 was valued at nearly £6 million, of which the London market took the major share. The C.G.T. liner, *Nor-*

mandie, was similarly valued whilst the new Cunarder, then still on the slipway, eventually broke all previous records. It was the astronomical value of these ships which in fact sustained the marine market during these otherwise difficult years.

If the dominant influence on the insurance industry during the inter-war period was the Great Depression, the other was the intensification of legal supervision and state intervention. It is convenient to begin by considering the case of industrial life assurance which was in many ways the category of business which attracted to itself the bulk of public criticism. In the last chapter we saw how the Liberal reformers sought a solution to the problem of supervision of insurance in a combination of state control with private enterprise. However, another group of reformers saw the role of the State in more positive terms, namely the Fabian Society which commissioned Sydney Webb to undertake an investigation into industrial life assurance. His report, which was originally published in the New Statesman in 1915, can be regarded as the first step in the literary onslaught to which industrial life assurance was to be subjected over the next thirty-five years. The criticisms which were subsequently made of the business are all found to some degree in this report together with the demand for nationalisation. One of the effects of Sydney Webb's survey was to induce Lloyd George's Coalition Government to set up a Departmental Committee of investigation under the chairmanship of Lord Parmoor in 1919. Its terms of reference were:

> 'to inquire into the business carried on by industrial assurance companies and collecting societies, exclusive of the issue of life assurance policies involving the payment of sums exceeding £50 on the death of the assured and of insurance business under the National Health Insurance Act and to report whether any amendment of the law is desirable.'

This was the first such body to deal solely with industrial life assurance and one of the more immediate consequences of its deliberations was the virtual abandonment of Gladstone's Post Office Insurance Scheme. At this time the Post Office collected premiums in the form of stamps affixed to cards which were handed in quarterly to an Office which handled Savings Bank business. Although the Committee examined the scheme with some sympathy, it was obvious that, if it was going to overcome its lack of success, which largely arose from the public's preference for door-to-door collection of premiums, it would have to be remodelled and reconstructed. As the Government saw no effective means of remodelling it, it was abandoned, as we have already noted, in 1928.

The major criticisms of industrial life business made by the Committee were those which had been made in the past and which were going to be made again in the future, namely, excessive expense ratios, excessive lapse rates and abuses connected with funeral benefits. These deficiencies were largely ascribed, as they were to be in the future, to overselling by agents. First, since the method of canvassing was considered to be the cause of many of the industry's troubles, the procuration fee paid to agents should be abolished. It was argued that agents should be given a minimum salary based on a fixed weekly collection, commission being paid on business acquired in addition to that. It was further suggested that companies might adopt the 'block' system of canvassing which had been pioneered by the Prudential. Previously, agents eager to earn commissions would canvass the same area as other agents even from the same company. Under the 'block' system each agent is allotted a defined piece of territory and precluded from seeking or accepting business outside its limits.

Secondly, the Committee, having noted that some offices were willing to grant free paid-up policies to policyholders whose policies lapsed after a long period, felt that under certain conditions receipt of such a paid-up policy, with the value calculated according to an official scale, should become a statutory right. It was recommended that the industrial life offices should be given five years to build up additional reserves to comply with this provision. Finally, it was suggested that industrial assurance companies, like friendly societies, should be required to make returns to the Chief Registrar of Friendly Societies instead of the Board of Trade in order to ensure that the whole of industrial assurance should be supervised by one body.

The immediate sequel to the Parmoor Report was the introduction of a Bill into the House of Lords by the Earl of Onslow in 1921. 'By this step, it was later explained in the House of Commons, the Government intended no more than to bring the substance of the Parmoor proposals into Parliamentary Debate and test public opinion with a view to actual legislation in a later session.'[9] The main provisions of the Bill were as follows. First, companies and societies should be supervised by an Inspector General of Industrial Assurance with wide powers of inspection and control. Secondly, expenses in the industrial branch should be limited to 40 per cent of weekly premiums and 25 per cent of other industrial life premiums.[10] Thirdly, policyholders should have the statutory right under certain conditions to a free paid-up policy.

This Bill met with an immediate and hostile reception from the offices which were particularly incensed by the second provision on expenses. Their argument was, that with such a wide divergence between the structure and nature of the business of individual offices, statutory regulation of expenses was unrealistic and unenforceable. But, as previously mentioned, once this Bill had served its purpose as a focus for debate the Government decided not to proceed with it, although it hoped to bring in an agreed measure at a later date.

However, the Government fell from power and it was left to the Conservative administration to bring in the Industrial Assurance Act of 1923. Under this Act the Chief Registrar of Friendly Societies became the Industrial Assurance Commissioner who was granted important statutory powers including the right to require offices to make returns to him. 'He might reject any returns with which he was not satisfied and give such directions for their amendment as he thought fit. If he had reasonable grounds for thinking that an offence had been committed, he could order an examination of the affairs of the office concerned and issue such directions and take such steps as he considered necessary to deal with the situation it disclosed; where a deficiency was revealed he could order a collecting society to be dissolved or apply to the court for an order to have the company wound up. He could reject valuation returns and—subject to the right of the office to appeal to the High Court—direct that such alterations should be made in them as were necessary to comply with the provisions of the Act. He could call for further information and, within certain limitations, could himself adjudicate upon disputes, referred to him by policyholders or assurance offices, which would previously have had to be taken to a court of summary jurisdiction.'[11]

The other important provisions of this Act were first, that the conditions, under which free paid-up policies and surrender values were to be granted, were enumerated and secondly, that industrial assurance for the purpose of the 1909 Act was from this time forward to be treated as a separate class of insurance which meant that a separate deposit of £20,000 was required and a distinct fund and revenue account to be recorded in the returns. However, the expenses limitation clause of the Onslow Bill was expressly excluded.

Despite this legislation industrial assurance was still under intermittent fire in the late 1920s. In 1928 the nationalisation of industrial life assurance was specifically referred to in statements of policy approved by the Labour Party in a document entitled 'Labour and the Nation'. A conference of the National Amalgamated Union of Life Assurance Workers in 1926 had supported nationalisation and the T.U.C. in 1927 had declared that: 'In the opinion of this Congress the time is opportune for an examination by the General Council and the unions concerned into nationalisation of industrial assurance and such other branches of private and social insurance as can be associated with it.'[12] However, the question of nationalisation was not referred to in the Labour Party's election manifesto in 1929, but in 1931 Mr. Philip Snowden, the Chancellor of the Exchequer, appointed Sir Benjamin Cohen to preside over yet another committee of inquiry. Its terms of reference were: 'To examine and report on the law and practice relating to Industrial Assurance and to Assurance on the lives of children under ten years of age, including the question whether any amendment of the law or any addition to it is desirable.'

The Committee did not consider nationalisation as such but did examine the kindred project of transferring all industrial assurance to a public utility corporation. They concluded that the difficulties were so great that they could not recommend it. Thus, while the Committee refrained from any discussion of nationalisation as such, some of the secondary arguments bearing upon the Labour Party's controversial views were given the first airing in official literature in this Report. For example, they drew attention to the fact that nearly all companies transacting industrial business also transacted ordinary life business. If, as had been proposed, the ordinary as well as the industrial business of these companies had been nationalised, the State would have found itself in competition with the companies which transacted ordinary, but not industrial, business. There was, of course, the possibility of nationalising all life assurance but the Committee recognised that this too would create difficulties. First, it had to be recognised that in the case of composite companies the staff employed on life assurance also gave part of their time to introducing clients to other aspects of the companies' business. There would be acute dislocation if life assurance were to be compulsorily severed from these associated activities. Secondly, a large proportion of the business of some companies was drawn from overseas and the companies transacting it were subject to the domestic laws of many states.

Having dismissed the idea of a public utility for these reasons, the Committee went on to consider some less drastic consolidation of industrial offices into groups which they considered would have the merit of eliminating wasteful competition between agents. However, it concluded that such a solution 'would be beset by many difficulties and that at the best it would not provide a cure for all the defects for which remedies are required'.[13] The Committee thus arrived at the point where, if it were to grapple with the problem of excessive expense ratios which was due to the extravagance of competition between the offices and between the agents, it had no alternative left but direct regulation of those ratios. It, therefore, recommended that a maximum ratio of 30 per cent should be fixed to cover expenses although the offices should be allowed a period of grace of seven years during which to reduce their expenses down to this level. The members of the Committee realised that there would be violent objections to this proposal but they considered that the objections were decisively outweighed by the consequential improvements in efficiency. In addition they gave their attention to many other problems of industrial life business which had been brought up in the past and which were to be brought up again in the future.[14]

The labours of the Cohen Committee did not produce any results in the form of legislative change, but the industry was not allowed to enjoy for long the absence of critical scrutiny for the next serious attack was launched in 1937 in the form of a book by Sir Arnold Wilson and Herman Levy.[15] Apropos the evidence of the Cohen Committee they made the following complaints:

> 'Four years have elapsed since the Cohen Report was published. It has never been specifically discussed in Parliament. The question has not figured in any party programme. The socialist groups of the Labour Party favour nationalisation. . . . They could not, however, carry with them the trade unions and the agents who value the control of the trade union approved societies: the Co-operative Societies who spend considerable sums on political activities would strenuously oppose any legislation which weakens the approved societies connected with the movement or merge them into a state service.'[16]

Their book had a considerable impact on the debate surrounding industrial assurance. Morrah argues that the book has many shortcomings including errors of fact and evidence of lack of impartiality, but inevitably it had an impact on public opinion because the book had no competitor of its own kind. The main criticisms found in this book are similar to those of the Cohen Report and they were to be heard again in the future: namely, the problems of expenses and lapses, abuses in funeral expense insurance and the dangers resulting from the power conferred by the control of large funds for investment. But the controversy was stilled, at least temporarily, by the outbreak of the Second World War and the companies enjoyed a respite from running the gauntlet of continual hostile attacks.

Another branch of insurance which received a considerable amount of official attention during the inter-war period was employers' liability. Immediately after the end of the war in 1919 a Departmental Committee was appointed under the chairmanship of Mr. (later Sir) Holman Gregory:

> 'to inquire into the working of the present system for the payment of compensation to workmen for injuries sustained in the course of employment and to consider and report whether it would be desirable to

establish a system of accident insurance under the control and supervision of the State; and to report further what alterations to the law be required to remedy defects which experience has disclosed or to give effect to their recommendations'.

The Committee was very disturbed by what it considered to be the excessive amount of profit which the companies had derived from employers' liability business, for it estimated that over the eight years from 1911 to 1918 average profits had amounted to 15·2 per cent of premium income. Consequently, in its Report it made the following recommendations. In the first place, the State should supervise the premium rates of insurance companies with a view to restricting their profits and expenses in workmen's compensation business. Secondly, mutual associations should be placed under the same obligations as insurance companies to set aside funds to meet outstanding liabilities and to provide returns and other information. Thirdly, compulsory employers' liability insurance should be introduced with certain exemptions. For example, employers with an annual average wage bill over £20,000 were entitled to claim exemption upon compliance with prescribed conditions. Finally, a Commissioner should be appointed to take charge of the supervision of insurance companies, mutual associations and self-insurers in certain matters, and to discharge all the duties in relation to workmen's compensation otherwise performed by a Government department.

Through the difficulties encountered in securing agreement among employers, employees and insurance companies, no immediate action was taken but in 1923 a new Workmen's Compensation Act was passed. In fact, it did not embody any of the four major recommendations but did deal with other minor recommendations including the raising of the income limit from £250 to £350 per annum below which non-manual workers qualified for benefit. This naturally brought many more workers within the scope of the Act. Some action was taken on the first of the major recommendations by securing the voluntary co-operation of the companies in limiting profits. The Government spokesman, Mr. Locker Lampson, explained the Government's attitude during the debate.

'I do not for a moment say that the principle of compulsory insurance is wrong . . . but it involves the creation of a great deal of machinery and additional cost and I think at the present time it would be inopportune to introduce it . . . the Holman Gregory Report also recommended that there should be state supervision of rates of premium . . . the Bill does not carry out that recommendation but I am glad to say that we have arranged that it shall be very largely carried out by voluntary agreement with the Accident Offices Association . . . this is to the effect that the loss ratio which the total amount paid by the companies belonging to the Association in the year in respect of compensation, including reasonable medical aid and legal expenses, bears to the total amount of premiums received by the companies in that year, is to be not less than 60 per cent or such other proportion not less than 60 per cent as may be agreed upon . . . and further, if the amount paid in respect of compensation falls short of or exceeds the above loss ratio, the companies will be bound to make a corresponding rebate, or will be entitled to make an additional charge, as the case may be, to the employers when the reset premium is paid.'[17]

The only other major legislation in this field before 1939 was the Workmen's Compensation (Coal Mines) Act 1934. Many coal miners had suffered hardships in the past because their employers became insolvent and were unable to meet their compensation obligations. Although the liabilities imposed by the various Acts were obligatory on every employer, there was no compulsion to insure those liabilities. This Act provided for compulsory workmen's compensation insurance in the coal-mining industry. Owners of mines could comply with the Act by insurance proper or by means of a 'compensation trust'. Under the latter arrangement a trust fund ensured the discharge of the owners' liabilities but the trustees were compelled to insure the excess of £1,500 for fatal injuries. Official uncertainties about the working of employers' liability insurance continued throughout the period and in 1938 the Government set in train yet another investigation by establishing a Royal Commission under Sir Hector Hetherington. However, its deliberations were interrupted by the outbreak of war and it was eventually superseded by the Inter-Departmental Committee under Sir William Beveridge in 1941, whose report will be considered in subsequent chapters.

So far we have considered legislative changes which were directed at particular sectors of the industry and now we turn our attention to the largely abortive efforts to subject the industry in general to closer and more effective supervision. Soon after the ending of the 1914–18 War it became clear that the 1909 Act had not achieved all that had been hoped of it. For example, it was possible to carry on marine business without being subject to the provisions of the 1909 Act provided that such business was not carried on in conjunction with any of the classes enumerated in it. During the war marine insurance premiums had been greatly inflated and large profits had accrued to the insurers in consequence. Large profits in any industry are always attractive to new entrants and marine insurance proved to be no exception. Thus the Depression and the reduction in tonnage which occurred in 1921 combined with a sharp increase in the cost of repairs hit an industry which was already suffering from excess capacity. Not surprisingly there were failures not only of specialist marine companies but of composite companies conducting other classes of business whose overall position was weakened by a poor marine account. These failures prompted the Labour Government in 1924 to appoint the Clauson Committee 'to inquire and report what amendments are desirable in the Assurance Companies Act, 1909'.

This Committee concerned itself with three main issues. First, with regard to deposits it admitted that the prime purpose was not to provide security for the policyholders directly, but indirectly by discouraging unsubstantial and speculative concerns from underwriting insurance business. Secondly, it believed that publicity arising from the requirement to render returns to the Board of Trade was the best protection for the policyholder. Thirdly, in respect of statutory funds the Committee, no doubt influenced by the difficulties of the marine branch, proposed that all companies should be forced not merely to maintain separate accounts on paper as required by the 1909 Act but to keep the assets distinct and earmark them for the class of policyholder from which they were derived. The views of the Committee were open to criticism on three grounds. First, experience had demonstrated that deposits did not fulfil even this limited function of discouraging undesirable new entrants; secondly, the insured most in need of protection were not likely to be sufficiently sophisticated to interpret company balance sheets; and, thirdly, some policyholders in strong departments would be subsidised at the expense of others. Although the Committee presented its Report in the form of a Bill (the Insurance Undertakings Bill) to Parliament in 1927, it never reached the Statute Book through a failure of the interested parties to agree. In retrospect the main interest of the Committee's Report resides in the fact that it considered, but rejected, a suggestion which was to crop up a great deal during the next fifteen years. When discussing what powers should be conferred on the Board of Trade in cases of 'apprehended insolvency', namely early recognition that a company might be in difficulties, it was suggested that some kind of advisory committee should be formed to act with the Board of Trade when some company was believed to be in danger of collapse. Such a provision would have required the Board of Trade to determine some criteria for judging 'solvency requirements'—a recurring topic in future years.

Only one of the Committee's recommendations led to further action and that was concerned with strengthening the Board of Trade's powers to effect the winding up of a company. Here the impulse to action arose from the failure of several rate-cutting companies which entered the market after compulsory third-party insurance became law.[18] These failures caused hardship both to their policyholders and to third parties many of whom were deprived of compensation. Greater powers were therefore given to the Board of Trade to bring about the winding up of a company by the Assurance Companies (Winding-up) Act, 1933, but unfortunately it worked clumsily. In 1935 *The Economist* was prompted to make the ironical comment that the Act's efficiency could be gauged from the fact that the two most recent failures (the Anglian and the London and General) had been known to be in difficulties for months, one of them actually reaching the point at which the salaries of staff could not be paid. In *The Economist*'s view the Act was a laughing stock for 'one company after another has tottered and tottered and finally fallen, while the Board of Trade has stood by with the Act in its hand and waited for the collapse'.[19] Not surprisingly, the Government responded by passing a further Assurance Companies (Winding-up) Act in 1935 with more teeth but without sufficient bite to quell criticism. The uncomfortable fact that between 1909 and 1935 fifty insurance companies transacting business in the United Kingdom had failed was sufficient evidence that the 1909 Act, which relied solely on deposits, had not brought adequate security for policyholders. In recognition of public disquiet the Government established yet another committee in 1936 'to consider and report whether any, and if so what, changes in the existing law relating to the carrying on of the business of insurance are desirable in the light of statutory provisions relating to compulsory insurance against third-party risks and by employers against liability to their workmen'.

This was the Cassel Committee which reported in 1937 and made far-reaching proposals for reform of the law. In the first place, all insurers should be licensed for one year at a time and the criterion for granting a licence should be the complete solvency of the insurer carrying the risk whether insurance company, Lloyd's underwriter or mutual indemnity association. Secondly, a central fund should be constituted as a second line of defence to meet the contingency of the insolvency of an insurer licensed to transact compulsory motor vehicle or aircraft business. Unfortunately, the labours of the Committee were largely set at nought by the outbreak of war. It can be truly said of the whole inter-war period that it was one of almost continuous official scrutiny and investigation of the insurance industry, which resulted in remarkably little effective restraint on the scope of its activities.

But in the growth and development of credit insurance, the birth of which we noted in the previous chapter, we observe the first example of a state-owned and operated insurance enterprise. In 1919 there was concern about the political and economic risks involved in re-opening trade links with those countries with which trade had been impossible during the war and a scheme was instituted to provide Government advances to exporters which were to be repaid when they obtained payment from a foreign buyer. This scheme was modified in 1921 and the first *guarantee* method was introduced. Under it the system of advances was discontinued and the Exports Credit Department of the Board of Trade was authorised to endorse bills drawn by British exporters on foreign purchasers. At the outset it was hoped that the scheme would give rise to profitable co-operation between the Export Credits Department and private firms conducting similar types of business. The Government, in effect, offered to reinsure risks undertaken by such institutions in financing foreign trade up to 70 per cent of the face value of the risk. 'Private institutions, however, refused to co-operate and agreed to recommend only to their clients that they should apply to the department for cover in cases where private firms were unable to give it. This, of course, left the department with only the worst risks. The losses suffered were rather heavy.'[20]

In 1926 its work was completely reorganised and its name was changed to the Exports Credit Guarantee Department. Subsequently, a number of Parliamentary committees found good reason for continuing the department on a temporary basis, while conditions were abnormal, but economic and political developments in the inter-war years never produced the degree of stability necessary for its demise. Until 1938 it was run on a strictly profit-making basis and it was able to transact business in spite of the existence of private firms because the scale of its operations and the assistance which could be placed at its disposal by the other departments of the Government, and particularly by those which maintained British representatives abroad, permitted it to insure risks which private firms could not touch. Its success may be judged by the fact that in the financial year 1933–34 the total value of British exports covered by the guarantees was about £7·5 millions, or less than 2 per cent of total British exports, whereas in the financial year 1936–37, the value of the guaranteed exports was £35 millions or more than 6·5 per cent of British exports.[21] It is not surprising, therefore, that in 1938 it was decided that the business of the department should be extended and the limit to the amount of guarantees which might be outstanding at any one time was raised from £26 millions to £50 millions. Since then it has been further strengthened from time to time so that, far from being wound up, it is still an integral and important contribution by the State to insurance services.

The same departmental committee of the Board of Trade which had recommended the establishment of the Exports Credit Department was also responsible for the Government sponsoring the creation of the British Trade Corporation. At its first meeting this body recognised the need for a credit insurance company. 'It having been brought to the directors' notice from evidence given before several departmental committees that there was a strongly expressed opinion that arrangements should be made for the insurance of commercial bills, the Corporation, after making extensive enquiries upon the subject, had decided to create a separate company that would be entirely under its control for doing the class of business referred to. It had therefore entered into an agreement with the Excess Insurance Co. Limited to transfer to the new concern the part of the Excess Insurance Company's business of this character and with the business to transfer also their underwriter, Mr. H. S. Spain, who had for many years past devoted his energies to credit insurance. It was hoped that the new undertaking would meet a genuine demand and it should be particularly useful to the smaller trader who was without the facilities which were possessed by the large merchant and manufacturer.'[22]

As a result the Trade Indemnity Co. Limited was registered on 5 March 1918 under the control of the British Trade Corporation. In 1924, however, it was decided to increase its paid-up capital and to interest a number of leading British insurance companies in becoming shareholders so as to enable the British Trade Corporation to surrender control. All went well for a time but the Great Depression and the economic nationalism of the 1930s which followed led to an increase in political and economic risks in the export trade against which commercial insurers found it difficult to insure. Consequently, this area of export credit insurance was largely left to the Export Credits Guarantee Department while the Trade Indemnity Company concentrated mainly on domestic business.[23]

It may occasion surprise that Lloyd's played virtually no part in the development of credit insurance but the explanation is to be found in one of the few scandals which have rocked Lloyd's during its long history. It concerned an underwriter named Stanley Harrison who became a member of Lloyd's in 1917 and after the war was involved in hire-purchase finance. During the early years after the Armistice over thirty finance companies were formed in the United Kingdom primarily to meet the demand for private motor vehicles. Their common practice was to buy cars and hire them out on easy terms to their eventual owners; at the same time they drew on the hirers for payment through bills of exchange of an appropriate length. A company requiring working capital would simply discount the bill, but since the finance companies were relative newcomers, it was obviously much easier for them to overcome the doubts of the discounter if the bill was backed by a credit insurance policy. At first the financiers seemed to have placed their business with companies but when they discovered that there was a small, but relatively cheaper, market at Lloyd's, they turned to certain of the underwriters there of whom Harrison soon became the busiest.

Harrison's downfall resulted mainly from a relationship which he established with a dubious finance company, the Industrial Guarantee Corporation. This company never had a great deal of capital but Harrison was rash enough to guarantee more than £2,000,000 of its bills for a premium income of a little over £20,000 and, as the company's position deteriorated, so did Harrison's. The crowning catastrophe for Harrison involved a fraud perpetrated by a Swede named Holsteinson. This fraud involved inventing a number of cars and charabancs, giving them imaginary engine and chassis numbers, drawing bills on the strength of their security, insuring them with Harrison and then discounting them with the help of Harrison's policy. At an opportune moment Holsteinson disappeared from the scene and was never seen in England again.

If this was not sufficient embarrassment in itself, Harrison was faced with another difficulty. Under normal circumstances he would have been able to go to the Chairman of Lloyd's and make a clean breast of his financial problems with his credit insurance account, but he himself had been perpetrating a fraud. He had been keeping two sets of books of which only one, which contained no information on his credit business, had been approved by Lloyd's auditors who on this evidence had given him the necessary certificate for carrying on his underwriting. He was then faced with the quandary that an admission that his credit business was in difficulties would have brought this fraud to light.

The affair eventually came to a head in October 1923 when a cheque of Harrison's was not honoured. The Chairman of Lloyd's immediately informed him that his underwriting accounts must be inspected again. The next day Harrison refused the auditors access to his books but later admitted to the Chairman that his financial position was hopeless. Although the officials of Lloyd's can be criticised for failing to detect these irregularities earlier, once they did know the true position they acted with commendable speed to protect the good name of Lloyd's. At a meeting of underwriting agents, A. L. Sturge, the then Chairman, did not beat about the bush when he told them that 'if we do not pay these bills, the name of Lloyd's will be seriously injured and will never recover during our lifetime'.[24] He called upon the underwriters to offer £200,000 to the Committee for immediate distribution to Harrison's creditors and they agreed to shoulder this responsibility in proportion to their premium income. In the event a special committee, which was established to deal with Harrison's outstanding credit debits, disbursed in all £367,787.

Not surprisingly the Harrison scandal had repercussions on the views of Lloyd's members about credit insurance many of whom wanted it abolished and outlawed. But this solution was not acceptable to all, especially Cuthbert Heath to whom we referred in the previous chapter, and a sharp clash of wills between Heath and Sturge ensued. However a compromise was eventually reached whereby credit insurance should be permitted but only by way of reinsurance with no policies being issued by Lloyd's directly to the public. Under this arrangement a merchant wishing to cover the solvency of a customer would have to take the risk to a company which might then, if it wished, obtain reinsurance with Lloyd's underwriters.

But, returning to the main theme, the insurance industry faced not only the challenges of the Great Depression and increased state supervision and control but also the growth of economic nationalism abroad during the inter-war years. 'A vast rash of legislation subjecting British insurers to various degrees of control, and their assets to various degrees of hypothecation, spread rapidly across the world.'[25] As free trade was abandoned in the desperate attempt to reduce unemployment at home, restrictions were placed on insurance and throughout the middle two quarters of this century the impediments have tended to increase both in number and effectiveness. These impediments can be broadly categorised as follows. In the first place, there are general restrictions on international trade, such as currency restrictions which make the transfer of funds in the light of underwriting experience and the transfer of profits increasingly difficult. Secondly, there is the practice adopted by a number of overseas countries of requiring insurance companies to keep a permanent deposit in the country in question which, however justifiable on other grounds, reduces the mobility of insurers' reserves and their ability to meet unexpected losses out of given total reserves. Thirdly, harassed ministers of finance often regard insurance companies as an easily accessible and tempting source of revenue and a support for the government bond market, and thus insurers' profits can be, and frequently are, attacked by foreign taxation. Faced with these threats the industry has frequently taken a long view and maintained its foothold in territories which, at least temporarily, have seemed to offer very poor prospects and in some cases patience has been rewarded. As a result British insurance has been able to add its capacity to the expanded needs of many local markets, particularly in South America, from which their disappearance was in the 1930s a distinct possibility.

The end of this period was clouded by the threat of another major conflict into which Britain inexorably would be drawn. The First World War, the 'war to end wars', had failed in its objective and in retrospect the Treaty of Versailles could be seen to have sown the seeds of the Second World War. Taken as a whole the inter-war period presented to the insurance industry one difficult problem after another. In 1921 came economic depression and in 1926 the General Strike; in 1929 Wall Street crashed and ushered in yet another, and this time much severer, depression; 1934 brought German re-armament, 1935 Italian aggression against Ethiopia, 1936 Civil War in Spain, 1927 a resumption of Japanese aggression against China, and all this against a background of changing British fortunes in the world economy. What is so surprising is that under such adverse conditions the British insurance market was able to make any significant progress at all.

APPENDIX TO CHAPTER IX

Coupon Insurance

It would have been inappropriate to include in our rather broad survey of events in the inter-war period a minor innovation in the marketing of insurance known as 'coupon insurance' but, since it may be of some interest, it is discussed in this short appendix. It refers to a practice adopted by many journals and newspapers of inserting a 'coupon' in their columns offering insurance (usually death benefit) to the reader under certain specified conditions. Although the first scheme of this nature was initiated by *Tit-Bits* in 1885, the practice did not become at all general until the early 1920s but by 1930 it was so well established that the national dailies had reached an agreement to offer their respective readers identical coupon schemes. They were usually undertaken by an insurance company for the publication in question as, for example, the Co-operative Insurance Society did for the *Daily Herald* in 1930, and were largely of two types. In the first type the premium was paid by the proprietor of the publication in question and the 'insured', when he found the coupon in that journal, merely completed it or complied with some other requirement. In the second, the insured himself paid the premium (usually known as the registration fee) and sent the completed form to the insurance company.

These insurances were not without their critics of whom W. A. Dinsdale is not untypical. 'The schemes are mainly for advertisement but they are not altogether satisfactory. The benefits are limited strictly to those accidents which satisfy the conditions of the coupon and no claim is admissible, for example, unless death occurs within one month. The premiums are so small for this "cut-price" insurance that they leave no margin for *ex gratia* payments.'[26]

The *Tit-Bits* scheme, mentioned above, will serve as an illustration of the generally restrictive nature of these schemes. The wording on the coupon in question read as follows: 'The proprietor of *Tit-Bits* hereby agrees that he will give one hundred pounds to the next of kin of any person, provided a copy of the current issue of *Tit-Bits* is found upon him or her at the time of the accident.' R. G. Garnett quotes another example which again illustrates their restrictive nature, namely a death benefit scheme entered into by the Co-operative Insurance Society with *Reynolds News* in 1936, whereby regular readers of that newspaper, who were also members of co-operative societies collectively insured with the C.I.S., received a sum equivalent to one-third of the amount payable by the C.I.S. under the collective life scheme.[27]

These coupon schemes were abandoned immediately after the outbreak of the Second World War and their demise was not unwelcome to many offices which had suffered such heavy losses from coupon insurance that they had adopted the practice of treating them as advertising expenses.

NOTES

1 *Industrialisation and Foreign Trade*, League of Nations (1945), p. 13.

2 W. Arthur Lewis, *Economic Survey 1919–1939*, Allen & Unwin, p. 81.

3 A. F. Noyes, ibid., p. 283.

4 D. E. W. Gibb, *Lloyd's of London*, p. 226.

5 The Spanish influenza epidemic swept the whole world with effects 'almost as sudden and as devastating as those of the plagues of former times'. (R. Blake 'Esto Perpetua', the Norwich Union Life Insurance Society, 1808–1958). The seriousness of the epidemic may be gauged from the fact that the Norwich Union's war claims in 1918 totalled £110,000 whilst deaths due to the influenza produced claims totalling £136,000. Other companies experienced similar losses.

6 In 1914 premium income amounted to £2,087,000 and by 1918 it had risen to £2,247,000.

7 E. V. Francis, ibid., p. 84.

8 Address to Annual General Meeting of Commercial Union Assurance Company in 1932.

9 D. Morrah, ibid., p. 89.

10 The Parmoor Committee had estimated that expenses and dividends absorbed 44 per cent of the premium income from industrial policies and inferred that therefore the policyholders recovered no more than 6¾d. out of every shilling they paid in premiums.

11 D. Morrah, ibid., pp. 97, 98.

12 R. G. Garnett, *A Century of Cooperative Insurance*, Allen & Unwin, p. 235.

13 Quoted by Morrah, ibid., p. 114.
14 The interested reader should consult the detailed account in Morrah, ibid., pp. 107–120.
15 Its title is *Industrial Assurance: An Historical and Critical Study*, O.U.P.
16 Sir Arnold Wilson and H. Levy, ibid., pp. 118–119.
17 *Hansard*, 30 May 1923, quoted by Raynes, ibid., p. 313.
18 The following companies failed: 1933 South East Lancashire Insurance; 1933 Hearts of Oak Assurance; 1933 Port of Manchester Assurance; 1935 Anglian Insurance; 1935 London General Insurance.
19 *The Economist*, 13 July 1935.
20 T. Balogh, *Financial Organisation, N.I.E.S.R.*, Cambridge, p. 161.
21 For a fuller account see F. H. Nixon, *The Banker*, February 1939.
22 W. A. Dinsdale, op. cit., p. 111.
23 Premium Income of Trade Indemnity grew as follows:

Year	Premium Income (£'000)
1918	12
1922	48
1926	153
1930	208
1934	164
1938	215

24 A. L. Sturge, quoted by D. E. G. Gibb, op. cit., p. 271.
25 A. F. Noyes, op. cit., p. 291.
26 W. A. Dinsdale, op. cit., p. 75.
27 R. G. Garnett, op. cit., p. 220.

Chapter 10

THE STRESSES OF THE SECOND WORLD WAR

'There is, in public affairs, no state so bad, provided it has age and stability on its side, that is not preferable to change and disturbance.'

(Michael De Montaigne)

'A state without the means of some change is without the means of its conservation.'

(Edmund Burke)

In this chapter and the next we are concerned with change, for it is change which provides the dominant background against which the events of the last thirty years have been acted out. We have already noted the effect of Britain's changing role in the world economy since 1914 and this must continually be borne in mind for it still remains a cogent force. But super-imposed upon this fundamental change are others which we shall note as we go along.

A vital source of change was, of course, the Second World War which differed in two important respects from the First. In the first place there was a marked extension of geographical involvement. As we have seen, the First World War was by and large confined to a relatively small geographical area, and damage to property was commensurately light though the loss of human life was on an appalling scale. The Second World War, on the other hand, was indeed world-wide in its scope, embracing the whole of Europe, North Africa, the Middle East, South East Asia, the Far East, the Pacific Islands and even Australasia; and the damage to property was commensurately heavy. The loss of human life was on a horrifying scale but, as compared with the First World War, the heaviest losses were sustained amongst the civilian population. This was in no small measure due to the second factor, the pace of technological change between the wars which brought the heavily-populated industrial centres into the firing line. Events in Spain and Abyssinia had prepared the world at large for the effects on land of total war and the bombing of Guernica, immortalised by Picasso, had provided an ugly and impressive example of destruction from the air. The long-range bomber loaded with high explosives was a new and terrible phenomenon.

Underwriters, having observed the havoc which German bombers had managed to create in a poor country with few rich cities and little concentration of wealth in its crowded areas, were made painfully aware of the enormous potential destructive power of bombs dropped on the rich industrial areas of Britain. As the clouds of war gathered, some of them had the foresight to take steps to deal with the problem.

In September 1936 Neville Dixey, the Chairman of Lloyd's, raised the problem of war risks with the Committee of Lloyd's which gave him the necessary authority to open negotiations with marine and non-marine underwriters and with the insurance offices. The outcome was an agreement that a clause, excluding war risks on land, should be drafted which every Lloyd's underwriter and every British company should be asked to sign. British marine underwriters were asked to confine the land war risks on cargo to forty-eight hours after discharge and continental companies were invited to join the concordat. At this stage life assurance, personal accident insurance and property in the U.S.A. and Canada were omitted from the provisions. Under the combined pressure of the Chairman of Lloyd's and the General Managers of the major tariff companies, which had always disliked war risks on land, the scheme was pushed through. Thereafter a war exclusion clause was inserted in every non-marine policy insuring property on land and not long after 500 foreign insurance companies fell in line with the British insurance market in declining to accept war risks.

There was also a vital difference between 1914 and 1938 in the provision of policies on cargoes. Whilst in 1914 most cargo policies contained what is known as the 'F.C. and S' clause which to all intents and purposes excluded war risks, in 1938 underwriters were heavily committed through the fashion which had arisen in the inter-war period of including war risks at nominal rates in almost all policies covering cargoes. However, with the onset of the Czechoslovakian and Albanian crises premiums covering voyages in the Mediterranean had risen sharply and were expected to go even higher.

This was the uncertain situation in 1939—for two years land war exclusion risks had been in force and the possibility of high cargo risks had arisen. It was obvious that the Government, which was anxious to ensure that the flow of trade (and particularly imports of raw materials) was not interrupted and that adequate stocks were maintained in Britain, could not allow this uncertainty to continue. So early in 1939 an Act was put through Parliament authorising the Board of Trade to reinsure 'King's enemy risks' (i.e. war risks) on ships, and cargoes by sea and air. The Board then arranged with the marine market that underwriters should accept the King's enemy risks offered to them exactly as in normal times but should reinsure them all with the Government. The plan worked so well that rates were kept down to reasonably low levels.

These reinsurance arrangements lasted for only a few months since, as soon as Hitler launched his 'Blitzkrieg' on Poland, the War Risk Insurance Office opened its doors to accept war risks direct. However, the Government was determined not to get caught as it had been during the First World War when its efforts to shield the insurance market from the impact of war had resulted in its being left 'holding the baby' of bad risks while the good risks were taken up by the private insurance market. It, therefore, came to a 'gentleman's agreement' with the companies and Lloyd's whereby a distinction was made between marine risks arising from voyages to and from Britain and voyages between overseas countries. In the first group, underwriters, if they were disposed to quote a rate, were required to quote one which was higher than the Government's published rate. This arrangement secured the Government against competition by rate-cutting and still made it possible for an insurer who objected to covering his risks with the British Government to insure on the open market. Business in the second group, on the other hand, could be underwritten at any rate the market chose to offer.

In 1939 measures were also taken to protect stocks, with the passing of the War Risks Insurance Act which introduced a war risk insurance scheme for commodities whereby the private insurance of stocks on land was prohibited by law. Thus the Government was granted a monopoly and, with a few minor exceptions, any trade was forced to take out cover with the Board of Trade. The insurance companies and the Corporation of Lloyd's were employed as Government agents to collect premiums and pass them on to the Board of Trade. Despite these extra burdens the companies discharged their duties with tolerance and efficiency. Then in 1941 came the War Damage Act which extended state involvement. The 1939 Act gave no cover to buildings, furniture, machinery, etc., and it was this gap which the 1941 Act was intended to fill. The Government's insurance scheme was extended to including buildings, business plant and equipment and private chattels. Buildings in the new Act were directly insured by the Government which instead of charging premiums added an extra impost of 2s. in £ on Schedule A Income Tax. Everything else was placed in the hands of the underwriters who acted as agents. The extension of the scheme to cover personal chattels immediately raised seemingly intractable difficulties one of which is referred to by D. E. W. Gibb:

> 'Was a tombstone, asked one of the brokers, a building or a chattel? If it was a building, it would come under Part I of the Act and insurance would be compulsory. If it was a chattel, it came under Part

II and the insurance was optional. The Board of Trade considered the point and decided that the tombstone was a building. But what of the coffin? Did that go with the stone? No. On the same authority it was a chattel falling under Part II of the Act so that there was no necessity to insure it. The stone and the coffin must go separate ways.'[1]

But these semantic excursions were nothing more than amusing diversions from the routine of day-to-day wartime business—business which, if we may judge from the figures, loomed larger with the passage of time. Although a large part of the rise in premium income could be attributed to the inflationary effect on values of the war itself, there is no doubt that a considerable increase in the volume of new business was the order of the day especially in the general branch. (See Tables at end of chapter.)

Life business had its own special problems for, not surprisingly, there was a sharp fall in new sums assured. Contracts of a long-term nature will only be entered into when it is possible to look ahead with some measure of certainty and that was transparently not the situation facing the average citizen of a country which was embroiled in a conflict only too likely to be fought with weapons of hitherto unimaginable powers of destruction. Consequently, many policyholders must have hesitated before committing themselves to payments for which they would continue to be liable during an unpredictable and hazardous future. Higher rates of premium due to lower interest earnings and increased taxation, in addition to less favourable prospects for bonuses on with-profits policies, added to the difficulties with which the offices had to contend. It might be thought that the rise in premium income throughout the war indicates that their problems have been overstated but this would be a misleading conclusion for new policies form only a small proportion of total assurances in force.

During the prolonged 'sitzkrieg', as the Americans so vividly described the period up to April 1940, the life offices granted cover against hazards without adding surcharges to premiums; but once real hostilities began with the attack on the Low Countries and France they had no option but to take account of the increased risk of mortality. Proposers in both the ordinary and industrial life branches were given the option of taking out a policy at the old pre-war rate but with restricted cover (typically, the amount payable was restricted to the premiums paid or the surrender value, whichever was the higher), or in the case of most offices, although not all, a policy which covered war risks in full at a higher premium. However, a number of insurers adopted a different approach. For example, the Scottish Widows introduced a scheme to cover war risks under participating policies without additions to the premium under which the cost of war claims was met out of reductions in with-profits bonuses. Other offices reduced the benefits of participating policies by the use of a formula. For example, the United Kingdom Provident and the Royal London Mutual stipulated that the amount payable on with-profits policies should be one-half of the sum assured plus accumulated bonuses if death was caused through enemy action.

Since it was obvious that policyholders would be faced with unusual problems in paying life premiums, early in 1940 the Government came to an arrangement with the life offices to ensure that they should be protected. The great majority of policies issued in the *ordinary* branch already contained a non-forfeiture clause which provided that, if the policyholder was unable to pay premiums, they could be met out of the surrender value of the policy. Under the Government's scheme their protection was extended to all classes of hardship even if the non-forfeiture clause did not appear on the policy. The arrangements also provided that all whole life and endowment policies should acquire a surrender value after two years' premiums had been paid, although the payment of three years' premiums was normally required under the conditions of some policies. Furthermore, where no surrender value was available to maintain the cover, the offices were required to treat the policyholder as generously as possible in the circumstances of each individual case in order to keep the policy in force as long as possible; they were also bidden to make all practicable arrangements to resuscitate policies after the war if they had unfortunately lapsed. From time to time reports on the working of these arrangements were made to the Board of Trade by committees, composed of representatives of the offices, which supervised the operation of the scheme.

In 1940 also similar steps were taken to protect the interests of *industrial* life policyholders by the enactment of the Industrial Assurance and Friendly Societies (Emergency Protection from Forfeiture) Bill which offered a much more satisfactory remedy for inevitable difficulties than that provided by legislation during the 1914–18 War. Under its provisions holders of industrial life policies which had been taken out more than two years before 1 September 1939, for sums assured of less than £50, who fell into arrears with premiums, could make application for protection from forfeiture on the grounds that default was due directly or indirectly to the war. The assurance company or society was to give the policyholder twenty-eight days' notice that he could make such an application in the event of default. If it was satisfied that default was directly or indirectly due to the war, the company or society could endorse the policy as being protected under the Act. If a policyholder's application was refused, he was given the right to appeal to the Industrial Assurance

Commissioner who was given the power to instruct that the policy should or should not be protected. Protected policies could not be allowed to lapse; however, the sum assured was to be reduced to compensate for the forgone premiums and for certain endowment policies the maturity date was deferred. The Act also provided that where a protected policy was forfeited or surrendered after the expiry of the period of protection, the provisions of the Industrial Assurance Acts, which gave policyholders the right to paid-up policies and surrender values, were to have effect subject to such modifications as the Commissioner thought necessary. He was given this power in order to prevent injustice to the main body of policyholders in the sense that owners of protected policies could refrain from paying premiums for lengthy periods and could subsequently allow the policies to lapse with no sacrifice on their part.

From the point of view of underwriting abroad the war meant the complete cessation of underwriting in many countries, which had a particularly severe impact on the fire and accident branches. Difficulties of communication by telegraph or letter, the exigencies of censorship, the practical impossibility of travel were all impediments of general application which took their toll on premium income. But they were of small significance compared with the rupture of insurance and reinsurance relationships with the markets of Germany, France, Belgium, Holland, Scandinavia, Italy and later the Far East, which previously had been of considerable aggregate importance.

Furthermore, war brought in its train in practically every country of the world an accentuation of the economic nationalism which had gradually been building up in the inter-war period. The problem was mitigated to some extent by the fact that business in the U.S.A. and the larger countries of the Commonwealth grew at a satisfactory rate. Moreover the Government attached considerable importance to the maintenance of the insurance companies' overseas business, which provided an important source of foreign exchange at a time when Britain's export trade was reduced to a fraction of its former total. The financial and foreign exchange regulations were framed in such a way as to provide facilities for overseas underwriting within the new framework of economic warfare which enabled the insurance companies to pursue their foreign business as and when opportunities presented themselves. British insurers also took advantage of every favourable turn of the war to reopen agencies and to recover business in territories released from enemy control.

Thus for example the London and Lancashire 'lost no time in reopening its business in Ethiopia and French Somaliland and reinstating its former native agent there in 1943 after the surrender of the Italian armies'.[2] Surprisingly enough the combined impact of adverse influences made little more than a dent on the overseas business. For example, by the end of 1941 the overseas revenues of the fire and accident departments of the Commercial Union actually showed considerable increases. 'The overseas fire revenue continued from there onwards to increase throughout the war. The overseas accident revenue suffered some reduction in 1942 and 1943, most of this being due to loss of income from private car insurance. But it rapidly picked up again in the last two years of the war. Growth of business in the United States, Australia, Canada and New Zealand accounted for this satisfactory progress. Workmen's compensation in particular was being actively developed in those countries owing to war-time conditions, and, in the United States especially, the Ocean and its subsidiary, the Columbia Casualty, were making rapid strides forward in most branches of casualty business.'[3]

An adverse influence of a different sort which, although it affected all categories of insurance, fell with particular severity on life assurance, arose from the methods adopted for financing the war. Here we must make a slight digression to explain the background. The policy adopted and made plain to all in the first year of the Second World War was that which gave rise to the phrase 'The Three Per Cent War'. In sharp contrast to the First World War the authorities decided that Government borrowing would be financed at low rates of interest. Among the reasons on which this decision was based was the belief that Government borrowing had been ill-managed in the 1914–18 war and the determination that the experience of these years would not be repeated. 'The confidence of this determination was based on the experience of cheap money during the thirties, when the monetary authorities achieved a mastery not previously paralleled, and by the belief that in the Second World War circumstances would from the beginning make possible a policy which the men of 1914 had not been able to contemplate. Lastly, some influence must be ascribed to academic thought on the rate of interest as a weapon of policy: academic opinion had during 1939 been afforded opportunity for expression, if not a hearing, in exalted circles and, perhaps with more effect, it had over a longer period been penetrating Governmental circles in its usual unnoticed way.'[4]

The basic cause of the differences in interest rate policies in the two wars is to be found in the fact that in the First World War the authorities continued to think of London as an open financial centre conducting its business broadly as usual; whilst in the Second War London's international weakness was perceived from the outset and had to be protected by both internal and external controls. The architects of financial policy were confident that strong exchange controls would prevent low interest rates from causing a flight of capital abroad, and physical controls and rationing would deaden their inflationary stimulus at home. 'They were aware that steady pursuit—to be successful, it had to be unflinching pursuit—of a cheap money policy would call at times for very careful handling, for a technical competence, indeed, which would itself be in sharp contrast to the unhappy bunglings of 1914–16. Their confidence in their technical mastery derived perhaps unconsciously from their success in enforcing a cheap money policy from 1932 to 1939.'[5]

There was a clear understanding that financial policy had to serve the main aim of commandeering real resources for directly warlike purposes such as the production of tanks, aircraft and naval vessels. In order to prevent private individuals making hampering demands on resources to satisfy their unimportant wants, the Government resorted to a variety of administrative controls. The ration book, not the purse, became the means of controlling individual consumption and citizens were forced to surrender their right to choose freely the sort of goods they wished to consume. The authorities' financial problem arose from the uneasy contrast between the high incomes earned by a population working long hours to produce military essentials and the very restricted range of goods made available for private consumption by the rationing system. Their main preoccupation was with the danger that the community's greatly increased holdings of money—their frustrated purchasing power—would burst through the dykes and destroy, or at least badly damage, the elaborate framework of the war economy by creating black markets and run-away inflation. In theory it would have been possible to siphon off all the excess purchasing power through taxation but this was hardly practicable since it would have involved such swingeing increases in taxes that there would have been damaging effects on incentives and the willingness to work. It was, therefore, decided to rely partially on taxation and to mop up the residual purchasing power through vigorous campaigns to increase savings. The problem here was that the public had to be offered some reward for surrending its liquid purchasing power but the Government was anxious to keep the cost as low as possible. Again, in theory, if the Government could have relied on the public to keep their savings in the form of hoards of currency or bank deposits, it would have been able to borrow at zero rates of interest. But this would have been too unrealistic and risky a policy for at any moment the public might have been tempted to use their accumulated hoards for a spending spree. Consequently, it became a major aim of financial policy to persuade the public to exchange their holdings of money for other forms of debt such as savings certificates, savings bonds and government securities. The inducement was to offer them some interest in return but to keep it as low possible, to minimize the cost to the Exchequer. Various devices were used such as so-called Tank Weeks and Aircraft Weeks in individual towns. These were accompanied by an enormous amount of official 'ballyhoo' designed to create the impression that, for example, our fighter aerodromes were full of intrepid pilots biting their nails in an agony of frustration at being unable to take off to do battle with the enemy because vital parts of their aircraft were missing. The culprits were Mrs. Smith and Mrs. Jones who were selfish enough to leave their money behind the clock or under the mattress instead of buying savings certificates. This was, of course, nonsense. The Ministries of Supply and Aircraft Production had long ago secured the necessary allocation of resources for the production of war weapons; the authorities were merely anxious to use these appeals to patriotism to siphon off purchasing power to prevent inflation and black markets.

The problem of minimising the cost was the psychological one of persuading the lenders that the authorities had the power and the will to maintain low rates of interest. A writer in *The Economist* suggested a plan of campaign early in the war. He pointed out that already the yield on perpetual stocks was down to $3\frac{1}{2}$ per cent and a comparatively small continued exertion would bring it still lower. Since the existing 3 per cent Defence Loan was within one and a half points of par, it should therefore be possible to issue a 3 per cent loan, possibly at a small discount, with a life of 15 to 20 years. 'If the first war loan were a security of this character, two advantages would be secured. The first would be to fix in the public mind the notion that 3 per cent is a reasonable rate for the Government to pay. And secondly, by keeping the life of the issue short, it would still be possible to keep up the pressure on the gilt-edged market, and as the long-term rate of interest fell, the life of subsequent issues could be gradually lengthened until it might eventually be possible to offer really long-term securities on a 3 per cent basis.'[6]

In pursuance of its policy the Government had the advantage that it was able to dictate certain rates particularly at the short end of the market and early on in the war the Treasury Bill rate was brought down to 1 per cent and pegged at that level. If necessary, the authorities had the power to maintain this rate by virtue of their own purchases, for the Bank of England had become well accustomed to open market operations in Treasury Bills. But the market in long-term securities presented more difficult problems: in fact the Bank of England was strongly opposed to operations in such securities in the ordinary course of events. 'In the very exceptional circumstances of early 1930 and early 1932 it had engaged in such operations, but on these occasions it had engaged on the same side as the weight of market opinion—i.e. its action had been to hasten and accentuate a market trend already incipient. Intervention against the market trend—which is what the Bank might have thought war-time action involved—is a very different kettle of fish; and central bankers who had grown up oppressed by the colossal size of the National Debt felt that if they once embarked on such operations they might have to go on and on, buying more and more securities thrown on the market by incredulous sellers. It is one thing to steady, by waving the hat of the Government broker, the slide in a momentarily demoralised market. It is quite another to try to stem an avalanche set in motion by a war to which no early end can be foreseen. The British authorities thought that, if they made such an attempt, the consequent inflation of the floating debt (since floating debt must replace the bonds unloaded by the investing public) would have immediate adverse effects on confidence, aggravating the situation with which they were trying to cope, and that it would also make post-war control of the credit situation much more difficult.'[7]

It was therefore important to enlist the support of the major institutional investors who formed the backbone of the market. Thus early in the war the Governor of the Bank of England, by arrangement with the Chancellor of the Exchequer, secured from the insurance companies, building societies and other investing bodies undertakings that they would invest all their available funds in Government bonds. It was the need to secure their co-operation that convinced the authorities that to force rates much below 3 per cent would create difficulties for many of the great financial institutions, who had become used to something like this level and whose financial structure was in some measure based on the assumption that rates would not go appreciably lower. 'Most obviously this was true of the insurance companies, whose premium rates were broadly based on this assumption. On the other hand it was realised that some institutions—notably the banks—could get along on much less than this, at any rate as their total resources increased. Bearing in mind the possibility of discrimination, the borrowing policy came to revolve round 3 per cent as the basic rate, the Treasury at the same time reserving to itself the right to squeeze money out of particular classes of institutions at lower rates.'[8]

The insurance companies loyally complied with this agreement and invested all their new money and additional sums from the sale and repayment of other securities in the Government tap issues. The result was that the companies provided approximately £600m. for the Exchequer and emerged from the war with almost 50 per cent of their assets in British Government securities. Although the decision not to push interest rates below 3 per cent was intended to show a tender regard for the problems of the industry, the consequence of this massive support had a serious impact on the yield on their funds, especially as rates of income tax were increased at the same time. Sir Robert Bignold,

Chairman of the Norwich Union, put the situation as follows: 'The investment of large sums in low-yielding securities and the repayment of many high-yielding investments has naturally had a serious effect on our net rate of interest. In 1938 after falling for several years this was still as much as £4 2s. 7d. per cent and in 1944 it was down to £3 8s. 1d. per cent.'[9]

The companies coped with their difficulties in three main ways. First, they assumed a lower rate of interest for the purpose of valuing their funds. Secondly, although they continued to pay bonuses, they did so at reduced rates. The allocation of 'reversionary bonuses', a system adopted by some life companies, has the effect of permanently increasing, with each bonus declaration, the amounts assured under the policies affected. It was thought prudent during the war not to commit the necessary reserves to this specific purpose, but to pay bonuses at reduced rates on policies under which claims were paid on death or maturity. At the end of the war these companies were able to use undistributed surpluses for the purpose of reversionary bonus allocations in respect of the war years. Thirdly, the distributions of profits to shareholders were reduced.

Their support of the gilt-edged market was not the sole contribution of the insurance companies to war finance. With few resources to spare for the production of exports, and heavy demands for imported raw materials to sustain war production and for food, the Government was faced with a constant problem of acquiring sufficient foreign currency to pay for them. It was not surprising that the authorities turned for help to the insurance companies with their extensive overseas assets. For example, South Africa acquired British holdings of their securities in exchange for gold exports. The Treasury compulsorily purchased the stock at market prices from the insurance companies and other private holders, who were offered cash or the chance of switching into the current 'tap' issue of Government securities. Similarly, a substantial proportion of heavy government expenditure in India was covered by the repayment of outstanding British loans.

This mobilisation of British insurance companies' investments overseas which were surplus to their local needs was comparatively easy but their 'tied' investments could not be so easily realised. The solution to this problem in the main area involved, the United States, was reached in 1941 when Mr. Keynes negotiated a loan from the Reconstruction Finance Corporation—the Jesse Jones loan.[10] This was for the sum of $425m. It was agreed that the collateral security should consist of the pledged shares of American subsidiaries of British insurance companies, listed securities of American corporations already vested in the United Kingdom Treasury, and both listed and unlisted securities not yet vested, in American corporations in which the percentage of British ownership was substantial. In addition there would be assigned to the Reconstruction Finance Corporation the earnings of United States branches of forty-one British insurance companies not incorporated in the United States. As these would not be represented by any pledged securities, the Reconstruction Finance Corporation sought a particular assurance against withdrawal of the assets during the currency of the loan. Thus, the crucial dollar gap was covered and the British nation at this moment of war-time financial crisis had every reason to be grateful that the British insurance industry had shown such unswerving determination in the past to expand its overseas business. It is interesting to note here that the British Government's eventual repayment of this loan in October 1951 was in no small measure due to the post-war dollar earnings of British insurance companies. Released from pledge, the securities were then returned by the Government to their owners.

In previous chapters we have noted the increasing propensity for the State to intervene in the insurance market and it might have been thought that during the war this trend would at least have been arrested. And in a sense it was but, as the war intensified, there was a growing tendency to seek consolation in the thought of a better social order to be achieved after and through victory and it was inevitable that this should involve a reappraisal of the existing national schemes of social insurances and allied services. In June 1941 the Government gave expression to this feeling by appointing a committee whose object was to lay the plans for developing what has now come to be called the Welfare State. It was an inter-departmental body under the chairmanship of Lord (then Sir William) Beveridge, consisting mainly of officials who were told to regard themselves as advisers and assessors. Thus it was that Lord Beveridge was the sole signatory of the conclusions propounded in *Social Insurance and Allied Services,* which was published in 1942; and the document is known, and will no doubt always be known, as the 'Beveridge Report'.

The Report was an attempt to mould into a harmonious system the group of social insurance services which had grown up empirically in response to diverse needs. They included National Health Insurance, Unemployment Insurance and Workmen's Compensation; and with them it was natural to class Contributory and Old Age Pensions. Unemployment and National Health Insurance had always been conducted on a compulsory basis for employed persons within certain limits of income. Health insurance cash benefits had been administered on behalf of the State by the approved Societies, some of which had been formed by, and affiliated to, the industrial assurance offices and were dependent largely on the agency staffs of these offices for the administration of the benefits.

This group of approved societies contained more than half the total membership. The State prescribed the standards of payment of workmen's compensation but did little more in this domain. The legal liabilities of employers to their workmen were taken over by insurance companies under policies privately negotiated. Thus the benefit rates paid in the various fields of insurance had not been correlated nor their administration made uniform. Not only did the Beveridge Report contain proposals for introducing much-needed uniformity into this 'hotch-potch' but also it made far-reaching recommendations for the reform of industrial assurance. This was the result of a specific request, made seven months after the appointment of the Committee, by the Minister without Portfolio, Mr. Arthur Greenwood, to consider the development of the National Insurance Scheme by way of adding death benefits. Industrial assurance, which had hitherto provided these benefits for its customers, was thus brought within the ambit of the inquiry. In the event it was this aspect of their work which had the most profound implications for the future of the insurance industry and was of most relevance.

Before we turn to consider Beveridge's proposals for industrial life assurance, we must mention briefly one of his recommendations which was of direct importance for another branch of the industry, namely that the existing system of Workmen's Compensation should be superseded. Instead provision for industrial disability should be made part of a uniform scheme of social insurance of a contributory character, whereby the benefits would be paid out of a central fund which would be maintained by contributions from employers, employees and the State, and administered by a Ministry of Social Security.

His major recommendations concerning industrial assurance were, first, that funeral grants should be included in National Health insurance benefits and, secondly, that the 'approved societies' which since 1911 had been the principal agencies for administering health benefits should be superseded by the State. Apart from these specific recommendations he was severely critical of the operation of industrial assurance and his strictures followed fairly closely the lines of the Parmoor Report of 1920 and the Cohen Report of 1933. For example, he observed conclusive evidence of excessive salesmanship by agents and challenged their place in the system when he said that 'it cannot be admitted that weekly collection of premiums is a permanent, indispensable requirement for securing regular voluntary contributions from persons of limited means'.[11]

He linked this criticism to that of high lapse rates and, although he conceded that there had been some improvement since the publication of the Cohen Report, he was satisfied that the scale of 'abortive' assurance was as formidable as ever. He also had a tilt at the level of expenses, calculating that for the years 1937–40 the cost ratio was 37·1 per cent which represented 7s. 6d. in the pound or 4½d. in the shilling of premiums received. He conceded that since 1912–17, the years for which the Parmoor Committee gave figures, the administrative cost had fallen by from one-third to one-eighth by 1937, although the reduction had not been achieved uniformly. However, he saw little scope for further reductions in costs so long as the business remained competitive. He, therefore, decided that reform must be sought along the line suggested by the Cohen Committee. It will be recalled that this body had ruled out, as impracticable, nationalisation of the business 'as it now exists'; but some members had recommended study of the possibility of widening the scope of State insurance to cover the contingencies hitherto met by industrial assurance. The Committee were convinced that 'if the changes which the due protection of the assuring public demands cannot be effected by less drastic measures, the difficulties in the transference of the business to a single organisation must be faced'.[12]

Lord Beveridge asserted that the result of his study was to suggest that such a resort to monopoly was the only way of 'retaining the good while curing the defects' and he therefore recommended the formation of an Industrial Assurance Board with a statutory monopoly of premium collection. This Board would take over and honour all existing policies of industrial assurance companies, would employ or compensate the staffs and shareholders and would control all the ordinary life business of the industrial offices. His case for a complete supersession of private enterprise rested on three arguments. In the first place, an insurance contract is for a long term of years; the customer cannot change his commodity if he is dissatisfied and therefore should be provided with disinterested advice. Secondly, industrial assurance was already so closely related to State insurance through the approved societies that it was easier to make the association closer than to break it. Thirdly, it was a feature of the business that it required little or no investment of capital.[13] Although these were his overt reasons for recommending nationalisation, he later conceded that the main reason for doing so was a desire to secure the services of outside staffs for his comprehensive scheme of social security.[14] Whichever is the true explanation, it is undeniable that Beveridge made the first authoritative recommendation for the taking over of industrial assurance by a state monopoly, although it was not an essential part of his scheme for social security, and his ideas for state control were taken up by others in the late 1940s as we shall see.

Having surveyed the main changes in the environment between 1939 and 1945 which affected the operations of the insurance companies, suffice it to say that they had to face all the other hazards and difficulties which were the common lot of commercial enterprises. These included the physical destruction of some of their premises and, more significantly, the loss of many valuable records.[15] Furthermore, they lost many senior and experienced members of staff to the armed forces, and in addition co-operated closely with the Committee set up early in 1942, under the chairmanship of Lord Kennet, to consider means of releasing manpower in banking, insurance and allied spheres. Particularly intractable problems faced industrial life assurance companies who had to reorganise their field staffs in order to maintain their services at a time when widespread distress caused by bombing lent a new urgency to the need for swift and sympathetic service. 'Agents and officials joining the Forces were replaced by temporary workers exempt from military service, by pensioners and by women collectors—in many instances the wives of members of the staffs. This was a costly operation since many employees absent on service were paid substantial allowances.'[16] The Kennet Committee recommended that offices should eliminate personnel engaged mainly in canvassing for new business: consequently in 1942 a standstill agreement mainly relating to fire and accident business was reached between the insurance offices. Nevertheless, they still had to cope with formidable obstacles in carrying on their existing business with smaller, inexperienced staffs who were faced with such problems as tracing policyholders' addresses with the much greater mobility of the population.

Under such conditions the industry's progress as revealed by the statistics on business transacted reflects great credit on its powers of resilience. In the early days of the war the outlook for the fire branch was indeed grim, for the companies had to meet claims on a heavy outcrop of fires due to an unexpected cause—the nightly blackout which made early detection difficult.[17] Claims also arose for other reasons such as the greater intensity with which industry was working; this led to carelessness on the part of operatives fatigued by heavy overtime and night work and inadequate maintenance of overheated machines, etc. Another serious effect on fire income came with the early air raids and accumulated throughout the war. The report of the Fire Department of the Commercial Union on activities in 1940 put the matter succinctly. 'The loss of property through enemy action has meant the loss of insurance coverage. As an example, in the raid on London on 29 December no fewer than 1,166 warehouses within one mile of the Royal Exchange were destroyed or so badly damaged as to render further fire insurance unnecessary.'[18] Without the War Damage Act, referred to earlier, there can be no doubt that the losses from German bombing, and especially incendiary raids, would have been insupportable. Another compensating factor was the revision of insured values, made necessary by inflation, which was only partially offset by the increase in payments on claims. Nevertheless it was a surprising achievement that premium income rose from £50m to £72m and expense ratios fell from 47 to 41 per cent between 1939 and 1945. (See Table at the end of chapter.)

In the accident branch experience was more erratic. Motor insurance felt the earliest and most severe restrictions of the war. Petrol was rationed and there were successive increases in its price; the rate of horse-power tax was raised and the production of cars for non-war purposes was severely curtailed. Not surprisingly, premium income fell. But this was more than counterbalanced by the large growth of activity in workmen's compensation. Claims experience was better than expected for a variety of reasons. First, high rates of pay were an inducement to workers to return to work as soon as possible after an accident. Secondly, the patriotic desire to play a full part in the war effort reduced periods of incapacity to a minimum. Thirdly, with increased earnings, premiums which were computed on the basis of wages, were increased substantially without a corresponding additional liability; even the higher rates of compensation did not entirely eliminate the margin provided. (See Table at end of chapter.)

The marine branch experienced a remarkable increase in premium income which rose by 300 per cent during the period. A certain proportion of this was attributable to the rise in values but much was the result of an increased volume of business. Strangely enough, despite the Government's lower rates for first category war risks, the market was nevertheless able to underwrite a considerable volume of business of that type, although, of course, the bulk of new business emanated from second category risks. Whatever the class of business, however, the market was always willing to offer its services—a willingness frequently exhibited in the face of extreme hazards which constitutes a remarkable tribute to British underwriting. Not surprisingly some heavy claims had to be met, one of which did not arise from loss on the high seas. It involved the *Fort Stikine* which arrived in Bombay in 1944 when the harbour was crowded with shipping, with a cargo of cotton and explosives. 'On the following day it suddenly caught fire. Frantic efforts were made to get the flames under control. They were unsuccessful and when the fire reached the holds, two terrific explosions shook the port and the city. In the harbour itself the burning cotton was blown in all directions, setting fire to and destroying nine other ships. In the city enormous damage was done to property and buildings partly through the blast and partly through the extension of the fire beyond the harbour. Five hundred persons lost their lives and a further thousand were injured.'[19] Such was the scale of the disaster that the fire underwriting companies agreed to make a voluntary contribution of 12½ per cent towards the liability assumed by the Government over the damage to property on land insured with them, and estimated to be £12m. But the total cost of the destruction of ships and cargoes, which amounted to £6m., was met by the whole marine market.

Life business also showed some tendency to expand during the war, almost the whole of the growth occurring in domestic business. Foreign business, of course, has never been of major importance to British life offices and the war effectively closed the door to British insurers in many parts of the world; only in the United States and Canada was it possible to attract new business. All in all, the expansion of premium income and the growth in the size of the life funds in such difficult and abnormal conditions, although new business fell, was gratifying.

Only an incorrigible optimist would have dared to forecast in 1939 that the British insurance industry would emerge from all the trials and tribulations of a modern war not only intact but with increased resources. While this was in no small measure due to the help and support of the Government, it was a tribute to the basic soundness of the industry.

NOTES

1 D. E. W. Gibb, op. cit., p. 235.
2 E. V. Francis, op. cit., p. 98.
3 E. Liveing, op. cit., p. 214.
4 R. S. Sayers, *History of the Second World War, Financial Policy*, 1939–1945, H.M.S.O. and Longman's, 1956, pp. 143, 144.
5 Ibid., p. 146.
6 *The Economist*, 20 January 1940.
7 R. S. Sayers, op. cit., pp. 173, 174.
8 R. S. Sayers, op. cit., p. 162.
9 Address to shareholders at Annual General Meeting, 29 May 1945.
10 Mr. Jesse Jones was head of the Reconstruction Finance Corporation.
11 *Social Insurance and Allied Services*, Beveridge Report, para. 185.
12 D. Morrah, op. cit., p. 162.
13 D. Morrah, ibid., p. 164.
14 W. Beveridge, *Full Employment in a Free Society*, George Allen & Unwin, 1944.
15 The Co-operative Insurance Society, for example, lost its branches at Swansea, Hull and Plymouth through bombing. See R. G. Garnett, op. cit., p. 225.
16 D. Morrah, op. cit., p. 139.
17 'In December 1942, James Darroch reported that the total loss by fire in Britain for each year since the outbreak of war *other than through enemy action*, had been greater than the average for the ten years preceding the war.' R. G. Garnett, op. cit., p. 226.
18 E. Liveing, op. cit., p. 212.
19 E. Liveing, op. cit., pp. 219, 220.

Table 29 (a)

COMPANIES ESTABLISHED IN THE U.K.
ORDINARY LIFE

£'000

	1936	*1937*	*1938*	*1939*	*1940*	*1941*	*1942*	*1943*	*1944*	*1945*	*1946*	*1947*	*1948*
Premiums*	98,072	99,739	102,077	99,459	96,404	95,549	99,841	103,598	109,469	117,496	134,533	158,854	172,981
Interest (less tax)	37,414	38,903	39,003	37,561	35,922	34,977	36,037	36,918	37,949	39,761	42,871	45,442	48,346
Commission and Expenses	12,692	12,975	13,254	12,874	11,847	11,894	12,122	12,059	12,232	13,829	18,258	22,057	24,223
Expense Ratio	12·9	13·0	13·0	12·9	12·3	12·4	12·1	11·6	11·2	11·8	13·6	13·9	14·0
Surrenders	8,348	8,118	9,249	10,300	9,990	6,806	5,796	4,946	5,141	7,032	11,682	11,583	13,696

* including considerations for annuities.

Table 29 (b)

COMPANIES ESTABLISHED IN THE U.K.
INDUSTRIAL LIFE

	1936	*1937*	*1938*	*1939*	*1940*	*1941*	*1942*	*1943*	*1944*	*1945*	*1946*	*1947*	*1948*
Premiums	53,629	55,792	57,997	59,835	62,189	63,557	67,963	72,186	75,701	79,392	83,562	91,161	97,103
Surrenders	4,549	4,556	4,634	3,977	23,41	1,310	996	978	1,059	1,723	3,068	3,670	5,468
Expenses	17,284	17,574	18,079	18,240	19,019	20,403	21,283	21,466	21,624	22,261	25,252	27,186	27,817
Expense Ratio	32·2	31·5	31·2	30·5	30·6	32·1	31·3	29·7	28·6	28·0	30·2	29·8	28·6

Table 29 (c)

COMPANIES ESTABLISHED IN THE U.K.
ORDINARY BUSINESS : NEW LIFE ASSURANCES

	1938	*1939*	*1940*	*1941*	*1942*	*1943*	*1944*	*1945*	*1946*	*1947*	*1948*
No. of Policies ('000)	604	476	334	399	391	368	369	378	675	759	674
Sums assured	253,806	193,172	125,198	145,268	161,106	167,487	176,450	201,750	398,423	517,257	511,653
New sums assured as % of 1938 figure	100	76·1	49·3	57·2	63·5	66·0	69·5	79·5	157·0	203·8	201·6

A number of comments can be made about the above tables.

(1) The generally lower wartime expense ratios in ordinary business can largely be accounted for by the fall in new business—new business involves the offices in initial expenses which obviously affect the expense ratio. This was sufficient to offset the higher expenses which could have been expected from retaining, on the payroll, staff serving in the forces.

(2) The greater variability of the expense ratio of the industrial offices during the war in part reflects the fact that new business was maintained to a considerable extent because of

(*a*) relative prosperity among the income groups for which industrial life caters.

(*b*) the very nature of the business has meant that outdoor staffs called for service have recently been replaced. (This did not happen in the ordinary branch).

(3) Since new business forms only a small part of total premium income, premium income has been maintained despite the fall in new business.

(4) The relatively small number of surrenders during the war largely reflects the measures taken by the government to help people who found difficulty in paying premiums.

Table 30 (a)

INSURANCE OTHER THAN LIFE
COMPANIES ESTABLISHED IN THE U.K.

ACCIDENT

£'000

	1938	*1939*	*1940*	*1941*	*1942*	*1943*	*1944*	*1945*	*1946*	*1947*	*1948*
Premiums	4,615	4,548	4,018	3,944	4,067	4,338	4,704	5,106	6,205	7,735	8,563
Commission and Expenses	1,903	1,910	1,743	1,664	1,719	1,722	1,828	1,954	2,472	3,048	3,308
Expense ratio	41·2	42·0	43·4	42·2	42·3	39·7	38·9	38·3	39·8	39·4	38·6

Table 30 (b)

FIRE

£'000

	1938	*1939*	*1940*	*1941*	*1942*	*1943*	*1944*	*1945*	*1946*	*1947*	*1948*
Premiums	49,532	49,609	51,027	54,455	56,305	59,929	65,054	71,777	88,285	108,626	127,606
Commission and Expenses	23,318	23,328	23,541	24,456	25,152	25,929	27,372	29,671	36,476	44,452	51,125
Expense Ratio	47·1	47·0	46·1	44·9	44·7	43·3	42·1	41·3	41·3	40·9	40·6

Table 30 (c)

MARINE

£'000

	1938	*1939*	*1940*	*1941*	*1942*	*1943*	*1944*	*1945*	*1946*	*1947*	*1948*
Premiums (Less Commission)	12,848	14,797	22,558	2,478	39,173	30,044	26,346	22,618	27,145	40,870	50,526

Table 30 (d)

MOTOR VEHICLE

£'000

	1938	*1939*	*1940*	*1941*	*1942*	*1943*	*1944*	*1945*	*1946*	*1947*	*1948*
Premiums	37,897	36,580	31,913	34,011	28,382	24,636	26,405	33,828	46,901	61,474	70,734
Commission and Expenses	14,688	14,478	12,841	13,261	11,683	10,083	10,322	12,742	17,541	22,506	24,981
Expense ratio	38·8	39·6	40·2	39·0	41·2	40·9	39·1	37·7	37·4	36·6	35·3

Table 30 (e)

MISCELLANEOUS ACCIDENT (INCLUDING EMPLOYERS' LIABILITY) £'000

£'000

	1938	*1939*	*1940*	*1941*	*1942*	*1943*	*1944*	*1945*	*1946*	*1947*	*1948*
Premiums	34,066	n.a.	33,221	37,216	39,471	45,566	48,239	49,861	57,992	73,150	73,898
Commission and Expenses	12,987	n.a.	12,835	13,643	14,755	15,918	10,331	17,074	19,523	24,239	25,481
Expense ratio	38·1	n.a.	38·6	36·7	37·4	34·9	33·9	34·2	33·1	33·1	34·5

Source: Board of Trade, *Annual Abstract of Statistics.*

Chapter 11

DEVELOPMENTS SINCE 1945

'In my opinion, contemporary British society is exceptionally vulnerable to the destructive allure of its own mythology. This is due, on the one hand, to the magnitude of the challenge to social adaptation posed by the loss of empire, the loss of industrial leadership and the political and economic changes in the world about us that have made a nation of fifty-odd million people a relatively small country instead of a relatively large one.'

Professor Harry G. Johnson

THE NEARER we approach the present day the greater is the risk, which all writers on contemporary history face, of being unable to present an objective assessment of the impact of events and of placing an incorrect emphasis on their significance. Moreover, the period from 1945 to 1970 is not a unified whole in the sense that the 1920s and 1930s are, for it embraces both a period of reconstruction and recovery and one of further growth which, however much it has fallen short of contemporary aspirations, has significantly increased the material welfare of the British people, the majority of whom enjoy the benefits of an affluence far beyond the imagination of their forbears in a period as recent as the early 1930s. In this, the last of the historical chapters, we make no attempt to treat events chronologically but adopt an eclectic approach whereby we discuss, first, changes in the general economic and political environment and, secondly, developments of particular significance for the insurance industry.

We have already noted how the First World War had a profound impact on the role of Britain in the world economy; the Second World War similarly accelerated the process of relative decline. Nevertheless, the ending of hostilities in the major theatres of war, including the Far East, ushered in a period which saw the renewal of hope for both material and immaterial progress—hope that was tinged with some foreboding in view of the magnitude of the obstacles which Britain faced in the post-war era. In the previous chapters we saw that in the darkest days of the war national morale was in no small part bolstered up by the prospect of a new social order after the war, the blueprint for which was laid down in a series of reports embodying ambitious plans for reform and reconstruction. Thus was hope sustained.

The Beveridge Report on social security was the first concrete response to 'the strong impulse to fuse the will to victory with aspirations for a better world after victory',[1] but it was soon followed in 1944 by the Government's White Paper on Employment Policy,[2] which marked a watershed in the development of official economic policy in that for the first time the Government openly committed itself to the objective of 'a high and stable level of employment after the war'. Other plans for social reconstruction included the Education Act of 1944 which established free secondary education for all; provisions for improved land use and town planning; and ambitious targets for the building of houses. In addition, considerable attention was given to international economic relationships and policies. In her endeavours to plan for a more peaceful and prosperous world Britain had the support of other countries whose governments and peoples shared the same feeling: that international economic relations had been among the least satisfactory aspects of the pre-war world in that 'they had undoubtedly contributed to poverty, unemployment, international hatred and war'.[3]

It was generally accepted that the obstacles and restrictions such as tariffs and quotas which had done so much to inhibit the growth of international trade in the 1930s should be removed as soon as possible. It was also considered essential to create an international monetary system in which countries would not be tempted to pursue 'beggar-my-neighbour' policies of exporting unemployment through competitive depreciation of their exchange rates. A consensus of opinion gradually emerged that an important feature of a stable international monetary system must be some type of international bank with the power and ability to provide a generally acceptable currency, on a sufficient scale to create the initial liquidity on which could be built a superstructure of mutual obligations that could carry a much higher level of international trade on the basis of similar national resources. The main protagonists in the early discussions were the British and the Americans whose distinctive solutions to the problem were a reflection of deep-seated differences in their attitudes to international trade policies—differences which were finally resolved at the historic Bretton Woods Conference in 1944. Keynes, the leader of the British delegation, put forward a plan for the creation of a new international unit of account, called *bancor*, with extensive overdraft facilities at a new international central bank; but in the event he had to surrender to American opposition to such a far-reaching solution. The final scheme was in two parts, one dealing with the problem of international liquidity by the creation of the International Monetary Fund and the other establishing the International Bank for Reconstruction and Development for the provision of long-term international lending. Those countries which subscribed to the agreement establishing the Fund bound themselves not to devalue their currencies, except under certain conditions to 'correct a fundamental disequilibrium', not to discriminate against other member states and, after a transitional period, not to place restrictions on current international payments.

Since extreme fluctuations in the prices of primary products had been a particularly disturbing aspect of pre-war international trade, a scheme was provisionally agreed for the stabilisation of commodity stocks through internationally managed buffer stocks. There were also protracted negotiations for the establishment of an International Trade Organisation, but these proved abortive largely because of serious divergencies of approach between Britain and America. ' "Why", the British were wont to ask, "were men to work for the *elimination* of preferences (which were characteristically British) but only for the *reduction* of tariffs (which were characteristically American)?" '[4] However, agreement was finally reached on the establishment of the more modest General Agreement on Tariffs and Trade which represented a substantial victory for the American viewpoint since it was designed to *eliminate* discrimination but only *reduce* tariffs. The failure to wring out of the Americans bigger concessions on tariffs had unfortunate consequences in that it made more intractable the dollar earning problem of Europe and the sterling area after the war.[5] Britain also undertook other international obligations including an agreement to share in the costs of the United Nations Relief and Rehabilitation Agency, which was designed to prevent starvation and disease from ravaging Europe, Asia and other parts of the world after the fighting stopped, and the International Labour Organisation, which was a survival of the old League of Nations.

In the formulation of all these plans for the reform and reconstruction of both the domestic and international social and economic framework Britain manifested a genuine hope for, and a dedication to the establishment of, a brave new world but nevertheless she approached the immediate problems of peace with considerable anxiety and foreboding. To put it in a nutshell, the Government was desperately concerned about the short-term prospects for the balance of payments. It was this preoccupation which led Britain to view America's emphasis on speedy post-war liberalisation of trade and payments with suspicion for 'having lost so many sources of her invisible earnings, and, at least temporarily, her power to produce for export, Britain foresaw the most dire threat to the pound sterling and to her balance of payments if freedom of trade and exchange were to be allowed too quickly'.[6] It must be admitted that in her anxieties Britain was somewhat exasperated by the knowledge that in the common cause she had made far greater sacrifices than America. 'The war caused the British standard of living to fall, the

American standard of living to rise; it caused a contraction of British exports, an accumulation of external debt and a run down of capital;[7] in America it had on the whole opposite effects.'[8] Against these losses there were few offsetting compensations with the exception of the creation of buildings, plant and machinery, largely paid for by the Government and intended for war production. 'There were also less obvious gains such as the virtual elimination of German and Japanese competition in international trade, at least for a few years, the rise in the labour force of the engineering industry, with its great export potential, and the spread of new skills among the working population.'[9] But these gains were insufficient to compensate for the fact that in the first place the gifts and borrowing which had enabled Britain to live beyond her means for so long would cease abruptly in the summer of 1945 and, secondly, her productive capacity could not immediately be geared to efficient production for export. Official forecasts were that consequently the deficit in the balance of payments might be £150m. in 1946, even with a very austere import programme, and was unlikely to disappear before 1951 when it might have accumulated to £1,250m. While this preoccupation with the foreign balance was understandable in 1945, it is interesting to note that it still appears as the dominant problem of British economic policy even now.

The Labour Government, faced with the prospect that the economy was likely to grind to a standstill for lack of fuel, raw materials and food unless large unrequited imports could be brought in to replace lend-lease supplies, had no alternative but to swallow its pride and turn to the Americans for a loan. Although the atmosphere in Washington during the negotiations was 'very much more frigid than during the war'[10] a credit of $3,750m. was granted on not ungenerous terms but one of the 'strings' attached had dire consequences. This was the obligation to apply the terms of the Bretton Woods agreement, not within five years after ratification, as originally agreed, but within a year of the actual granting of the loan, i.e. by July 1947. In insisting on this the Americans completely underestimated the extent of the problem of dollar shortage which was a reflection of the fact that in a war-ravaged world the U.S.A. was the only source of supply for many raw materials and goods. Consequently, when sterling was made convertible in July 1947, as required by the terms of the Loan Agreement, almost every country with sterling earnings hurried to convert them into dollars and a large part of the dollar loan drained away. From then on the possibility of the devaluation of sterling was always on the cards, although the day of reckoning was postponed until 1949 mainly because the Americans, having belatedly recognised the magnitude of the dollar shortage, made—with the Marshall Plan—an act of unparalleled generosity. Britain's foreign exchange reserves never recovered from the drain in 1947 and, when the relaxation of controls at the end of 1948 and the booming home demand made inroads into the precarious balance of payments, a sustained attack on sterling began in international markets and forced Sir Stafford Cripps, the Chancellor at that time, to devalue the pound from \$4·03 to \$2·80.[11]

We have concentrated on the problem of the balance of payments in the immediate post-war years because it was the clearest and most immediate manifestation of the extent to which Britain's commitment to total war had left her debilitated and had eroded further her economic strength relatively to the United States and the 'white' dominions such as Canada and Australia. But, when one is reviewing the whole post-war period, it is inexcusable to concentrate exclusively on this aspect for there are other important objectives of economic policy no less deserving of our attention. We propose, therefore, to enumerate these briefly and to evaluate our relative success in attaining them.

We may take as a useful starting point the five aims of economic policy which the Radcliffe Report listed in their consideration of the effectiveness of monetary policy.[12] They are: a high and stable level of employment; reasonable stability of the internal purchasing power of money; steady economic growth and improvement of the standard of living; some contribution, implying a margin in the balance of payments, to the economic development of the outside world; and finally a strengthening of London's international reserves, implying a further margin in the balance of payments.[13]

We have already seen how in 1944 the Government committed itself to the acceptance 'as one of their primary aims the maintenance of a high and stable level of employment after the war'.[14] In the attainment of this objective all post-war Governments of either political complexion have achieved a degree of success which would have appeared utterly unrealistic and utopian to their predecessors. So successful indeed has our post-war experience been as compared with pre-war that it is difficult to appreciate from the vantage point of 1969 why, for example, Keynes conceived the idea of the notorious post-war credits as a useful weapon in the armoury for alleviating a post-war slump. (See Table 31.) In his work, *Full Employment in a Free Society*, Beveridge foresaw that unemployment caused by changes of job, and by slow adaptation of industrial structure, could seldom fall below 3 per cent of those wishing to work; so that 3 per cent was held to be the minimum ratio of unemployed to workforce that could realistically be defined as 'full employment'. At the time it seemed to be no more than a pious hope. Yet since then the ratio, except for brief cold spells in 1946–7 and 1962–3 has never reached 3 per cent; 'at $2\frac{1}{2}$ per cent, Governments have trembled, and for elections $1\frac{1}{2}$ per cent is dangerously high'.[15] Moreover, Britain has been more successful than comparable countries such as the U.S.A., Italy and Western Germany for most of the period, although the latter has been more successful in the 1960s, having kept the unemployment rate below 1 per cent.[16] By any standards, however, Britain has triumphantly attained her objective in the post-war period, although some writers have cast doubt on the extent to which the success may be attributed to

Table 31

CRUDE UNEMPLOYMENT RATES FOR THE U.K.

Year	%
1931	21·5
1938–9	12·5
1948–50	1·6
1951–3	1·7
1955	1·2
1957	1·6
1959	2·3
1961	1·6
1963	2·2
1965	1·3
1967	2·2
1968	2·3
1969	2·5

Sources: Mitchell and Cole, Monthly Bulletin of Statistics.

Government policy. For example, R. C. O. Matthews has suggested that at least 'part of the reason for low unemployment in the post-war period has been the trend increase in the scarcity of labour relative to capital'.[17] But, whatever the reason, this aspect of British economic performance must be judged a success.

The same, however, cannot be said of our performance in achieving reasonable stability of the internal purchasing power of money, for since 1949 it has been poor by any standard. Inflation has advanced upon a broad front, with no major group of commodities escaping from its impact, and in even the best years has proceeded at a rate of at least 3 per cent per annum despite official attempts to halt the process. It is true, of course, that Britain's experience has not been unique, for inflation has been a common feature of all industrialised countries since the war. Nevertheless, over the whole post-war period the rate of inflation has been higher than in other Western countries with the exception of France;

since 1958 the disparity has been less marked but the comparison is still unfavourable. However, to a considerable extent the failure to curb inflation represents the cost of the success of employment policies.

In evaluating the performance of the British economy in achieving steady economic growth and an improvement in the standard of living it is possible to use various standards of comparison which show it in very different lights. By the standards of Britain's own past the rate of economic growth has been faster than perhaps during any previous period in her history. 'Industrial production, the key factor, rose, according to one calculation, by 3·7 per cent a year in 1948–60, compared with 3·1 per cent in the inter-war years, 1·6 per cent in 1877–1913 and just over 3 per cent earlier in the 19th century, when the population increase was much faster.'[18] Since 1960, despite several years of stagnation, it has risen from 95 to 123 by the end of the second quarter in 1969. (1963 = 100, seasonally adjusted.) There has been a similar growth in Gross Domestic Product per head of the population which has risen at a rate of just over 2·2 per cent per annum between 1949 and 1969, which is sufficient to produce a doubling in 30 years. Such an increase in output is naturally reflected in a broadly comparable improvement in the average level of consumption, per head of the population, which has increased by over 35 per cent in the last 15 years partly with the help of improved terms of trade. Moreover, the increased availability of real resources has been

Table 32

INDUSTRIAL COUNTRIES: CONSUMER PRICES

1963 = 100

Year	*U.S.A.*	*Canada*	*Japan*	*Belgium*	*France*	*W. Germany*	*Italy*	*U.K.*
1958	94·5	93·9	78·9	94·1	80·6	89·9	85·5	89·5
1959	95·1	95·0	79·7	95·2	85·0	90·8	85·1	90·0
1960	96·6	96·2	82·6	95·6	88·1	92·1	87·1	90·9
1961	97·7	97·1	87·0	96·6	91·1	94·2	88·9	94·0
1962	98·8	98·3	92·9	97·9	95·4	97·1	93·1	98·0
1963	100·0	100·0	100·0	100·0	100·0	100·0	100·0	100·0
1964	101·4	101·8	103·9	104·2	103·4	102·3	105·9	103·3
1965	103·0	104·3	110·7	108·4	106·0	105·8	110·7	108·2
1966	106·0	108·2	116·4	112·9	108·9	109·5	113·3	112·4
1967	109·0	112·0	121·0	116·2	111·8	111·1	116·9	115·2
1968	113·6	116·7	127·5	119·3	116·9	113·1	118·5	120·6
1969 (Sept.)	121·2	123·0	136·9	124·6	125·2	116·1	122·6	127·6

Source: National Institute Economic Review, November, 1969, Table 18.

used to raise the rate of fixed capital formation more sharply and the cumulative effect of 15 years' investment is a rise in the country' capital stock of about one-half. All this must be judged highly satisfactory.

It is only when these achievements are compared with those of similar industrial countries in the same period that complacency is shattered. In particular, many of the countries of Western Europe, once they had made good the ravages of war, have experienced rates of growth in Gross Domestic Product per head of the population of as much as 5 or 6 per cent. As a consequence, since 1953 Britain has been surpassed in income per head by France, West Germany, Norway and Denmark; and in particular her failure to use her potential as well as, for example, France, Italy and West Germany is distressing. While in the 1950s Britain at least had the consolation that her rate of growth was slightly better than that of the U.S.A., in the 1960s this no longer applied for the latter shot ahead. This poorer performance caused a substantial economic loss, the magnitude of which may be gauged from the fact that if Britain had enjoyed European-type growth an additional personal disposable income per head, man, woman and child, of between £125 and £250 a year in 1969, would have been available. 'The discussion about the failure of the economy to grow is therefore a discussion about the loss of economic welfare of this order of magnitude. Even then, this calculation still excludes such other related losses as the breaches of international and internal contracts, the loss of goodwill and of confidence in labour relations, and the severe diminution of political independence, all of which were the result of the failure to expand real output at European rates.'[19] There has been no shortage of explanations for Britain's relative failure but it is beyond the scope of this book to embark on a detailed discussion of them; suffice it to say that 'we must take care not to assume that everything was wrong, or to put it in other words, that the fault lay with the economy in the aggregate, with the general direction in which it moved or the stage of historical development in which it found itself'.[20]

The last two of the Radcliffe Report's objectives are both concerned with the balance of payments and may be conveniently treated together, particularly as it was in foreign trading relations that the weaknesses of the British economy continually manifested themselves. Moreover, it can be argued that the constant, and in some respects unhealthy, preoccupation with the balance of payments led to the 'stop-go' policies which must bear considerable responsibility for the failure to achieve a higher rate of growth. Here as in other aspects of British economic performance it is deceptively easy to confuse myth with reality. It is a commonplace to berate our exporters for their failure to sell their goods abroad more effectively: a closer examination of the record reveals that by certain standards their achievements by no means deserve to be belittled. For, in fact, the post-war foreign trade balance was exceptionally strong compared with other periods as may be judged from the following evidence. First, the immediate post-war task of raising exports by some 75 per cent above the pre-war level was astonishingly achieved by 1950. Secondly, whereas at the end of the 19th century British exporters were covering about 75 per cent of the total import bill, under the spur of the post-war export drive the percentage has consistently been pushed beyond the 90 per cent level. Indeed, during the years 1956–59 the gap was almost plugged with the percentage reaching 99 per cent and even in the past ten years or so the average has been around 96 per cent. In other words at a time when Britain has been lurching from one sterling crisis to another, Britain's visible exports have been covering a greater share of the import bill than ever before in her industrial history. Thirdly, British exports were highest and grew faster in those branches of production, such as chemicals, vehicles and engineering, in which the exports of other nations were at their most buoyant and this is hardly evidence of structural weakness. On the other hand it cannot be denied that the very fast growth in world trade provided exceptionally favourable conditions for the expansion of exports and it can be argued that British exporters, although they did well, nevertheless failed to take full advantage of the situation. In support of this view there is the undeniable fact that Britain's share of world exports in manufactures has been declining for most of the post-war period; for, while in 1948 it formed 29·3 per cent of the aggregate export of these goods by the eleven top industrial nations, this pro-

Table 33

SHARES OF CERTAIN COUNTRIES IN EXPORTS OF MANUFACTURES OF THE TOP 11 INDUSTRIAL COUNTRIES

Year	*U.S.A.* %	*U.K.* %	*Western Germany* %	*France* %	*Japan* %
1958	23·3	18·1	18·5	8·6	6·0
1960	21·6	16·3	19·3	9·7	6·9
1964	20·4	14·2	19·7	8·9	8·3
1965	20·5	13·5	19·2	8·8	9·4
1966	20·2	12·9	19·5	8·6	9·8
1967	20·5	11·9	19·7	8·5	9·8
1968	20·2	11·1	19·5	8·3	10·7
1969 (3rd. qtr.)	19·6	11·1	19·3	8·2	11·4

Source: *National Institute Economic Review*, November, 1969, Table 20.

portion had fallen to 11·1 per cent at the end of the third quarter of 1969. In contrast, W. Germany's proportion was only half Britain's in 1950 but caught up with it by 1957 and by the end of 1968 had reached 20 per cent.

Invisible earnings did not do quite so well, but not so badly as is often assumed. The returns from 'portfolio' investments showed a sad decline from their former importance in Britain's balance of payments. Civil aviation showed a small surplus year by year but net income from shipping, once a very large net earner of foreign currency, was negative in the 1960s. Travel and private transfers were becoming negative items. But some other sources yielded relatively more than before the war. Profits of direct investments of British firms, especially those of oil companies and mining companies, agency, commission and premium earnings of the City of London and authors' royalties kept up well. As a result invisible earnings continued to make a sizeable contribution to the balance of payments. 'Between them, these current items on private account created a strong positive balance year by year. By themselves, they would have placed Britain in a similarly favourable position as West Germany and France in the 1960s and would have made unnecessary the destructive restrictionist policies which the British economy had to endure.'[21] Why then the recurring and debilitating balance of payments crises which have been so damaging to national morale because they have come to be regarded 'not only as a painful affliction but also as a symptom of an organic malaise of the British body economic?'[22] The short answer is to be found in two items, Government expenditure and net foreign investment; and the former is much the more important. Professor Postan has outlined the consequences admirably:

> 'Throughout the post-war period the United Kingdom carried burdens of foreign payments and obligations heavier relative to its national income than those borne by any other European country. Many of these burdens originated in the international role Britain preserved or assumed (the precise verb is a matter of choice) after the war. Some of them, above all, the upkeep of the Army of Occupation in Germany (its cost exceeded £80m. in 1964), fell upon Britain as a victor in the war; others arose from lingering imperial commitments. Although during this period Britain liquidated the bulk of her dependent empire, she still preserved some vestiges of her colonial past in the Eastern Mediterranean, in the Middle East and in South East Asia, which entailed expenditure on bases and troops, subsidies to local rulers, and a succession of colonial or post-colonial wars in Palestine, Malaya and Cyprus, Suez and Aden. The fact that some of these obligations

appeared inescapable and helped to preserve whole parts of the world from lapsing into chaos or from being taken over by the Communist powers did not make them any less burdensome.'[23]

In the event the burden has been considerable and increasing; for Government expenditure of foreign exchange was on the average not much above £100m. in the early fifties and by the middle sixties it had grown to almost £500m. (See Table 34.) The other negative item, which was of smaller absolute size and grew much more slowly, was net foreign investment. Until they had been greatly reduced by liquidation during the war, British foreign investments were very large but they were manageable in that they gave rise to a current flow of annual income from abroad. After the war foreign, especially American, investment in the United Kingdom became sufficiently great to produce an outflow of profits and interest payments which in some years was more than half as great as Britain's income from its own foreign investments. 'At the same time the balance of payments continued to bear the weight of resumed transfers of British capital abroad for investment. In some years, more particularly in 1958, 1959, 1960 and 1963 the outflow of funds on this account outpaced by a large margin the inflow of foreign investment into the United Kingdom; and by all appearances Britain was fast resuming her pre-war role of an international lender and exporter of capital.'[24] Here we must lay another mythical ghost to rest for, far from Britain living off the rest of the world in this period, the rest of the world can be said to have been living off Britain!

Although the benefits to Britain from investing abroad may be a matter of controversy, there can be little dispute about the short-term burden on the balance of payments which prompted the Labour Government to place restrictions on direct investment outside the sterling area in July 1965.[25] In addition to the private capital transfers, there were also official investments of which the most important were the 'sterling balances' which arose from yet another of Britain's liabilities—the sterling area, a liability which is perhaps inescapable, perhaps economically valuable, but nevertheless quite burdensome. These sterling balances were a war-time creation which arose out of the expenditure by British forces in such countries as India and Egypt and since 1950 they have never moved far from the £3,500m. mark. Their significance is that they represent a large volume of foreign debt and incur the implicit obligation to defend a medium of payment for a volume of transactions greatly in excess of Britain's own foreign trade, her own receipts from abroad and of her own gold and foreign exchange reserves.

We are now in a position to summarise the main features of Britain's

Table 34

U.K. BALANCE OF PAYMENTS, 1950–1968
(£ million)

Year	Visible Trade Balance	Invisibles, Profits, Interest, etc. (net)	Other (net)	Total Private Current Balance	Government Current Transaction	Total Current Balance	Total Capital (net)[1]	Balance of Current and Capital Transactions
1950	(− 51)	(+159)	(+334)	(+442)	(−136)	(+306)	—	—
1951	(−689)	(+147)	(+327)	(−215)	(−150)	(−365)	—	—
1952	−279	+252	+251	+224	− 61	+163	−134	+ 29
1953	−244	+229	+226	+211	− 66	+145	−194	− 49
1954	−204	+250	+202	+248	−131	+117	−191	− 74
1955	−313	+174	+122	− 17	−133	−115	−122	−177
1956	+ 53	+229	+101	+383	−175	+208	−187	+ 21
1957	− 29	+249	+157	+377	−144	+233	−106	+127
1958	+ 29	+294	+243	+566	−219	+347	−196	+151
1959	−118	+266	+228	+376	−227	+149	−255	−106
1960	−408	+240	+192	+ 24	−282	−258	−192	−450
1961	−153	+263	+227	+337	−332	+ 5	+ 68	+ 73
1962	−104	+346	+244	+486	−359	+127	− 98	+ 29
1963	− 80	+394	+179	+493	−382	+111	−148	− 37
1964	−537	+413	+157	+ 33	−432	−399	−370	−769
1965	−272	+470	+158	+356	−447	− 91	−203	−294
1966	−136	+422	+189	+475	−470	+ 5	−102	− 97
1967	−635	+415	+287	+ 67	−466	−399	−116	−515
1968	−796	+436	+403	+ 43	−462	−419	− 39	−458

Source: Central Statistical Office, *United Kingdom Balance of Payments.* (Annual) Figures for 1950 and 1951 are drawn from *United Kingdom Balance of Payments 1946–1957* (1959) and *Key Statistics*, and have not been corrected in the same way as the later figures.

[1] Minus means net overseas investment; plus means net disinvestment. Figures for 1967 from C.S.O., *Financial Statistics*, 71 (March, 1968).

post-war payments position. If we ignore for the moment Government expenditure, the British economy produced sufficient surplus to have sustained both a rapid growth at home and net investment abroad. 'Burdened, however, as it was by the political fact of heavy and rapidly growing Government spending and lending abroad, the current balance was too small to sustain a heavy net foreign lending programme as well.'[26] Britain's ability to compete in foreign markets and to export its produce abroad was higher than before the war and higher than that of many other industrialised nations but it did not rise sufficiently fast to be able to carry the burdens of the post-war liabilities incurred, whether wisely or unwisely, for an amalgam of political and economic reasons. That the burden was insupportable was finally recognised by the decision to devalue in 1967—a decision which the Labour Government attempted unsuccessfully to delay by incurring an even heavier volume of official foreign debt. Since then, there has been a striking improvement in the balance of payments and on the threshold of the 1970s the surplus on current account is running at an annual rate of over £600m. Not surprisingly, this is being hailed as a triumph for economic policy and evidence that the nightmare of 'stop-go' is at an end but this would be premature and misguided, for not only may the surplus be short-lived but also there are other important yardsticks by which to judge performance. It is difficult to gainsay that the improvement in the balance of payments has been purchased at the cost of a higher level of unemployment which, however utopian by Beveridge's standards, is now unacceptably high. Moreover, the rate of inflation is if anything accelerating because Britain is still unable to absorb wage increases in higher productivity and the rate of economic growth after two years of stagnation is only slightly above 2 per cent. By comparison with that of other countries similarly placed, British economic policy, the attempt to control the economy as a whole, must be judged a failure—a marginal failure but a failure for all that.

These economic events have been enacted against a political backcloth, the chief characteristics of which have been, first, the bi-polarisation of the world into two spheres of influence dominated on the one hand by the major Communist states, the Soviet Union and China and, on the other, by the U.S.A.; secondly, the retreat from colonialism by the European powers and thirdly, connected with this, the emergence of an intense nationalism among the underdeveloped countries of the 'Third World'. The co-operation between the Allied Powers in their pursuit of victory over Germany and Japan had raised hopes of fruitful cooperation for the establishment of a new world order through the United Nations but these were soon to be falsified when the Soviet Union made clear its intention to enforce its own political philosophy on the territories liberated by the Red Army, including East Germany. With the creation of the Iron Curtain, of the existence of which Sir Winston Churchill had warned the world in his speech at Fulton, Missouri, in 1946, Poland, Czechoslovakia, Hungary, Rumania, East Germany and the former Baltic States were at one fell swoop removed from Western European and American influence. Then in 1949 came the triumph of Mao Tse-Tung in China, which in terms of population represented an immense addition to the strength of Communism, although subsequently he has so emphasised his independence of the Soviet Union that there has been a serious possibility of military conflict. Since the organisation of the United Nations had been based on the assumption of continuing cooperation between the major powers, the emergence of the Cold War and the refusal of the United States to contemplate the admission of China has greatly hindered its development as an effective arbitrator in world disputes especially where the interests of the Soviet Union and the U.S.A. clash.

Britain, as a major colonial power, began the retreat from colonialism with the courageous, if risky, decision to grant India her independence in 1947, although she had to make a major concession to the Moslem leader, Mr. Jinnah, by agreeing to partition and the creation of Pakistan, a two-part state separated by hundreds of miles. The process of disentanglement from an imperial past was gradually extended to Africa and other parts of Asia and is now almost completed, although occasionally atavistic yearnings for the glory that was gone have manifested themselves in adventures such as the Anglo-French escapade at Suez in 1956. This sometimes painful adjustment to changed circumstances has now been given an air of irreversibility by the decision to withdraw from defence commitments east of Suez, except for the retention of a token force at Singapore. Other colonial powers have similarly bowed before the forces of anti-colonialism with varying degrees of reluctance; only Portugal clings with tenacity and at increasing cost to her territories such as Angola and Mozambique. The scale of the transformation from a colonial to a post-colonial era may be judged by the fact that within fifteen years of the end of the Second World War over sixty new countries gained formal independence.

Emancipation from alien rule was accompanied by a growing political consciousness within these countries and the political struggle itself has fanned the flames of nationalism. Moreover, they entered political independence with a backlog of deep poverty, with little accumulated capital or experience of industrialisation and with only a vague understanding of the complexities of rapid change in their societies and economies. Many considered political independence and economic development synonymous, unaware of the long and slow process by which the power and affluence of the industrialised countries had been reached. 'Rarely, if ever, has the world faced and absorbed political change on so large a scale in so short a time. As European and other countries had done earlier, the new African and Asian countries faced conflicting political, sectional, and cultural pressures in trying to build viable nations. Some countries were torn by internal disruption; in others the political framework proved unequal to the stress; but, compared with what history might have led the world to expect, the turmoil has been limited.'[27]

Undoubtedly the emerging nations and the low-income countries everywhere faced a problem of immense magnitude. All the manifestations of underdevelopment, low levels of technology, high illiteracy rates, low savings ratios, high birth rates, inefficient public administration and political instability, seemed to be a vicious circle from which only a fortunate few might hope to escape. Happily, as the Pearson Commission has pointed out, these fears have proved groundless for 'the record of the past twenty years proves that economic development is feasible, given adequate effort and sound policies'.[28] In actual fact between 1950 and 1967 the less developed countries as a group increased their total production of goods and services by an annual average rate of 4·8 per cent. In many cases the great efforts necessary to improve material well-being have had to be stimulated by emphasis on the individual citizen's commitment to nation building, and the consequent nationalistic fervour has at times led to policies designed to limit the freedom of action of foreign companies to repatriate profits, particularly financial organisations which rely on attracting the people's savings. Not surprisingly, an international business such as insurance has borne the brunt of the political expression of nationalism.

Such are the political and economic influences: namely bi-polarisation in world politics; the demise of colonialism; emergent nationalism in the underdeveloped world; full employment; inflation and Britain's relative failure to readjust her economy fully to the forces released by the Second World War and the consequent balance of payments crises, which have combined to shape the fortunes of the British insurance industry in the post-war world. While some of these influences, such as inflation, have created problems, these have been dwarfed by the beneficent effects of the growth in real income, which, however disappointing by international standards, has been faster than in any previous period of our history; the consistently high level of employment; and the great increase in the size of the capital stock. Not surprisingly, the growth in insurance as measured by premium income has broken all past records and on the face of it the industry's response to the challenges and opportunities of the post-war world has been magnificent. Even after due allowance has been made for inflation which, particularly since 1950, has had a major impact on the growth of claims and costs as well as premium income, the expansion of life assurance and motor insurance in particular has been spectacular. The former is obviously closely linked with the growth in real income which has also influenced the structure and nature of the business. Originally, as we have seen, life assurance evolved as a means of protection against the contingencies of death but the growth in real income has provided an increasing margin which, after the need for essential protection has been fulfilled, has been channelled into investment

Table 35

PREMIUM INCOME OF MAJOR BRANCHES, 1945–1968

Year	*Ordinary Life*	*Industrial Life*	*Fire*	*Marine Aviation and Transit*	*Accident Personal*	*Motor*
1945	109,500,000	79,392,000	71,777,000	48,547,000	5,106,000	33,828,000
1969	1,160,000,000	286,000,000	1,053,000,000*	181,000,000	—	633,000,000

* Includes non-motor accident 1969 figures are not directly comparable.

Sources: *Insurance Directory and Yearbook,* British Insurance Association.

through the life branch. This has been accomplished by the use of the endowment policy in its many forms, some of the more recent of which explicitly recognise the need for protection against endemic inflation by means of a link with equities. Furthermore, increasing affluence during the years of full employment has made people less tolerant of the prospect of relative poverty in old age and less willing to rely on the minimum benefits provided by the Welfare State, so that there has been a rapid burgeoning of occupational pension schemes, many of which have been arranged through collective assurance with the life companies.

The motor vehicle had, of course, become a common feature of everyday life before the war, for in 1938 there were over 3m. licenced vehicles on British roads of which almost 2m. were private motor cars. But the spectacular growth in vehicle ownership came after the war and, more especially, after the termination of petrol rationing in 1950. By 1955 there were about 6½m. licensed vehicles on the roads of which 3½m. were private cars; by 1968 these figures had further increased to 14½m. and nearly 11m. respectively.

With increasing material welfare and the rise in the nation's capital stock the demand for fire insurance rose correspondingly. There was a similar advance in those countries such as the U.S.A., Canada, Australia, New Zealand and South Africa which have for many years provided the major source of income from overseas. The experience of the Commercial

Union Assurance Group in the first half of the post-war period was typical. 'Indeed, the rise in results from accident and fire underwriting in these territories was to be little less than prodigious. In Canada, for instance, the net accident premium income rose from some £594,000 in 1946 to over £3,200,000 in 1958, while in the same period the net fire premiums rose from £320,000 to nearly £1,237,000. In Australasia the net premium income increased in round figures from £530,000 to £3,500,000 and the fire from £450,000 to £2,000,000.'[29]

Marine underwriting is particularly sensitive to fluctuations in international trade, which has expanded to record levels throughout the post-war period and carried premium income with it. The return to peaceful conditions found the world's shipping capacity so debilitated that a vast ship-building programme was launched. The expansion was not confined to cargo-carrying vessels; passenger traffic came into its own again, at least temporarily, and typical of the new liners which were commissioned was the Caronia, insured for £4m. in 1948. By 1951 most European countries possessed shipping tonnages comparable with, or even exceeding, those of 1939 and world shipping was actually 27 per cent larger in volume than immediately before the war. The average size of ships has increased sharply and so have insurable values. For example, Sir Arthur Rogers, Chairman of the London and Lancashire, remarked in 1951 that the value of the hull and cargo of a 7,000–8,000 ton vessel sailing from Australia equalled the pre-war insurable value of the 80,000 ton *Queen Mary*. Size and value have continued to escalate to such an extent that at the beginning of the 1970s naval architects are planning to build tankers of 1m. tons. Since the early 1950s passenger traffic has inexorably declined but with the virtual doubling in the value of world trade since 1957 the growth of cargo traffic has more than compensated.

The cause of the decline in passenger traffic by sea has been the phenomenal rise in international air travel, which has now become the accepted method for covering long distances. The number of aircraft flights into and out of the U.K. has increased from 66,000 in 1945 to 336,000 in 1968 and the number of passenger miles from 302,000,000 to 8,758,000,000. Consequently, aviation underwriting has become a significant source of income at least for the relatively small group of insurers involved. Immediately after the end of the war some of the insurance companies, whose interest in aviation insurance had hitherto been confined to their role as shareholders of the specialist companies, decided to underwrite under their own names and at the same time several new specialist syndicates were formed at Lloyd's with a resultant intensification of competition on the London market. Up to 1950 underwriting results were somewhat mixed mainly because of the activities of war-time pilots who attempted to establish themselves as charter operators, often with inadequate capital for the safe and efficient operation of the surplus war planes of which their fleets were composed. Furthermore, the aircraft industry was switching over rapidly to the development of new planes and on the assumption that the new generation of civil aircraft would be operationally safer, the underwriters were continually being pressed to reduce their rates. Whilst efforts were made to offset the countervailing power of the operators, nothing materialised until 1949 when the Aviation Insurance Offices Association was formed with a membership of eight companies. This helped to alleviate the situation since it enabled the underwriters to pool experience and methods, but it was clearly laid down in its constitution that it was not to be a rate-fixing body. Nevertheless, it was able to exert considerable collective pressure to keep rates up on the first generation of jet aircraft, on the grounds that insurers had little idea of their probable safety record and caution was justifiable in the light of experience with the Comet I. To the extent that their worst fears proved groundless, aviation underwriting was consequently that much more profitable especially in the late 1950s and early 1960s.

However, this period of spectacular growth has not been devoid of challenges which the insurance industry has faced with varying degrees of success. The first challenge was that of reconstruction and the re-establishment of connections with territories which had been severed by the war. In general these were successfully accomplished in a relatively short time, although the spread of Communism in Eastern Europe and China and the emergence of nationalism in Asia had the effect of depriving the industry of some of its pre-war markets.

In the early post-war years the life branch faced another challenge which was of peculiar significance to it alone and that was the continuation and intensification of the 'cheap-money' policy pursued during the war. The Labour Government had inherited a structure of low rates as a legacy from war finance and found compelling reasons for disturbing them as little as possible. In the first place, there was the problem of servicing the greatly enlarged National Debt of which a substantial proportion was composed of short-term securities. Secondly, the average life of the dated stocks was considerably shorter than it had been in 1919 and in nearly every year up to 1961 there was a large number of securities awaiting redemption. Thirdly, there was a general fear that shortly after demobilisation there might be a serious fall in the level of economic activity and a rise in unemployment such as had occurred in 1921. Fourthly, the Government had been returned to power with a commitment to nationalise the basic fuel industries, road and rail transport and the iron and steel industry; the lower interest rates could be forced, the smaller the future burden of payments on the compensation stock which would have to be issued. Finally, a Labour Government had a natural bias in favour of low rates of interest which by contributing to the 'euthanasia of the rentier' would play their part in aiding the general policy of diminishing existing inequalities of income.[30]

In retrospect the policy was extremely misguided for it paid insufficient attention to the facts that the British public had emerged from the war with a greatly increased volume of liquid assets which were only prevented from exerting strong inflationary pressure by physical controls, and that there was a widespread desire for the early abolition of these controls. In the event Dr. Dalton's drive for cheaper money was abandoned when the deposits of the eleven clearing banks had risen by £900m. and the monetary authorities became increasingly nervous about losing control of the money market.[31]

Nevertheless it gave the life companies some anxious moments for even before the adoption of Dr. Dalton's ill-starred policy, they were becoming increasingly embarrassed by, and preoccupied with, the problem of falling interest rates. Premiums are calculated at certain assumed rates of interest and there is normally a considerable lag between changes in the latter and adjustments in the former. This lag works to the advantage of the companies when interest rates are rising and to their disadvantage when they are falling. The intensification of cheap money in 1946 followed a period of 15 years in which interest had been falling steadily and premiums gradually rising. Much of the business undertaken during the 1930s and the war had been underwritten at premiums much below those ruling in 1946. It is little wonder that the prospect of even cheaper money intensified their problems. 'The seriousness of the situation may be judged from the fact that in 1947 the largest life office had to transfer its entire investment reserve fund of £9·6m. and a further £3m. from profits on investment account to the assurance funds in order to permit a valuation of the funds on a 2 per cent basis in the ordinary branch and a 2½ per cent basis in the industrial branch. In 1947 companies, which were earning less than 2 per cent net on their funds, had many outstanding policies which were uneconomic. Eventually, they were forced to protect themselves by raising premiums and reducing ordinary reversionary bonuses on with-profit policies well below the pre-war level.'[32] With the passage of time and the apparently inexorable rise in interest rates the problem has receded to such an extent that the investment managers of the 1970s, observing yields of over 9 per cent on government securities, must find it difficult to comprehend the preoccupations of their predecessors.

A recurring theme in the history of the insurance industry has been the extent of state control, and the early post-war years witnessed the most formidable attack yet experienced on its freedom of action. The case for the nationalisation of industrial life assurance, which, as we saw in the previous chapter, was originally put forward during the war by Lord Beveridge, was taken up by Ian Mikardo in 1948 in a pamphlet entitled *The Second Five Years—a Labour Programme for 1950*. The arguments in favour of such a step included the familiar ones such as the profusion of overlapping services, over-selling, the high rate of lapses and a new one, namely, the failure of the companies to use their considerable financial power derived from their funds in the national interest. Since the distinction between ordinary and industrial assurance was a legal, and not a functional, one, Ian Mikardo argued that it would be impossible to effect an artificial separation which would leave either of the two branches in private hands.

The campaign was taken a stage further at a meeting in Transport House early in 1949 when the possibility of nationalising the whole of the insurance industry was considered and rejected on the grounds that 'the risk of disturbance to foreign business, particularly with dollar resources in mind, was too great'.[33] The next step was to consider the possibility of taking over the whole of the industry's life business but it was immediately realised that the problem of separating the various branches of the business was a serious obstacle since practically all the companies which were engaged in non-life underwriting also had substantial stakes in life assurance. Consequently the discussion of the scope of potential nationalisation was then limited to industrial life assurance, but even such a less ambitious project was not straightforward, because some of the major industrial offices had extensive overseas connections and interests in general business and practically all of them had expanding overseas branches. Nevertheless, the final decision was to take over the 14 industrial-ordinary life offices in their entirety with all their existing domestic and overseas interests in both life and general business. Significantly, the National Union of Cooperative Insurance Society Employees (a section of the Transport and General Workers Union) was the only union at the meeting to voice apprehension about these proposals.[34]

By the time the Labour Party's annual conference was held in 1949 the emphasis had switched from socialisation or nationalisation of industrial life assurance to the vaguer idea of conversion into a public service primarily for the purpose of rounding off the social services. Again there was opposition from the Cooperative Movement for one of their members, J. S. Worrall, argued that the Cooperative Insurance Society was in effect 'a consumer organisation, as all profits were returned to its members; it provided a great social service, and the Labour Party was proposing to nationalise an already collectively-owned and democratically-controlled institution'.[35] Behind the scenes the Cooperative Insurance Society had been putting considerable pressure on the Labour Party to abandon its proposals on the grounds that they were unlikely to benefit the policyholders. In particular their directors were sceptical as to whether the Labour Party plan would succeed in reducing the costs of premium collection, especially as it was letting it be assumed that it could at one and the same time reduce costs and leave agents' terms unaffected. But their greatest cause of dissatisfaction was that, while the non-profit making Cooperative Insurance Society was to be one of the 14 nationalised companies, 134 small organisations were omitted from the scheme and would be free to develop and compete against the nationalised body. There was also opposition from the trade unions included in the National Federation of Insurance Workers, 9 out of 12 of which declared themselves opposed to nationalisation at a conference held on 27 October 1949, mainly because the insurance workers were afraid of redundancy and the loss of pension rights.[36]

This persistent opposition was not long in producing results for on 23 November, 1949, the National Executive of the Labour Party issued a statement to the effect that it had been decided to convert industrial assurance into a public service by means of mutual ownership. In other words the proprietary companies were to be compulsorily converted into mutual companies under the supervision of an Industrial Assurance Board, but this modified scheme suffered from the defect that it offered little prospect of effectively reducing administrative costs since 'any wasteful form of competition between agents of rival offices would probably be just as keen between a score of mutually-owned offices as it would be between the existing companies, mutual or proprietary'.[37] It was more than likely that all the faults attributed to the existing system would be produced in the new one and the only benefit accruing to policyholders would be the distribution of the rewards which previously had been received by the shareholders of the proprietary companies. However, it was claimed that all would benefit under the new proposals whereby insurance funds and their investment would remain in private hands while the Government would 'guarantee and accept complete responsibility for all existing policies'.[38]

This modification of the original proposals failed to draw the teeth of opposition from the Cooperative Insurance Society and the agents, and in the event the plans for public ownership in any form were quietly dropped, although lip service was still paid to the idea in the Labour Party's pamphlet *Challenge to Britain*, published in 1953.

Although no reference was made to nationalisation or 'mutualisation', it was categorically stated that 'we are convinced that a publicly-organised industrial assurance service would give better value and security to policyholders, sharply reduce administrative costs and provide a channel for further savings'.[39] This proved to be the last reference to the subject in official Labour Party policy statements. There can be little doubt that this change of heart was in no small part attributable to the hostility of the agents, for the Labour Party 'cowered before the prospect of opposition from 60,000 agents organised in 400 anti-nationalisation committees . . . it vacillated, compromised and finally collapsed'.[40] Nevertheless, whatever the balance of forces, the Cooperative Insurance Society played a critical role out of keeping with being merely one insurance office in many, and was largely instrumental in forcing the Labour Party to recognise that there are fundamental differences between social insurance[41] schemes which are more a social service financed by taxation masquerading as insurance and the activities of insurance companies.[42]

Although the threat of nationalisation receded, the industry has continued to be the subject of further legislative control during the post-war period in the form of the 1946 and 1967 Acts. Briefly, the 1946 Act accepted the main recommendations of the Cassel Committee and extended the application of the 1909 Act to marine, aviation and transit insurance; increased the initial capital requirement to £50,000 and tightened up the requirements for solvency by stipulating that an insurance company would in future be deemed insolvent if its assets did not exceed its liabilities either by £50,000 or one-tenth of its premium income in its last financial year. The stimulus for further legislation arose in the 1960s from public anxiety over the failure of some newcomers to the motor insurance market, in particular the Fire, Auto and Marine, the London and Cheshire and the Irish-American companies. The 1967 Act attempted to prevent a repetition of these unpalatable events by insisting among other things that the initial capital requirement should be raised to £100,000 and by increasing the powers of the Board of Trade to control the entry of new firms and to prevent existing companies from continuing to transact business whenever their solvency is in doubt.[43]

The other major challenges which the insurance has had to face are the effects of inflation on expenses and claims and the impact of technological change on the size of individual risks. The major effect of inflation on life insurance has been to raise the costs of acquiring new business, and to force the companies to pay more attention to the need to shield their policyholders from the erosion of the value of their policies through a shift in their investment policies towards assets which offer better protection against the falling value of money and a greater emphasis on the bonus element in with-profit policies. In general insurance, in which selling expenses and commissions absorb a considerable proportion of the premiums, the pressure on costs has been inexorable; at the same time claims, particularly in the fire and motor markets, have escalated. Unfortunately, for a variety of reasons some of which were outside the insurers' control, such as legislative restraints in the United States, and others which were not, such as the inflexibility of the tariff system, premiums have not always been quickly adjusted in response to rising costs.[44]

The technological revolution has posed the biggest challenge of all to general insurance, which happens to be one of the fields in which its consequences are manifested rather spectacularly. 'Insurance for 2,000 years was marine insurance; only in the last 300 has there suddenly arisen a need for new types of cover, other than for shipwreck, piracy and so on. For 2,000 years, ships did not change much. Size crept up; means of locomotion altered periodically, but these gradual changes did not upset the principles and methods of insuring hulls and cargoes. Now suddenly —bulk carriers. Size has abruptly multiplied by a factor that takes ships into a different world, and their insurance with it.'[45] The increasing scale of liability, the big risk, has also become an important feature of fire business. Not only has vastly more expensive equipment been installed in factories but of even greater significance has been the trend, with automation and other techniques of mass production, towards long and uninterrupted lines of machinery under a single factory roof with few of the natural fire barriers of the past. Consequently, fire risks have not just got bigger, they have completely changed in character. Again the development of aviation has created a completely new type of risk. 'In 1900 only a lunatic would have suggested that by 1975, not only would man have learnt to fly, not only would insurance cover for this inconceivable mode of transport have grown to 20 per cent of that for marine insurance, but that insurers would have been asked to give cover to a man on the moon.'[46] Here too the scale of risk has changed dramatically with the arrival of the Jumbo Jets on the scene.

That the response of general insurers to the twin challenges of inflation and technological change has not been completely successful is shown by the manner in which the very profitable expansion of the first decade after the war has given way to the profitless expansion of the subsequent years. This has provided the stimulus to make a more vigorous attack on expenses particularly in the difficult North American market and one of the solutions has been to form bigger units. Consequently after a lull of thirty years a wave of amalgamations has been sweeping the market since the late 1950s. The first new merger came in 1956 when the Guardian

Table 36

MAJOR AMALGAMATIONS OF INSURANCE COMPANIES SINCE 1956

Year	*Companies*
1956	Guardian—Licences and General
1957	Guardian—Caledonian
1958	British Life Office—Reliance Mutual
	Eagle Star—Threadneedle
1959	Commercial Union—North British and Mercantile
	Sun—Alliance
	Norwich Union—Scottish Union
	Royal Exchange—Atlas
1960	Northern—Employers Liability
	Guardian—Union of Canton
	National Employers Mutual—National and Colonial
	Eagle Star—Navigators and General
	Eagle Star—Removers and General
1961	Royal—London and Lancashire
	Eagle Star—Army, Navy and General
	Legal and General—British Commonwealth
	Norwich Union—Parcels and General
	Royal—British America
1963	Yorkshire—Scottish Insurance
1965	Sun Alliance—London
1966	Eagle Star—City of London
1967	General Accident—Yorkshire
	General Accident—London Provincial Marine and General
1968	Guardian—Royal Exchange
	Commercial Union—Northern Employers
	Prudential—Mercantile and General

Sources: *Insurance Directory and Year Book.*
The Policyholder.
Post Magazine and Insurance Monitor.
Economist Insurance Supplements.

acquired Licences and General but the process did not really gain momentum until 1959. In that year the Commercial Union acquired the North British and Mercantile, the Sun merged with the Alliance, Royal Exchange took over Atlas and Norwich Union acquired Scottish Union. 1961 saw an even more significant merger when the Royal and the London Lancashire pooled their assets to form the largest insurance group in the United Kingdom. A striking feature of the list of companies in Table 36 is the predominance of composite companies, for only one specialist company, namely British Life taken over by Reliance Mutual, appears. This serves to emphasise that the compelling force behind the recent spate of amalgamations has come from the fire and accident departments, anxious to reduce their expense ratios by diversifying geographically and increasing the range of insurance services.

Unfortunately, it is by no means clear that the policy has succeeded in its objectives. Admittedly, the benefits cannot be expected to accrue immediately since there must inevitably be teething troubles especially during mergers with neither of the original managements wishing to be dominated by the other. Nevertheless, since a considerable number of the

Table 37

EXPENSE RATIOS AND UNDERWRITING RESULTS OF SELECTED COMPANIES

(i) *Fire Business*

Company Group	*% Growth of Premiums 1963–7*	*Commission and Expenses as a % of premiums. Change from 1964 to 1967 (minus sign = reduction in expenses)*	*Underwriting results as % of premiums. Change from 1964 to 1967 (plus sign = improvement minus sign = deterioration)*
Royal	+ 28·1	−2·4	+ 2·3
Commercial Union	+ 25·4	−2·9	+ 4·3
General Accident	+ 33·5[1]	+1·7	+ 3·8
Northern and Employers	+ 28·9	−0·2	+ 2·9
Guardian	+ 31·2	−4·4	+10·8
Eagle Star	+112·5	+0·1	− 0·9
Royal Exchange	+ 6·4	−2·4	+ 6·7
Phoenix	+ 42·3	−1·5	+ 4·7
Norwich Union	+ 18·5	−5·7	+ 5·7
Sun Alliance and London	+ 14·8	+1·3	+ 3·5

(ii) *Accident Business*

Royal	+ 36·2	−1·6	+ 1·5
Commercial Union	+ 38·0	−3·4	+ 3·1
General Accident	+ 33·4[1]	−0·5	+ 3·7
Northern & Employers	+ 26·4	−0·8	+ 3·5
Guardian	+ 38·6	−1·4	+ 2·2
Eagle Star	+ 72·4	+0·7	+ 1·4
Royal Exchange	+ 20·6	+0·2	+ 3·7
Phoenix	+ 32·8	−2·1	+ 4·0
Norwich Union	+ 13·4	−1·2	+ 7·4
Sun Alliance & London	+ 27·9[2]	−2·5	+ 2·3

Source: The Policyholder, 9 August, 1968.

[1] This represents increase in combined premiums of General Accident and Yorkshire for 1963.

[2] Represents increase in combined premiums of Sun-Alliance and London for 1963.

amalgamations occurred between 1956 and 1961, the companies concerned should have been able to reap some of the benefits by, say, 1968. An attempt was made to assess such benefits in the issue of the *Policyholder* dated 9 August 1968 in the manner shown in Table 37. During the period 1963 to 1967 the growth of fire and accident premiums of the two companies not involved in the 1959–1961 round of mergers, namely the General Accident and the Phoenix, were better than at least half of the merged companies. Similarly, their average underwriting results for the period from 1964 to 1967 and the improvements in those results over the period were better than the average for all ten companies. It should be stressed that this evidence is inconclusive and does no more than suggest that the actual benefits from mergers may have fallen somewhat short of expectations. Nevertheless, it serves to emphasise that amalgamation into stronger units is only a partial solution to the challenges facing general insurance and it is yet to be demonstrated, as we see in subsequent chapters, that the industry has found the remedies to the problems which beset it in the 1960s.

It is somewhat ironical that, because this history of the British insurance industry ends at this particular juncture, we find it, after centuries of triumphant evolution to a position of acknowledged dominance in the international market which is the envy of its foreign competitors, uncertain about its future and hesitant about the measures to be taken to ensure that it is sufficiently flexible and responsive to meet the challenge of modern technology. It is unfortunate that in its middle age, when it was suffering slightly from hardening of the arteries and was understandably complacent about its past performance, it should suddenly have been forced to come to terms with an environment which was experiencing more technical changes in a decade than had occurred in the previous half century. Thus we observe the paradox that while the industry has enjoyed a period of unparalleled expansion since 1945, its profit record, with the notable exception of life assurance, is, to say the least, dubious. An analysis of the causes of this paradoxical situation is one of the tasks now awaiting us in our study of the contemporary industry.

NOTES

1 W. K. Hancock and M. M. Gowing, *British War Economy*, H.M.S.O. and Longmans, 1949, p. 534.

2 Cmnd. 6527.

3 S. Pollard, *The Development of the British Economy, 1914–1967*, Edward Arnold, 1969, 2nd edition, p. 352.

4 A. J. Youngson, *Britain's Economic Growth, 1920–1966*, Allen & Unwin, 1967, p. 155.
5 A. J. Youngson, op. cit., p. 156.
6 S. Pollard, op. cit., p. 354.
7 F. W. Paish estimated the loss of capital at £9 milliard in 1948 prices, *Post-War Financial Problems and Other Essays*, 1950, p. 150.
8 A. J. Youngson, op. cit., p. 153.
9 A. J. Youngson, op. cit., p. 157.
10 S. Pollard, op. cit., p. 357.
11 For a more extensive discussion, see S. Pollard, op. cit., passim.
12 Cmnd. 827, para. 69.
13 Cmnd. 827, ibid.
14 Cmnd. 6527, para. 1.
15 M. Lipton, *Assessing Economic Performance*, Staples Press, 1967, p. 128.
16 M. Lipton, ibid.
17 R. C. O. Matthews, 'Why has Britain had Full Employment since the War?', *Economic Journal*, Vol. LXXVIII, September 1968, p. 568.
18 S. Pollard, op. cit., p. 408.
19 S. Pollard, op. cit., pp. 435, 436.
20 M. M. Postan, *An Economic History of Western Europe, 1945–1964*, Methuen, 1967, p. 79.
21 S. Pollard, op. cit., pp. 450, 451.
22 M. M. Postan, op. cit., p. 67.
23 M. M. Postan, op. cit., p. 68.
24 M. M. Postan, op. cit., p. 70.
25 The C.B.I. later commissioned Professor W. B. Reddaway to undertake an investigation, subsequently published as *Effects of U.K. Direct Investment Overseas* by Cambridge University Press. One of his main conclusions was that the continuing annual gain to the balance of payments, including both profits and induced exports, for every £100 of direct overseas investment worked out on average at only £9.
26 S. Pollard, op. cit., p. 454.
27 *Partners in Development, Report of the Commission on International Development,* Lester B. Pearson, et. al., Pall Mall Press, 1969, p. 26.
28 *Partners in Development*, ibid.
29 E. Liveing, op. cit., p. 242.
30 For a fuller discussion see Clayton and Osborn, op. cit., pp. 88, 89.
31 See C. M. Kennedy, 'Monetary Policy', in *The British Economy* (1945–1950), edited by G. D. N. Worswick and P. M. Ady, Oxford University Press, 1952.
32 G. Clayton and W. T. Osborn, op. cit., p. 92.
33 R. G. Garnett, op. cit., p. 237.
34 R. G. Garnett, op. cit., p. 238.
35 R. G. Garnett, op. cit., p. 239.
36 R. G. Garnett, op. cit., p. 257.
37 R. G. Garnett, op. cit., p. 263.
38 Michael Young, *The Future of Industrial Assurance: Labour's Proposals for National Ownership by the Policyholders*, Transport House, 1950.
39 *Challenge to Britain*, Labour Party, 1953.

40 H. Hopkins, *The New Look: A Social History of the Forties and Fifties*, 1963, p. 371.

41 W. A. Robson, *Nationalized Industry and Public Ownership*, 1962, p. 19.

42 For a fuller and more authoritative account of the issue of nationalisation, see R. G. Garnett, op. cit., pp. 232–266.

43 In February 1970 the Midland, Northern and Scottish was requested to stop selling policies under its 'Alpha' Plan. Later in the year it went into liquidation.

44 This is extensively discussed in Chapter 13.

45 *The Economist Insurance Supplement*, 1969, p. vii.

46 Ibid.

Part IV

THE CONTEMPORARY INDUSTRY

Chapter 12

THE ANATOMY OF THE CONTEMPORARY BRITISH INSURANCE INDUSTRY

> 'Ahem!' said the Mouse, with an important air. 'Are you all ready? This is the driest thing I know. Silence all round, if you please.'
>
> Lewis Carroll

THE CONTEMPORARY insurance industry has grown from the modest origins which we have described to a position where it provides protection against a multitude of risks, which not long ago were considered to be the direct responsibility of individuals, such as legal liability for defective products and losses from bad debts. At the same time the market has grown so that contemporary purchasers of insurance include all types of business organisation, local authorities, public corporations, societies and individuals while the sellers of insurance exhibit a bewildering variety of form, size and function with a highly developed system of intermediaries linking the two sides of the market.

The British industry has also developed a wide-ranging international business which has such a high reputation for probity and expertise that it is variously estimated that as much as 70 per cent of non-life premiums and 10 per cent of life premiums originate overseas. Furthermore, the British insurance industry is heavily involved in the 'wholesale' reinsurance market and London is the premier international centre. Reinsurance is a device for spreading the larger risks and can be defined as an agreement made between two parties, called the ceding company and the reinsurer respectively, whereby the ceding company agrees to cede, and the reinsurer agrees to accept, a certain fixed share of a risk upon terms as set out in the agreement. In 1964 the leading British reinsurance companies received the following premium income in respect of their fire and accident business.

Company	*Premium Income £m.*
Mercantile and General	12·2
Victory	7·2
Reinsurance Corporation	6·8

In addition Lloyd's and the reinsurance departments of British and foreign insurance companies transact a considerable volume of reinsurance business through the London market.

As has been intimated, a bewildering variety of risks are nowadays covered by the device of insurance, and classification presents certain problems. The two main types of insurance, namely personal and property are listed in Table 38. It should be noted that some of these categories cover wider risks than their actual title suggests; for example, fire insurance may embrace insurance against damages from civil disturbances, storms, earthquakes and other special risks.

Table 38

A CLASSIFICATION OF INSURANCE

A. Personal Insurance: Loss of income or increased expenditure through:

DEATH	SURVIVAL	ILL HEALTH	UNEMPLOYMENT
Life	Juvenile	Sickness	Unemployment
Burial	Old Age (Pensions)	Invalid	
		Accidental Injury	
		Maternity	

B. Property Insurance: Loss resulting from damage to, or destruction of, property.

TANGIBLE PROPERTY	INTANGIBLE PROPERTY
Fire	Credit (Bad Debts)
Flood and Storm	Title and Mortgage
Marine	Corporate Bonding
Motor Vehicles	Business Interruption
Aircraft	Loss of Profits
Crop and Livestock	Market Loss
Property Depreciation	Strikes
Embezzlement	Compensation
Forgery	Public Liability
Burglary	Employers Liability
Theft	Reinsurance
Plate Glass	
Boiler	
Radiation	

Another convenient classification is one which distinguishes life assurance from the other categories which have many features in common. The convention, which is used in the industry, is to describe all forms of insurance other than life as 'general insurance'. The characteristic feature of all forms of general insurance is that the contract is an annual one. The premium is paid in return for the promise of an indemnity if the specified contingency occurs during a given year; if there is partial damage, an indemnity is paid to cover the actual loss. The contract in life assurance is usually a long-term one and the premiums are normally paid over a period of years. While it is theoretically possible to provide life cover on an annual basis, there are serious disadvantages in practice.

Since most life assurance policies are bought for the purpose of family protection in the event of death or to make provision for old age, a contract which terminated each year would prove quite inadequate and most inconvenient. A family man needs a long-term contract at a reasonable premium which he knows in advance and for which he can provide in his annual budget. A second, and perhaps more significant, distinction is that those who take out a long-term life assurance policy expect to make a claim on the insurer because the event on the occurrence of which the claim is paid, e.g. death or the attainment of a given age, is certain to happen. The only uncertainty arises from ignorance about *when* death will occur. On the other hand, in general insurance the particular contingency against which protection is sought—burglary or fire, for instance—may never happen to the individual policyholder. It is this distinction which is the basis for using 'assurance' when describing the various types of life business and 'insurance' for general business.

The main categories of life assurance contracts are, first, 'whole-life' policies under the terms of which premiums are paid during the whole of the insured's life in return for an agreed sum payable at death. Premiums for life assurance may, however, be paid for a limited term or even in a single payment by special arrangement. The second important type of life assurance is endowment assurance under which the insurer contracts to pay a given sum at the end of a specified period or at death, whichever occurs first. There are also 'pure' endowment policies which do not include any death benefit. Another type of contract issued by life assurance companies is the annuity which provides a guaranteed income for life in return for a given 'lump-sum' payment. These forms of contract can be, and are, combined in a variety of ways, the range and scope of which is continually being increased by actuarial virtuosity and ingenuity; they are often issued for specific purposes as in the case of 'Death Duty Policies', 'Family Income Policies', 'Pension Contracts', 'Educational Annuities' and 'House Purchase Policies'. Although in general these contracts are long-term, short-term assurances are also available which give cover if death occurs within a specified period. A further distinction, which has a legal basis, may be made between 'ordinary' and 'industrial' life assurance—a distinction which depends primarily on the methods and frequency of payment of the premiums. Ordinary life assurance premiums are paid usually by bankers' order to the insurer once a month or less frequently. In contrast, industrial life assurance premiums are generally collected from the policyholders' homes every week by a large staff of agents, both full-time and part-time. While many ordinary life premiums are only paid annually, and some industrial life premiums are paid monthly, there is a legal limit of two months on the interval between payments in the latter case. Another legal distinction is that industrial assurance concerns, as defined in the Industrial Assurance Act of 1923, may issue policies within certain limits for the funeral expenses of a child, parent, grandparent, grandchild, brother or sister of the insured. In ordinary life assurance a person may only insure his own life and that of his wife. By and large the practical distinction is that industrial assurance provides a service for wage-earners and ordinary life assurance for salary-earners and the higher income groups.

A relatively new type of life assurance, which has developed rapidly since its inception in 1931, is group life assurance. Schemes for providing death benefits and pensions can be, and are frequently, financed by funds initiated by the employers, or by trustees appointed by them and the employees, but many medium-sized and small firms prefer to transfer the responsibilities for devising and managing these schemes to assurance companies. In certain cases, instead of group life assurance, use is made of a collective or group system of individual endowment assurances under which the sums assured may be used at maturity to purchase individual annuities.

In recent years many life assurance organisations have developed house purchase schemes either by advancing mortgages on their own account or by providing decreasing term assurance in collaboration with building societies who are making the advance. Such loans are liquidated by the borrower over a term of, say, 15, 20 or 25 years, by uniform monthly payments, including both interest on the outstanding loan and capital instalments. The instalments of capital are small at first but gradually increase as diminishing sums have to be deducted from the monthly total to pay interest on the outstanding loan. Many building societies are prepared to advance a larger sum so that it shall include a single premium for a term assurance of diminishing amount equal to the outstanding loan. In the event of the death of the borrower before repayment the assurance company then repays the loan and the property becomes free from debt for the benefit of his survivors. Finally, a large amount of life assurance is transacted every year for the purpose of providing collateral security for loans from banks and other financial institutions. Such loans may be for personal consumption or may be required for business or professional purposes.

In view of the immense variety of types of insurance contract it is not surprising to find that the insurers, themselves, appear in many different guises and forms of organisation. According to current legislation in the United Kingdom individuals who are members of an approved association (of which the only example extant today is Lloyd's), societies, companies and mutual associations may transact business as insurers, in some or all of the four conventional classes of business, namely life, fire, accident and marine. First, let us consider the companies which form the largest section of the whole market and include both companies which are incorporated under the various Companies Acts and those which are incorporated in other ways such as by Royal Charter or by private Acts of Parliament.

At the time of writing there are approximately 500 companies operating in the United Kingdom, of which about 400 are incorporated in Great Britain, 50 in other Commonwealth Countries and the remainder elsewhere abroad. Of these some 275 U.K. and Commonwealth-registered companies, accounting for over 95 per cent of the premium income of the whole company market, are members of the British Insurance Association. A further distinction in the company sector may be made between proprietary companies, which are owned by shareholders and include some of the largest companies in each branch, and mutual companies which are owned by their policyholders who receive the profits and are technically responsible for any losses although in many cases their liability is limited by guarantee. Many of the largest companies transacting ordinary life assurance are mutuals. Yet another distinction, which is not as important as it once was, may be drawn between 'tariff' and 'non-tariff' companies. Tariff companies are those which have entered into an agreement to charge the same basic minimum premium rates for the same basic cover and to adhere to common rates of commission for brokers and agents. Such companies which have bound themselves to a tariff agreement for some categories of their fire insurance business are members of the Fire Offices Committee.[1] Prior to October 1968 agreed tariffs for motor insurance were operated by members of the Accident Offices Association but since that date, when ten of its leading members asked for the dissolution of the tariff agreement, the distinction between 'tariff' and 'non-tariff' companies has had no real validity.

Secondly, there are the 6,000 underwriting members of the Corporation of Lloyd's who are organised into marine and non-marine syndicates and take a pre-arranged share of any risk accepted by each syndicate although an individual member undertakes unlimited liability only for his share of the risk. Their activities are supervised and controlled by the Committee of Lloyd's, consisting of 12 elected members, whose main responsibility is to ensure that both prospective and existing underwriters comply with stringent financial and other regulations. A distinctive feature of the organisation is that underwriters are not allowed to deal directly with the public but only through recognised Lloyd's brokers who are also elected by the Committee. Brokers wishing to place insurance walk round the underwriting room at Lloyd's with slips of paper on which are written details of the risks for which cover is required and underwriters who are prepared to underwrite all or a proportion of the risks, initial the brokers' slips for the appropriate sums. Given the preponderant interest of the members of Lloyd's in marine insurance, it is not surprising that over 75 per cent of their premium income, which in 1967 amounted to £610m., emanates from overseas. However, they transact most types of business and in recent years they have become increasingly fierce competitors in the motor branch in which their premium income has increased six-fold since 1950. An important exception is life assurance which usually involves entering into long period contracts which are not easily accommodated by Lloyd's distinctive organisation. The underwriting members of Lloyd's are joined together into a number of syndicates which vary in size. All the members are personally responsible for the insurances accepted by their syndicate and are parties to the contract of insurance between themselves and their insured, even if they do not actually underwrite themselves. Every syndicate is represented by one man who has a seat in The Room and is known as the underwriting agent. He possesses the necessary professional expertise for evaluating risks and quoting appropriate rates and is thus responsible for the financial welfare of the members of his syndicate which depends upon his underwriting skill. It is customary to describe this underwriting agent as 'the Underwriter' and the members composing the syndicate as 'Names'. It is a fundamental feature of the mode of transacting business at Lloyd's that each syndicate divides its total responsibility between its members in certain pre-arranged shares. Whenever the underwriter accepts a risk, he does so on behalf of his whole syndicate with every member receiving his allotted share. An important aspect of this division of risks amongst the members of a syndicate is that their liability is not joint but several. This means that each is liable for his own share but is not liable for the share of any of the other members of his syndicate. On the policy this is given effect by the words 'Each for himself and not one for another.' Since for one reason or another, such as death or resignation, the personnel of Lloyd's syndicates must change from time to time and because the liability of each member is on an individual basis, such syndicates can enter into contracts only for definite and comparatively short periods. Only seven syndicates out of 270 write a small volume of short-term life assurance under a policy which provides for the payment of a certain sum in the event of the assured's dying within a year.[2]

Thirdly, there are over 100 mutual associations which have usually been formed to cover the special risks of members which arise out of some trade or occupation. They range from some plate-glass associations with annual premium income barely in excess of £1,000 to the large Protection and Indemnity Clubs formed to cover certain marine risks for shipowners which are not normally insurable in the commercial market.

Fourthly, there is a heterogeneous group of societies providing some type of insurance including over 9,000 Friendly Societies, 89 Collecting Societies and many trades unions which offer some form of benefit for their members. The distinction between friendly societies and collecting societies is based on the fact that the former are concerned with sickness assurance and the latter with industrial life assurance which brings them within the ambit of the Industrial Life Assurance Acts. So although all Friendly Societies are overseen by the Registrar of Friendly Societies, usually the two functions are performed by separate societies. Their recent history has been one of efforts, or failures, to expand the range of other types of business which they may carry on. 'Within certain limits these include ordinary life assurance, and policies for medical or institutional treatment as well as their traditional business of mutual sickness benefits. Just as in sickness insurance their main rival is the state, so in most other profitable fields the societies have to face the competition of commercial insurance companies as well as other forms of mutual associations (such as those run by many professions) not registered as Friendly Societies.'[3] In this competition the one great advantage of being registered as a friendly society—exemption from all forms of tax—is coupled with stringent regulations specifically designed to prevent them from straying too far on to ground already covered by commercial insurance companies. Until 1966 they suffered from the severe handicap that the largest sum for which they could insure a policyholder's life was £500 (plus bonuses) even if more than one policy was issued but this limit has now been raised to £2,500. Another serious obstacle in their path is that they are not allowed to merge with each other. At present only full-blooded takeovers, with one society completely absorbed by another and losing its identity, are permitted. Furthermore they are unable to convert themselves into ordinary companies without involving themselves in a web of legal complexities which make this virtually impracticable at the moment. A predictable consequence of these handicaps is that there are far too many small societies which are scarcely viable and are lacking in dynamism. It is for this reason that it is difficult to dissent from the harsh verdict of *The Economist* on the friendly society movement that 'it has seemed to have as much alacrity as a mammoth stuck in a glacier'.[4] Not surprisingly, their total premium income is 'small beer' compared with that of the insurance companies or even Lloyd's.

The insurance companies, which form the dominant sector of the insurance market, may be distinguished according to function. First, there are the composite companies which transact all the various classes of business; this category includes many of the largest companies in the industry of which all are proprietary with the exception of four mutuals. Secondly, there are the general companies which do not transact any life assurance. Thirdly, there are the specialist companies which underwrite only one class of risk such as many of the mutual associations or, in a wider sense, companies transacting insurance in only one branch, the outstanding examples of which are the specialist life companies including twenty-five mutual companies. Finally, it should be noted that only a handful of companies, 15 in 1968, transact industrial life assurance and the majority of these are composite companies although six reinsure all their general business through other companies.

In view of the dominance of the company sector it is important to look at its growth and the development of its structure in recent years. The relevant figures on growth are shown below in Table 39.

We now turn to an examination of the distribution of this total business between the various companies in the course of which we consider the degree of concentration in the company sector at various selected dates and the changing relative position of the leading companies. The simplest picture of the degree of concentration in the industry is given by examining the cumulative percentage of the total insurance in force

Table 39 (a)

ORDINARY AND INDUSTRIAL LIFE BUSINESS

(£m)

	1935	*1938*	*1955*	*1960*	*1965*	*1967*	*1968*
Premium Income[1]	161	176	493	734	1,100	1,353	1,509
Life and Annuity funds at end of year[2]	1,269	1,467	3,618	5,432	8,640	10,311	11,389

[1] Includes consideration for annuities.
[2] Includes life business of collecting societies.

Table 39 (b)

ANNUAL RATE OF GROWTH

(cumulative percentage)

	1935–38	*1938–55*	*1955–60*	*1960–65*	*1965–68*
	%	%	%	%	%
Premiums	3·0	6·3	8·3	8·4	11·1
Life and Annuity funds	4·9	5·4	8·5	9·7	9·7

Table 39 (c)

NON-LIFE BUSINESS

(£m)

	1935	*1938*	*1955*	*1960*	*1965*	*1966*	*1967*	*1968*
Premium Income[1]	107[2]	142	626	921	1,289	1,378	1,493	1,792
General Funds at end of year	118[2]	150	487	628	783	813	926	1,085

[1] Includes income from capital redemption business.
[2] Figures not directly comparable with other years.

Source: *Annual Abstract of Statistics.*

which is transacted by the top company, the top two companies, and so on. This is done in Table 40. It will be noted that up to 1953 the degree of concentration increased across the board; however, between 1963 and 1965 the increase in concentration appears to have been confined to the top two companies and to be largely attributable to the rapid growth of the Legal and General. The top company has been the same throughout, namely the Prudential, but there has been some jockeying among the companies for the next four positions as is shown in Table 41.

When we examine the distribution of the industrial assurance business between the participating companies, we find that although the total number of companies engaged in industrial life assurance is small and has remained more or less constant, a considerable degree of deconcentration has occurred. Once again the Prudential has maintained its domi-

Table 40

DISTRIBUTION OF ORDINARY LIFE ASSURANCE AMONG THE TOP COMPANIES

(by sums assured)

Rank of Companies	*Cumulative percentage of total assurance in force*				
	1937	*1948*	*1953*	*1963*	*1965*[1]
	%	%	%	%	%
Top Company	12·4	17·3	18·0	18·0	18·7
Top 2	18·5	24·1	29·2	28·9	30·4
Top 5	33·4	38·8	43·9	45·7	44·9
Top 10	48·5	54·6	59·1	62·3	58·9
Top 20	67·9	73·3	75·9	80·9	76·7

[1] Latest year for which figures are available.

Source: Board of Trade: *Summaries of Insurance Business.*

Table 41

RANKS OF LEADING COMPANIES IN GROUPS : ORDINARY LIFE AND ANNUITIES

(on basis of sums assured)

	1929	*1948*	*1953*	*1963*	*1965*
1.	Prudential	Prudential	Prudential	Prudential	Prudential
2.	Pearl	Legal & General	Legal & General	Legal & General	Legal & General
3.	Norwich Union	Sun Life	Norwich Union	Standard Life	Norwich Union
4.	Refuge	Pearl	Sun Life	Norwich Union	Standard Life
5.	Sun Life	Norwich Union	Standard Life	Sun Life	Sun Life
6.	Scottish Widows	Refuge	Pearl	Commercial Union	Pearl
7.	Commercial Union	Royal	Co-operative	Royal	Co-operative
8.	North British	Commercial Union	Royal	Pearl	Mercantile & General
9.	Royal	Scottish Widows	Scottish Widows	Scottish Widows	Guardian
10.	Legal & General	Co-operative	Commercial Union	Eagle Star	Yorkshire
11.	U.K. Temperance	Standard Life	Refuge	Co-operative	Scottish Widows
12.	Alliance	North British	Eagle Star	Guardian	Friends Provident
13.	Scottish Provident	U.K. Temperance	North British	Yorkshire	Scottish Amicable
14.	London Life	Royal Exchange	U.K. Temperance	Royal Exchange	Northern
15.	Standard Life	Britannic	Britannic	Mercantile & General	Commercial Union
16.	Eagle Star	Alliance	Alliance	Friends Provident	Equity & Law
17.	Phoenix	Scottish Provident	Scottish Provident	Northern	Royal
18.	Northern	Eagle Star	Royal London	Refuge	U.K. Provident
19.	London & Lancs.	Royal London	Royal Exchange	London Assurance	Refuge
20.	Atlas	London & Manchester	Yorkshire	Scottish Amicable	Clerical & Medical

Source: Board of Trade: *Summaries of Insurance Business.*

nant position at the top but there have been changes in the positions immediately following; perhaps the most striking aspect has been the growth of the Cooperative Insurance Society from eleventh position in 1925 to second position shortly after the end of the Second World War. Since the industrial life assurance companies are in competition with the friendly societies of which there are approximately 80 still in existence,

Table 42

DISTRIBUTION OF INDUSTRIAL LIFE ASSURANCE BUSINESS AMONG THE TOP COMPANIES

Rank of Companies	*Cumulative percentage of total sums assured*				
	1925	*1937*	*1953*	*1963*	*1968*
	%	%	%	%	%
Top 1	53·5	46·4	42·8	38·8	36·1
Top 2	66·4	59·6	57·0	54·7	57·2
Top 5	87·8	85·8	85·3	82·8	83·3
Top 10	98·3	99·1	98·6	98·2	98·2

Source: *Report of Industrial Assurance Commissioner.*

Table 43

RANK OF INDUSTRIAL ASSURANCE COMPANIES AND COLLECTING SOCIETIES IN 1968

(on basis of sums assured)

All Companies		*Major Collecting Societies*	
1. Prudential	(1)[2]	1. Liverpool Victoria	(4)
2. Co-operative	(2)	2. Royal Liver	(9)
3. Pearl	(3)	3. Scottish Legal Life	(12)
4. Royal London Mutual	(5)	4. City of Glasgow	(17)
5. Refuge	(6)	5. Aberdeen & Northern	(20)
6. Britannic	(7)	6. Tunstall & District	(21)
7. United Friendly	(8)	7. Blackburn Philanthropic	(22)
8. London & Manchester	(10)		
9. Wesleyan & General	(11)		
10. Salvation Army	(13)		
11. Standard Mutual	(14)		
12. Blackburn	(15)		
13. Reliance Mutual	(16)		
14. Pioneer[1]	(18)		
15. National Life	(19)		

[1] Taken over by Vehicle & General in 1968.
[2] Figures in brackets show the ranking for companies and societies combined.

Source: *Report of Industrial Assurance Commissioner.*

it is useful to rank companies and societies both separately and together as is done in Table 43.

In non-life business, for which premium income is a more appropriate measure of size, the picture revealed by Table 44 is one of a marked increase in the degree of concentration between the immediate post-1945 years and 1963 which is not surprising in view of the spate of mergers during the late 1950s. The apparent decrease in concentration between 1963 and 1965 is surprising but is probably explained in part by the absence of important mergers during the period (see Table 43, p. 226). It is unfortunate that we do not possess comprehensive figures for later

Table 44

DISTRIBUTION OF NON-LIFE INSURANCE AMONG THE TOP COMPANIES

(on basis of premium income)

Rank of Companies	*Cumulative percentage of premium income*			
	1929	*1948*	*1963*	*1965*
Top 1	18·0	15·6	20·7	19·7
Top 2	30·5	25·0	31·4	30·3
Top 5	48·2	40·6	53·8	52·3
Top 10	70·3	60·8	74·6	71·1
Top 20	90·3	81·5	89·3	84·7

Source: Board of Trade: *Summaries of Insurance Business.*

years but, since the rate, at which amalgamations have occurred, has accelerated once again, it would be surprising if they did not reveal a further increase in the degree of concentration. The Royal and the Commercial Union have maintained their supremacy over the last forty years but there have been considerable changes among the rankings of the companies immediately below them as is shown in Table 45.

The insurance companies, unlike Lloyd's, transact business both directly with the public or indirectly through intermediaries of which there are two main categories, namely full-time insurance brokers and part-time agents. To maintain and expand both their direct and indirect sales most companies have developed a comprehensive system of branches which is supported by a sales organisation in the field consisting of full-time, salaried inspectors whose task it is to canvass firms, members of the public, agents and brokers for business. To distinguish between the two categories of intermediaries namely agents and brokers, is not easy, although it has been suggested that the former act for the insurer while the latter act for the insured. Since, however, both are paid for their

Table 45

THE RANKS OF THE LEADING COMPANY GROUPS IN NON-LIFE BUSINESS

(on basis of premium income)

	1929	*1948*	*1963*	*1968*
1.	Royal	Royal	Royal	Royal
2.	Commercial Union	Commercial Union	Commercial Union	Commercial Union
3.	Royal Exchange	General Accident	General Accident	General Accident
4.	Employers Liability	Phoenix	Northern & Employers	Guardian Royal Exchange
5.	Phoenix	London & Lancashire	Sun Alliance	Sun Alliance & London
6.	General Accident	North British	Guardian	Eagle Star
7.	London & Lancashire	Royal Exchange	Royal Exchange	Phoenix
8.	North British & Mercantile	Employers Liability	Phoenix	Norwich Union
9.	Northern	Northern	London Assurance	Prudential
10.	Sun Office	Sun Office	Norwich Union	Co-operative
11.	Norwich Union	London Assurance	Eagle Star	Mercantile & General
12.	Alliance	Alliance	Prudential	National Employers
13.	London Assurance	Norwich Union	Co-operative	Vehicle & General
14.	Eagle Star	Prudential	Yorkshire	Legal & General
15.	Yorkshire	Yorkshire	National Employers	Friends Provident
16.	Atlas	Eagle Star	Mercantile & General	Pearl
17.	Guardian	Atlas	Provincial	United Friendly
18.	Scottish Union	Guardian	Legal & General	Refuge
19.	Prudential	Scottish Union	Pearl	Britannic
20.	Caledonian	Caledonian	Cornhill	Sun Life

Sources: For 1929, 1948, 1963 Board of Trade: *Summaries of Insurance Business.* For 1968, *The Policyholder*, September, 1969.

services by the insurer in the form of a commission, this yardstick proves not to be particularly helpful. Suffice it to describe the existing structure of the intermediary market as follows. At one end of the spectrum there are accountants, bank managers, estate agents, building societies, solicitors and others who hold agencies with one or a limited number of insurance companies with whom they place business for their clients and who can be clearly distinguished as part-time agents. At the other end of the spectrum there are the firms of Lloyd's brokers who possess the exclusive right to place business on the floor of Lloyd's and who include amongst their ranks a few with an international clientele and an annual premium income of more than £20m. Between these extremes there is a heterogeneous group of individual firms which may be roughly classified as brokers or agents according to whether the placing of insurance is their main activity or not. Not surprisingly, it is impossible to get accurate information on the relative importance of agents and brokers, although it is widely believed that currently more than 50 per cent of premium income in general insurance originates through brokers.

Since there are no legal obstacles in the way of newcomers establishing themselves as brokers in the British insurance market and, in particular, no system of licensing, it is impossible to obtain accurate information on the number of practising brokers. However, some indication may be gleaned from the membership of the various brokers' organisations, three of which have existed for some time. In December 1967 these were as follows:

Association	*Membership (Dec. 1967)* Firms	*Individuals*
Lloyd's Insurance Brokers' Association	234	—
Corporation of Insurance Brokers	1,295	3,250
Association of Insurance Brokers	725	1,500

However, some allowance has to be made for the fact that there is some overlap in the membership of these bodies and one official estimate is that there are approximately 2,000 broking firms who are members of the last two brokers' organisations. During 1967, to complicate the situation further, two new brokers' organisations were formed, namely the Federation of Insurance Brokers and the Institute of Insurance Brokers. In March 1968, the former announced that its investigations had revealed that at that time there existed in Britain over 5,200 broking firms including the 2,000 already referred to. It is equally difficult to obtain information on the range of size of broking firms, although, with the trend in recent years for major firms to seek a quotation on the Stock

Exchange, our knowledge of their scale of operations has been radically improved. It appears that at the top of the range there are some 50 firms which handle an annual premium income in excess of £10m., the largest in order of size being C. T. Bowring (market capitalisation of £38·4m.), Sedgwick Collins (£19·6m.), Price Forbes (£13·4m.) and Staplegreen Insurance (£13·2m.). Judged by market capitalisation these giants are around 10 to 20 per cent of the size of the big insurance companies and their annual premium income is in the region of £100m., some of it being derived from branches and subsidiary companies overseas. During recent years when the technological revolution has been posing particularly difficult problems for the insurance industry, the larger broking firms have shown considerable initiative in developing special new types of insurance and seeking out underwriters and companies who will underwrite them. They have also been instrumental in developing links with insurance companies through acquisition, two examples being the take-over of the Crusader Insurance Company by C. T. Bowring and Company and that of the Minster Insurance Company by Robert Bradford and Company.[5] The motive behind these steps towards vertical integration is the desire to achieve reductions in administrative costs arising from the use of computers, economies in marketing and the provision of guaranteed access to the market for insurers. Since we are now primarily concerned with the structure of the market, we shall postpone until a later chapter a discussion of the impact of the brokers on the competitive process but at this juncture it is worth noting that the entry of a large number of suburban and provincial brokers into the market in recent years has made it easier for new insurers to establish themselves without incurring the considerable expense of establishing a comprehensive branch network.

It is even more difficult to collect information on the number of part-time agents although they possess their own representative body, namely the Corporation of Insurance Agents. In 1965 this Corporation took the initiative in forming the Standing Joint Committee of Insurance Agents to act, on behalf of both the Corporation and those professional bodies whose members hold insurance agencies, in negotiations with insurers on matters of common interest. It is the Chairman of this Joint Committee to whom we are indebted for one of the few estimates of the number of part-time agents in the United Kingdom, for in 1967 he calculated that there were approximately 160,000 of them. In addition there are the so-called 'own-case agents' who have come into existence through the practice whereby any sizeable industrial or commercial firm or public authority which places its insurance directly with an insurance company may obtain an agency, either in its own name or in the name of a senior official, in order to obtain a discount equivalent to the commission normally payable to the broker or agent. A curious aspect of the intermediary market which may be noted here is that the part-time agents are paid much the same level of commission as brokers despite the fact that they make greater demands on insurers for assistance in handling transactions, especially when they merely introduce business. While part-time agents are extensively used throughout the various insurance markets, we must call attention to the distinctive position in industrial life assurance in which it is the practice of the major companies to rely mainly on full-time agents in the field to collect premiums on existing policies and to attract new business.[6] To sum up, insurers make use of a variety of different types of marketing organisations which are the result of the composition of their business and their historical evolution. Those composite companies which normally transact all types of general insurance and life assurance are found to rely on a chain of regional offices and agents for marketing their products. This does not mean that they deal exclusively through these agents for they will always accept business from brokers but they will tend to be agent-orientated. At the same time those companies which rely mainly on brokers are unlikely to have many, if indeed any, agents, although they will not be averse to a certain amount of direct selling. Thus, the majority of insurers differ only in the relative emphasis placed on the use of brokers and agents, the exception being the Lloyd's syndicates with their exclusive reliance on marketing through brokers.

The existing marketing structure of an insurer has been moulded and influenced by its early history since even the largest composite companies began life by selling mainly one type of insurance. If their initial entry was into the life assurance market towards the end of the last century, they found it desirable to maintain personal contact with the insured by establishing a network of agents and regional offices which was conveniently at hand for later penetration of the market in general insurance. On the other hand the specialist insurers of more recent origin, who have entered the industry through accident insurance in which personal contact is considered to be less important, have tended to rely on brokers rather than a network of branches and agents which would have made initial entry considerably more expensive.

Finally, we must make a brief reference to the characteristics of the consumers of the products of the insurance industry. These extend from individuals, who are the predominant purchasers of life assurance, to large private companies and public corporations with extensive property interests to protect who are the major consumers in such branches as marine insurance. The major influence on the demand for life assurance and general insurance is the level of real income with which both are positively associated. There are two principal reasons for this relationship. First, as real income per head increases consumers may be expected to allocate an increasing proportion of their expenditure to the consumption of services such as insurance. Secondly, the economic and technological progress associated with an increasing national income implies that for both individuals and firms there are larger property values to protect and new types of risk for which insurance cover is sought. Corroborative evidence of this may be found in such estimates as have been made of the income-elasticity of demand for non-life insurance in the United Kingdom, Western Europe and North America. For example, a study by the Swiss Reinsurance Corporation gives the following results for the years 1958–65.

Table 46

INCOME—ELASTICITY OF DEMAND FOR NON-LIFE INSURANCE IN SELECTED COUNTRIES

Country or Region	*Income-elasticity of demand for non-life insurance*
EFTA countries	1·48
EEC countries	1·51
U.K.	1·32
U.S.A.	1·13

Source: Swiss Reinsurance Corporation, Experiodica No. 12 (31 12 1966), Population, Gross National Product and the Insurance Industry in EFTA and EEC 1958–65 (quoted by R. L. Carter, Competition in the British Fire and Accident Insurance Market, Unpublished Ph.D. thesis of University of Sussex).

The remarkable growth in life insurance since the Second World War, which we have already noted, would also indicate that the income elasticity of demand for life insurance is almost certainly greater than one.[7] This conclusion is supported by the evidence in the following table which shows that premium income has been a growing proportion of personal income in recent years.

Moreover, if we are to judge by North American standards, there is still plenty of scope for further expansion of the insurance market since, for example, life insurance in force in Canada and the United States represents 195 per cent and 164 per cent of national income respectively as compared with 98 per cent in the United Kingdom;[8] there is no reason to believe that, when income per head in the United Kingdom reaches the existing levels in North America, a similar relationship will not obtain here.

Table 47

RELATIONSHIPS BETWEEN PERSONAL DISPOSABLE INCOME AND EXPENDITURE ON LIFE ASSURANCE IN THE U.K.

	Total Personal Disposable Income[1] *£m*	*Expenditure on Life Premiums* *£m*	*(2) as % of (1)* %
Year	*(1)*	*(2)*	*(3)*
1957	15,341	396·9	2·6
1961	19,552	532·3	2·7
1964	23,383	759·1	3·2
1967	27,559	1080·8	3·9
1968	29,304	1224.0	4.2

[1] Total personal income less taxes on income (but not additions to tax reserves) national insurance and health contributions.

Source: National Income Blue Book, 1968.

While income is a major determinant of the demand for the services of insurance, legal requirements also play a role in certain branches, especially motor insurance. For, as we have noted in Chapter 9, the motorist is compelled by the Road Traffic Act to insure himself against his legal liability for causing injury or death to third parties. Although it is in principle possible for motorists to limit their insurance to such 'Third Party Cover', the great majority in fact pay the small additional premiums necessary to provide protection against the risk of the loss of their vehicles through fire or theft. It is understood that the provision of this basic cover currently accounts for about 15 per cent of the premium income arising from the insurance of private motor vehicles in the United Kingdom and results in the demand for private motor insurance being highly price-inelastic.

Not all consumers purchase insurance cover through the market : many of the largest concerns in the United Kingdom adopt the device of self-insurance. For many years Government Departments have chosen to assume certain insurance risks themselves and more recently the National Coal Board and British Rail have followed suit. R. L. Carter in a survey of local authorities discovered that as a general rule they are tending to retain more risks and have established their own insurance funds for this purpose.[9] As private industry has become more cost-conscious in recent years, more and more of the larger companies have turned to the assumption of risk as a means of lowering the costs of insurance. As R. L. Carter has pointed out, the large firm will discover that its risks fall into three categories. First, there are those cases where so many small individual items are exposed to risk that the frequency of loss may be calculated with reasonable accuracy and the maximum amount of any individual loss is so small that adequate provision may be made by treating any losses as normal operating expenses. An obvious example is the risk of breakage to the plate glass windows of a multiple chain store. Secondly, at the other extreme there are the big risks which would have such a catastrophic effect on the firm's operations that insurance through the market is essential. Thirdly, there are the risks which lie in between these two extremes. Other things being equal, the larger the firm the more feasible it becomes to handle the risks in the third category through self-insurance.[10] For this reason the practice of employing full-time insurance specialists has been growing among large firms to such an extent that in 1964 the British propensity to spawn associations manifested itself yet again in the formation of the Association of Insurance Managers in Industry and Commerce.[11]

Some very large companies have taken the further step of forming or acquiring their own 'captive' insurance companies, an outstanding example being Unilever's ownership of the Blackfriars Insurance Company.[12] It is a solution which is only available to the giant corporation with widely diversified interests, for it alone can provide its captive insurance company with a large and well-balanced volume of high quality underwriting such as will be acceptable to the reinsurance market. If these conditions are satisfied, an efficient captive insurer may avoid the dangers inherent in the operation of self-insurance funds, such as the tendency to set aside inadequate sums to cover the risks assumed, the danger of funds being absorbed in the business so that sufficient liquid assets are not available when a large loss occurs, and the lack of proper protection against catastrophes.[13]

NOTES

1 Currently, there is a tariff agreement embracing comprehensive household insurance but recently the Fire Office Committee announced its abandonment as from 1 January 1971.

2 On 18 November 1970 Mr. Harry Mance, the Chairman of Lloyd's, revealed to a general meeting of members a scheme to promote a limited liability company to be known as Lloyd's Life Assurance. It appears that under this scheme the underwriting agents will be able to subscribe for shares in the new company out of the premium trust funds of their members but will not themselves write long-term life business.

3 *The Economist*, Insurance Supplement, July 1965, p. xxii.

4 Ibid.

5 In the case of Lloyd's such links have existed for a long time in that all Lloyd's brokers are in some way or other connected with the various underwriting syndicates.

6 Their remuneration usually consists of a salary plus commission. It has been estimated that 18 per cent of commissions are paid out to company agents in the U.K.

7 A rigorous analysis would have to distinguish between substitution and income effects.

8 *Life Insurance Fact Book*, 1969, Institute of Life Insurance (New York), p. 98.

9 R. L. Carter, 'The Insurance Practices of Local Authorities', *Local Government Chronicle*, 14 August 1965.

10 R. L. Carter, op. cit., p. 273.

11 In 1966 a member of the Council of this body estimated that approximately 300 industrial and commercial companies employed full-time insurance specialists.

12 I.C.I. operates through the Imperial Chemicals Insurance Company which has a premium income in excess of £100m. per annum.

13 See R. L. Carter, op. cit., p. 284.

Chapter 13

THE COMPETITIVE SITUATION

> 'In the private enterprise sectors of the economy, producers should be made to compete; for a main justification for private enterprise is that, because of competition, producers have every incentive to produce in the most economical manner the things which are most needed.'
>
> Professor James Meade

IN THIS chapter we shall be concerned with the competitive behaviour of the insurance market as manifested in the extent of price competition, the ease of entry and the pressure exerted on insurers by intermediaries and the ultimate purchasers. In this case as in others it is appropriate to treat life assurance separately from general insurance since there are important differences in their respective markets and the processes of price formation. As has already been noted, the bulk of life assurance with the important exception of group pension schemes is sold to individuals, while a significant segment of the demand for general insurance emanates from business organisations, some of which employ their own specialist insurance staff, and various public bodies.

An immediate consequence of this difference in the respective markets is that the degree of consumer ignorance is markedly greater in life assurance than in general insurance. This is partly because there is a bewildering variety of different products and partly because the determination of the premium involves the application of sophisticated statistical techniques. Let us first consider the question of the variety of the products. With the exception of term insurance whereby the insurer agrees to pay out a fixed sum only if the policyholder dies within a specified period, all life assurance policies are a combination of insurance and investment whereby the insurer, instead of guaranteeing payment on premature death, contracts to pay out *whenever* the policyholders die or if they *survive* for a stated number of years. Since the policyholders are therefore insured against the risk of early death and also have the certain promise of a sum of money at the end of a stipulated period, it follows that only part of the premiums, which they pay, represents the purchase of pure insurance cover, the remainder being accumulated to ensure the disbursement of the final payment. In performing their insurance function the life assurance companies and societies are unique but in their investing function they face competition from a variety of other financial intermediaries, such as investment trusts, savings banks and building societies, which also cater for the public's demand for safe channels for the investment of their savings. But their ability to offer the public an element of insurance in addition to the custody and management of savings represents a substantial advantage in their competition with other savings institutions.

Having established that an element of investment exists in the majority of life assurance contracts, we should note some other distinctions. The first is between whole life assurance and endowment assurance. Under the former type of policy the insurer contracts to pay out a fixed sum on death while under the latter the payment occurs after the lapse of a stipulated period, and it is designed primarily to provide protection against the risk of poverty in old age. In order to provide maximum protection against a serious fall in money income after retirement, policyholders frequently take the benefits accruing to them in the form of an annuity rather than in a lump sum. Old people who, either because they have no dependants or for some other reason, desire to supplement their income for the rest of their lives by living off their capital, are faced with the difficulty that they do not know how long they will live. If they optimistically assume that they have many years to live, they may consume their capital so slowly that, when in fact they die, a substantial part of it is still untouched; thus their standard of living will have been unnecessarily depressed. On the other hand, they may pessimistically underestimate their powers of survival, consume their capital too quickly and find that their declining years are unnecessarily burdened with poverty. Such problems may be overcome by purchasing an annuity from a life office which can offer its annuitants a guaranteed income for the rest of their lives considerably in excess of the interest yield on the capital surrendered. Life offices, which engage in selling endowment assurances combined with annuities, or deferred annuities as they are usually called, have to enter into contracts which last for sixty, seventy and even eighty years.

The extreme form of pure endowment assurance is not very common and the more usual practice is to sell policies which contain an element of life as well as endowment assurance. The insured's dependants are given a small measure of protection against the risk of poverty through his early death, and he himself is given a larger measure of cover against poverty in old age, though neither receive as much financial protection as they would from a purely life assurance policy in the first case and a purely endowment policy in the second. Another important distinction is between 'with-profits' and 'without-profits' policies. In the latter the insurer contracts to pay a fixed sum of money either in the event of the policyholder's death or on his attainment of a certain age, but in the former he offers to pay a certain sum plus an additional bonus the size of which will depend on the profitability and success of the insurer's operations. A modern variant of with-profits endowment policy, which came into existence about fourteen years ago, is one which is linked to unit trusts in such a way that the amount which is paid out on the expiry of the policy depends not on the profits of the insurance company but on the performance of the unit trust to which the policy is linked. In some versions the same objective is sought by the establishment of a special investment fund by the insurance company. These schemes are specially designed to appeal to policyholders who are liable to pay surtax, or at least tax at the standard rate, because they receive the same tax concessions as are available on other life assurance premiums. Sufficient has now been said to show that the possibility of combining the two elements of insurance and investment in differing proportions means that the would-be insurer is faced with a bewildering variety of different policies from which to choose. In making his choice, which must depend on individual needs and circumstances, he has to consider not only the premium or price but also the type of cover which he is being offered. A difference in the premiums charged by two separate companies may, or may not, reflect real differences in the products being offered.

Having demonstrated the heterogeneous nature of the products, we must now turn to a consideration of the determination of premiums. A distinguishing feature of life assurance policies is that in contrast to general insurance policies they last for many years during which the premium remains constant, although the risk, for which insurance cover is sought, does not. While in theory life assurance policies could be written on an annual basis, there are practical reasons why in the vast majority of contracts this is not done. The basic difficulty arises from the very elementary, but highly significant, fact that the probability of death rises with an increase in age. Consequently, a man who tried to cover himself annually would find that the cost of a given amount of insurance would rise steadily with age until in his late fifties it would become relatively very expensive. Even worse, if a sudden deterioration in his health seriously reduced his expectation of life, he would find it difficult to buy adequate cover because he would consequently be charged a very high premium. On the face of it this problem can be overcome by the insurance company offering to provide a given amount of insurance cover for a given period of years on the payment of equal annual premiums. Unfortunately, this device does not deal with the problem that the healthiest policyholders may be continually tempted by other insurance companies to transfer to them unless they can somehow be bribed to stay with the original insurance company. This can be done by withholding part of each man's insurance cover in the earlier years of the contract and restoring it in the later years, so that the insurer is getting rather too little insurance for his money to begin with and too much later on. In principle most life policies involve some retention of the current benefit, although the degree to which this is done varies according to the type of policy. An immediate consequence of this practice of postponing the payment of a portion of the current benefit is that an accumulating fund to meet future liabilities becomes an essential part of the life assurance business. In the earlier years the premium income paid by a group of policyholders will exceed current claims and expenses and the insurance fund will gradually rise to a peak until in the later years current claims plus expenses overtake premium income and there is a gradual process of decumulation until the last survivor of the original group dies. The basic nature of this process is shown in Figs. 1, 2 and 3. Figs. 1 and 2 show how premium income falls and the cost of claims rises and then falls as a result of deaths among an original group of policyholders. The direct effect of these two influences on the rate of accumulation of the insurance fund is shown in the upper graph in Fig. 3. The investment of the accumulated fund, however, provides the company with an important additional source of income, the effect of which can be observed in the lower graph of Fig. 3. The significance of such prospective interest earnings is that it enables the insurer to make some reduction in the level of premiums for the benefit of the policyholders. If the actuaries, with a mixture of skill and luck, are exactly correct in forecasting mortality rates and the average level of interest earned, the fund will just be exhausted by the payment of the claim arising from the death of the last surviving member.[1]

We have now established that the accumulation of funds in life assurance plays an essential part in the fulfilment of long-term contracts for the payment of equal annual premiums. But there is a second and more important reason. As agents and intermediaries for the collection of the public's savings, they become liable to repay the capital sums entrusted to them plus interest at some fixed date in the future. The funds, which thus accrue to them from endowment assurance premiums, are earmarked to cover future liabilities which can only be met if they are kept intact and allowed to increase at the compound rate of interest assumed at the time of the contract. Consequently, it would be entirely wrong to assume that at any time these funds were a surplus which could be drawn upon with impunity. It is possible for a life office, with an apparently large fund available, to be technically insolvent, in so far as the fund is

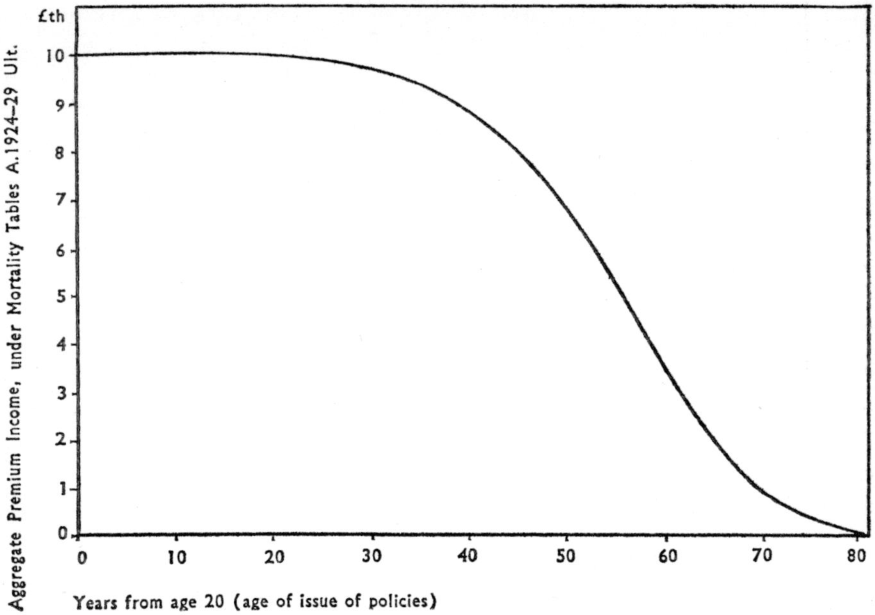

FIG. 1. *Aggregate Premium Income from a Group of 1,000 Whole Life Policies (at £10 p.a.)*

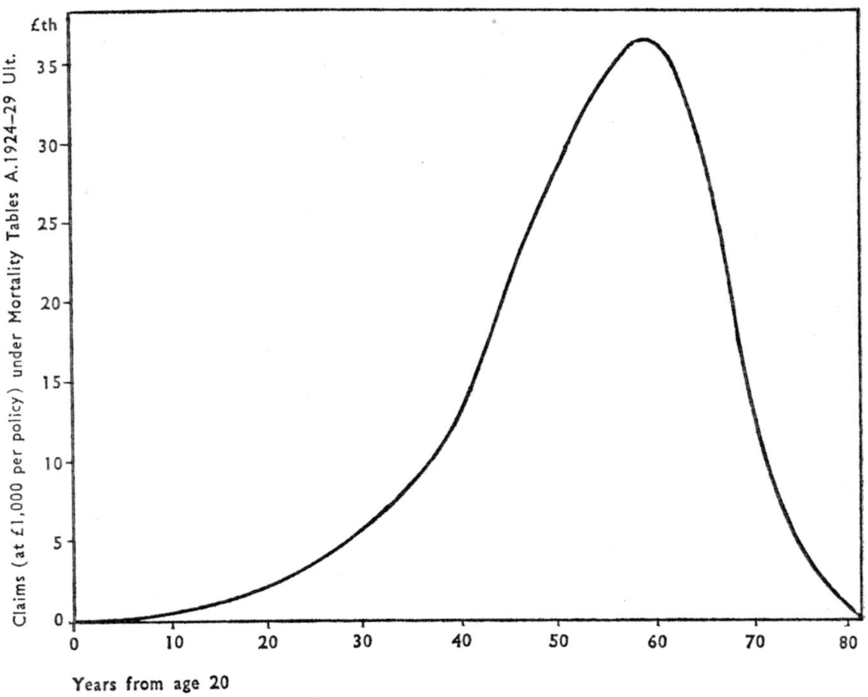

FIG. 2. *Claims under a Group of 1000 Whole Life Policies (issued at age 20)*

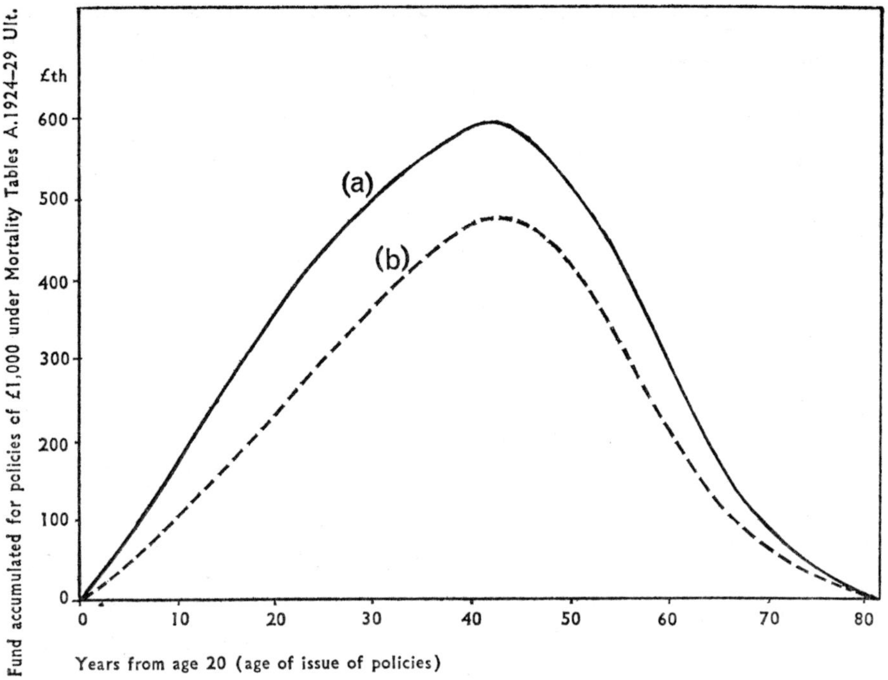

FIG. 3. *Fund Accumulated for a Group of 1,000 Whole Life Policies*

Notes: (a) Accumulation without interest: premium approx. £20 p.a.
(b) Accumulation with $2\frac{1}{2}$% interest: premium approx. £10 p.a.

less than necessary to meet future liabilities even when allowance is made for its growth at the assumed rate of interest.

This technical discussion has been necessary to establish the point that the major determinant of the price or premium of life assurance contracts is the need to accumulate a fund which is large enough to meet all future liabilities. The ultimate size of the fund depends upon two main flows, the inflow of premium income and interest earnings minus tax and the outflow of claims and expenses. The volume and time trend of claims depends upon the rate of mortality experienced by the insurer; in practice this is calculated by actuaries who use mortality-tables which take into account all the principle factors, namely age, sex, and class of life of which the rate of mortality is a function. The largest part of a life office's cost comprises items of a variable nature, the most important being those incurred in selling through agents or brokers who are paid by commission. This is a heavy charge on the first premium, for current market practice is to pay an initial commission of up to 2 per cent which is calculated in relation to the basic sum assured. Such payments to agents are only one element in the cost of selling life assurance, since in addition the companies have to defray the costs of their own sales staffs both at their head offices and in their branches who have the essential task of servicing the agents. Even when a policy is sold direct, as is the usual custom in the industrial branch, insurers will have their own sales costs to meet. In addition there are the expenses involved in paying fees to doctors for the usual medical examinations, which are incurred whether the policy is accepted or not, and the administrative costs of preparing and processing the policy documents. Finally, it is the usual practice to include some contribution to the overhead costs of the central administration. Given the calculation of the size of the outflow arising from the assumed mortality experience and expenses, the next step is to fix the rate of premium which will yield a fund large enough, after allowing for growth at a given rate of interest, to meet the estimated claims as and when they occur.

Having established the basic principles involved in the determination of premiums, we would naturally expect to find that in practice there exist a large number of different prices for the many categories of life policies available. Broadly speaking there are three major determinants of any given premium. First, it depends on whether the insured is purchasing term insurance, whole life or endowment assurance; secondly, it varies according to the age of the insured and the duration of the contract; and a third source of variation arises from the choice between a with-profits and a without-profits policy, the former being the more expensive. Even when these three factors are constant, as in the case of a man in good health taking out a 25-year endowment policy without profits at the age of 35, there is still a surprising range of different premiums charged by different insurers which appears to be caused mainly by differing assumptions about mortality, interest earnings and expenses. In seeking to explain such differences it is convenient to distinguish between *gross* premiums and *net* premiums, the basic principle for the determination of the latter being 'that the present value of the premiums must always be equivalent, at the outset, to the present value of the benefits to be provided by the insurance'.[2] Thus the level of net premiums largely depends upon expected mortality and the assumed rate of interest. Most companies have in recent years used the A 1924–29 mortality table as the basis of their calculations, but they are, of course, at liberty to vary premiums from the level indicated by this table to allow for variations in their expected mortality from the average.[3] Although such variations were surprisingly large in the past, it is understood that nowadays they are quite small.

Another important influence which causes variations in premiums is the difference in the yields which the insurers succeed in obtaining from the investment of their funds. Some evidence of this is provided in Table

48 although it must be remembered that the variation in the interest rates assumed by insurers for the purpose of calculating premiums is normally less than that in the rates earned, particularly in recent years when interest rates have been rising rapidly. A third important cause of variation arises from the different loadings added to net premiums in order to obtain the premiums actually charged. The difference between gross and net premiums represents the provision for expenses and an additional margin of reserve for contingencies. Even when due allowance has been made for these influences, the variation in premiums between insurers is substantially greater than might have been expected, as is shown below.

Table 48

GROSS YIELDS ON FUNDS FOR 39 BRITISH LIFE OFFICES (1968)

		Gross Yield %
Mutual Life Offices		
Company with highest yield:		
U.K. Provident		8·16
Company with lowest yield:		
Clerical, Medical and General		6·42
	Average	7·07
Proprietary Life Offices		
Company with highest yield:		
Sun Life		7·06
Company with lowest yield:		
General Life		6·44
	Average	7·13
Industrial-cum-Ordinary Life Offices		
Company with highest yield:		
Pearl		7·53
Company with lowest yield:		
Brittanic		6·79
	Average	7·17
Composite Offices		
Company with highest yield:		
Caledonian		7·47
Company with lowest yield:		
Yorkshire		6·67
	Average	7·08

Source: *The Economist* Insurance Supplement, July, 1969.

The comparison of premiums for with-profits policies is a much more precarious exercise since insurers adopt the practice of loading the premiums with an additional payment to earn the profit for eventual distribution. Since this surcharge, designed to provide the with-profits bonuses, varies considerably, it follows that policyholders would be mistaken in choosing policies on the basis of current level of bonuses declared, for a large bonus may simply be the result of a comparatively large initial bonus loading.

It would have been an extremely onerous task to assemble all the information necessary to undertake a comparison of existing premiums for the different types of policy and much beyond the capacity of the present writer. Fortunately, the Consumers' Association have in recent years carried out an exhaustive survey the results of which were published in their supplement to *Which* on Life Insurance. Their main conclusion is that policyholders in general receive somewhat less for their money than they could for two main reasons. First, they exhibit a widespread cautious preference for the types of policy which place greater emphasis on the element of insurance than of investment. Secondly, they seem to be woefully unaware of the vast differences in the value for money which they could obtain if they made their choice of policies more rationally.

On the first point the following tables show the percentage of total *ordinary life* sums assured accounted for by specific types of policy.

Table 49

DISTRIBUTION OF TYPES OF POLICY IN ORDINARY LIFE

	Whole Life		*Endowment*		*Others*	
Year	*with profits* %	*without profits* %	*with profits* %	*without profits* %	*with profits* %	*without profits* %
1937	18·5	9·7	47·1	9·9	1·8	12·9
1948	11·6	8·9	47·2	13·7	2·2	16·4
1954	9·7	7·5	38·4	20·9	2·1	21·5
1958	9·9	7·2	34·4	20·9	2·7	25·2
1960	9·0	6·4	31·7	19·9	2·5	30·4
1961	8·4	5·9	31·6	18·9	2·7	32·5
1962	8·4	5·9	30·7	17·0	3·1	35·0
1963	8·2	5·8	29·8	15·5	3·3	37·4
1964	8·3	5·9	29·5	14·5	3·2	38·5
1965	8·4	5·8	29·3	12·1	3·0	41·4
1966	8·3	5·6	27·8	11·6	3·2	43·5
1967	8·5	5·7	27·2	10·4	3·1	45·0
1968	8·2	5·7	25·5	9·1	3·3	48·3

Source: Annual Abstract of Statistics.

Table 50

DISTRIBUTION OF ALL POLICIES IN ORDINARY LIFE

	Ordinary Life	
	without profits	*with profits*
Year	%	%
1937	32·5	61·4
1948	39·0	61·0
1954	49·9	50·2
1958	53·3	47·0
1960	56·7	43·2
1961	57·3	42·7
1962	57·9	42·2
1963	58·7	41·3
1964	58·9	41·0
1965	59·3	40·7
1966	60·7	39·3
1967	61·1	38·9
1968	63·0	37·0

Source: Annual Abstract of Statistics.

Table 51 gives the rate of growth of sums assured in the two categories for recent periods in ordinary life assurance.

There is reason to believe that the tables above do not give an accurate picture of the changing preferences of policyholders over time. The 'Other' Group accounts for a considerable proportion of the sums assured

Table 51

RATES OF GROWTH OF WITH-PROFITS AND WITHOUT-PROFITS IN ORDINARY LIFE

(Sums Assured)

		Years	
Type of Policy	*1937–48*	*1948–56*	*1956–68*
	%	%	%
With Profits	34·5	63·4	265·3
Without Profits	78·2	179·8	468·6

Source: Annual Abstract of Statistics.

in the 'without-profits' category which is not entirely surprising since it includes, first, a considerable volume of 'schemes' business which has generally been written on a without-profits basis, and, secondly, term assurance much of which provides large sums assured for comparatively small premiums. Table 52 overcomes this problem by concentrating on whole-life and endowment policies.

Table 52

RATE OF GROWTH OF WITH-PROFITS AND WITHOUT-PROFITS ASSURED (ORDINARY LIFE) PER CENT, WHOLE LIFE AND ENDOWMENT POLICIES ONLY

Type of Policy	*Years* 1937–48	1945–56	1956–68
	%	%	%
With Profits	33	61	250
Without Profits	71	170	138

Source: *Annual Abstract of Statistics.*

Nevertheless, the general impression remains that 'we remain a cautious bunch in these islands, not easily seduced by the cult of equities and bounding property values despite a generation of continuous inflation'.[4]

As far as the problem of the value of money provided by the policies of different companies is concerned, the Consumers' Association undertook a number of investigations which involved the analysis of the policies of some 90 to 100 companies selling ordinary life assurance. The tables below are derived from this analysis and purport to show the best and

Table 53

I. TERM INSURANCE

Ranking	*Level Term Sum Assured for man aged:*		*Convertible Term. Sum assured for man aged:*		*Decreasing Term Sum assured at outset for man aged:*		*Family Income Benefit Annual Income for man aged:*	
	25	*45*	*25*	*45*	*25*	*45*	*25*	*45*
	£	£	£	£	£	£	£	£
Best	37,377	6,023	32,432	5,738[4]	63,878	12,114	4,720	913
Worst	10,900[1]	3,870[2]	12,370[3]	3,615	21,423	7,531	1,660	517
Difference	26,447	2,153	20,062	2,123	42,455	4,583	3,060	396

The policy conditions to which the above figures refer are premiums of £5 per month for a 20 year term.

Source: *Which,* Supplement on Life Insurance, September 1967.

[1] Logomia (for members of NALGO and their families). The next lowest figure is £14,844.

[2] Logomia. The next lowest figure is £4,340.

[3] Medical Sickness (for Doctors and Dentists). The next lowest figure is £13,775.

[4] Convertible for first fifteen years only.

Table 54

II. WHOLE LIFE POLICIES

Ranking	*Without profits* Policy held until death. Man aged: 25	45	*Policy held until death. Man aged 45* Estimated sum at death	Guaranteed sum assured	*With profits* Estimated surrender value after 10 years	*Policy held until death. Man aged 45* Estimated sum at death	Guaranteed sum assured
	£	£	£	£	£	£	£
Best	6,676	2,780	12,373	5,166	587	3,887	2,273
Worst	3,500	1,800	5,022	1,504[1]	297	2,266	1,023
Difference	3,176	980	7,351	3,662	290	1,621	1,250

All the above policies require the payment of a premium of £5 per month.

[1] Double bonus policy.

Source: *Which*, Supplement on Life Insurance, September, 1967.

Table 55

III. ENDOWMENT INSURANCE

Ranking	*Without Profits* *Policy held to maturity* *Man aged:* 25	45	*With Profits* *Policy held to maturity* *Man aged:* 35	*Estimated surrender value after 10 years*	*Death after ten years* *Estimated sum payable*	*Guaranteed sum insured*	*Past Performance 1952–67 Approx. sum*
	£	£	£	£	£	£	£
Best	1,591	1,459	2,073	710	1,579	1,430	1,386[1]
Worst	1,250	1,100	1,446	487	1,217[1]	740[1]	954
Difference	341	359	627	223	362	690	432

The above policies are for premiums of £5 per month for a 20 year term.

[1] Double bonus policy.

Source: *Which*, Supplement on Life Insurance, September, 1967.

worst terms available from various types of policies. In some cases the best (or worst) terms are offered by companies catering only for special groups such as nurses or local government officers. Where this is the case, the next best (or worst) alternative has been used. The survey comprised all British and foreign companies writing ordinary life assurance in the U.K.

It should be noted with regard to Table 53 and the subsequent ones that if the policyholder required much less insurance and for which he would pay a much smaller premium than in the examples shown (such as a £4,000 decreasing term insurance to cover a house mortgage), the rank order of the companies is unlikely to be the same and the differences between them would not be anything like as great.[5]

Table 55 purports to show the amount of insurance which could be bought by men aged 25 and 45 seeking without-profit policies and men aged 35 seeking with-profits policies, assuming that they wanted a 20-year term and paid premiums of £5 per month. There are obvious difficulties in attempting to make fair comparisons of with-profits policies since

Table 56

BEST AND WORST PERFORMANCES

Amounts paid out on life policies of annual premium of £50, taken out by a man aged 29.

Year	*Whole Life Assurance* £	*Spread* £	*Endowment Assurance* £	*Spread* £
1950	4,292–3,042	1,250	1,988–1,654	334
1955	4,436–3,228	1,208	1,942–1,680	262
1960	4,892–3,332	1,560	2,238–1,652	586
1965	5,263–3,463	1,800	2,364–1,655	709
1970	7,489–3,661	3,828	3,183–1,899	1,284

In the case of whole life assurance it is assumed that the policy was taken out in 1930 on a with-profits basis by a man who died in 1970.
In the case of endowment assurance it is assumed that the policy was taken out in 1945 and matured in 1970.

Source: *The Economist,* Insurance Supplement, July 18, 1970, p. xxiv.

ideally one needs to be able to predict future rates of bonus. The calculations by *Which* are based on the assumption that existing interim rates of bonus will remain unchanged in the future for the sake of convenience in computation and that the policyholder has an average expectation of life (48 years for a man aged 25 and 29 years for a man aged 45). As an additional check, the writers of *Which* examined the past performance of with-profits endowment policies by estimating the final sum obtained in 1967 for a 15 year endowment policy taken out in 1952 by a man aged 35 for a premium of £5 a month.

The *Which* results may be compared with a similar investigation carried out by *The Economist* for earlier periods, see Table 56.

If a purchase price of £2,500 is assumed, the percentage return shown below is the rate quoted by the various companies in the investigation.

Table 57

IV. IMMEDIATE ANNUITIES: PERCENTAGE RATES OF RETURN

	Annuity bought for £2,500 by man aged:		
Ranking	*50*	*65*	*75*
	%	%	%
Best	8·2[1]	11·7[2]	17·3[3]
Worst	7·1	10·4	15·4
Difference	1·1	1·3	1·9

[1] Royal National Pension Fund for Nurses. The next best was 8·1%.
[2] The next best was 11·5%
[3] The next best was 16·9%.

Source: *Which*, October, 1967.

For purposes of comparison it is convenient to convert the above rates of return into the amount of money received per annum as is done in Table 58.

A diagrammatic illustration of the range of variations in premiums for 68 companies incorporated in the U.K. is given in the histograms shown in Figs. 4, 5, 6 and 7.

The figures quoted in the various tables reveal a situation in which by any standards there are such remarkable divergencies in market prices that it is surprising that competitive forces have not driven down the more highly-priced policies. The probable explanation of the persistence

Table 58

IMMEDIATE ANNUITIES: MONEY RATES OF RETURN

	Annuity bought by a man aged:								
Ranking		*50*			*65*			*75*	
	£	s.	d.	£	s.	d.	£	s.	d.
Best	205	0	0[1]	292	10	0[1]	432	10	0
Worst	177	10	0	260	0	0	385	0	0
Difference	27	10	0	32	10	0	47	0	0

[1] Royal National Pension Fund for Nurses.

Source: *Which*, October, 1967.

Premiums charged by 68 U.K. companies per £1,000 assured for without profits whole life policy for man aged 30

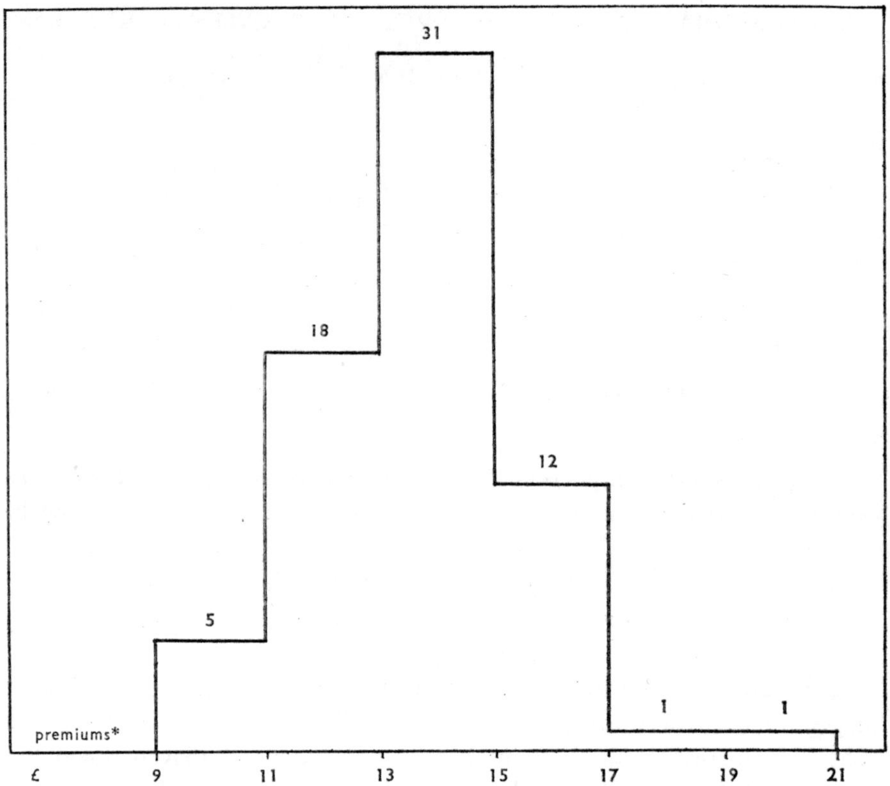

Source: *Stone and Cox Life Assurance Tables, 1969*

FIG. 4. *Whole Life without Profits, 68 companies (incorporated in U.K.)*

Premiums charged by 68 U.K. companies per £1,000 assured for 20-year endowment policies (without profits) for man aged 30

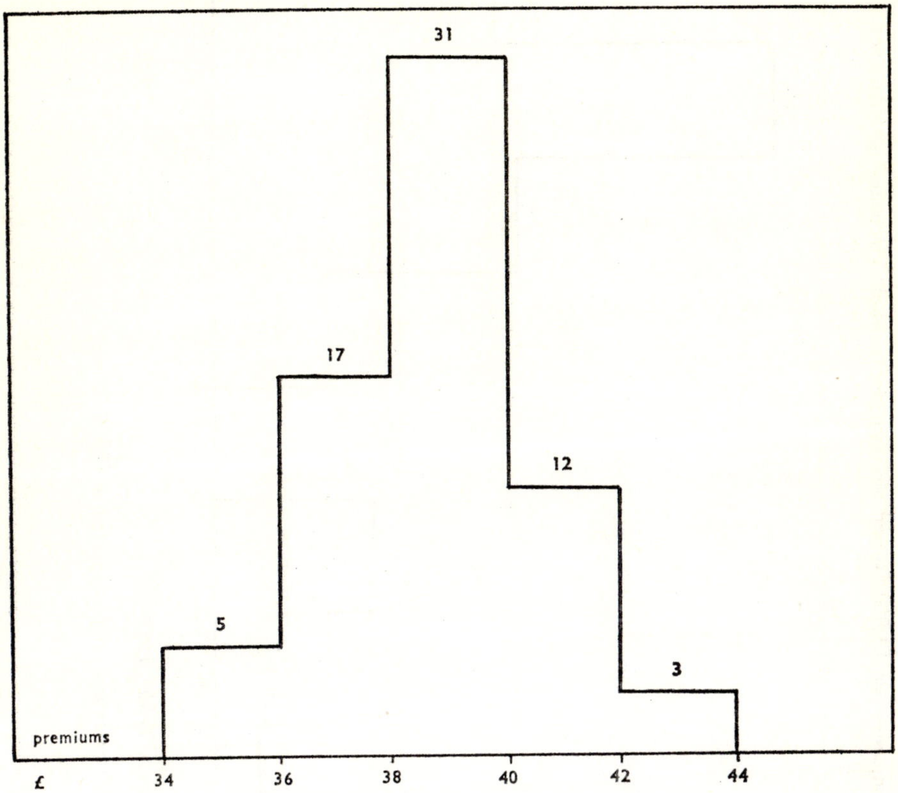

Source: Stone and Cox Life Assurance Tables, 1969

FIG. 5. *20-year Endowment without Profits, 68 companies (incorporated in U.K.)*

Premiums charged by 80 U.K. companies per £1,000 assured for with profits, whole life policy for man aged 30

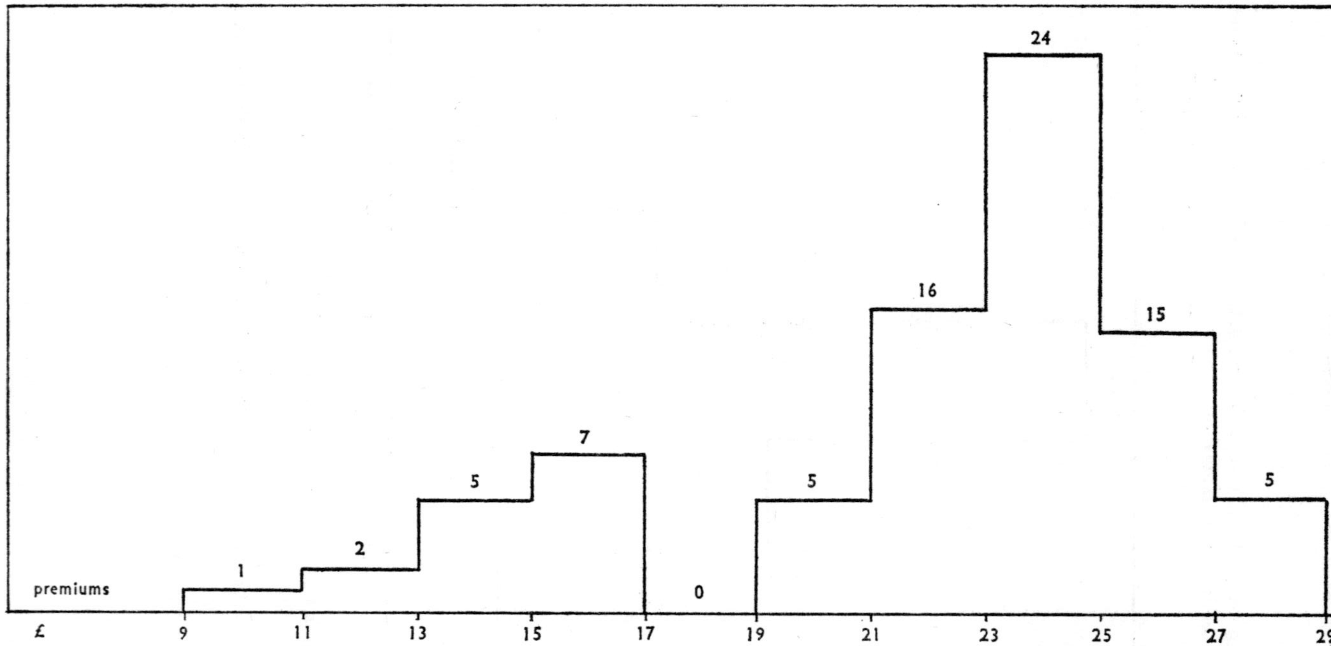

Source: *Stone and Cox Life Assurance Tables, 1969*

FIG. 6. ***Whole Life with Profits, 80 companies (incorporated in U.K.)***

Premiums charged by 80 U.K. companies per £1,000 assured for 20-year endowment policies (without profits) for man aged 30

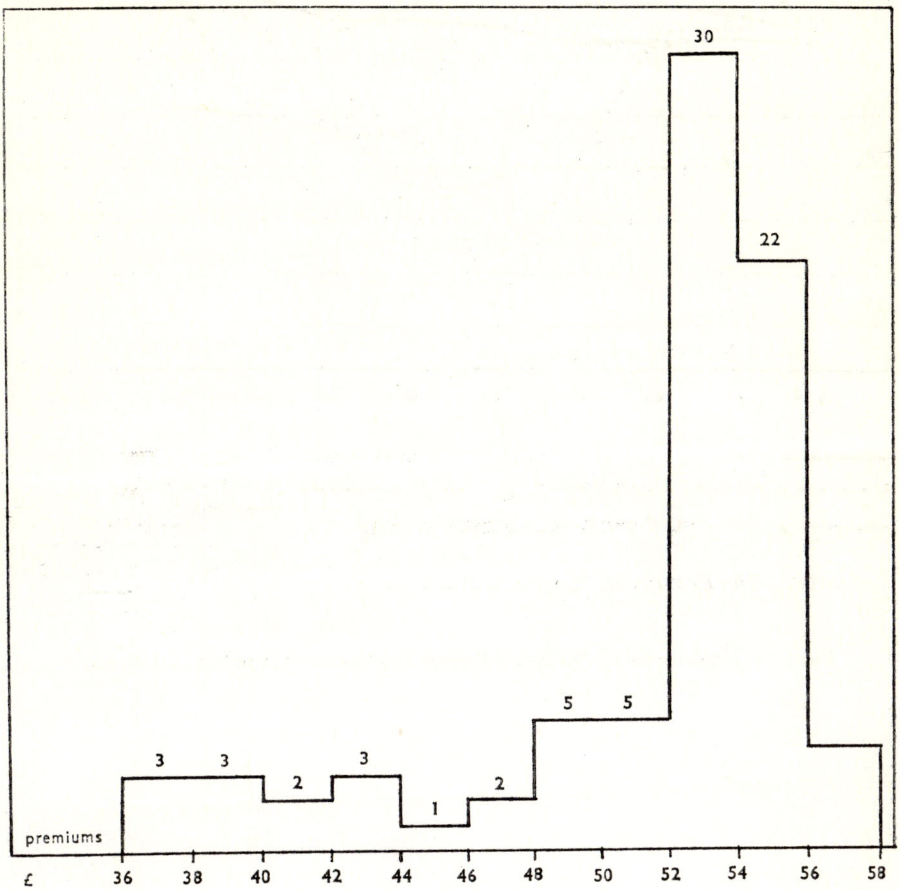

Source: *Stone and Cox Life Assurance Tables, 1969*

FIG. 7. *20-year Endowment with Profits, 80 companies (incorporated in U.K.)*

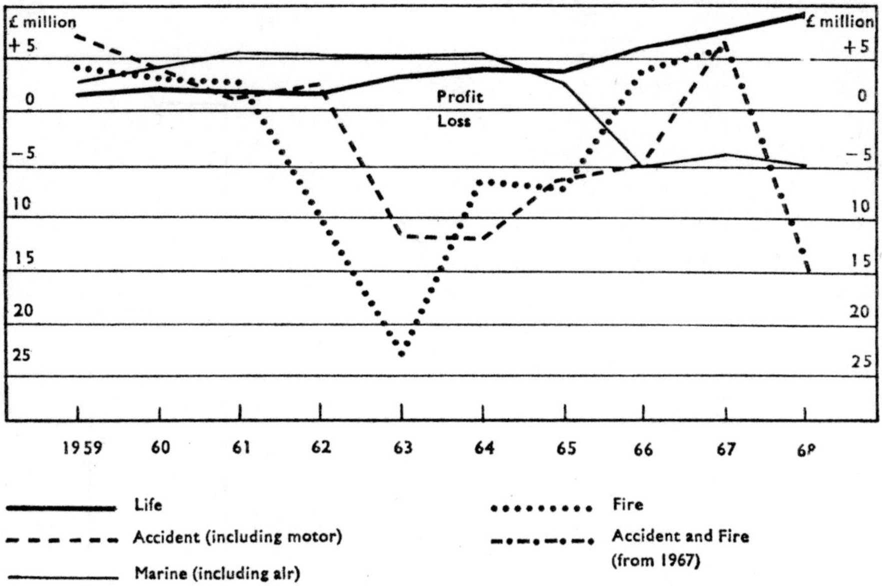

Source: *The Economist,* Surveys of Insurance

FIG. 8. *Underwriting Profits of British Insurance Companies, 1956–1968*

of such discrepancies is that the market for life assurance is very imperfect for reasons which are derived from the demand side and from the structure of the intermediary market. It would appear that the vast majority of policyholders are woefully ignorant of the prices of the different products and make very little effort to 'shop around'. Admittedly, this is not easy, given the existing methods of selling through agents and brokers who derive their fees from the insurers and not the public. It is not surprising that the *Which* supplement offers the following advice to the consumer: 'Although insurance brokers, solicitors, bank managers and others will offer you advice about which of the hundred or more companies to choose, you may not find it easy to judge when such advice is truly expert and independent, and when it is not. So what you need is comprehensive comparative information about the value-for-money of different companies—either as a direct guide on which companies to get quotations from, or as a check on any recommendations made to you by insurance brokers or otherwise.'[6]

It is not without significance that some of the companies with the most competitive prices pursue a policy of not paying commissions while others pay a smaller commission than the average. Furthermore, since the sale of whole-life and endowment policies usually offers the prospect of considerably higher commissions than term assurance, the risk that particular policies and particular companies may be recommended to clients for the wrong reasons is considerable. If our conclusions about the degree of imperfection in the life assurance market and the causes of it are correct, greater competition can only be ensured by methods designed both to improve consumers' knowledge through the efforts of bodies like the Consumers' Association and to reform the organisation of the intermediary market. In concluding this discussion of pricing in life insurance it should be observed that while all our evidence has been drawn from ordinary life assurance, *prima facie* there is reason to believe that the competitive situation in industrial life assurance is no better especially since consumer ignorance is probably greater in that market and a larger proportion of policies are sold through agents employed by one company.

In general insurance the problem of price formation is very different mainly because the contracts are short-term, usually for a year or less, with the result that the sale of current policies does not mean incurring liabilities which will not have to be met for many years. Like life assurance companies, general insurance companies have accumulated funds but, whereas in the former they play an essential part in the fulfilment of the contract, in the latter they are in the nature of a safeguard in order to meet exceptional variations in the incidence of claims. These general funds may be thought of as being composed of two parts, one being unexpired premiums and the other the reserve fund. The size of the fund arising from the accumulation of unexpired premiums depends on the regularity with which the insured make their payments. If, for example, an insurance company arranges for its policyholders to pay their premiums at the beginning of each quarter and if losses occur at regular intervals throughout the year, the fund in hand would fluctuate between three-eighths $[(\frac{1}{4} \times \frac{3}{4}) + (\frac{1}{4} \times \frac{1}{2}) + (\frac{1}{4} \times \frac{1}{4})]$ of the annual premium income immediately before the receipts of the quarter's premiums, and five-eighths $[(\frac{1}{4} \times 1) + (\frac{1}{4} \times \frac{3}{4}) + (\frac{1}{4} \times \frac{1}{2}) + (\frac{1}{4} \times \frac{1}{4})]$ immediately after. If this staggering of payments were carried further and put on a daily basis, the insurer would always have approximately one-half of the annual premiums at his disposal. Although such an arrangement would ensure that funds would be available to meet variations in the incidence of claims throughout the year, it might not be enough to meet exceptional catastrophic losses on a scale large enough to bring about insolvency. Hence common prudence suggests the need to build up a special contingency or reserve fund.

The typical insurance company which offers cover against such heterogeneous risks as fire, burglary, injury and loss of goods in transit is essentially organised in this way. Where it is a limited company, the shareholders' capital after the provision of the necessary premises and equipment is invested to earn as high a yield as possible compatible with the function of providing a reserve to cover the main insurance operations. Premiums, which are usually paid on an annual basis, are fixed at a level sufficient to cover expected claims plus expenses and to yield a margin of profit the size of which will be determined by competition. Shareholders' dividends are derived from this margin of profit, from the interest earned on the investible portion of the unexpired half of the premium income, and from interest earned on the reserve fund. However, in practice companies may incur a loss on their underwriting operations without being forced to dip into their reserve funds provided that the deficiency is covered by interest earnings. In fact this has frequently been the position of the major British general insurance companies, for in the eight years from 1962 to 1969 inclusive only once did they achieve a profit on their underwriting operations.[7]

Having established that the investment fund has a different function in general insurance, we can now turn to the factors determining the level of premiums. Broadly speaking, general insurers pursue a full cost pricing approach given by the following equation:

$$\text{Premium} = \text{Claims} + \text{Commission} + \text{Expenses} + \text{Surplus}$$

Table 59

RESULTS OF 9 MAJOR INSURANCE COMPANIES[1]

£mm.

	1962	*1963*	*1964*	*1965*	*1966*	*1967*	*1968*	*1969*
Non-life premiums	838·3	887·7	963·8	1,042·8	1,110·5	1,206·6	1,392·6	1,499·3
Underwriting profits from:								
Fire Business	−10·0	−23·2	−6·0	−7·0	3·4	5·3	−13·4 (Fire and Accident combined)	−36·0 (Fire and Accident combined)
Accident Business	2·3	−11·9	−12·1	−6·3	−4·8	6·2		
Marine Business	5·0	4·9	4·8	1·9	−4·3	−3·2	−4·7	1·4
Total underwriting profits	−2·7	−30·2	−13·3	−11·4	−5·7	8·3	−18·1	−34·6
Net interest income	36·5	38·1	41·0	69·1	73·0	80·5	90·3	103·2

Source: *The Economist*, Insurance Supplement, July, 1970, p. x.

[1] Companies are Commercial Union, Eagle Star, General Accident, Guardian Royal Exchange, Norwich Union, Phoenix, Prudential, Royal, Sun Alliance and London.

It can be seen that the premiums determined by this equation are essentially dependent upon two variables, the estimation of claims arising from the losses likely to be incurred, and expenses, since both the commission and the surplus, or profit margin, are expressed as proportions of the premium. In defining premiums and claims, however, we have to allow for the practice of reinsurance. Net premiums are equal to gross direct premiums less premiums on reinsurance ceded *plus* premiums on reinsurance accepted, whilst claims are equal to claims paid and outstanding less claims payable by reinsurers *plus* claims payable on reinsurance accepted. The latter is the major item on the right-hand side of the equation and typically accounts for between 55 and 65 per cent of a general insurer's total costs. The prediction of losses is more difficult than in life assurance because it is less easy to achieve accurate measurements of probability through the application of the law of large numbers. Obviously, the larger the volume of underwriting, the less the uncertainty but, as is well known, even the largest British general insurance companies have had their calculations plunged into disarray through particular catastrophes. In practice, the volume of claims arising from a particular year's trading is usually not finally determined until two years have elapsed, particularly in the case of marine insurance. The next most important component is selling costs which, including commission and other allowances to agents, typically account for between 15 and 21 per cent of total costs. Thus, the variable costs arising from these two sources amount to 80 per cent or more of total costs. The remainder of expenses consists of administrative costs such as maintaining policy records, collecting loss statistics and preparing accounts. It should be noted here that in principle there exist potential economies of scale which might be expected to influence price determination. First, the sales expenses of a large established company are likely to be lower than for a small company, especially one which is trying to enlarge its share of the market. Goodwill is an important asset in that the well-known reputable company with established local connections with brokers has a built-in advantage in attracting new business. Hence one would expect that the small company must devote proportionately more effort and expense to attracting new business and extending its sales organisation. In practice, as we shall see, new entrants have attempted, with some success, to overcome this disadvantage by avoiding the expense of establishing large networks of branches and dealing through brokers whose interest has been stimulated by the offer of higher commissions. Secondly, the larger company is able to take advantage of technical economies arising from the use of accounting machines and computers and economies derived from the use of highly specialised staff. Thirdly, the larger the company, the larger the

Table 60

UNDERWRITING PROFIT AND LOSS OF BRITISH COMPANIES
£'000

	1948	*1950*	*1956*	*1957*	*1958*	*1959*	*1960*	*1961*	*1962*	*1963*	*1964*	*1965*	*1966*	*1967*	*1968*
FIRE	9,801	16,907	4,627	3,832	7,683	4,937	7,335	5,309	−8,963	−21,673	−5,257	−5,734	4,896	7,624	−4,035
Motor	−233	16,131	−11,997	−10,600	−9,408	−1,441	−4,053	−4,909	−5,811	−15,755	−18,684	−11,944	−8,908	113	−9,568
Personal Accident	946	1,084	1,538	870	1,085	1,690	1,629	1,189	920	98	1,118	1,482	1,715	2,063	n.a.
Miscellaneous Accident	7,410	8,033	9,855	9,365	9,196	11,428	8,939	9,223	11,306	4,741	9,026	8,572	5,978	6,081	n.a.
TOTAL 'ACCIDENT'	8,123	25,248	−604	−365	+873	11,677	6,515	5,503	6,415	−10,916	−8,540	−1,890	−1,215	8,257	n.a.
MARINE[1] [2]	+3,664	+4,826	+5,180	+4,367	+2,750	+3,019	+4,929	+6,875	+7,570	+7,453	+6,610	+669	−6,729	9,352	−9,884
LIFE[3]	+3,299	3,455	6,739	5,508	4,600	7,720	6,077	6,979	11,739	10,865	9,316	15,099	13,243	11,220	n.a.

[1] Transfers to or from profit and loss.
[2] including aviation where companies report marine and aviation together
[3] see below:

Source: (*a*) Fire and Accident: *Post Magazine and Insurance Monitor.*
The figures above are for direct business that is exclusive of reinsurance companies.
(*b*) Marine: *The Policyholder.*
(*c*) Life: *Annual Abstract.*
The figures above are for the sum of (1) shareholders' surplus and transfers to profit and loss account from ordinary life business; (2) shareholders' surplus from industrial life business

number of risks which it can retain for its own account. Not only is it able to accept a larger share of good risks but also to reduce relative costs because the expenses of handling an individual risk do not necessarily increase in proportion to premiums, for certain administrative costs remain virtually the same whatever the premium. Moreover, a larger company has less need to rely on the reinsurance market because with its greater size its own retentions of larger individual risks can be increased in the expectation that a larger volume of business will produce more stable claims costs. To sum up, the general insurer has to determine its price policy in the light of three attributes of its costs, first, the element of uncertainty in the magnitude of the major component, claims, which tends to diminish with size; secondly, the high proportion of variable costs; and thirdly, the existence of economies of scale. In theory, if a general insurer can identify the better risks within the broad classes of premium rates to which most of its competitors adhere, then it should be possible to fix lower premium rates and attract a considerable volume of business. But in practice it would appear that the average economies of scale are regarded as insufficient to bring about any dramatic reductions in costs for an established company, and the size distribution of existing companies is such that a company intent on increasing its share of the market by premium reductions would 'trigger off' retaliatory price-cutting by companies of equal or larger size to prevent any substantial change in market shares. The case for avoiding price competition is strongly reinforced by the element of uncertainty concerning the probable volume of claims when changing social, economic and industrial conditions can, and do, significantly upset trends in losses. Such uncertainty induces in insurers a reluctance to pursue the objective of maximum profits by price-competition and a preference for a less risky existence at normal, or a little above, normal profits. Moreover, the early history of the industry has given practical demonstrations of the dangers of price-cutting with the frequent bankruptcies of insurers, especially during the second half of the 19th century when over 300 companies foundered. Not surprisingly, the propensity to combine and to eliminate the risks of price competition has always been a powerful influence in general insurance, particularly in the fire and accident branches. We now turn to an examination of the effect of tariff agreements, in these two branches, which is justified, first, on the grounds that together they form the major source of general premium income and, secondly, because they provide a contrast in that the major tariff agreement in accident insurance, the motor one, has collapsed whereas in fire insurance it survives.

A tariff in motor insurance was first introduced during the early years of this century when a collective agreement was thought to be necessary in order to protect both the companies and the public from the dangers of excessive price-cutting and consequential company failures. It was controlled by the Accident Offices Association, which was founded in 1906,[8] and was adhered to by the vast majority of insurance companies for many years. But from the middle 1950s when the tariff companies controlled two-thirds of the market there was a steady decline in their market share until 1968 when it had fallen as low as 30 per cent. With the share of the Lloyd's syndicates in the market more or less constant at about 15 per cent, this meant that the non-tariff companies had moved into a dominant position and had almost doubled their premium income during the 1960s. Nevertheless it is true to say that up to the moment when the tariff agreement eventually collapsed, the tariff companies acted as price leaders.

Although the actual procedure of the Accident Offices Association was shrouded in secrecy, it would appear that they took as their starting point the collection of statistics on losses from their members and then made an allowance for expenses, based on the experience of the average company. However, before the premium rate was finally fixed, a surcharge was added for profits; but the probable income from the investment of funds to cover unexpired risks and outstanding claims was apparently not taken into account. An element of flexibility was introduced by fixing the basic premiums with regard to seven regions, seven engine sizes and three classes of user and providing machinery for the review of rates in individual cases.[9] The Association, having fixed the minimum premiums for the various classes, also laid down the permissible 'no claim discounts' to be offered to policyholders. It also controlled closely the type of cover provided by their members and even laid down the actual wording to be adopted in the clauses of the contract.

On the other hand, the non-tariff insurers were completely free to fix their own premium rates and provide as much, or as little, cover as they chose. In practice they seem to have adopted the policy of basing their premiums on those of the tariff companies with a standard reduction of between 5 and 10 per cent. This had the advantage of overcoming the problem of obtaining reliable statistics on losses, since an insurer needs a very large underwriting portfolio before his own experience of losses can provide a reliable guide. Evidence that the non-tariff companies treated the tariff companies as price leaders is provided by the way in which tariff changes were introduced in 1966. In July of that year the A.O.A. announced changes both in the basic premiums and the size of 'no claim discounts' which had the effect of almost eliminating the existing price advantages of the non-tariff insurers, who, however, immediately retaliated by improving their own rates and discounts. With regard to cover, the non-tariff companies appear to have attempted to improve their claims experience by limiting their liability, although in view of the wide range of policies available it is difficult to make a valid generalisation.

However, the Consumers' Association, when it surveyed motor insurance in 1966, found support for the A.O.A's claim that their members were concerned with providing the public with reasonable cover for it concluded that, while there was not a great deal of difference between the cover offered by the tariff and the best non-tariff companies, the policies of the tariff companies were in general the best.[10] It also found that, when service was judged by the speed with which claims were settled, the tariff companies consistently showed up in a better light than either Lloyd's syndicates or the non-tariff companies. To sum up, the market situation could be described as one in which the tariff companies were selling a high quality product at a fixed price in competition with a cheaper one of widely varying quality. From the point of view of the public interest, it can be argued that the motor tariff system was damaging because, in so far as the expense loading used in fixing the tariff was not based on the lowest-cost company, it fostered inefficiency since it impeded the expansion of the larger lower cost companies which were prevented from exploiting their economies of scale. On the other hand it was beneficial in that it imposed high standards of quality on all participating companies, although it may at the same time have inhibited innovation through the slowness of the A.O.A. in adapting policies to meet changes in the social and legal environment.

In October 1968 ten of the largest tariff companies requested the A.O.A. to consider the case for the abandonment of the tariff agreement and this move heralded its collapse. A major cause of this fundamental change in the market's competitive structure was the poor underwriting results in recent years as shown in Table 13 and Chart 1. (More up to date figures for nine major companies have been given in Table 12.)

Of course, these figures refer to world-wide business and it is, unfortunately, difficult to obtain accurate figures on domestic motor insurance, but it is widely believed that the overall profit ratio on domestic underwriting during the 1960s has been on average a little under 1 per cent. Certainly, the industry was so much concerned about the lack of profitability in motor underwriting that the British Insurance Association took the initiative in commissioning McKinsey & Company, the management consultants, to carry out an investigation and recommend a programme of action for improving profit rates. Their report, which was published in May 1965 was based on a thorough analysis of the industry's operations and concluded that fundamental reforms were essential, especially in the measurement of risks and price-determination.

By implication it constituted a highly critical evaluation of the industry's performance, for it made recommendations for improvements in almost every aspect of the business from underwriting methods to the efficiency of management and the ways of remunerating their intermediaries. There were five basic recommendations. First, the British Insurance Association should establish a unit to collect and collate statistics on losses and claims; secondly, drivers, rather than cars, should be the basis of rating; thirdly, insurers should increase their efforts to control the costs of repairs and to influence the design of vehicles; fourthly, the 'no claims discount' should be abolished; and, fifthly, commissions should reflect more accurately work actually undertaken.

The tariff changes implemented in 1966 by the A.O.A., to which we have already referred, were the first concrete results of the Report and incorporated some of its recommendations. First, a group rating approach for fixing premiums was adopted in that the factors taken into account in measuring risk were the characteristics of a particular vehicle such as speed and acceleration and the cost of repairs. Secondly, the A.O.A. recommended selective increases in premiums, especially for drivers with bad claims experience and for those under 25 whom McKinsey had discovered were responsible for 27 per cent of all claims. But the more radical proposals such as the abolition of the 'knock-for-knock' agreements for claims above £100 and of the 'no claims discount' were ignored. In the case of the latter they moved in the opposite direction to that recommended by increasing the scale of no claims discounts for the very significant reason that in this matter they felt particularly vulnerable to the competition of the non-tariff companies.

The McKinsey Report can be said to have played a part in the eventual breakdown of the agreement in that it called into question the whole basis of rating hitherto applied by the A.O.A.; but it was not the major factor, which was surely the competitive threat from the non-tariff companies. Their success could be attributed mainly to their ability to exploit the deficiencies of the tariff agreement in not making a sufficiently sharp distinction between the risks of insuring good and bad drivers. Thus, they were able to direct their marketing efforts to seducing the drivers who were 'good risks' from the tariff companies, by the attraction of lower premiums, and excluding 'bad risks' through the imposition of larger compulsory excess payments on young or inexperienced drivers. So successful was this policy that, although they charged lower prices and paid higher commissions, they were still able to make greater underwriting profits because their proportion of claims through losses was substantially lower, and to make serious inroads on the market share of the tariff companies.[11]

Not surprisingly, the more efficient tariff companies became increasingly restive at their inability to retaliate because they were tied to a minimum price agreement which reflected the average costs of all members including the less efficient. This is an inherent weakness of any collective price agreement, which cannot be eliminated, but even so the tariff agreement might have survived had the A.O.A. been much more flexible and speedy in implementing changes. As *The Economist* commented, 'it, (the tariff structure) has come increasingly to resemble the Maginot Line—formidable but inflexible and progressively more irrelevant to the real problems'.[12] Through the need to convince the 'sleepers' of the need for any change, there was a long delay before reforms considered desirable by the 'thrusters', were implemented. There was not only the problem of the time-lag in adopting measures to meet the competition of the non-tariff companies, but also the lack of stimulus to innovation in that the members had very little incentive to produce new ideas which, if accepted, would immediately be available to all members. The freedom of non-tariff companies to innovate was dramatically illustrated in 1968 by the introduction of the 'Alpha' and the 'D.C. Plan' which used revolutionary methods for fixing premiums based on careful statistical analysis of past losses.[13] As the established tariff companies pondered ways and means of countering this new threat of further selective attacks on their markets, the more dynamic ones realised that there was little hope of making an adequate response if they had to work through the A.O.A. Moreover, the larger groupings, which had resulted from the mergers of Guardian and Royal Exchange and the Commercial Union and Northern and Employers in 1968, felt that they were now sufficiently large to dispense with what had once been the greatest advantage of membership of A.O.A., namely, access to adequate loss statistics. Thus, the tariff structure finally collapsed having succumbed to the increasing threat of selective competition.

It is obviously premature to make a realistic assessment of the competitive structure which has emerged since then because the situation is extremely fluid. But one thing is certain : it has ushered in an era of innovation and experimentation with profound effects on the entire range of the industry's activities. In the first place, the more dynamic of the ex-tariff companies have taken full advantage of their new freedom, to devise special schemes which are primarily designed to win back the high quality business lost to the more successful non-tariff companies prior to 1968 by selective appeals to certain sections of the market. Their strategy is to use the inducement of low premiums to entice back a sufficiently large number of these good risks in order to improve the balance of their underwriting portfolios. Consequently, there has been a plethora of special plans such as Royal's 'Economy Policy', Prudential's 'Top Driver Policy', Guardian's 'Red and Blue Plans', and Royal Exchange's 'Diploma' which have the common feature of embodying restrictions designed to discourage the young or inexperienced driver, particularly those with bad accident records, and the owners of sports cars. The inducements to the good drivers have taken the form of price-cuts, which had the effect of making their premiums between 5 and 10 per cent lower than the average premiums of the old non-tariff companies; and an improvement in benefits such as more liberal medical and legal expenses. An essential prerequisite for this attack on the high quality section of the market was the identification of good risks by more careful and sophisticated analysis of loss statistics and a consequential reassessment of the criteria used in determining premiums. Inevitably, since the collapse of the tariff agreement deprived insurers of the benefit of easy access to the statistics provided by members of the A.O.A., they have had to fall back mainly on their own resources. However, the British Insurance Association has made an attempt partially to fill the gap by using a computer to collect and analyse statistical information for distribution to its members, although its sources are for technical reasons limited to the largest companies. Despite the difficulties of acquiring adequate statistical data there is no doubt that insurers are showing commendable enterprise and ingenuity in devising more rational methods of risk assessment.

Generally speaking, the larger ex-tariff companies have been responsible for the innovations while the others have been content to make minor changes such as the provision of increased 'no claims discounts' and wider cover. At the same time the former non-tariff companies, who had so successfully enlarged their share of high quality underwriting, have not deemed it necessary to defend their share of the market against this onslaught by radical changes in the price and nature of their products. However, Bradford-Pennine is an exception in that it introduced a new policy on 1 January 1969, which placed greater emphasis on the age and experience of the driver.

The second important consequence of the collapse of the tariff agreement has been a revolution in methods of marketing with special emphasis on direct selling to the consumer and the elimination of intermediaries. Here we can detect the influence of the McKinsey Report which, in recommending a review of the methods for remunerating intermediaries, called attention to the danger of duplication of administrative work. The most extreme example of direct selling is that of Midland, Northern and Scottish which employed nationwide advertising to market its 'Alpha' policy.[14] Although the ex-tariff companies have not gone so far in this direction, some have adopted the practice of selling directly to their customers through retail shops, such as the arrangement made by the Royal with Selfridge's, and have mounted extensive advertising campaigns making extensive use of 'brand' names to launch their new-style policies.

The basic philosophy behind the strategy of the ex-tariff companies who have been making most of the running appears to be that lower premiums are compatible with profitable underwriting providing that costs can be lowered by reducing claims and expenses. It is a strategy which relies heavily on the assumption that the 'good risks' driver is sufficiently price-conscious—an assumption which would appear to have some justification when it is recalled with what ease some of the new 'cut-rate' insurers such as Fire, Auto and Marine were able to acquire a substantial underwriting portfolio. While the subsequent failure of some of these companies may have made the public wary of cheap motor insurance, this is much less likely to be the case when the companies concerned are household names such as the Royal, the Royal Exchange and the Guardian. But, even if the pricing policy is successful in attracting more high quality business, it does not follow that the consequential reduction in claims will be sufficient to outweigh the increase in other expenses which the new marketing policy demands. While the technique of direct selling has the advantage of eliminating the cost of commissions, it requires substantial backing through national advertising which has in some cases involved a sharp increase in selling costs. Moreover the policy of direct selling has the disadvantage that it may so alienate the brokers that business is lost in that section of the market which remains broker-orientated, especially as the plethora of new schemes has made it difficult for them to keep abreast with developments. The prospect of achieving an adequate reduction in costs has been rendered even more improbable by the continuing rise in the costs of repair and the imposition of Selective Employment Tax. Consequently, the argument of some brokers that the insurers are attempting to market their products at uneconomic prices would seem to be justified and the newly-acquired freedom from the restrictions of the tariff agreement, while it may have stimulated innovation and improved the methods of risk assessment, has done nothing to put motor underwriting on a more profitable basis. It may well be that some of the large ex-tariff companies have deliberately chosen to attract back the 'good-risks' drivers on temporarily uneconomic terms in the hope that their allegiance can still be retained when the inevitable revision of rates takes place.[15] However that may be, it is obvious that the collapse of the tariff agreement had led to the kind of price war the avoidance of which was its original *raison d'être*, and the consequential adverse effects on profitability and the future capacity of the industry are not in the long-term interests of the consumers whatever the short-term benefits may be.

Since many of the criticisms of the motor tariff apply with equal force to that operated by the Fire Offices Committee which was formed a hundred years ago, it is unnecessary to discuss the effect on the competitive situation in such detail. Like the A.O.A. the Fire Offices Committee has always regarded its main task to be that of fixing minimum premium rates and to this end they employ approximately 650 different classes which they consider enable them to discriminate fairly between risks. Moreover, although class rating is taken as a guide to the degree of exposure to a given risk, each individual risk is subject to differential rating within the class according to its physical features. This is a more flexible method of rating and in so far as, first, the physical features selected for rate adjustments do have a bearing on the risk with no important features omitted and, secondly, the modifications to rates are an accurate reflection of the expectation of losses, this form of rating is an improvement on class rating. Although the Committee's methods of procedure are wrapped in secrecy, it would appear that risks are classified according to industry or trade such as retail shops, engineering plants, boot and shoe factories, etc. Although there have been revisions to individual tariffs in the light of modern industrial developments, in general they tend to reflect Britain's pre-war industrial structure and do not sufficiently take into account the special features of the major modern industries such as chemicals, plastics, synthetic fibres and rubber, so that an important sector of the industrial market does not come under the tariff agreement. The F.O.C. also addresses itself to the task of standardising policy conditions, fixing rates of commission and determining discounts for installing sprinklers and other appliances for protection against fire. It also coordinates the tariff offices' relations with non-tariff offices and the rest of the market and in particular operates a restrictive practice which is currently being examined as part of an investigation into the supply of fire insurance in the U.K. by the Monopolies Commission. This is known as the 65/35 rule whereby the tariff offices insist that they collectively should be allowed to take at least 65 per cent of any large risk which the market is required to cover, or none of it. Originally, the F.O.C. operated on a world-wide scale, along with the Royal Navy and the Colonial Office with foreign insurers participating, where appropriate, as associate members. These golden days have passed with the development of local markets abroad.[16]

Competition from non-tariff insurers has never been as severe as in motor insurance since for many years the tariff companies controlled more than 90 per cent of the market as measured by premium income.

But in the late 1950s and early 1960s it became more intense, especially for the larger risks, as the non-tariff companies greatly increased their capacity, and the tariff companies' share fell below 90 per cent.

Table 61

COMPANY FIRE PREMIUMS

	1928 Premiums £'000	%	*1963* Premiums £'000	%	*1967* Premiums £'000	%
Tariff Companies	57,192	95·0	267,255	85·0	469,308	81·6
Non-tariff Companies	2,863	4·8	41,825	13·3	95,653	16·6
Mutual Companies	159	0·2	5,495	1·7	10,584	1·8
Total	60,214	100·0	314,575	100·0	575,545	100·0

Source: Insurance Directory and Year Book.

Note: There is reason to believe that these figures overstate the tariff companies' share in the market for, first, they include overseas business and, secondly, they exclude Lloyd's syndicates.

This intensified competition produced a flood of applications to the F.O.C. for special discounts for insurances of exceptional importance and the shortage of capacity threatened to undermine the attempts to enforce rigid adherence to the 65/35 rule. Such was the position in 1963 when losses on fire underwriting reached the disastrous figure of £21,673,000 which was a salutary antidote to traditional complacency. To be fair, however, insurance companies had already become uncomfortably aware that the inexorable rise in losses through fire was due to a radical change in circumstances and that the increase in wastage consisted almost entirely of fires in industrial and commercial premises which involved total damage in excess of £10,000 in each case. Tables 62 and 63 indicate the nature of the problem.

The main causes of this rapid rise in the cost of damage through fire appear to be the following: First, there is a trend towards heavier concentrations of increasingly valuable goods in the very large unpartitioned areas of modern factories and warehouses, which with the use of highly combustible materials like plastics, greatly increases the risk of fire; secondly, there is evidence of growing public carelessness; thirdly, higher standards of living imply the use of more electrical goods and electrical machinery with a consequential increase in the risk of fire through faulty wiring; fourthly, the criminal offence of arson is becoming much more prevalent.

Whatever the causes, the alarming increase in losses and the disastrous

Table 62

ESTIMATED FIRE LOSSES IN THE U.K.

Year	*Amount* £mm.
1950	19·6
1955	27·6
1958	24·1
1959	44·2
1960	43·8
1961	37·5
1962	55·6
1963	66·4
1964	76·7
1965	75·1
1966	82·3
1967	90·0
1968	100·0
1969	120·0

Source: *Insurance Directory and Year Book.*

Table 63

5-YEAR TOTAL OF ESTIMATED LARGE FIRE LOSSES 1961–66

Industry Group:	£mm.
Textiles	21·6
Engineering and Electrical Goods	19·1
Chemical and Allied Industries	13·1
Distributive Trades—retail	11·6
Distributive Trades—Wholesale	10·5
Paper, printing and publishing	10·4
Miscellaneous manufacturing	8·9
Distributive trades—others	6·6

Source: *Economist Insurance Supplements.*

underwriting results convinced the insurance companies that the structure of their fire premium rates gave firms little or no incentive to incur expenditure in reducing fire risks. Accordingly in 1963 a comprehensive overhaul of the structure of premiums was set in train while as an interim step a 15 per cent surcharge was imposed on premiums for commercial and industrial property. Rates for houses and flats were left alone but those for business property were increased substantially in 1964 and likewise again in 1966, making premiums on average about 30 per cent more expensive. These changes have ushered in both a new era of co-operation embracing all insurers and a contraction of market capacity as insurers have reviewed their underwriting policies and reinsurance arrangements. Consequently, the F.O.C. now claim that the threat of non-tariff competition is no longer serious and special discounts are rarely granted.

The current position in the fire insurance market is that for industrial and commercial risks price competition is firmly controlled through a collective tariff structure, whereas as from the end of 1970 the household tariff has been abandoned. It has collapsed for reasons similar to those which led to the demise of the motor tariff, since it has proved deficient in two main respects. First, it has proved to be unwieldy and inflexible in meeting the challenge of changing circumstances and, secondly, collective action has not been forthcoming where it ought to have been in reforming the remuneration of agents and brokers. Table 64, which is now solely of historical interest, gives some comparisons for 1969, when the tariff was still in force, between the rates charged by the tariff companies for comprehensive house and contents policies, including protection against fire, and those of some non-tariff competitors. Despite this evidence of considerable disparities in market prices, the overall position appears to have been one of price-leadership by the tariff companies whose rates were broadly accepted by the rest of the market as a

Table 64

HOUSE AND BUILDINGS AND CONTENTS INSURANCE

Company	*Minimum Rate for each £100 of cover* *Buildings*		*Contents*		*Total cost of £6,000 buildings, £2,000 contents excesses deleted, no discounts*		
	s.	*d.*	*s.*	*d.*	*£*	*s.*	*d.*
Tariff Companies	2	6	5	0	16	10	0
Lloyds	1	9	4	0	11	5	0
Central Heating Policy	1	3	3	6	9	5	0
Co-operative	2	0	4	0	13	15	0
Cornhill	2	3	4	6	13	15	0
Trident	1	6	5	0	11	10	0
Vehicle & General	2	0	4	0	10	0	0

Source: *Money Which,* December, 1969, pp. 144, 145.

standard of reference. Since conditions were different from those existing in the motor market prior to the abandonment of the tariff, it does not seem likely that there will be a similar outbreak of price-cutting. The future of the industrial and commercial tariff, which obviously is under scrutiny, is a much more controversial matter and will clearly not be decided until the Monopolies Commission makes its report. Suffice it to say that there is a much stronger case for its retention, albeit in a modified form, as is discussed in Chapter 17 (p. 362).

The degree of competition in any market is a function not only of the strength of competitive forces among existing sellers but also of the potential threat of competition from new entrants. Consequently, we have to take into account the ease with which new insurers can enter the market by considering the nature and severity of the obstacles in their path, but let us first consider the facts on entry as shown below, which on the face of it would suggest that entry has been reasonably easy. There are a variety of motives which may induce a prospective entrant to take the plunge and enter an industry. First, he may be attracted by evidence that existing firms are earning above normal profits; secondly, he may conclude after examining an industry's performance that most established firms are operating inefficiently; thirdly, he may have developed either a different product for which he is convinced there will be a large demand or improved methods of production or distribution which should enable him to operate at lower than average costs.

Table 65

NEW COMPANIES REGISTERED FOR THE TRANSACTION OF INSURANCE BUSINESS IN GREAT BRITAIN REGULATED BY THE INSURANCE COMPANIES ACT, 1958

Year	*British*	*Foreign*	*Total*
1957	—	4	4
1958	5	8	13
1959	3	2	5
1960	6	8	14
1961	6	6	12
1962	9	9	18
1963	16	15	31
1964	19	7	26
1965	17	4	21
1966	23	4	27
1967	13	4	17

Source: Board of Trade.

While the first may possibly have influenced entrants to life assurance in recent years, it certainly cannot have been an important inducement in most branches of general insurance. Much more potent attractions were the prospects of taking advantage of the industry's inefficient and inflexible pricing and marketing policies which provided scope for enterprising innovations.

In economic literature the obstacles to entry are defined as those factors which create advantages for established sellers over potential entrants to the market. The first important obstacle to be considered is the legal requirement under the Companies Act 1967 whereby an insurance company must have a minimum paid up capital of £100,000 before it receives the authorisation of the Board of Trade. However, this 100 per cent increase in the capital requirement which was stimulated by the failures of Fire, Auto and Marine, and Irish American, remains a relatively low barrier in comparison with the initial capital requirements of many manufacturing and extractive industries.

The second barrier to entry arises from economies of scale which, if they are large, may render it extremely difficult for a new entrant to gain a foothold in the market by undercutting established sellers. There are formidable statistical difficulties in making meaningful inter-firm cost comparisons, which are discussed at greater length in the next chapter, but the evidence for what it is worth suggests that, while in life assurance there exists a significant relation between size and expenses, in general insurance economies of scale are not particularly great. Since one of the difficulties in estimating expense ratios from aggregate data is the possibility that the premium income and expenses of several large firms may introduce a bias into the results, the figures in Table 66 which

Table 66

EXPENSE RATIOS AND SIZE OF COMPANY, 1963
ORDINARY LIFE

Size of Company (measured by premium income in £m.)	*£5m. and over*	*Between £5m. and £10m.*	*Less than £0·5m.*
Average Expenses Ratio %	13·5%	15·9%	25%

Source: Board of Trade.

are based on a sample of 30 companies attempt to take this into account. Johnston and Murphy in an earlier study[17] also found that, after allowing for the influence of new business and participation in group pension schemes, there remained a significant relation between size and expenses, the expense ratio declining on the average with the size of company. On the other hand, the impression of increasing efficiency with size is not so clear in general business, as is shown in Table 67 which gives the figures for fire and accident business for a sample of 62 companies in 1963. In fact, the correlation between the log of premiums and the expense ratio is—0·1831 which is insignificant at the 5 per cent level. R. L. Carter in a more detailed analysis of fire and accident business between 1962 and 1964 also concluded that the scale curve is fairly shallow and for composite companies with extensive branch networks economies of scale may

Table 67

EXPENSE RATIOS OF 62 COMPANIES
IN FIRE AND ACCIDENT 1963

Size of Company (measured by premium income £m.)	*Over £9m.*	*£9m. to £0·6m.*	*Below £0·6m.*
Expense Ratios	35·2%	35·6%	39·0%

Source: Board of Trade.

exceed 5 per cent, but not more than 10 per cent, of premium income. (See Table 68.)

We may tentatively conclude that, while economies of scale in life business may have acted as a deterrent to new entrants, they were not sufficiently great to have constituted a serious obstacle in general business.

A third barrier to entry to the general insurance market arises from accessibility to the reinsurance market where the over-riding consideration in fixing the rate of commission or premium for any class of reinsurance is the direct insurer's past claims experience. Since by definition the new insurer cannot provide such information and there is always the danger that it will tend to underwrite a badly balanced portfolio, the reinsurer has every inducement to load the premium rate for excess losses to compensate for the greater uncertainty. On the other hand, once the reinsurer relies on the acquisition of new business for expansion, competition for such new business to some extent restrains this tendency to load rates for newcomers. Sometimes, in the hope of establishing long-term profitable connections, reinsurers are prepared to nurse a new insurance company through its early difficult years, provided that it will respond by not seeking the lowest reinsurance premiums at each renewal as many have tended to do in recent years. Furthermore, an insurer, who is unable to obtain satisfaction on the London Market, is always free to seek reinsurance cover abroad. Thus far we have been considering new entrants as firms who are entirely new to insurance business but there is a type of entrant to the market whose position in relation to reinsurance would be as favourable as that of an established British company of comparable size. This is the overseas insurance company which on entering the British market could extend its existing reinsurance arrangements, in which British insurers could conceivably already be interested, to embrace its new area of operations. With the backing of its overseas business it

Table 68

COMBINED COMMISSION/EXPENSE RATIOS OF BRITISH COMPANIES: THREE YEARS' AVERAGE 1962–1964

		Tariff Companies			*Non-Tariff Companies*			*All Companies*		
	Premium Income	*No. of Co's.*	*Average of Expense Ratios*	*Standard Deviation*	*No. of Co's.*	*Average Expense Ratios*	*Standard Deviation*	*No. of Co's.*	*Average Expense Ratios*	*Standard Deviation*
FIRE	Fire Premiums									
	under £1m.	7	39·4	3·84	18	43·3	11·33	25	42·6	10·04
	£1m.—£10m.	5	48·0	3·0	5	41·9	3·11	10	45·3	1·61
	£10m.—£50m.	8	45·6	1·81	1	41·1	—	9	45·1	2·21
	over £50m.	1	44·7	—	—	—	—	1	44·7	—
ACCIDENT	Accident Premiums									
	under £1m.	7	34·4	8·33	10	34·7	6·62	17	34·5	7·38
	£1m.—£10m.	4	37·8	2·34	10	35·5	4·13	14	36·2	2·82
	£10m.—£50m.	8	37·7	1·67	2	32·5	1·75	10	36·6	2·68
	over £50m.	3	35·1	1·43	1	32·1	—	4	34·4	1·79
MOTOR	Motor Premiums									
	under £1m.	5	33·8	7·52	7	38·1	11·99	12	36·3	11·0
	£1m.—£10m.	4	34·5	1·45	9	34·5	4·05	13	34·5	3·47
	£10m.—£50m.	8	35·9	0·8	2	31·8	1·78	10	35·1	1·97
	over £50m.	3	34·3	1·85	1	30·7	—	4	33·4	2·22

Source: R. L. Carter, op cit., p. 56.

Note: The terms 'tariff' and 'non-tariff' were a valid basis for differentiating between companies at this time but now are rapidly becoming obsolete.

would probably enjoy even better terms than a small established British company.

Finally, we must consider what have been the two most serious barriers to new entrants in the past, namely the advantages of established sellers in differentiating their products and the organisation of the intermediary market. The observed preference for established insurers, perhaps less marked nowadays, may be attributed mainly to the intangible nature of a product the quality of which can be assessed only to a small degree at the moment of sale. Consequently, easy access to the insurer tends to be highly valued by some members of the public and in this respect the large established insurers with their network of branch offices and agents possess a considerable advantage over new companies. The result is that new companies must frequently be prepared to incur higher selling and advertising costs and to charge lower premiums but even this is not a simple matter because the suspicion of cheap insurance in an era when several new companies have failed is such that it may be difficult to discover the correct strategy.

With regard to the organisation of the market, on the one hand, the innate conservatism of many brokers yields an advantage to established insurers, but on the other hand the substantial increase in the number of provincial brokers in recent years has provided new companies with the opportunity of obtaining national representation without the burden of incurring the heavy costs of establishing a large number of local branches and appointing part-time agents. Certainly, some of the more thrustful of the new companies have succeeded in making serious inroads into the ex-tariff companies' share of the motor accident market by relying on provincial brokers. Thus, it would appear that the organisation of the market has been of declining significance as a barrier to entry during the 1960s.

Of course, potential competition does not arise solely from the entry of new companies, but also from the creation of new Lloyd's syndicates, which presents fewer problems. An application to form a new syndicate must be made to the Committee of Lloyd's which would have to satisfy itself about the qualities and the experience of the persons in charge of underwriting and, more significantly, to be informed of the number of underwriting members who would be prepared to join it. This latter requirement is sufficient to debar an application for membership from someone who simultaneously wished to form and run a new syndicate without previous experience of Lloyd's because few, if any, members would be prepared to risk entrusting their capital to a totally inexperienced syndicate. But, if permission is granted, a new syndicate is in a more fortunate position than a new company for, from the outset, it shares the reputation of the whole Lloyd's market so far as the insuring public is concerned. Even in its relationship with Lloyd's brokers, who are its sole source of business, the new syndicate has an advantage as compared with a new company in its relationship with brokers in general because one or more Lloyd's broking firms are frequently involved directly, or indirectly, in the syndicate's formation and, in any event, its underwriter will be well-known and will have established connections on the Lloyd's market. Thus the only significant barrier to the entry of a new syndicate is the capital requirement which Lloyd's lays down for new underwriting members.

In forming conclusions about the conditions of entry it is important to emphasise that new entrants to the insurance market are not a homogeneous group and the initial disabilities, from which they are likely to suffer, differ between Lloyd's syndicates and companies and even between British and foreign companies. Moreover, differences will arise depending on the range of business which the new entrant proposes to underwrite; for example, a new entrant who offers a comprehensive service by underwriting all classes of risk may gain acceptance from the intermediaries more readily than say, a specialist motor company. In general, however, the conditions of entry to the British insurance market in recent years have been such that newcomers have suffered from certain disadvantages which neither in theory nor in practice have proved to be a serious deterrent.

Let us now turn to a consideration of the potential influence of the countervailing power of buyers on the competitive situation. *A priori* one would expect countervailing power to be of a greater significance in the general insurance market than in that for life assurance, for whereas in the former the buyers range from individuals whose insurance needs can be covered for a premium of a few pounds a year to large companies who spend more than £200,000 per annum on insurance, the typical purchaser of life assurance is the single individual who is not in a strong bargaining position. A possible exception arises in the case of companies who operate their pension schemes through insurance companies and can offer new long-term business on a sufficient scale to make a significant difference to an insurer's premium income, although the tendency for the largest companies to administer their own pension funds obviously reduces the impact of such countervailing power.

In general insurance evidence of the exercise of some countervailing power is easier to find. For example, certain trade and professional associations and many major industrial and commercial firms have been able to secure special terms and discounts for their members and employees respectively and in July 1967 the Automobile Association announced plans to provide cheaper motor insurance for its members by forming its own insurance company with a Lloyd's syndicate acting as underwriter. Again, retailers who have collaborated in forming wholesale organisations to combat the threat of competition from super-markets, have as a by-product been able to negotiate collectively with insurers for special schemes. However, it is among larger buyers that the exercise of countervailing power is most clearly seen for the scale of annual expenditure on insurance by the major industrial companies and public authorities is such that they have both the incentive and the bargaining power to secure reductions in premiums. As we have already noted, many large organisations employ their own insurance specialists who have the knowledge and expertise necessary for effective bargaining. This was clearly demonstrated in 1965 when the F.O.C. introduced differential commissions and many of the large companies employing insurance specialists were able to obtain the highest commissions which were originally intended only for approved brokers. Moreover, during the discussion of the causes of underwriting losses in recent years it has frequently been asserted that the inadequate rates being charged for large risks, particularly in fire, were the result of pressure from large buyers.

We must also consider the exercise of countervailing power by intermediaries, particularly brokers, which is a matter of considerable controversy in the industry. On the one hand, the insurers allege that pressure from brokers has led to uneconomic price-cutting from time to time; on the other hand, the brokers vehemently argue that it is not in their own interests to force down premiums below an economic level since the profitability of broking is dependent on securing a high rate of renewals in order to offset the considerable expense of obtaining new business. If this were to be secured by a policy of forcing down premiums, the insurers would announce a substantial increase in premiums at the earliest opportunity thus persuading the insured to take their business elsewhere. Not surprisingly, it is extremely difficult to get firm evidence on the effect of brokers' pressure but it is clear that at times they do foster reductions in premiums and succeed in keeping them at a lower level than they otherwise would be, particularly for individual general insurance where the buyer's bargaining power is weak. 'But there is less reason to believe that brokers are solely responsible for forcing rates down to uneconomic levels; before a lower rate can be obtained, an insurer must either have made the offer or be prepared to agree to the broker's request. Also so long as the public takes differences in premiums into account in comparing policies, there will be both new and established insurers willing to use price competition and brokers will give them business.'[18]

In conclusion, in life assurance there are few serious structural obstacles to blunt the impact of competitive forces but such is the degree of consumer ignorance and inertia that big disparities in premiums are a persistent feature of the market. In general insurance, tariff agreements have in the past had an inhibiting effect on competition and efficiency but as they begin to crumble the major risk appears to be excessive price competition with deleterious effects on profitability and the future capacity of the industry.

NOTES

1 For a more detailed explanation see G. Clayton and W. T. Osborn, *Insurance Company Investment*, George Allen & Unwin, 1965, Ch. 3.

2 H. E. Raynes, *Principles of British Insurance*, p. 85.

3 J. Johnston and G. W. Murphy, 'The Growth of Life Assurance in the U.K. since 1880', *Proceedings of Manchester Statistical Society*, 1956–57, p. 40.

4 See *The Economist*, Insurance Supplement, 24–30 July 1965, p. xxii.

5 *Which*, Supplement on Life Insurance, September 1967, p. 25.

6 *Which*, Supplement on Life Insurance, September 1967, p. 20.

7 For a more detailed discussion of these problems see G. Clayton and W. T. Osborn, op. cit., pp. 37–43.

8 The tariffs in several types of accident insurance such as personal accident and sickness have never been under the control of the Accident Offices Association.

9 It has been variously estimated that the Accident Offices Association used to deal with almost 1,000 applications per annum for special ratings.

10 See *Which*, January 1966, p. 13, where evidence is provided that the policies of four non-tariff companies and one Lloyd's syndicate were subject to serious restrictions especially with regard to liability for passengers' injuries.

11 The spectacular growth of the Cornhill Insurance Company and Vehicle and General in recent years is testimony to the success of a policy of selectivity.

12 *The Economist*, Insurance Supplement, July 1968, p. x.

13 The Alpha scheme was introduced by the Midland, Northern and Scottish Co. which based the premium solely on the age of the policyholder; the D.C. Plan was an innovation by General Accident with cover confined to the policyholder and his spouse.

14 In February 1970 it was ordered by the Board of Trade to cease selling new policies but it was later allowed to resume normal trading. However, in November 1970 it went into liquidation.

15 Early in 1970 several major companies announced substantial increases in their rates. Later in the year most companies gave advanced warnings of further increases in the future.

16 For a fuller discussion see *The Economist*, Insurance Supplement, July 1968, p. x.

17 'The Growth of Life Assurance in the U.K. Since 1880', *Proceedings of the Manchester Statistical Society*, 1956, pp. 37–42.

18 R. L. Carter, op. cit., p. 249.

Chapter 14

THE PERFORMANCE OF THE INDUSTRY

'Our analysis of the deficiencies in the performance of British industry is certainly consistent with a need for something more than general increases in effective competition.'

Richard E. Caves

HAVING DEVOTED a considerable amount of space to an analysis of the industry's competitive situation, it is our intention in this chapter to make a brief evaluation of the current performance of the industry by the use of other criteria such as expense ratios, profitability, progressiveness, cost-price relationships and capacity. At the outset it must be recognised that a rigorous and definitive analysis is rendered impossible by deficiencies in the statistical information available.

First, existing legislation does not make it mandatory for companies, in filing their returns with the Board of Trade, to distinguish between the results of their activities in different areas. For example it is impossible to compare premium income and underwriting profits in the domestic market with those in overseas markets. Unfortunately, the companies themselves are not prepared to remedy these deficiencies in the official statistics by voluntarily providing data which would enable commentators to distinguish between premium income derived directly and that emanating from reinsurance activities, although the B.I.A. now provides consolidated data on the distribution of premium income (excluding marine, aviation and transport) between the U.K., U.S.A. and the rest of the world. Meaningful comparisons between Lloyd's and the company sector are difficult because Lloyd's publish information on premium income *net* of brokerage, discounts and commission whereas the companies give *gross* figures; furthermore, Lloyd's do not discriminate between fire and other general insurance activities.

Secondly, accurate inter-company comparisons are impossible, through disparities in reinsurance practices which cannot be identified because published data is *net* of reinsurance transactions, that is premiums and losses are given minus payments to, plus payments from, reinsurers.

Thirdly, in the general branch there are significant differences between companies in treatment of provisions for unexpired risks and estimation of outstanding claims which can vitiate comparisons of profitability.

Since efficiency in insurance, as in any other industry, is basically concerned with providing the maximum output from the minimum input of resources, assuming that we have access to the necessary information, we might in theory be able to measure this efficiency by comparisons between different insurers now and over time. But, apart from the statistical problems which we have already noted, there are other inherent difficulties. For example, since the basic function of both life and general insurers is to assume risks on behalf of the insured, it might be thought that the attainment of maximum efficiency simply requires that the transfer of risks should be accomplished with the minimum use of resources in assessing premiums, administering policies and processing claims, etc., but this neglects the importance of service. Most insurers believe, whether justifiably or not, that a complete insurance service involves not merely the transfer of risks but also the provision of ancillary services such as advice on the amount of cover and the speedy settlement of claims, which can only be achieved by the establishment of a local branch or broker network and consequential increases in administrative costs. There are many other administrative and selling expenses which yield little tangible satisfaction to the insured, because they are incurred to persuade prospective buyers to purchase insurance from one insurer only, and involve far more expenditure than is necessary to provide the public with sufficient information to make rational choices between the products of different insurers. An adequate measure of efficiency requires rational discrimination between useful and superfluous services provided by insurers, but in practice this is impossible and we are forced either to ignore the problem or to fall back on subjective and arbitrary distinctions. A second and more intractable difficulty arises from the dual nature of an insurer's activities. We have already noted how the majority of life assurance contracts comprise a combination of insurance with investment so that the insurers' investment policies make a vital contribution to the efficiency of their operations but even in non-life business, despite the emphasis traditionally placed on underwriting results, investment earnings also have a significant bearing on profitability. Consequently, since in both branches successful investment policies form an integral part of insurers' operations, it follows that ideally any measure of efficiency should take them into account but unfortunately attempts to do so come up against difficult conceptual and practical obstacles.

Having called attention to the difficulties involved in assessing efficiency in the insurance industry, let us nevertheless make an attempt in the full knowledge of the limitations of the exercise and begin by examining life assurance. In our analysis of the competitive situation we have already observed a marked discrepancy in the final value of the proceeds of maturity for 'with-profit' endowment policies and the variations in the cost of providing a given sum either at maturity or on death for 'without profit' policies. Since there is little variation in mortality experience, differences in performance must have their origin in variations either in operating costs or returns on investment. The conventional method of comparing the former is to use crude expense ratios but there are various pitfalls to be avoided in using them as a measure of relative efficiency. These pitfalls are less important in industrial life assurance than in ordinary life assurance because the type of business transacted varies less between industrial life than ordinary life offices. The chief fallacy to avoid is the prevalent assumption that expense ratios are higher in industrial life assurance than in ordinary life assurance because the premiums are collected by house-to-house calls. This is incorrect as is shown by the fact that, although the premiums on ordinary life policies issued by industrial life offices are also collected by house-to-house calls, the ordinary life expense ratios of industrial life offices are lower than the ordinary life expense ratios for similar business issued by the life offices not transacting industrial life business.[1] The major proportion of expenses in life business are incurred in selling and servicing policies and also in collecting and accounting for premiums and it can be demonstrated that the higher average expense ratio in proportion to premiums in industrial life assurance arises solely from the smaller average size of policy and the greater frequency of payment of premiums. If expenses are broken down according to number of policies issued, the number of policies in force and the number of premiums collected, expenses per item of work are lower in industrial life assurance as a result of the greater simplicity and standardisation of policies and the economies of mass production.[2] Contrary to widely held beliefs, the collection of premiums by house-to-house calls is materially cheaper than collecting premiums through the post.

In comparing the ordinary life expense ratios of companies it is important to pay particular attention to the following significant causes of variations. First, allowance must be made for the distribution of pension scheme business between the companies, since expense ratios for this class of business are materially lower than for individual policies. Currently, about one-half of total premium income in ordinary life assurance in the U.K. arises from pension schemes but the distribution varies greatly between one company and another (in fact, from nil to 90 per cent). Secondly, account must be taken of the ratio of new business to existing business for the obvious reason that the expense of selling and issuing policies absorbs a large part of the first year's premium so that a rapidly expanding and successful company writing a large amount of new business in relation to its existing business will tend to have a high crude expense ratio. The third important influence is the average size of policy

Table 69

CRUDE EXPENSE RATIOS OF MAJOR INDUSTRIAL-CUM-ORDINARY PROPRIETARY LIFE COMPANIES

Company	*Ordinary Branch*						*Industrial Branch*					
	1963	*1964*	*1965*	*1966*	*1967*[3]	*1968*[3]	*1963*	*1964*	*1965*	*1966*	*1967*[3]	*1968*[3]
	%	%	%	%	%	%	%	%	%	%	%	%
Brittanic	16·0	16·5	16·3	16·0	15·0	16·4[2]	33·8	33·6	34·1	36·1	36·3	36·0
London and M/c.	20·1	19·7	18·0	17·2	17·5	18·5[2]	35·1	34·9	33·2	34·4	35·4	37·1
Pearl	22·9	23·8[1]	23·1	21·5	22·1	23·8	31·3	32·6[1]	31·7	31·3	31·4	32·0
Prudential	17·1	17·1	17·6	18·0	18·5	19·1	30·9	30·1	30·7	31·2	32·8	32·8
Refuge	16·3	16·1	16·5	15·6	15·5	16·3	36·4	35·6	35·2	33·5	34·8	36·9

Source: Published Accounts.

[1] In 1964 expense ratio of Pearl was inflated by special bonuses paid to staff and pensioners to celebrate the company's centenary.

[2] In the ordinary branch the increased new business of Britannic and London and Manchester was a major factor causing increases in the expense ratios.

[3] The ratios for all companies in 1967 and 1968 have been adversely affected by Selective Employment Tax which is estimated to cost about 1 per cent of premium.

issued by the company for the reasons already discussed. Even though allowances may be made for the last two influences, the difficulty of obtaining information on the relative importance of pension schemes both in new and old business does not make the attempt to obtain standardised expense ratios particularly rewarding or illuminating. Tables 69 and 70 give some information on expense ratios which must be interpreted in the light of all the reservations mentioned.

The points to note about Table 70 are, first, that expense ratios, excluding selling expenses, varied from 7·4 per cent to 19·4 per cent while total expense ratios varied from 7·9 per cent to 30·2 per cent; secondly, that the two companies which do not pay commission, namely the Equitable and London Life, have outstandingly good figures; and, thirdly, the largest mutual company, the Standard Life has the lowest expense ratio of the remaining companies.

These two tables should be seen in conjunction with Table 66 in the previous chapter which revealed a tendency for expenses to decline with size of company. It will be recalled that J. Johnston and G. W. Murphy,[8] after allowing for the effects of new business and pension schemes on company data for 1952, found that there was a significant relation between size and expenses but unfortunately we have been unable to apply their techniques to the results of the more recent years, when pension schemes had become relatively more important, through deficiencies in the available data. However, of the ten companies with expense ratios of over 21 per cent in Table 70 only four came in the top ten for growth between 1963 and 1968 and the other five 'high-expense-ratio' offices (Royal, Phoenix, Marine and General, Scottish Equitable and Pearl) were well below average size. The only firm conclusions we can draw from these inter-company comparisons are, first, that improvements in the statistics are an essential pre-requisite for adequate analysis, although on the face of it the variations in crude expense ratios are greater than one would expect after due allowance for the composition of business, and bear some relation to size; and, secondly, that selling and marketing expenses are an important source of such variations.

When we turn to a consideration of profitability, we must note that profits are even more arbitrary in life assurance than in most commercial activities since they depend upon two sets of estimates, namely estimates of future liabilities and estimates of future income, and companies may, and do, vary in the degree of caution which they exercise in making these estimates. Nevertheless, the surplus, which is revealed by the periodic valuations of assets and expected liabilities, is the best measure of profitability available and to a major extent its size is determined by the excess of the net interest earned over the amounts required to

Table 70

ORDINARY LIFE ANNUITY AND CAPITAL REDEMPTION BUSINESS OF 39 BRITISH LIFE OFFICES

	Premium income 1963 £mn.	*Premium income 1968 £mn.*	*Expense ratio* excl. commission 1968 (%)*	*Expense ratio* inc. commission 1968 (%)*	*Fund end 1968 £mn.*	*Fund growth 1963-1968 %*	*Fund growth 1958-1968 %*	*Gross yield§ %*
Mutual Life Offices								
Clerical, Medical & General	4·8	13·4	9·6	15·1	109·0	102	219	6·42*
Equitable	4·6	7·7	7·9	7·9*	90·8	73	171	6·94
Friends' Provident	10·4	23·9	10·9	17·4	220·0	71	229	6·69
London Life	4·7	8·2	9·4	9·4	93·7	47	115	7·08
Marine & General	1·6	2·8	16·8	25·6	23·9	73	176	6·74
National Mutual	2·3	4·1	16·1	23·9	44·6	75	207	7·10
National Provident	5·2	7·9	14·7	20·5	90·5	61	173	7·06
Norwich Union	38·7	56·6	12·6	18·7	536·3	61	172	6·99
Provident Mutual	4·9	8·2	13·1	18·5	63·8	67	148	7·23
Scottish Amicable	14·7	21·9	13·5	18·1	206·6	70	217	6·88
Scottish Equitable	3·8	7·1	16·3	24·0	67·3	81	186	6·88
Scottish Life	5·0	8·6	13·4	20·6	73·1	77	215	6·98
Scottish Mutual	3·4	6·7	12·7	19·4	54·9	91	217	7·20
Scottish Provident	6·7	9·8	12·5	18·4	117·1	54	146	7·45
Scottish Widows'	18·1	29·0	9·3	13·9	322·1	60	180	7·56
Standard Life	45·6	66·2	9·4	12·9	692·8	71	198	6·91
UK Provident	6·7	10·4	11·2	16·3	125·8	69	160	8·16*
Average/Total	181·2	292·5	*11·4*	*16·4*	2932·3			*7·07*
Proprietary Life Offices								
General Life	4·9	8·7	14·5	23·5	66·2	88	252	6·44*
Equity & Law	11·3	16·3	15·4	22·6	183·5	54	209	7·89
Sun Life	27·1	38·5	12·8	17·8	361·9	65	176	7·06*
Average/Total	43·3	63·5	*13·7*	*19·8*	611·6			*7·13*
Industrial-cum-Ordinary Life Offices†								
Britannic	5·8	7·1	‡	16·2	71·2	33	151	6·79*
Co-operative	15·4	23·3	7·4*	18·2	185·2	64	87	7·44
Lond. & Manchester	4·9	6·2	11·8	18·3	58·5	22	82	7·15
Pearl	18·9	25·2	14·2	23·6	233·4	52	131	7·53*
Prudential	89·2	137·4	12·6	19·1	1180·9	67	174	6·97
Refuge	10·7	12·2	10·9	15·5	117·4	27	59	7·07
Royal London	5·4	6·5	10·1	21·4	68·8	34	75	7·25
Average/Total	150·3	217·9	*12·0*	*19·3*	1915·4			*7·17*
Composite Offices								
Atlas	5·5	8·7	11·6	17·5	89·3	54	136	7·34
Caledonian	2·8	4·3	13·3	19·2	52·7	55	223	7·47*
Commercial Union	17·3	36·4	11·4	17·0	349·3	69	149	7·19
Eagle Star	22·3	30·6	8·1	13·3	331·6	58	180	7·04
Guardian	14·5	19·5	14·2	23·0	228·2	79	340	7·05
Legal & General	64·8	99·4	11·3	16·7	934·8	65	178	6·69
Northern	9·8	14·4	10·6	15·6	125·0	66	123	7·30
Phoenix	6·8	10·9	19·4*	25·7	112·7	57	150	7·11
Royal	11·3	17·7	18·4	30·2*	264·9	59	139	6·92
Royal Exchange	6·1	7·8	10·9	15·5	81·1	51	138	7·42
Sun-Alliance & London	9·6	17·0	16·2	22·2	168·9	46	110	6·75
Yorkshire	8·7	16·5	10·4	18·5	146·4	70	199	6·67*
Average/Total	179·5	283·2	*12·2*	*18·4*	2884·9			*7·08*

* The proportion of premiums absorbed by expenses of management (including or excluding commission paid to agents and brokers). This ratio is affected both by the office's own efficiency and by its mix of business. Pensions business, in particular, is cheaper to administer (per £ of premiums) than ordinary life assurance business. † Excluding 'industrial' branch life assurance. ‡ Not available.
§ On ordinary life and annuity funds only.
Source: The Economist, Insurance Supplement, July, 1969.

build up the actuarial reserves from which the office's liabilities will ultimately be met. Thus the higher the yield on investment, the greater the surplus, other things being equal. Table 70 shows that in 1968 gross yields varied from 8·16 per cent to 6·42 per cent. A second influence is the level of operating expenses, which we have already discussed, while a third is the level of capital profits which is derived from the periodical writing up of the value of ordinary shares and real property in their portfolios and is the more significant, the greater the relative importance of equity investment. Finally, the surplus over and above the sums necessary to meet contractual liabilities will be larger, the greater the proportion of 'with-profit' business, and it is essential to allow for this in any comparison of profitability. Broadly speaking, the rise in the value of equities in the 1950s and 1960s and the more recent rise in interest rates have both contributed to the high level of profitability of life assurance in recent years, especially of those companies which moved into equity investment early. The great disparity in the proceeds of with-profit endowment policies, which we noted in the previous chapter, is largely attributable to the relative success of the companies' investment policies which are an important influence on the size of the surplus. By the standards of the best some companies have put up a distinctly poor performance and must be judged relatively inefficient.[4]

In general insurance the conventional method for carrying out inter-company comparisons is the ratio of management expenses plus commission to total premiums but it suffers from many of the weaknesses which we have discussed in its application to life assurance. In particular, 'administration and sales costs show considerable variation between different classes of risk and between direct and reinsurance business. Therefore, variations in different insurers' product-mixes could largely invalidate some inter-company comparisons and changes taking place within an individual company could upset comparisons over time.'[5] Similarly, S. L. Lengyel has pointed out that the work carried out by an insurer and the conditions under which it is performed vary between both classes of business and companies and he singles out eight possible causes of short-run cost variations.[6]

The figures shown in Table 71 should, therefore, be interpreted in the light of these reservations, but it should be noted that they tend to confirm the results of our analysis of 62 firms in 1963, namely a slight tendency for efficiency to increase with size. Table 72 shows how, spurred on by poor underwriting results and the impact of corporation tax in recent years, the leading British composite companies have made discernible progress in cutting their costs and rationalising their fire and accident underwriting.

Table 71

EXPENSE RATIOS OF 16 BRITISH OFFICES
FIRE, ACCIDENT AND MISCELLANEOUS INSURANCE, 1969

Company	*Premiums* £*m.*	*Expenses* %	*Commission* %
Century	15·7	20·9	18·7
Commercial Union	320·8	16·9	17·8
Co-operative	23·3	20·5	16·8
Cornhill	15·0	18·1	15·9
Eagle Star	69·9	18·0	17·7
General Accident	179·5	17·3	17·5
Guardian Royal Exchange	153·5	18·6	17·0
Legal & General	15·9	28·7	14·7
National Employers Mutual	22·8	22·9	14·4
Norwich Union	53·7	34·7[1]	—
Pearl	11·9	29·0	15·3
Phoenix	77·1	18·0	17·2
Provincial	13·3[2]	22·5	—
Prudential	45·7	23·3	14·4
Royal	352·3	17·9	16·7
Sun-Alliance & London	123·2	20·0	17·0
All	1,493·5	18·4[3]	17·0[4]

[1] Includes commission.
[2] Premiums after deduction of commission.
[3] Excluding Norwich Union.
[4] Excluding Norwich Union.

Source: *The Economist,* Insurance Supplement, July, 1970.

Dr. R. L. Carter has made a brave and pioneering attempt to take into account the opportunity cost of capital employed and to apply three measures of efficiency, namely a profits/inputs index, an output/inputs index and a financial efficiency index to the 1966 results of the ten leading composite companies. For all three indices the comparison of the individual firm's results was with the average of the ten instead of with the average of the industry as a whole. See Table 73.

As Carter points out, it would be rash to draw firm conclusions from an analysis of only one year's results but two points are worth noting. 'First, among these large companies with non-life premium income ranging from £41m. to £267m. the dispersion of efficiency is considerable and, secondly, the results tend to confirm the impression of mild economies of scale among the large composite companies.'[7]

In considering profitability it is useful to begin with the yardstick that profits must be sufficient to cover the opportunity costs of the factors

Table 72

EXPENSE RATIOS OF LEADING BRITISH COMPOSITE COMPANIES

	1954	*1960*	*1963*	*1964*	*1965*	*1966*	*1967*	*1968*	*1969*
Non-life premiums (£m.)[1]	472·8	750·5	887·7	963·8	1,042·8	1,110·5	1,206·6	1,392·6	1,499·3
Net trading profits (£m.)[2]	7·0	−1·0	−27·2	−17·8	−19·3[1]	−12·0[1]	1·7[1]	−19·5	−28·0
Expense ratios % [3]	40·3	38·5	38·5	37·7	37·0	36·9	36·2	35·2	35·2

Source: *The Economist*, Insurance Supplements.

[1] Before tax.
[2] From all departments after pension provision and tax.
[3] Fire and accident departments.

employed in providing the services of insurance including the potential earnings on capital after necessary allowance for the degree of exposure of that capital to risk. In theory, insurance companies by careful application of the law of large numbers to homogeneous groups of statistically measurable risks should be able to reduce the residual uncertainty, especially by the judicious use of reinsurance, to a very low level. In practice, the uncertainty has been increased, partly by their own failings in collecting loss statistics and developing scientific principles for rate-fixing, and partly by official limitations on their freedom of action in the important American market.[8] Nevertheless, even after account is taken of the possible incidence of catastrophic risks, general insurance can be classified as a relatively low-risk activity and a satisfactory rate of return on capital employed should not greatly exceed the return on Government securities.

Table 73

MEASURES OF EFFICIENCY—10 LEADING COMPOSITE COMPANIES BASED ON 1966 accounts

Company	*Profits/input*	*Output/input*	*Financial Efficiency*
1. Company One	0·9860	0·9841	1·0011
2. Company Two	1·0015	1·0138	0·9922
3. Company Three	0·9780	0·9792	0·9967
4. Company Four	1·0300	0·9736	1·0061
5. Company Five	0·9982	1·0217	1·0033
6. Company Six	1·0207	1·0003	0·9995
7. Company Seven	0·9882	1·0437	1·0014
8. Company Eight	1·0079	1·0203	1·0004
9. Company Nine	1·0226	1·0033	1·0044
10. Company Ten	1·0110	1·0133	1·0132

1·000 is average performance.
Below 1·000 is above average performance.
Above 1·000 is below average performance.

Source: R. L. Carter, op. cit. p. 315.

Unfortunately, there are both conceptual difficulties in defining capital employed, since insurers' funds are acquired both from shareholders and policyholders, and also practical obstacles in calculating it arising from deficiencies in the published statistics. Shareholders subscribe the funds required for the acquisition of necessary capital assets, including working capital, but a substantial proportion of a new entrant's capital resources is required to provide sufficient free assets to meet the statutory minimum solvency margin. Subsequently, free reserves may be accumulated from undistributed profits and, together with the share capital, these funds are known as the policyholders' surplus. Policyholders' contributions to insurance funds consist of the sums retained by insurers in the course of their underwriting operations to cover contingent liabilities in the form of unexpired risks and outstanding claims. 'Like the policyholders' surplus, policyholders' funds are permanently available for investment because other than in exceptional circumstances payments for expenses and claims can be met from current premium income. One difference between the two sources of funds lies in their contribution to an insurers' earnings. The policyholders' surplus simultaneously finances the underwriting operations, thus making possible the flow of premium income and also provides an independent source of income from its investment. Policyholders' funds arise out of the underwriting operation and only make a contribution to earnings in so far as they are invested. Therefore, in measuring underwriting efficiency the appropriate figure for capital employed is the policyholders' surplus.'[9]

The practical obstacles in examining the profitability of general insurance arise from the need to rely on the published accounts of individual companies which can, and do, use different accounting conventions. In the first place, insurers enjoy a considerable amount of freedom in allocating expenses to different branches of their business and in their treatment of such expenses as pension contributions and taxation. Secondly, the use of different methods for valuing liabilities in the form of unexpired risks and outstanding claims provides scope for individual judgement in estimating profits. Thirdly, existing company legislation confers considerable freedom on British insurers for using profits from the sale of investments to write down the book values of their portfolios.[10]

With all these reservations in mind let us now consider the available data on profitability. Fig. 9 supplements the information already provided in Tables 59 and 60 in the previous chapter and emphasises how profitable fire and accident business was in the early 1950s and how sharply results deteriorated in 1956. Since then profit-ratios (e.g. total underwriting results as a percentage of premium income) have been negative, although some improvement can be detected in recent years despite a deterioration in the results from marine (including aviation) underwriting. Given our inability to distinguish between domestic and overseas business, it is open to question how far the observed unprofitability is attributable to the difficult trading conditions in the American market but there is a reasonable presumption that it has been a major factor. What is perhaps more significant, as we discuss in more detail in Chapter 16, the British companies have been much less successful than U.S. companies in paring down their expenses as a contribution to improved profitability.

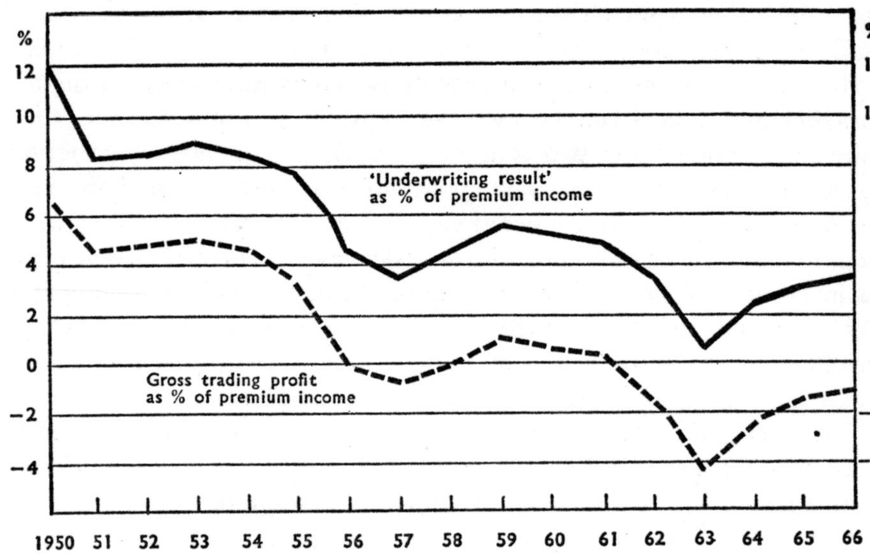

Source: Read, Hurst-Brown and Company's Insurance Shares, 1967.

FIG. 9. *Results for 11 leading Composite Companies*

Notes: (1) Trading Profits are defined as transfers from underwriting accounts less pensions and all other charges.

(2) Underwriting result is defined as trading profit plus earnings on investment of reserves for unexpired risks and unsettled claims.

The major conclusion to be drawn is that since the middle of the 1950s underwriting for the majority of companies was an unprofitable affair and even the profitable results from a few companies (e.g. in 1968, the Norwich Union and the Prudential made profits) were far from satisfactory when expressed as a percentage of premium income.

Their performance does not appear in a more favourable light when the rate of earnings on capital employed is estimated as was done by Read, Hurst-Brown and Company in their survey already referred to. They made this calculation by adding to the companies' published capital and reserves an estimate of the appreciation of investments based on three assumptions, first, that the market values of equities in 1954 was double the book value at that time; secondly that these equities and subsequent purchases moved in step with the Dow-Jones average and the *Financial Times* index; and, thirdly, that other investments have remained at the value stated in the accounts. The results are shown in Table 74 below, which confirms how profitable an activity underwriting was in the early 1950s and how low the return on capital was in recent years in relation to acceptable standards in other industries. Given this evidence of the

Table 74

RATES OF RETURN ON CAPITAL EMPLOYED

Year	*Capital and Reserves*	*Book Value of Equities*	*Estimated Appreciation*	*True Capital Employed*	*Total Gross Profit £m.*	*% To Capital Employed*
1950	138	42	37	175	40	23
1951	141	49	51	192	36	19
1952	148	57	47	195	40	21
1953	158	68	52	210	44	21
1954	183	80	80	263	45	17
1955	192	94	108	300	44	15
1956	204	106	110	314	31	10
1957	210	118	112	322	30	9
1958	217	130	112	329	37	11
1959	251	151	191	442	48	11
1960	288	182	235	523	51	10
1961	332	212	257	589	53	9
1962	350	227	225	575	45	8
1963	350	245	274	624	23	4
1964	364	269	340	704	41	6
1965	364	302	358	722	50	7
1966	370	340	289	659	59	9

Source: Read, Hurst-Brown and Company, Insurance Shares, 1967 (privately circulated).

relatively unsatisfactory performance of the industry, it is interesting to look at the range of individual results. J. Plymen and S. Pullen have published the results of an investigation into the relationship between the pre-tax profits of ten major composite companies and the real value of shareholders' assets (unfortunately not clearly defined) in 1966, a year in which results were much better than in the preceding four years. They calculated that the earnings on capital employed were as follows:

3 best offices	9·3%
4 average offices	6·7%
3 worst offices	3·9%

As they somewhat acidly observe, even for the best three offices the financial results were only just adequate and left no scope for building up reserves. 'Considering that the shareholders' assets under present conditions should be invested to produce some 5 to 6 per cent, it appears that for some half of the ten offices 1966 results were worse in terms of profits than would have been obtained merely by investing the shareholders' capital without undertaking any insurance activities at all.'[11] All in all, the non-life companies deserve no more than 'gamma minus' when their performance is judged by the criterion of current profitability.

The progressiveness of an industry may be judged by the degree of energy and inventiveness it displays both in improving productive and distributive processes in order to increase efficiency and in developing new and improved products. This implies that insurers, if they are to be judged progressive, must be alive to the nature of technological, economic and social changes in industry, commerce and the whole environment of the community which expose the insured population to new types of risk and induce demands for protection against novel combinations of risk; at the same time they must be unremitting in their search for opportunities to introduce and apply improved techniques for measuring risks so as to increase the accuracy of rate-fixing and to bring what were considered previously to be uninsurable risks within the ambit of their activities. Any verdict on the performance of the insurance industry as judged by this criterion must inevitably be somewhat subjective, especially since there is such a paucity of information on such matters as the procedures for fixing rates and assessing risks in general insurance; nevertheless it is possible to make some attempt at evaluation even if one is forced to rely more than is desirable on general impressions.

In the task of developing new products both life assurance and general insurance companies can be legitimately criticised for their failure to use modern techniques of market research so as to be adequately informed of the types of cover which are most suitable for the needs of the insured. Nevertheless, the life companies have not been inactive in devising new combinations of endowment and whole-life policies to meet specific purposes as in the case of Death Duty Policies, Family Income Policies, Pension Contracts, Educational Annuities, and House Purchase Policies, which have emerged from the application of considerable actuarial virtuosity. At the same time they can be accused of being slow to realise that the man-in-the-street is becoming increasingly concerned about the impact of inflation on his savings and is tending to place more emphasis on policies as a means of investment. *The Economist* has from time to time been particularly critical of the companies on this score, especially in their response to the success of the unit trust movement; for existing life assurance companies have been very slow off the mark with equity-linked life policies, and 'their unadventurous selling methods and deadly boring advertising (slanted too much towards death and old age and not enough towards saving) have given opportunities to others'.[12] It later commented with ironical amusement on the indecent haste with which the more decorous and old-fashioned companies later climbed on the band wagon of unit-linked life assurance policies after vainly trying to warn the public of the pitfalls of all equity policies.[13] Although these criticisms are perhaps excessively severe, there is little doubt that the companies have been slow to adapt themselves to a world in which the more sophisticated policyholder is well aware that 90 per cent of a life policy premium is allocated to investment and only 10 per cent to provide life cover. They have not proved flexible enough to remedy the real weakness of the conventional with-profits policy, which is that the policyholder gets no guarantee that the profits earned on his share of the fund will go to him after due allowances for the insurance element in the contract since this depends on the arbitrary decisions of the insurer. To quote from *The Economist* again, 'life offices are selling two quite separate (or separable) products; life cover and investment expertise. These two things are tied together to form the life assurance policy—only because the life assurance tax relief makes it worth doing so. But the policyholder of tomorrow will increasingly demand that the prices of these two items should be shown separately.'[14]

Judged by the number and variety of new types of risk currently being underwritten compared with the situation just after the end of the Second World War, the British general insurance industry should largely be absolved from any criticism of lack of progressiveness. For example, there have been notable advances in liability and loss of profits insurance. Nevertheless, there is evidence that the driving force behind such changes has originated not so much within the companies themselves as from the larger firms of brokers who have frequently taken the initiative in developing special new types of insurance, have found underwriters and companies who will cover the risks and have then gone out and actively sold the new types of policy to industrial and commercial customers. Sometimes indeed innovations, especially in the industrial and commercial field, have been introduced as a result of the initiative of the insured themselves. But, whatever the origin of the changes, British insurers have been reasonably responsive and their record for product innovation in the post-war period must be adjudged a respectable one.

With regard to improvements in the processes of production and distribution we have already commented on the propensity of insurers to cling to out-dated methods of rate-fixing, selling and marketing. Only in recent years have companies taken steps to eliminate wasteful processes involving intermediaries and experimented with direct selling to customers where appropriate. But now the position is changing rapidly and experimentation is the order of the day. In one particular sphere of their activities they cannot be accused of being slow to take advantage of the benefits of modern technology: that is in the application of computers to the many routine operations which are a normal feature of the insurance business. Thus, one is left with the overall impression of an industry which may have been slow to react to the quickening pace of change in the outside world but is now much more alive to the benefits to be derived from a flexible and responsive attitude to innovation.

Turning to cost-price relationships, we are as usual faced with the difficulty that there is a paucity of information about the process of price determination, particularly in general insurance. But what evidence we have suggests that in both life and general insurance the insurers adopt uniform cost-plus pricing policies and do not attempt to fix premiums in relation to marginal costs. Even if they wished to, in many cases they lack the necessary information because, until recently, they have not expended much effort in costing the different methods of selling insurance and in particular have failed to use market research for demand forecasting, so that they are uncertain not only about the costs of acquiring additional business but also about the potential revenue which could thereby be generated. The consequent adoption of cost-plus pricing policies has the disadvantage that it renders insurers less alive to market opportunities and the costs of alternative methods of operations so that they may consequently fail, first, to scrutinise costs as closely as desirable with adverse effects on their efficiency, secondly, to exploit new sources of demand and, thirdly, to adjust prices quickly enough to ensure that capacity is adequate to meet demand.

Another aspect of cost-price relationships which is of importance is the extent to which prices, even if they are related to average total costs rather than marginal costs, are fairly discriminating in that they reflect real differences in the costs of assuming the burden of risks on behalf of the insured. The economic objections to price discrimination which cannot be thus justified are, first, that it leads to the waste of economic resources in that the demand for some goods and services is relatively stimulated while that for others is relatively depressed, and, secondly, it leads to the redistribution of income arising from the effects of one group of consumers subsidising another. Of great practical importance is the impact of unfair price discrimination on risk management. Direct measures to prevent or reduce losses will be adopted only to the extent that the necessary expenditure is likely to show a relatively better return than other methods of risk avoidance including insurance, either because they completely eliminate the risk for less cost than the premiums incurred in transferring the risk to an insurer or, more usually, because they reduce the expectancy of loss to such a degree that the present discounted value of future savings in expenditure on premiums arising from a reduction in rates more than offsets the cost of such measures.[15] But, if premiums are higher than can be justified by real costs, then the insured are to that extent induced to devote more time and effort to the prevention of losses than is really merited, and vice-versa if premiums are relatively too low. In either case there is a misallocation of resources.

In considering the extent to which such undesirable price discrimination occurs in the British insurance industry, it is necessary once again to distinguish between life and non-life insurance. The criteria for the determination of life premiums are sufficiently scientific in that, even though life offices may differ in their assumptions about future rates of interest and consequently in the premiums they charge, they do not discriminate in the terms which they offer to policyholders whose age and other circumstances are sufficiently alike. But in general insurance the position is very different and, although it is difficult to obtain proof of price discrimination, since the outside observer does not have access to the highly-confidential information on the processes of rate-fixing, there is a fair amount of circumstantial evidence that they are not sufficiently scientific to avoid the danger of undesirable price discrimination. In the first place, until recently no attempt was made to collect statistics on losses on an industry basis which is an essential *sine qua non* for accurate rate-fixing. Consequently, insurers instead of trying to discover what factors affect the size of particular risks have tended to charge just whatever rate produces an overall profit for each broad class of risk. Secondly, if premiums are to reflect real costs, then classes and class ratings must be kept under continuous review, but the tariff associations have not proved to be sufficiently flexible to do this until they were goaded into action by competition from non-tariff insurers, whose success was largely due to more accurate and more responsive pricing policies, and by deteriorating underwriting results. Thirdly, there is reason to believe that there has been discrimination in favour of large buyers of insurance, sometimes through pressure from brokers, sometimes through the exercise of the insured's own countervailing power, which on occasion has led to the acceptance of bad risks at totally uneconomic premiums.[16] This is not only unfair to small insurers but also inhibits the use of adequate preventive measures to limit losses. Fortunately, while this has been the position in the recent past, the general insurance industry is now much more aware of the need for adequate loss statistics and improved methods of costing and rate-fixing so that its performance as judged by the criterion of cost-price relationships is improving.

Finally, we turn to a consideration of the insurance industry's capacity in the sense of the number of risks which it is capable of underwriting. The concept of capacity is much easier to grasp when applied to a manufacturing industry such as radio and television which, with given capital equipment, can only increase output up to a certain finite limit even with the most intensive use of productive facilities. The insurance industry is able to produce a much more variable output of services in relation to its fixed assets, although this flexibility is tending to decline as the relative importance of fixed costs increases with the application of such modern management devices as computers. Nevertheless, its capacity may be limited in two senses either because the insurer's net assets, which provide the necessary protection against an unexpectedly high level of claims, are insufficient in relation to premium income or because it is unable to absorb the larger risks which the public wishes to transfer to it.

In the United Kingdom the volume of business which insurers are capable of underwriting at any moment of time is limited by the capital reserves at their disposal in relation to the solvency requirements of the 1967 Companies Act. Again, we have to make the customary distinction between life and non-life insurance. There is as yet no problem of inadequate capacity in the life branch because, first, the incidence of losses is so much more predictable, through the application of actuarial science, than in the non-life business that the magnitude of unexpected claims is small and in any case may be defrayed from current premium income and, secondly, life assurance has been so profitable in recent years that there has been no difficulty in building up reserves. But the situation in non-life insurance is not so happy for, although insurers are able to comply easily with the requirements of the 1967 Companies Act, in recent years the industry's reserves have been falling in relation to premium income. The deterioration, which was to some extent reversed in 1968 by the writing up of the book value of investments and by revealing hidden reserves (see Table 75), has been occurring steadily for some time (see Table 76). The underwriting capacity of Lloyd's cannot be

Table 75

PREMIUM INCOME AND RESERVES OF
9 LEADING COMPOSITE COMPANIES

Year	*Premium Income*	*Statutory Minimum Reserves*	*Reserves as shown in Accounts*
1967	£1,206m.	£123·8m.	£392·1m.
1968	£1,392m.	£141·9m.	£787·1m.
1969	£1,499m.	£152·2m.	£698·1m.

Source: *The Economist,* Insurance Supplement, July, 1970, p. xii.

Table 76

GROWTH OF BUSINESS AND CAPACITY, 1956–1965

	Premium Income	*Gross Assets*	*Net Assets*
British companies	80%	54%	—
American insurers	89%	81%	78%
American insurers (1956–66)	98%	82½%	61%
Lloyd's	69%	(no. of members: 39%)	

American figures exclude marine business

Source: *The Economist,* Insurance Supplement, July, 1968, p. vi.

measured accurately since it depends upon the personal wealth of members but it is probable that this has grown by more than the 39 per cent growth in membership between 1955 and 1965. Nevertheless underwriting losses in recent years have put pressure on many members whose resources are now stretched to the limit. Since, despite some recent relaxations in the rules, the amount which each member may underwrite is effectively determined by the size of his deposit, there is now a serious shortage of capacity which is especially acute in the fire and accident sectors but not too serious in the marine branch. On a conservative estimate it is calculated that 750 new members will have to be recruited each year for the next five years to ensure that underwriting capacity is adequate. Hence, in 1968 it was decided that men from outside the

Commonwealth would be considered for membership and in 1969 the seriousness of the situation was underlined by the decision to admit women to this hitherto exclusively male preserve. But the principle of unlimited liability has so far proved to be a serious deterrent and the number of applications for membership has been disappointing.

With regard to companies the problem is probably more serious than Tables 75 and 76 reveal, because gross assets include claims unpaid and unexpired premiums which increase in line with premium income and should properly be deducted to arrive at an estimate of the companies' underlying capital and free reserves. 'So the rise in the capital and free reserves must have been slower still: one authoritative estimate puts it at 45 per cent only.'[17] In any case the total volume of business which an insurer is capable of underwriting is only one dimension of its potential capacity and within the industry the concept is normally used in relation to the size of the individual risk which an insurer can accept and, more specifically, which it can retain for its own underwriting account without recourse to reinsurance. In fact the arrangement and availability of reinsurance is a major determinant of capacity. Whether or not it has been caused by the difficulties of access to the reinsurance market on reasonable terms, the British insurance market's diminishing ability to absorb large risks has become a major cause for concern. It is largely attributable to the growth of modern technology which is creating individual risks of a magnitude undreamed of only a few years ago. For example, the largest oil tankers afloat have grown from 20,000 tons in 1948 to 31,000 tons in 1956 and to over 500,000 tons in the 1970s while there has been a similar growth in the size of passenger aircraft culminating in the Jumbo Jets which have just come into service. These ships and aircraft are not only in themselves considerably more expensive than those which they are rendering obsolete but they magnify many times over the legal liabilities which could conceivably arise from an accident.[18] In the past pooling arrangements have been adopted for coping with such large risks as happened in 1956 when a special Committee, representing the whole British insurance market including Lloyd's, was established to underwrite property and liability insurance for atomic energy installations at home and abroad. In the future such consortia could be organised on an international scale but eventually a situation is only too likely to arise when either commercial insurance will be unable to offer full coverage or the industry will need a substantial injection of new capital. It is this prospect which provides such a compelling need for the insurance companies to improve their return on capital over that attained in recent years if they are not to discover that recourse to the capital market can be painfully expensive.

In conclusion, it may appear that the verdict on the industry's performance, particularly in non-life insurance, must be critical but there are mitigating circumstances which in all fairness should be noted. If the industry can be accused of being slow to respond to change, it must be emphasised that the very success of the British insurance industry in the past can be attributed to the application of a shrewd blend of conservatism and enterprise in assuming risks, the nature of which changed but slowly. In the last twenty-five years the technological revolution has wrought changes in the market for risks on a scale and at a speed which are without precedent in the industry's long history and have, not surprisingly, demonstrated the need for new and unaccustomed managerial techniques.

NOTES

1 From information supplied by the Cooperative Insurance Society.

2 I am indebted to Mr. A. Duval, Actuary of the Cooperative Insurance Society for information on this point.

3 Op. cit., pp. 38, 39.

4 Johnston and Murphy investigated the relationship between size (measured by sums assured) and profit rate (defined as Surplus ÷ Premiums) for 30 companies in 1953 after allowing for the relative importance of with-profits business. 'We find a simple correlation of 0·5679 between profit rate and the percentage of with-profits business, which accords with expectation. The partial correlation between size and profit rate with the percentage of with-profits business held constant is −0·3150 which just falls short of the 5 per cent significance level. The data suggests a tendency for profit rate to decline with size of company, but the relationship is not statistically very strong and it would be desirable to carry out a similar analysis for other years to see if this pattern persisted.' Op. cit., p. 46. I in fact carried out another analysis on data for 30 companies in 1960 and 55 companies in 1965; the simple correlations worked out at 0·6113 and 0·5819 and the partial correlations at −0·3249 and −0·1641 respectively. This hardly strengthens the hypothesis that the profit rate declines with size of company.

5 R. L. Carter, op. cit., p. 309.

6 S. J. Lengyel, *Insurance accounts: an economic interpretation and analysis,* F. W. Cheshire Limited, 1947, Ch. 6.

7 R. L. Carter, op. cit., p. 316.

8 This is discussed at length in Chapter 16, p. ??

9 R. L. Carter, op. cit., pp. 306, 307, where this whole question is extensively discussed. It should be noted that the financial efficiency index which Carter employed in analysing the 1966 results of 10 composite companies includes both policyholders' funds and policyholders' surplus.

10 See R. L. Carter, op. cit., pp. 320, 321.

11 J. Plymen and S. Pullen, 'Insurance Profitability: past, present and future', *Policyholder*, 20 September 1968, p. 1442.

12 *The Economist*, Insurance Supplement, July 1967, p. vi.
13 *The Economist*, Insurance Supplement, July 1968, p. xxxi.
14 *The Economist*, Insurance Supplement, July 1969, p. xiv.
15 For a more extensive discussion see R. L. Carter, op. cit., pp. 346, 347.
16 See *The Economist*, Insurance Supplement, July 1969, p. viii.
17 *The Economist*, Insurance Supplement, July 1968, p. vi.
18 The total sum at risk in a fully-loaded Boeing 747 has been estimated to be not far short of $100m. See *The Economist*, Insurance Supplement, July 1965, p. vii.

Chapter 15

INSURANCE AND THE CAPITAL MARKET

> 'Control over property has gravitated to the managers of the financial institutions because they perform a function which is valuable to society. Their function is to distribute among the generality of people the wealth which the corporations (that is, the big industrial companies) are creating.'
>
> Father Paul Harbrecht

THE INSURANCE companies' importance as investors is derived from their function as intermediaries in the capital market who collect and administer savings on behalf of a large body of individual policyholders. As a first step in evaluating the relative importance of these savings, it is useful to begin by noting that they are part of personal savings: one of the three main categories of savings, the others being company saving and Government saving. The relative importance of the three categories in recent years is shown in Table 77. Before the war the Government's contribution to total saving was either very small or negative; companies

Table 77

SOURCES OF GROSS SAVING IN THE U.K.

% of total each year

	1938	*1948*	*1952*	*1956*	*1960*	*1964*	*1966*	*1967*	*1969*
Persons	56	2	17	25	29	31	32	32	26
Companies	60	65	64	63	63	58	48	53	61
Government	−16	33	19	12	8	10	19	15	13

Source: National Income Blue Book.

accounted for about two-thirds of total gross saving and the personal sector for half. In the immediate post-war years the pattern was completely changed: although company saving retained its relative position, Government saving displaced personal saving as the contributor of the other third when the public went on a spending spree after the years of wartime austerity. Since 1952 personal saving has shown a remarkable recovery and now accounts for about one-third of the total. But this underestimates the importance of personal savings in the capital market, for the savings of other sectors largely by-pass the market. Companies use their savings mainly to finance their own investment and the same is true of the nationalised industries; the savings of the Central Government, in so far as they are not used to finance its own capital expenditure, are lent to other parts of the public sector. Thus personal savings are the only large pool of mobile funds which can be channelled through the market to meet the needs of either public or private investment.

Table 78, which traces the growth of personal saving in recent years, shows the magnitude of the rise and the irregular way in which it has taken place. For it more than trebled between 1948 and 1951, and again between 1951 and 1952; it rose by nearly 60 per cent between 1955 and 1956 and doubled between 1959 and 1961.

The statistical obstacles in the way of breaking down aggregate personal savings into the various purposes for which they are used are formidable but it is possible to deduce that certain items absorb a very large proportion of total personal savings. First, a major proportion is used for the double purpose of providing protection both against the risk of dying too soon and of living too long and accrues in the hands of assurance companies and pension funds. A second important use is for capital formation in personally-owned businesses and farms. Various savings surveys have confirmed the impression that private owners of enterprises save more heavily than other people, even when allowance is made for the fact that on average they belong to the higher income groups. The third major use of savings is for the purchase of houses but since much of this is carried out by private persons increasing their indebtedness to life assurance companies, building societies, etc., it is impossible to estimate how much of their current net savings private individuals are putting into the housing sector. See Table 79.

Another way of looking at personal savings is to identify the assets which the personal sector acquires with the savings. In the process of channelling their savings into various outlets private individuals buy a large amount of intermediary claims of varying marketability. The only substantial part of personal savings which does not involve the creation of intermediary claims is that which is used for capital formation in privately-owned businesses and farms. A great part of the remainder is used to acquire commercial bank deposits, various forms of National Savings, building society shares and deposits, insurance company policies and the obligations of unit trusts, investment trusts and industrial companies. There is a variety of ways in which the different forms of assets might be classified into different groups for economic analysis. One possible arrangement emphasises the distinction between increases in assets resulting from 'contractual' saving on the one hand and, on the other, assets acquired through the channels of spasmodic or 'once and for all'

Table 78

PERSONAL DISPOSABLE INCOME AND SAVING

£ million and percentages

	1948	*1949*	*1951*	*1952*	*1955*	*1956*	*1959*	*1961*	*1964*	*1966*	*1967*	*1969*
(1) Personal Disposable Income[1]	8,676	9,108	10,331	11,148	13,598	14,605	16,951	19,552	23,383	26,484	27,559	31,023
(2) Personal Saving[2]	41	126	114	380	486	766	834	1,722	1,924	2,252	2,191	2,405
(3) (2) as % of (1)	·47	1·4	1·1	3·4	3·6	5·2	4·9	8·8	8·2	8·5	7·5	7·8

[1] P.D.I. equals total personal income less payment of U.K. taxes on income, national ins. etc. contribution and taxes paid abroad and additions to tax reserves.

[2] Saving before providing for depreciation and stock acquisition but after providing for additions to tax reserve.

Source: *National Income and Expenditure* 1970, Table 19; 1968, Table 22.

acts of saving but the distinction is not an easy one to make. Thus, a certain amount of National Savings, especially through the 'Save as you Earn' scheme, qualifies as 'contractual' while, on the other hand, a large proportion of the repayments to building societies must represent premature repayments such as occur when an existing house changes hands.

It is obvious that contributions paid to life assurance companies and pension funds are contractual saving but it would be wrong to assume that they can be calculated by simply adding up all insurance premiums and superannuation payments in a given period. 'The proportion of such premiums or contributions which are used to pay the costs of administration must be allocated to consumption. The remainder of a premium also ranks as consumption where the contingency insured against is loss or accident; such a premium is simply part of the cost of maintaining the insured asset intact and is no more saving than the provision for repair or replacement of assets which wear out.'[1]

But in all those cases where the premiums or contributions are paid by deferring present consumption in order to ensure a certain level of future consumption when death or retirement or the attainment of an agreed age occurs, such premiums or contributions, after the deduction of costs and profits, represent saving. There are certain statistical complications in estimating the sums saved for the purposes of superannuation, especially in the case of Government schemes where various categories of civil servants and teachers are promised pensions but do not suffer any deduction from current salaries. But, generally speaking, the sums saved for pensions are transmitted either to a specially constituted fund or to an insurance company and it is logical to include as part of current savings not only the contributions which the employees pay out of their salaries but also those which the employer pays on their behalf.

But the total of premiums and contributions cannot be treated as the net savings passing through these particular financial institutions. A small part, as we have noted, must be treated as consumption in so far as it is used to defray the costs of administration. On the other hand, an addition must be made in respect of the interest accruing on the funds accumulated in the past. That part of interest earnings which is needed to pay the future benefits to 'without-profits' policyholders and to pay bonuses to 'with-profits' policyholders should be treated as income that is withheld and ploughed back as savings on behalf of policyholders. A relatively small part in the case of proprietary companies is paid out to shareholders or held as undistributed profits, in which case it must be treated as part of company saving. Thus, apart from this minor qualification, the net increase in the sums accruing in the hands of superannuation funds and life assurance companies may be taken as repre-

Table 79

USES OF PERSONAL SAVINGS IN THE U.K.

	1951	*1952*	*1954*	*1956*	*1957*	*1958*	*1959*	*1960*	*1961*	*1962*	*1963*	*1964*	*1965*	*1966*	*1967*	*1968*	*1969*
Gross saving minus capital repayments and tax reserves	−1	306	261	663	634	488	664	1,050	1,517	1,406	1,449	1,647	1,883	2,038	1,957	1,796	1,924
Used for:																	
Life Assurance and Pension Funds	314	351	437	514	579	649	717	816	869	934	1,074	1,157	1,163	1,241	1,378	1,523	1,535
Investment in businesses and farms	211	205	242	226	200	238	224	259	278	238	270	209	261	306	359	441	409
New private housing	58	99	221	289	296	314	382	466	520	522	541	670	688	650	688	733	648
Unidentified	−584	−349	−639	−306	−441	−713	−652	−491	−150	−288	−436	−389	−229	−159	−467	−899	−668

Source: *National Income and Expenditure*, 1970 and earlier issues.

senting the net saving of the personal sector which arises from this source. Table 80 presents these data.

As might be expected, the contractual element in saving is much less volatile than the non-contractual one but, underlying the year-to-year fluctuations, there has been a marked change in their relative importance. In the early part of the period contractual saving was the dominant element, reaching 98 per cent of the total in 1955 and 105 per cent in 1958. Complete figures for the earlier period are not easily obtained but there can be little doubt that during most of the first post-war decade, non-contractual personal saving was negative. From 1959 to 1961 total saving grew much faster than contractual saving and the proportion of contractual saving fell to only 50 per cent. The process was reversed in 1962 and, since then, there have been relatively small fluctuations about an average of 60 per cent. Until recently it has been difficult to get accurate figures of the sums accruing through private pension funds but with the improvement in the availability of financial statistics, which was one of the most beneficial effects of the Report of the Radcliffe Committee on the Working of the Monetary System, it would appear that superannuation funds account for approximately one-third of total contractual saving.[2] This implies that life assurance funds have accounted for approximately 40 per cent of total personal savings in recent years.

Table 80

SAVING THROUGH LIFE ASSURANCE AND SUPERANNUATION, 1955–1968

Year	*(1) Net Increase in Funds £m.*	*(2) Personal Saving*[1] *£m.*	*(1) ÷ (2)* %
1955	477	486	98
1956	514	766	67
1957	579	759	76
1958	649	616	105
1959	717	834	86
1960	816	1,317	62
1961	869	1,722	50
1962	934	1,548	60
1963	1,074	1,671	64
1964	1,157	1,924	60
1965	1,163	2,124	55
1966	1,241	2,252	55
1967	1,378	2,197	63
1968	1,523	2,191	70
1969	1,535	2,405	64

[1] Saving before providing for depreciation and stock appreciation but after providing for additions to tax reserves.

Sources: *National Income and Expenditure,* 1970; *Board of Trade,* 1968.

Contractual saving in its various forms contains a very strong 'built-in' potential for growth and, barring major changes in government policy, this is likely to continue. The future trend in the relative importance of contractual and non-contractual savings will, therefore, depend on whether the latter can match, or even exceed, this growth rate and this in turn will depend largely on government policy, including the level of and distribution of taxation.[3] It seems likely, however, that non-contractual saving will play a more significant role in the future.

Besides engaging in current saving and investment, the personal sector is concerned in a great number of borrowing and lending transactions and purchases and sales of existing assets. The net effect of these in 1969 may be summarised as follows:

Table 81

ALLOCATION OF PERSONAL SAVINGS 1969

		1969 *£m.*
Saving[1]		2,311
Plus	Capital transfers and addition to resources	278
		2,589
Less	Taxes on Capital	−571
	Investment in Fixed Capital and Stocks	−1,207
	Net Increase in Financial Assets	811

[1] Before providing for depreciation and stock appreciation.

Source: *National Income Blue Book,* 1970.

This net gain of £811m. was composed of the following transactions.

Table 82

ACQUISITION OF FINANCIAL ASSETS BY PERSONAL SECTOR

	£m.
Increase in assets of life assurance and pension fund	1,535
Increase in liquid assets	1,365
Sales of Stock Exchange securities	−324
Increase in mortgage and hire-purchase liabilities	−900
Sales of existing land and buildings	−237
Decrease in other assets	−628
Total	811

Source: *National Income Blue Book,* 1970.

These tables demonstrate very clearly that the only major type of financial assets which the personal sector has been acquiring, in addition to the obligations of life assurance companies and pension funds, are liquid assets such as currency and bank deposits, deposits with building societies and hire-purchase finance companies, National Savings and local authority debt. It should also be noted that persons were net sellers of stock exchange securities even after allowing for the substantial purchases of unit trust units. Thus the practice of private individuals in the United Kingdom of directly purchasing Government and company securities has been largely transformed into one in which they prefer to entrust an increasing proportion of their savings to a variety of financial intermediaries. (See Tables 83 and 84.)

Table 83

SALES OF STOCK EXCHANGE SECURITIES BY THE PERSONAL SECTOR

£ million

	1963	*1964*	*1965*	*1966*	*1967*	*1968*	*1969*
Government Securities	231	88	91	17	237	259	−85
Company and Overseas securities	575	660	773	573	679	751	595
Less purchases of unit trust investments	−60	−77	−59	−105	−84	−258	−186
Net Sales	746	671	805	485	832	752	324

Source: National Income and Expenditure, 1970, Table 70.

We have now established that since the early post-war years the contribution made by the personal sector to the total volume of savings, which is the only large pool of mobile funds available to be channelled to the capital market, has been growing both absolutely and relatively. Within the personal sector institutional investors play an important role in assembling a large part of the community's savings and allocating them to various investment outlets. As such forms of saving continue to grow, the investment activities of the institutions accepting them have more and more impact on official policy and exert greater influence over the amount and type of securities offered in the capital market. Our figures show that of particular significance is the investment behaviour of the insurance companies which are quantitatively the most important, for their decisions about the proportion of their current funds which they are prepared to place at the disposal of the public sector have implications

Table 84

NET ACQUISITIONS OF LIQUID ASSETS BY THE PERSONAL SECTOR

£ million

	1963	*1964*	*1965*	*1966*	*1967*	*1968*	*1969*
Notes & Coin	42	71	84	34	61	72	74
Bank deposits	358	458	512	250	740	682	308
Deposits with building societies	490	501	657	726	1,090	762	890
Deposits with H.P. Finance Houses	8	24	30	12	−10	−1	−2
National Savings	318	358	74	−35	125	77	−113
Local Authority Debt (inc. temporary and longer term[1])	104	120	217	123	31	104	181
	1,320	1,532	1,574	1,110	2,037	1,696	1,338

[1] Excluding quoted securities and negotiable funds.

Source: *National Income and Expenditure, Blue Book,* 1970.

for the operation of monetary policy and debt management. Also their size gives them great power in directing the flow of capital and their relative preferences for the various forms of private debt and for the obligations of different types and sizes of company have a qualitative effect on capital formation.[4]

In considering the investment behaviour of life assurance companies we have to recall that in fulfilling their long-term contracts they are exposed to the risk that unexpected changes in interest and dividends may produce a smaller yield on their total portfolio than that assumed when the premiums were fixed. This so-called yield risk consists of two parts. First, there is the capital-value risk—the possibility that the liquidity position of the company will be such that the security must be sold before maturity and a capital loss sustained. Secondly, there is the income-risk—the possibility that market interest rates will change, either during the course of future premium receipts or at the time securities mature and the funds must be reinvested. These two forms of income-risk derive from different circumstances. In the first case, the risk is caused by promising an interest return at the outset but delaying the receipt of the premiums, and hence the investment, until some future date. This is the unique risk of the life assurance contract. The second, or recontract, risk arises because a specific income is desired for a longer period than the maturity of the asset chosen.[5]

In practice, capital-value risk, although it received considerable attention in early discussions of the principles of investment, is of secondary importance. The demand for capital-certainty and marketability is closely connected with the liquidity position of the companies which is a function of the cash inflow. Since today's premium inflow is largely determined by the rate of sales of policies in the past, the future cash inflow may be calculated from the rate of sales up to the present. The past rate of growth of British assurance companies has been such that, on the average, premium income inflow has been more than twice the outflow of claims, thus providing a natural built-in liquidity sufficient to withstand emergency demands for cash with remarkable little strain. Since it has been calculated that recent sales have been running at such a level that, even if no new policies were sold, the life fund would continue to grow for at least ten years and would not return to the original level for over twenty years, it can be said that the precautionary motive for liquidity hardly exists for assurance companies. Similarly, the demand for liquidity arising from the speculative motive is very weak mainly because the sheer weight of their investible income means that they tend to be price-makers in the capital market. The investment managers of the largest British life assurance companies each have more than £1m. of net income to invest every week of the year; if they hold off the market for even a few weeks, they will have such embarrassingly large funds to allocate to investment that prices in some markets may be turned against them if they try to make quick purchases—and time is always pressing. We can, therefore, conclude that for life offices the speculative motive is as weak as the precautionary motive, so that portfolio liquidity can easily be satisfied by placing a nominal amount to their funds in short-term government securities. In the vast majority of their investment decisions it can be said that the liquidity attributes of various assets are barely considered.[6]

Since the unique risk of life assurance is that of entering into a contract which promises an interest return from the outset although the receipt of premiums, and hence the investment, will be delayed until some future date, it is not surprising that much attention has been given to the problem of minimising income-risk. Immediately after the 1939–45 War investment managers were much concerned with such devices as 'matching' and 'immunisation' to combat the problem of falling interest-rates and were relieved to discover that it was theoretically possible for an assurance fund to achieve a large measure of protection. But in practice they appear to place little emphasis on the need to minimise income-risk for a variety of reasons of which one of the most important stems from the part played by the bonus loading element in with-profits premiums. This provides a reserve which can bear the brunt of any initial failure to earn the rate of return assumed when the without-profit policies were written. Provided that bonus declarations are flexible, companies are in a position to ride-out a fall in yields over a long period. At the same time the interests of with-profits policyholders make the objective of income-certainty undesirable, for it eliminates the possibility of profits as well as losses. In many of their contemporary activities the life offices' functions are not dissimilar to those of investment trusts and any policy which has a bias against profit may reduce their competitiveness with other financial institutions.

Given that minimisation of capital-value risk and income-risk are not important objectives of investment policy, it would seem that life assurance companies can be regarded as adopting a particular investment pattern by following the simple objective of maximising expected yields. There is little reason to believe that the pursuit of this simple maximisation rule is modified to any great extent by the need to obtain portfolio diversification in order to reduce the risk of default. 'It would appear that diversification only becomes a primary objective of policy when investment managers are choosing the ordinary shares of particular companies to hold in their equity portfolio. The picture which thus emerges is of income-conscious investors who strive to maximise their earnings by selecting their assets from a range of eligible investments, eligibility being determined by limits set on the amount of risk acceptable on any given asset.'[7] This aim of maximising expected yields operates under two constraints. First, many British companies face exchange risks through the international scope of their operations and it is sometimes prudent to ensure that liabilities in one currency are covered by assets expressed in that currency. Secondly, through the existence of different bases of taxation there is scope for choosing investments which are more suitable for one basis than for another.

So far we have been discussing the principles for the investment of life funds, which are quantitatively much the most significant, but general funds, which amounted to £m.1,335 at the end of 1968, are by no means negligible. Since they serve the different purpose of meeting unexpected claims during any given year, it is not surprising to discover that there is a strong demand for cash arising from the transactions motive which is a major point of difference in their investment behaviour. But apart from this the investment pattern of the two funds is surprisingly similar. General insurance companies, subject to an over-riding demand for readily marketable assets, behave as income-conscious investors who strive to maximise their earnings. The major contrast between the investment patterns of life and non-life funds is the emphasis on marketability which is reflected in the general funds' higher proportion of medium-dated gilt-edged stock and the smaller proportion of debentures, preference shares, mortgages and real property. The greatest similarity between the two funds is revealed by the demand for ordinary shares to satisfy the objective of maximising expected yields and hedging against inflation. The aim of maximising expected yields on a portfolio of adequate marketability is subject to a serious constraint in the form of a great variety of local regulations imposed by foreign governments. Since more than half of the assets of British insurance companies' general funds are held outside this country and are subject to a variety of restrictive influences, from which life funds are largely immune, the actual distribution of assets deviates to a considerable extent from that which, given full freedom of action to pursue their portfolio objectives, they would choose.

Having completed our discussion of the portfolio objectives of insurance companies, let us briefly consider the merits and demerits of the various categories of available assets. First, British Government and Government guaranteed securities have the great advantage for income-cautious investors that they offer complete security of income up to the date of redemption. Thus, provided that at the time of purchase the yield is greater than that assumed in the current premium, they are an attractive asset for a life assurance company. It is true that the expected yield may fall short of the apparent yield if, before the date of redemption, enforced sales should become necessary during a period of rising interest rates. Such a risk of capital loss among gilt-edged stock is at its greatest with irredeemable securities, as those life offices which purchased 'Daltons' in 1947 have learnt to their cost. Fortunately, as we have noted already, the danger that a life assurance company, whose business is expanding, may have to realise capital losses through sales of Government securities is remote. The real disadvantage of gilt-edged stock lies elsewhere, in that they offer no protection against inflation, which has clearly been a major problem since the war. It is a disadvantage which has become progressively more serious as the assurance companies have tended more and more to provide the services of investment trusts and to undertake more and more pension business in which the real value of the annuity is of crucial importance.[8] In general insurance the liabilities are short-term, rarely extending beyond three years, and because of the nature and financial magnitude of some of the risks involved, it is essential that substantial assets should be held in readily realisable form. The gilt-edged market meets this requirement because it is so large and active that opportunities always exist for buying and selling. Consequently, although the reasons may differ, all insurance funds will hold a substantial proportion of gilt-edged securities despite their inadequacy as a protection against inflation.

Non-Government fixed-interest stocks, of which industrial debenture and preference stock are the chief examples, are a suitable outlet for the investment of life funds particularly if they are redeemable. Prior to 1913 they were viewed with more favour than Government securities, the majority of which at that time were undated. For a long period after that they declined in popularity mainly through a reduction in their supply. This hypothesis is supported by the renewal of interest since 1965 when, owing to the impact of corporation tax, industrial companies have found it more advantageous to raise capital in this form. Debentures offer considerable security of income and, if dated, a large degree of capital-safety, but suffer from the same disadvantage as gilt-edged in that they offer no protection against inflation. They also suffer from other disadvantages. First, they sometimes carry a wide range of optional dates of repayment which reduce their attractiveness for investment managers, particularly those who are wedded to the principle of 'matching'. Secondly, they are not actively bought and sold in the market except immediately after they have been issued when they can still be bought free of stamp duty. Consequently, debentures are not a very flexible form of investment.

Preference shares, the friendless orphan of the Stock Exchange, suffer from a variety of disadvantages. They are usually undated but often at the same time carry the option of repayment which may be used, as in the past, to the disadvantage of the lender. This uncertainty, combined with the narrowness of the market, leads to considerable fluctuations in capital values while at the same time income-security is not as great as for Government securities and debentures. Finally, like all fixed-interest stock, they provide no hedge against inflation. Such a formidable array of disadvantages must be counteracted by a sufficient margin of yield over that obtainable on Government securities to make them suitable assets.

Equities suffer from the disadvantage that they are subject to serious fluctuations in capital value, which have been reduced in post-war years by the greater emphasis on full employment as a major objective of Government policy. On the other hand, they offer protection against the hazards of inflation and a share in the increase in profits and dividends which an expanding economy yields, although they do involve considerable administrative costs. The real justification for a substantial holding of equities is to secure a high expected yield in the form both of capital appreciation and dividends. This cannot be achieved without attempting to estimate the future prospects of a wide range of companies as a basis for selection. The existing portfolio of ordinary shares must be constantly reviewed and, if necessary, the composition must be changed in the light of current prices and future prospects. For these purposes an expert staff is essential.

Another type of equity investment, which provides a good hedge against inflation, is real property of which some companies, notably Norwich Union and Legal and General, have been active purchasers in recent years. In one respect property is superior to ordinary shares in that it enjoys greater stability of value but its main disadvantage is that it is not easily marketable and is particularly sensitive to political influences. Insurance companies usually confine their investments to blocks of high-class property such as offices, flats and shops combined with either offices or flats on good sites which, although freer from political control than house property, are subject to restrictions on development imposed by the Town and Country Planning Authorities. There are considerable administrative costs involved, in that the supervision and administration of land and property interests require the services of a specially skilled department. For this reason there are wide divergencies of practice among insurance companies in the extent to which they invest in property and some of them virtually neglect this field.

Finally, mortgages are an important category of assets. Their chief advantages include a low capital-value risk as compared with all quoted securities and a satisfactory yield. Against this they suffer from the disadvantages of considerable income-risk and poor marketability. They tend to be rather short-term investments, for the option of replacement means that the borrower may choose to liquidate his liability at a time when opportunities for reinvestment at a satisfactory yield are poor. They also suffer from the same disadvantage as real property in that the administration of loans and mortgages demands skilled supervision especially in those cases, admittedly rare, where the security is doubtful. The conflict between advantages and disadvantages produces a great variety of attitudes among the companies.

In view of the marked differences in the objectives served by life and general funds, it might be assumed that there would be equally sharp differences in the nature of the assets which make up their respective portfolios but this is not the case. In the basic cleavage between fixed-interest and equity investments very little difference can be discerned, although within their fixed-interest portfolio the life funds do concentrate upon much longer-dated stocks and in the general funds mortgages are not much sought after. At 31 December 1969 the life fund assets were made up as to 22·3 per cent in ordinary shares and 11·4 per cent in property, making 33·7 per cent in equity-type investments; in the general funds ordinary shares represented 27·5 per cent of the whole and property 6·0 per cent giving 33·5 per cent in the equity category. Fixed-interest investments represent the balance in each case. The reason for this uniformity in the pattern of investments probably rests on the need for general funds to secure the maximum long-term return on assets through equity investment in order to enhance the growth in shareholders' dividends over and above what may or may not be provided by the purely insurance operations. Moreover, the introduction of corporation tax in the 1965 Finance Act gave the general companies an additional incentive to invest in ordinary shares, and also in preference shares, for the benefit of the freedom from further corporation tax which ordinary and preference dividends paid by U.K. companies enjoy in the hands of a corporate recipient (i.e. so-called franked income).

Although we are primarily interested in contemporary investment policy, it is useful to note how the relative importance of the main types of asset have changed during this century as is shown in Table 85 which is based on the old series of statistics published in the Board of Trade Journal and the Annual Abstract of Statistics. Since 1962, as a result of the promptings of the Radcliffe Committee, the Board of Trade has been publishing details of the assets of insurance companies, calculated on a slightly different basis from that for previous data. One novel and useful feature of these recent statistics is that they are given in both book and cash values. Taking a broad view of investment behaviour since the Second World War, the outstanding features are the relative decline in the importance of British Government securities and the corresponding rise in equity investment including both ordinary shares and property; in the rest of the fixed-interest category there has been a steady rise in the relative importance of both mortgages and debentures. The dominant position occupied by British Government securities immediately after the war was the direct result of the agreement between the Government and the industry whereby all new money was channelled towards the public sector and, with the emphasis on cheap money at that time, it was a major objective of the companies' policy to seek out other more rewarding outlets for their money—an objective which was rendered less easily attainable by the Labour Government's policy of nationalisation. Given the evidence of the risk of continuing inflation and the changes in the characteristics of their business, it is not surprising that at varying dates during the 1950s many, if not most, insurance companies decided to divert a very significant proportion of the funds becoming available for investment towards ordinary shares and property. This policy has not been pursued with unshakeable inflexibility and it is interesting to note that during recent years (with the notable exception of 1968) there has

Table 85

ASSETS OF BRITISH INSURANCE COMPANIES[1]

	1913	*1937*	*1946*	*1951*	*1956*	*1960*	*1964*	*1968*
Total Assets (£m.)	—	1,745	2,526	3,590	5,207	7,156	10,102	14,832
Structure of Assets: (% of Total Assets)								
Mortgages (including Policy Loans)	1·6[2]	13·9	5·9	8·7	11·4	12·4	14·8	14·8
British Government Securities	0·9	21·4	39·9	31·7	23·4	18·5	16·6	13·7
Debentures }	30·6 (Debentures and Preference Stocks and Shares)	16·1	10·3	10·4	12·9	13·7	15·2	15·9
Preference Stocks and Shares }		8·2	7·9	7·4	6·7	5·1	4·0	2·6
Ordinary Stocks and Shares	3·4	9·9	9·6	11·5	15·9	21·2	22·3	25·0
Land, House Property, Ground Rent, etc.	—	5·5	4·7	6·4	7·9	8·6	9·0	9·4

[1] All insurance companies established within Great Britain.
[2] Including property.

Sources: *The Economist*, 1913; *Board of Trade*, 1937–68, *Annual Abstract of Statistics*.

Table 86

FINANCIAL ASSETS HELD BY INSURANCE COMPANIES

	1961 £m.	%	*1962 £m.*	%	*1964 £m.*	%	*1966 £m.*	%	*1968 £m.*	%	*1969 £m.*	%
Total	7,099		7,689		9,132		10,596		12,720		13,771	
Public sector securities	2,138	30·1	2,311	30·1	2,580	28·2	2,712	25·6	2,961	22·5	3,152	22·2
Ordinary	1,462	20·6	1,572	20·4	1,933	21·2	2,199	20·8	2,943	22·4	3,238	22·8
Preference	362	5·1	371	4·8	399	4·4	426	4·0	347	2·6	327	2·3
Debentures	886	12·5	981	12·8	1,313	14·4	1,735	16·4	2,184	16·6	2,290	16·1
Mortgages and Loans (*a*)	662	9·3	715	9·3	800	8·8	904	8·5	1,052	8·0	1,114	7·8
(*b*)	411	5·8	467	6·0	603	6·6	838	7·9	1,001	7·6	1,123	7·9
(*c*)	21	0·3	21	0·3	26	0·3	25	0·2	32	0·2	37	0·3
Overseas Govt. etc. securities	106	1·5	112	1·5	119	1·3	106	1·0	139	1·1	123	0·9
Land, property, ground rents	675	9·5	730	9·5	851	9·3	1,084	10·2	1,349	10·2	1,539	10·8
Other	44	0·6	39	0·5	49	0·5	63	0·6	5	0·0	22	0·2
Cash and short term assets	116	1·6	106	1·4	146	1·6	123	1·2	188	1·4	246	1·7
Agents balances	216	3·1	263	3·4	312	3·4	382	3·6	519	3·9	560	3·9

been a discernible weakening in the companies' appetite for ordinary shares by comparison with what they invested a few years earlier.[9] New investment in ordinary shares in respect of the companies' United Kingdom operations were on average £170m. per annum between 1959 and 1961 whereas the figures for the most recent years were as follows:

Table 87

INSURANCE COMPANIES' ALLOCATION OF NEW MONEY TO ORDINARY SHARES

(cash value) £m.

1962	*1963*	*1964*	*1965*	*1966*	*1967*	*1968*	*1969*
86	119	156	86	103·4	99·6	223·7	148·1

Source: Board of Trade.

The reduction in the pace of investment in ordinary shares between 1965 and 1967 was to some extent taken up through increased investment in property which averaged £100m. a year during this period compared with an average of £65m. between 1959 and 1961.

So far as fixed-interest securities are concerned, the insurance companies are now substantial investors in industrial debentures mainly by subscribing to new issues. The figures below show how this item has moved in recent years.

Table 88

INSURANCE COMPANIES' ALLOCATION OF NEW MONEY TO DEBENTURES

(cash value) £m.

1962	*1963*	*1964*	*1965*	*1966*	*1967*	*1968*	*1969*
99	146	189	206	231·4	185·4	218·1	122·3

Source: Board of Trade.

Their policy with regard to mortgages tends to be the passive one of responding to the pressure of demand which is a function of the relative availability of funds from the building societies and, consequently, it is possible to detect a 'scissors' movement between the building societies' advances on mortgages and those of the insurance companies.

Since the process of reducing the proportion of British Government securities from the high war-time levels was more or less completed in the late 1950s, the policy of the companies appears to have been to treat it as a residual item and to direct an increased flow of funds towards this category only when other outlets are either unavailable or are con-

Table 89

INSURANCE COMPANIES' ALLOCATION OF NEW MONEY TO BRITISH GOVERNMENT SECURITIES

(cash values £m.)

1962	*1963*	*1964*	*1965*	*1966*	*1967*	*1968*	*1969*
149	98	88	48	21	219	120	107

Source: Board of Trade.

sidered unattractive, although in the last few years a more positive attitude has developed as yields have reached historically very high levels. Certainly, the sums invested have shown considerable annual fluctuations as Table 89 demonstrates.

Thus far we have been looking at the companies' investment policy from the point of view of their choice of assets but this provides little information on their relative importance in different sectors of the capital market. In principle this can be obtained by looking at the capital market in terms of either stocks or flows, but there is much to be said for using the 'flow of funds' approach, because in general it appears that they change the structure of their assets not so much by switching their existing holdings as by altering the disposition of their newly-acquired funds. This means that to a great extent the present pattern of investments has been determined by investment decisions which were taken a long time

Table 90

NET INVESTMENT OF INSURANCE COMPANIES

(cash values £m.)

	1963	*1964*	*1965*	*1966*	*1967*	*1968*	*1969*
Mortgages including policy loans	93	135	183	159	92	144	201
British Gov. Sec.	98	88	47	22	219	120	107
British Municipal, Overseas Gvt. and Municipal Secs.	33	2	16	−12	2	14	33
Debentures	146	189	205	230	186	218	122
Preference Shares	23	14	15	2	−32	−21	−4
Ordinary Shares	119	157	87	102	99	225	148
Other	−1	3	—	−1	—	1	2
Property	62	57	90	118	95	121	186
Cash, etc.	44	28	−19	−6	45	−1	47
	617	673	624	614	706	820	842

Source: Board of Trade Journal.

ago; a change in preferences for assets has to be maintained for a considerable number of years before it makes much impact on the relative proportions of different categories of assets.[10] The actual flow of funds into the different available channels is shown in Table 90.

It will be noted that all categories of assets benefited from the increased flow of funds made available by the insurance companies in every year, the only important exception being preference shares. Undoubtedly, the most striking feature of the whole post-war period has been the great contribution made by the insurance companies to capital formation in the industrial sector. Some indication of their relative importance in

Table 91

INVESTMENT OF NEW MONEY IN ORDINARY SHARES

(£m.)

	1963	*1964*	*1965*	*1966*	*1967*	*1968*	*1969*
Insurance companies	119·0	157·0	86·0	103·4	99·6	223·7	148·1
Pension Funds— Public Sector	38·1	41·3	37·1	34·0	36·6	61·7	83·6
Pension Fund— Local Authorities	35·6	34·0	36·0	33·7	38·1	52·3	52·6
Pension Fund— Private Sector	102·9	133·4	101·6	124·4	121·9	167·0	83·2
Investment Trusts	67·5	67·8	−29·7	3·4	86·5	101·2	−99·6
Unit Trusts	42·2	61·7	62·1	93·1	82·6	196·9	131·9

Source: Board of Trade and Financial Statistics.

different sectors of this industrial market is given in Table 92 which compares the supply of new funds to each sector from the insurance companies with the demand from that sector as represented by new issues. It must be understood that such a comparison does not mean that the insurance companies actually bought this proportion of new issues; on the contrary the figures represented their purchases of both new and existing securities in each category. Nevertheless, in broad terms the table emphasises very clearly their overwhelming importance, especially in the supply of fixed-interest capital. Their significance as a source of equity capital is underlined by the comparison with the sums provided by the other major institutional investors, although it should be noted that the private pension funds, which traditionally are much more heavily committed to equity investment, usurped the place of the insurance companies as the most important source of equity capital in 1965, 1966 and 1967. However, this sustained buying of ordinary shares has as yet had surprisingly little impact on the insurance companies' share of the total equity capital

Table 92

NEW ISSUES AND NET INVESTMENTS BY INSURANCE COMPANIES

	Debentures			Preference			Ordinary		
	New Issues (1)	*Net Investment £m. (2)*	*(2) as a percentage of (1)*	*New Issues (1)*	*Net Investment £m. (2)*	*(2) as a percentage of (1)*	*New Issues (1)*	*Net Investment £m. (2)*	*(2) as a percentage of (1)*
1963	271·5	146	54	14·7	23	153	163·9	119	72
1964	234·0	189	80	10·7	14	127	168·9	157	93
1965	454·6	205	45	3·2	15	500	45·5	87	193
1966	479·5	230	48	16·4	2	12	142·5	102	72
1967	343·5	186	54	5·7	−32	n.a.	72·6	99	135
1968	309·5	218	70	3·1	−21	n.a.	363·7	225	62
1969	397·4	122	31	—	−4	n.a.	195·0	148	76
1963–1969	2,490·0	1,296	52				1,452·1	937	65

of quoted companies, which is still no more than 11 per cent, but this is an average figure and understates their greater relative importance as shareholders in the most rapidly expanding sectors of British industry which have been more dependent on new issues of capital than the rest.[11]

Another aspect of their equity policy which deserves attention is the extent to which they act counter-cyclically in the timing of their purchases. It has been argued by various writers that the present organisation of the Stock Exchange whereby there exist good facilities for short-term speculation combined with only limited facilities for long-term speculation may be dangerous and may be responsible for excessive swings in prices which are not justified by underlying economic conditions.[12] A possible remedy would be for 'the institutions, which have an incentive to take a long view and the professional analysts qualified to do so, should intervene more actively in the market'.[13] This requires that they should always be prepared to sell stock when in their view the current price is excessively high in relation to long-term prospects and vice versa. At one time it was believed that the insurance companies are so hard-pressed in selecting investments for their new money that they do not behave as traders but buy securities to hold for income and are extremely reluctant to sell stock which they consider to be fundamentally sound, even though the current price is excessively high in relation to long-term prospects.[14] However, the improvements in statistical information since 1962 show that, whatever was the position in the past, they are now much more active investors. See Table 93. To some extent this trend reflects

Table 93

INSURANCE COMPANIES' TURNOVER IN ORDINARY SHARES

£m.

	1962	*1963*	*1964*	*1965*	*1966*	*1967*	*1968*	*1969*
Purchases	183	243	266	206	220	313	595	520
Sales	97	124	109	119	118	214	370	372
Net Acquisition	+86	+119	+157	+87	+102	+99	+225	+148
Turnover	280	368	375	325	338	527	965	892

Source: Board of Trade and Financial Statistics.

the surge of mergers but an increased readiness to job around in the market has obviously played an important part. This increased activity does not mean that they behaved counter-cyclically for, as Fig. 10 shows, their equity buying during the period from 1964 to 1968 followed closely the movement of equity prices, although their appetite appears to have slackened in the last quarter of 1968 as the bull market reached its peak.

Such a conclusion, however, must be extremely tentative for, given the importance of the insurance companies as price-makers in the market, the observed movement of equity prices reflects variations in the strength of their demand; furthermore, since rights issues, which insurance companies find particularly attractive for building up their portfolios, are more prevalent during bull markets, it would be surprising if their net acquisitions did not tend to increase concomitantly.

From discussions with investment managers it would appear that they

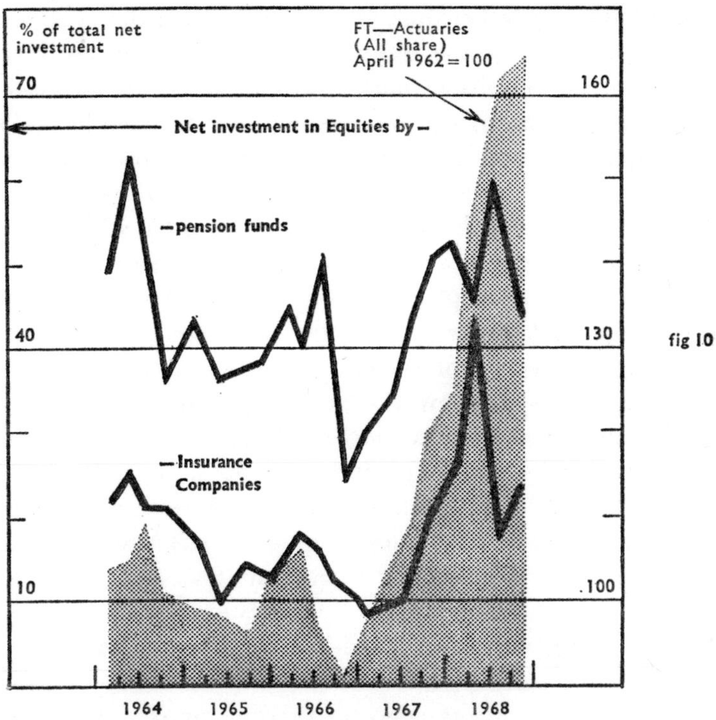

Source: *The Economist*, Insurance Supplement, 1969.

FIG. 10. *Insurance Companies' Share Purchases in Relation to Price Changes*

adopt the following criteria in selecting equities. First, they are only in very exceptional cases prepared to consider buying unquoted shares or the shares of companies registered overseas. Secondly, they dislike investing in companies whose fortunes are tied up with one particular commodity (or even a small group of commodities), particularly if that commodity is subject to considerable price fluctuations. This criterion effectively rules out a large number of British registered companies which operate mines and plantations overseas. Thirdly, they try to confine their investments to companies whose directors are known to be wise or at any rate unquestionably prudent, and in particular they are not displeased by a cautious dividend distribution policy. Fourthly, they insist on being minority shareholders and aim, if possible, to hold less than 3 per cent, and certainly not more than 6 per cent, of any one industrial company's equity. Fifthly, they do not want more than a tiny fraction of their total funds to be invested in any one company. Finally, they prefer their assets to be either dated or readily marketable and are prepared to lock up at most only a very small fraction of their total assets in securities of doubtful marketability.[15]

We must also remember that, in addition to their direct contribution to the finance of industry, the insurance companies play an important indirect role in the new issue market. For in acting as underwriters they have immensely strengthened its organisation and have helped to reduce the 'economic distance' between lender and borrower. Issuing houses prefer them to many other underwriters because of their large resources and their willingness to hold the securities on offer with the result that they usually underwrite more than half of any new issue. They are particularly active in support of placings which are attractive to insurance companies because they make possible the purchase of securities in blocks of convenient size, usually of £5,000 or more.

Fig. 11 attempts to show the pattern of investment in the various sections of the fixed-interest market including Government securities, company debentures and loans and mortgages. It tends to confirm the impression that, although insurance companies were net buyers of long-dated Government securities in every quarter except two, they treat them as a residual form of investment. Between 1965 and 1966 there was a marked shift towards Government securities and by the third quarter of 1966 these, along with other fixed-interest investments, were absorbing almost the whole of their inflow of new money. Early in 1967, mainly through fear of 'missing the bus' in the bull market, they turned their backs abruptly on gilt-edged stock but 'returned later with a much reduced appetite'.[16] The second feature of their policy towards gilt-edged is that their net acquisitions are the outcome of active switching operations, for in 1965 and 1966 their turnover of Government securities amounted to £500m. per annum, rising to £850m. in 1967 and £1,100m. in 1968, while their net inflow rose only by one-third. It used to be thought that only a few companies were prepared to give the meticulous attention to the gilt-edged market necessary for the pursuit of a profitable switching policy but it now appears that they are more numerous. Finally, Fig. 11 confirms the importance of the insurance companies' contribution to the debenture market which was maintained at a consistently high level throughout the period.

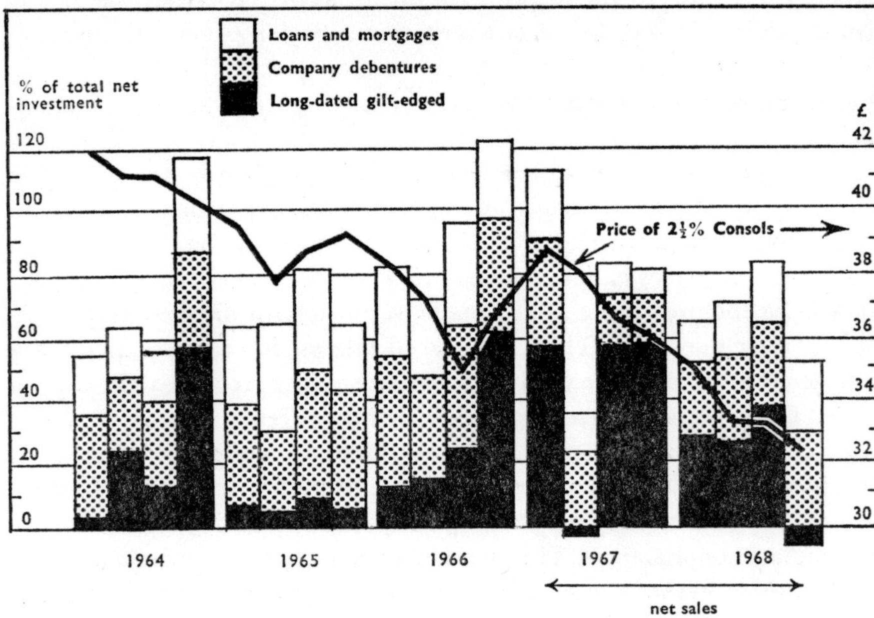

Source: *The Economist,* Supplement on Insurance, July, 1969.

FIG. 11. *Net Investment in Fixed-Interest Assets by Insurance Companies*

Let us now summarise this discussion of the role of the insurance companies in the capital market. In considering their role as collectors of savings we found that for most of our period savings administered by them accounted for more than 50 per cent of total personal saving, which itself comprises the only large mobile pool of funds for the capital market. What is more the volume of life assurance in particular is growing. Since 1945 the assets of all insurance companies have grown by an average of 8 per cent and there is no evidence yet of any slackening in the pace of expansion. Thus, there is every likelihood that the insurance industry will continue to control a large proportion of personal saving for many years to come. A second feature of their role as savers is that the savings they administer are contractual and, therefore, relatively stable. This means that the investment managers of life companies must frame their policies in the knowledge that week by week funds will remorselessly flow in as a result of past sales of policies.

In investing these funds the investment managers of life funds do not pay particular attention to the avoidance of capital-value risk and income-risk but follow the objective of maximising expected yield. There is little reason to believe that this maximisation rule is modified in practice by the conscious pursuit of portfolio diversification to avoid the risk of default, except in the case of ordinary shares. So far as general funds are concerned, the picture is surprisingly similar except that they have a greater transactions-demand for cash and place greater stress on marketability.

In the actual execution of policy the basic problem is the choice between equity and fixed-interest investments, which is strongly influenced by relative changes in expected yields. For much of the 1950s the life insurance companies had a voracious appetite for ordinary shares but they appear for the time being to be broadly satisfied with the existing proportion in their portfolios. Their diminished interest in ordinary shares was first detected at the time of the appearance of the 'reverse yield gap' in 1959. The position of general funds is slightly different in that the introduction of corporation tax in 1965 gave them an additional incentive to purchase ordinary shares. A second feature of their investment behaviour is that they aim at all times to keep fully invested and do not normally accumulate cash balances. Thirdly, they do not appear to operate countercyclically on market swings, although the interpretation of the statistical evidence is very hazardous, and are influenced more by longer-term aims than by short-term market movements. Fourthly, within the category of fixed-interest investments British Government securities appear to be a residual item, the volume of purchases being dependent on balances available after other assets, such as debentures, have been acquired. Finally, it was at one time believed that they did not actively trade in securities and altered the composition of their portfolios by changing the allocation of their new money to attain their objectives. However, the improved statistical information available since 1962 suggests that this conclusion needs to be modified.[17]

NOTES

1 G. Clayton and W. T. Osborn, op. cit., p. 26.

2 For example, during 1963 net acquisitions by insurance companies amounted to £617 while those of pension funds were £310 1s. See J. G. Blease, 'Institutional Investors and the Stock Exchange', *District Bank Review*, No. 151, September 1964, p. 41.

3 See E. Victor Morgan, 'Personal Saving and the Capital Market', *District Bank Review*, No. 163, September 1967, p. 10.

4 For a more theoretical discussion of the role of the financial intermediaries, see G. Clayton and W. T. Osborn, op. cit., pp. 28–35.

5 For a fuller discussion, see Clayton & Osborn, op. cit., pp. 59–87.

6 For a more extensive treatment, see Clayton and Osborn, op. cit., pp. 63–70.

7 Clayton & Osborn, ibid., p. 81.

8 See Clayton and Osborn, op. cit., pp. 116-119.

9 A distinction here should be noted between life and general funds. While life funds may have lost their appetite to some extent, the provisions of the 1965 Finance Act have provided general funds with a greater incentive to buy ordinary shares.

10 As we shall see, this appears to be less true than it was in the past.

11 For a more detailed analysis see Clayton and Osborn, op. cit., pp. 167–179.

12 See E. Victor Morgan, *The Stock Exchange*, pp. 271–272 and Clayton and Osborn, op. cit., pp. 233, 234.

13 E. Victor Morgan, op. cit., p. 272.

14 See Clayton and Osborn, ibid., p. 235.

15 For a more detailed analysis see Clayton and Osborn, op. cit., pp. 183, 184.

16 *The Economist*, Supplement on Insurance, July 1969.

17 See Clayton and Osborn, op. cit., p. 221.

Chapter 16

THE INTERNATIONAL ROLE OF BRITISH INSURANCE

> 'While Britain acquired new sources of visible exports, the invisible ones, which had once more than balanced our international payments, languished. Britain was simply no longer the centre of the world's commercial and financial system, nor its major maritime carrier.'
>
> E. J. Hobsbawn

We have already had cause to comment on the international character of the British insurance industry and have shown how during the 19th century in particular it showed commendable enterprise and initiative in penetrating the markets of the world so that it has become one of the most international of all British industries. We now turn to a brief consideration of the size and nature of the contribution made to Britain's invisible earnings from these international activities.

In the first place, as we saw in the last chapter, the investment managers of both life and general funds in pursuing their investment objectives choose to invest a proportion of their assets in foreign securities, the income from which constitutes a credit item on the invisible account of the balance of payments and makes a significant contribution to the industry's foreign earnings. Unfortunately, although the Board of Inland Revenue provides global estimates to the Central Statistical Office of the interest and dividends received on foreign government and municipal stocks, and/or paid through U.K. paying agents and coupon dealers,[1] there is no way of separately identifying in these estimates the portfolio income received by insurance companies which is submerged in the total for portfolio investment receipts. However, the British Insurance Association estimated that in 1965, given that the book value of its members' foreign investments were £454m., the net income was approximately £25m.—a figure which must have increased quite sharply in recent years as a result of devaluation and the rise in interest rates in the major international centres.

Secondly, and more importantly, there are the foreign earnings which are directly derived from their primary function of satisfying the foreign demand for insurance cover. The contributions from the various sectors of the market differ considerably in importance. While, as we have already noted, the business of British life assurance companies is predominantly domestic in origin, about 25 companies transact ordinary life business overseas on a significant scale. In the past few years this source of business has in fact been expanding at a slightly faster rate than that originating in the United Kingdom and in 1967 provided slightly more than 10 per cent of the total premium income of British life assurance companies. This foreign life business is much more heavily concentrated than its domestic counterpart, since four companies, namely, the Prudential, Standard Life, Norwich Union Life and Legal and General, in recent years have controlled more than 75 per cent of the premium income.

But it is general business, mainly fire, accident and marine, which is the principal source of direct foreign earnings. Since, unfortunately, the statistics still do not differentiate between domestic and foreign premium income, we are forced to rely on such indirect evidence as that given by the British Insurance Association to the Radcliffe Committee on the Working of the Monetary System, in which it was estimated that approximately two-thirds of premium income from general business emanated from the underwriting of foreign risks. Although in the ten years since the publication of this Report there has probably been a slight decline in the proportion of overseas income, it appears reasonable to estimate that currently overseas business contributes 60 per cent of total premium income. While British insurance companies transact general business in a great many countries, certain countries, especially the U.S.A. and Canada, are the major sources of income. In 1967 the branches and local subsidiaries of British companies in the United States wrote premiums in that country valued at $1,075m. which is equivalent to approximately 41 per cent of the total overseas premium income of U.K. companies in respect of general insurance, while business in Canada, Australia, and other Commonwealth countries accounted for a further 30 per cent. As in the case of life assurance the business is heavily concentrated in the hands of a few companies; for example, in 1967 four large composite groups, namely the Royal, Northern and Employers, General Accident and Commercial Employers Union[2] accounted, with their American subsidiaries, for over 90 per cent of the premiums earned by British companies in that country.[3]

In view of Lloyd's interest in general business, it is clear that this is another important source of foreign income. Business derived from foreign clients by Lloyd's underwriters and brokers yields income in two forms, namely from policies underwritten in the market and from brokers' commissions. Unfortunately, once again statistical obstacles make it difficult to give accurate figures of the volume of foreign business. 'However, figures are available to show that U.S. and Canadian dollar business has for a considerable period of time represented approximately 50 per cent of Lloyd's total premium income, and it is reasonable to estimate that other foreign business accounts for a further 25 per cent. Accordingly, Lloyd's net premium income from all overseas business (on the basis that it is equal to 75 per cent of total premium income) has progressively increased from approximately £130m. in 1955 to approximately £216m. in 1965.'[4] If we apply the same method of calculation as used by the Committee on Invisible Earnings to more recent data, it would appear that Lloyd's currently earns more than £350m. from overseas.

Income from brokers' commissions arises from the fact, which we have already noted, that all business at Lloyd's has to be negotiated through accredited Lloyd's brokers. 'Sometimes foreign business is commissioned directly from a U.K. broker but more often than not through an overseas agent or subsidiary of the broker. In the former case, the U.K. broker would expect a commission of about 20 per cent of premium income; in the latter about 5 per cent. Lloyd's estimate that foreign earnings of brokers in respect of insurance business transacted at Lloyd's is currently well in excess of £10m. In addition, brokers earn commission from non-Lloyd's business and sometimes from business transacted between overseas clients and overseas insurance companies.'[5] In addition to the direct insurance business, derived from overseas by insurance companies and Lloyd's, a small amount of foreign cover is provided by mutual indemnity companies whose activities are generally confined to the shipping industry, but their total premium income is no more than a few million pounds.

While quantitatively these direct operations of Lloyd's and the foreign agencies, branches and subsidiaries of insurance companies are much the most important source of foreign income, there are two additional sources which must be mentioned. First, there is the income from the reinsurance market of which London is the recognised centre; secondly, there are the earnings from the placing of foreign risks by brokers with the insurance companies at their head offices in the U.K. and with the underwriting syndicates at Lloyd's. Although in the past this was the usual method whereby overseas risks were underwritten, such business, which is known in the industry as 'home/foreign', is now of minor importance since, where a significant volume of business is obtained from any overseas territory, it is normally transacted through a branch office, subsidiary company or agency. The inability to obtain any estimate of the volume of this business is rendered even less important by the fact that 'home/foreign' earnings from marine underwriting, including aviation and transit, are already incorporated in the returns to the Board of Trade.

Until the publication of the Report of the Committee on Invisible Exports was published there was no precise indication of the industry's contribution to the balance of payments but, since then estimates have been published by the Central Statistical Office which (including portfolio income) give the following picture:

Table 94

ESTIMATED OVERSEAS EARNINGS OF THE U.K. INSURANCE INDUSTRY

(£m.)

	1965	*1966*	*1967*	*1968*	*1969*
Companies home/foreign underwriting business and income on direct and portfolio investment	46	66	78	90	111
Lloyd's (underwriting and interest)	14[1]	20[1]	45[1]	74[1]	91[2]
Brokers	21	23	27	35	41
U.K. net insurance income overseas *including* portfolio income	81	109	150	199	243
U.K. net insurance income overseas *excluding* portfolio income	50	78	115	161	200

[1] Three year average.
[2] Two year average.

Source: Table 57, *U.K. Balance of Payments, 1970 (The Pink Book)*, C.S.O.

This table shows that the insurance industry's average yearly contribution to Britain's invisible exports in these five years has increased sharply and now represents approximately one-half of the total of all British invisible exports by the financial sector.

It is clear, therefore, that British insurers' interests in overseas markets are of fundamental importance, not only to themselves but to the economy generally but, although they make a gratifying contribution to invisible earnings, it is pertinent to enquire whether their performance could not be improved. At the outset it should be emphasised that the industry has operated under certain handicaps in recent years of which the most significant has been the growing tendency of overseas governments to place various legislative controls on domestic insurance operations which have, directly or indirectly, operated to the disadvantage of the British insurance market. While there are strong reasons why developing countries should wish to harness the funds arising from insurance business for their development programmes, the measures which they take to ensure that this happens, such as legal requirements about the proportion of funds to be invested locally, unfortunately tend to reduce the flexibility and thus the competitiveness of British insurers even though in terms of international economic welfare this may be a price which ought to be paid. Overseas operations have been developed to their existing scale on the assumption that insurers would be free to transfer funds from one market to another as the need arises. Since the principle of insurance consists of the accumulation of funds from many sources to cover a wide spectrum of risks, any regulations which have the effect of splitting up reserves into a number of separate funds, restricted to one particular country, inevitably reduce efficiency. However, while such regulations may have inhibited the growth of British insurance in the underdeveloped world, they can have had only a marginal impact on total overseas business since this is heavily concentrated in the United States and the so-called 'white' Commonwealth countries. Since a detailed examination of recent experience in all these markets would require a book in itself, we shall limit ourselves to a brief survey of the American market which is not only quantitatively the most significant but also has been a major cause of poor underwriting results from overseas operations in the past decade, especially in motor and industrial fire insurance.

Although the premiums derived from American business constitute an extremely important element in the total premium income of some major British companies, the U.K. industry currently controls only a minor segment of the American market, for in 1966 the volume of business underwritten by branches and local subsidiaries and affiliates represented a mere 4·8 per cent of total premium income. What is even more striking is that their relative importance has fallen rapidly since 1946 when they accounted for 10·9 per cent of total business. (See Table 95.)

Table 95

DISTRIBUTION OF GENERAL INSURANCE BUSINESS IN THE U.S.

	1946 Net Premiums $m.	%	*1966* Net Premiums $m	%
U.S. Proprietary Companies	2,622	64·7	14,058	63·8
U.S. Mutual Companies	879	21·7	6,017	27·4
U.K. Companies	441	10·9	1,048	4·8
Lloyd's and others	109	2·7	876	4·0
Total	4,051	100·0	21,989	100·0

Source: Best's *Insurance Guides.*

The causes of this declining market share are various but the major one, which has also affected the American proprietary companies, has been competition from two groups, first, those companies which sell insurance direct to the public without agents and without brokers and, secondly, the mutual companies which have built up an enviable reputation for the rapid settlement of claims without involving the insured in protracted legal proceedings. With regard to competition from direct-selling insurers the British companies appear to have been slow, as they have been in the domestic market, to remedy some of the obvious deficiencies in their marketing policies. Several British companies which have withdrawn from the American market in recent years realised too late that their agents and brokers were more concerned with the commissions they received than the quality of the business which they introduced or the accuracy of the insurance proposals which they put forward. 'What is essential is a much greater caution in the selection of American representatives, a much more searching enquiry into their backgrounds and reputations and a greater reticence in according to them a freedom of insuring risks on the insurer's behalf without reference to him.'[6] Moreover, the need to scrutinise critically the use of agents and brokers in the U.S. is even more urgent than in the United Kingdom because the power of agents is greatly strengthened by the organisational features of the market, including legal recognition that the right to renew contracts rests with them rather than with the underwriters. This right has provided agents with a useful bargaining weapon, for the threat of switching business has frequently been successfully employed to raise commissions which amount to as much as 30, or even 40, per cent of premium income.

But more disturbing than the decline in the British industry's relative share of the world's largest insurance market are the poor underwriting results as shown below. These have been attributed by the industry to the same causes which have led to disappointing results in the home market, namely progressive deterioration on motor business due to inflationary increases in the costs of repair, and an equally relentless tendency towards higher risk of loss from fire underwriting which stems in part from an increase in both the incidence and damage from fire in new buildings. There are additional hazards in the American market such as hurricane damage which was responsible for the disastrous results in 1965. In that year large areas of the United States were devastated by Hurricane Betsy which inflicted losses of $700m.—even more than the San Francisco earthquake—of which $30m. was borne by British insurers.

The task of making underwriting more profitable in the U.S. is rendered more difficult by the paradox that the country, with the most

Table 96

U.S. BUSINESS OF BRITISH INSURANCE COMPANIES AND THEIR AMERICAN SUBSIDIARIES

$'000s.

Year	*Total premium income* *(1)*	*Underwriting profits* *(2)*	*Interest earnings* *(3)*	*Total Earnings in U.S.*[1] *(2) + (3)* *(4)*	*Earnings remitted home %*
1957	770,850	–58,373	42,893	–15,480	—
1958	776,667	–34,404	44,771	10,367	138
1959	806,890	– 8,258	46,604	38,346	57
1960	842,782	–12,423	49,780	37,357	72
1961	855,301	–18,554	52,959	34,405	77
1962	867,046	–10,859	54,199	43,340	48
1963	907,319	–32,414	57,861	25,447	72
1964	936,765	–47,536	60,662	13,126	167
1965	990,519	–49,653	63,515	13,862	247
1966	1,047,812	–16,177	69,314	53,137	56
1967	1,075,353	–11,037	75,796	64,759	48

[1] Gross interest, dividends and rents less investment expenses.

Source: Best's *Insurance Guide.*

dedicated commitment to the capitalist ethic, subjects the insurance industry to a rigorous form of supervision which prevents increases in rates without prior approval of the insurance commissioners of the various states. This system creates special problems for insurers, for not only is there need to convince the state insurance authorities of the case for increasing rates, but also the administrative process itself inevitably involves considerable delays. With regard to the former, insurers have to overcome the political unpopularity of rate increases of which the state insurance commissioners, whose appointments are political, are only too well aware. Although resistance to increases is not universal, in certain states it is firm and unyielding while in others there have been compromises whereby the state insurance commissioner has sanctioned smaller increases than those asked for. In other cases the commissioners have demanded that income from investments arising from the premium reserves for motor business should be included in the rating calculations. But whatever may be the attitude of individual insurance commissioners, there is the problem, which is common to all states, that when new rates are eventually agreed they may be based on statistical information which is two years out of date. Given the unfavourable influences affecting motor and fire underwriting to which we have already alluded, such a lag in adjusting rates is sufficient to ensure continuing losses for many years to come. One of the consequences of this ponderous and unwieldy system of rate regulation is that inevitably the appropriate levels of premiums for some classes of risk are above the permitted ceiling and, therefore, unacceptable to most insurers. This increases competition for the better risks, particularly in the commercial field, which becomes so intense that undercutting below the permitted maximum rate leads to unprofitable underwriting. This has induced two state insurance departments—in Massachusetts and New York—to call a halt to the practice of cutting legally filed rates by more stringent supervision.

The response of many U.S. insurance companies has been, among other things, to review their marketing policies, to make a vigorous attack on costs, and to take advantage of what are believed to be considerable economies of scale. Certainly, some companies have been reasonably successful in reducing expense ratios; for example, the Continental Insurance Company of New York, which bought a stake in the Phoenix Assurance Company in 1963, succeeded in reducing its expense ratio by one and a half percentage points over the two years to March 1965 on premiums of some $500m. Nevertheless, sheer size is not necessarily a solution for if a group becomes too large for central control its costs may increase; more significant for the reduction of expense ratios appears to be a steady annual increase in premium income within the optimum size for a fire and accident (or casualty) company in the U.S. which appears to lie within the range of $400m. and $1,000m. a year. Only the Royal Group of existing British companies falls within this range at present.

Certainly, the desire to reduce expense ratios by increasing the size of the American underwriting account was a powerful influence on the process of amalgamation in the 1950s and 1960s which led to the eventual dominance of the three composite groups, namely the Royal, General Accident and Commercial Union. Despite this there is evidence that the British companies have been less successful than their American counterparts in reducing costs although, owing to statistical inadequacies, the evidence should be interpreted 'with a pinch of salt'. In 1968 J. Plymen and S. Pullan presented a paper, to the annual conference of the Chartered Insurance Institute, on Insurance Profitability in which they attempted a comparison between the operating results of British and American companies, although a direct comparison may be misleading because of variations in the composition of their underwriting accounts. For a valid comparison it is necessary to compare the British companies' loss and expense ratios class by class with the U.S. averages, calculating for each company 'standard ratios' reflecting what the experience would have been if the average U.S. results had in fact been applied to that company's particular pattern of business. For the year 1965 the combined U.S. results of the 10 leading British composite companies were as follows:

Table 97

LOSS RATIOS AND EXPENSE RATIOS, 1965

	10 British Companies	*Standard Ratios*
	%	%
Loss Ratios	68·9	69·3
Expense Ratio	35·8	33·4
	104·7	102·7

Source: *The Policyholder,* 20 September, 1968, p. 1442.

Plymen and Pullan point out that the poorer performance of the British companies is attributable to higher expenses since the loss ratios are in fact slightly below the corresponding American figures. 'The cause of these higher expenses may well be the relatively small size (by U.S. standards) of most of the British companies' U.S. operations.'[7] Further, they show the changes in the expense ratios of the same British companies in respect of their world-wide operations in comparison with those for all U.S. stock companies between 1956 and 1966. While the U.S. companies have achieved a dramatic reduction in their expense ratios, particularly in the fire department, the British composites appear to have been much less successful in reducing expenses although, since these are global figures, an improved performance in the American market may have been somewhat marred by poorer results elsewhere. To sum up, while all insurers in the American market have been operating under

Table 98

AVERAGE EXPENSE RATIOS, 1956–1966

	10 U.K. composite companies		*U.S. Stock Companies*	
	Fire	*Accident*	*Fire*	*Accident*
	%	%	%	%
1956	45·7	36·8	45·7	33·4
1966	43·0	33·4	38·3	27·9
Reduction 1956–1966	2·7	3·4	7·4	5·5

Source: *The Policyholder,* 20 September, 1968, p. 1442.

severe handicaps, the American domestic companies have been more successful in adapting their marketing and operating policies to improve their performance. In countering this criticism British insurers would no doubt retort that, although in the eleven years between 1957 and 1967 underwriting losses amounted to the staggering figure of $300m., nevertheless their total earnings after allowing for investment income have amounted to $318m., a substantial proportion of which has been remitted home to the benefit of the U.K. balance of payments.

But it nevertheless remains doubtful whether in recent years their flow of income has been commensurate with the insurance industry's massive investment in the American market. More significantly there is evidence, although admittedly scanty, that the rate of return on capital employed in the 1960s has been well below 10 per cent even when true capital employed is defined as published capital and reserves plus estimated appreciation of investment portfolios.[8] From the point of view of the use of resources it may be asked whether it would not be better for the industry to cut its losses and either repatriate its capital, to the great benefit of the capital account of the balance of payments, or deploy it elsewhere in other overseas countries where future returns on capital appear to be more promising. Certainly, this has been the response of some companies for the Yorkshire and the Norwich Union decided to abandon their American operations in 1958 and 1963 respectively, while others limited the range of their activities by selling their subsidiaries or reinsuring their outstanding business with other American companies.

However, two points should be made about the feasibility of redeploying the capital funds in the domestic market. First, the immediate benefits to the balance of payments can easily be exaggerated, for a significant proportion of the industry's large holdings of U.S. securities represents prepaid premium income and claims outstanding, but not settled, and is therefore inseparable from the companies' underwriting operations. Secondly, the British insurance industry has deliberately pursued a policy of penetrating world markets in order to achieve greater stability in their profits, on the assumption that the factors determining profits in different countries are sufficiently independent so that it is possible to offset gains in one region against losses in another. If this is a valid justification for engaging in overseas operations, it follows that the alternative to remaining in the American market is to expand in other overseas markets. But, as we have already seen, the U.S. market provides 40 per cent of the general insurance overseas premiums of British companies and it is inconceivable that such a volume of business could be quickly replaced by expansion into other smaller overseas insurance markets. If the larger British companies were to attempt to withdraw from the American market, there would inevitably be a sharp fall in their total premium income with adverse effects on their efficiency and their expense ratios in particular so that it is hardly a policy to be seriously contemplated; but for the smaller companies it might be the most rational decision to take.

Given that the larger companies have little alternative but to remain in the American market, they will have to improve their competitive position if they are to earn a reasonable rate of return on their capital employed. This will only be achieved by the most vigorous and sustained efforts to reduce operating expenses further through, for example, increased mechanisation, but in addition certain deficiencies must be eradicated. First, particular attention will have to be given to the development of new and flexible marketing policies, especially direct selling to the public of personal insurance; for commercial risks, which require greater expertise in the measurement and assessment of risk, it will still be necessary to work through the agency system but, as we noted earlier, the companies will have to be more selective in their choice of agencies than some of them have been in the past. Secondly, it is imperative that they should obtain a stake in the life assurance market, for all the major competing American companies, which either own subsidiary life companies or have substantial holdings of their equity capital, have been marketing with great success package policies covering a variety of risks combined with life cover. It is obvious that the Commercial Union's successful bid for Northern and Employers' in 1968 was to some extent motivated by the fact that the latter had an interest in an American life company. However, even if British insurers succeed in eliminating their weaknesses, they will be hard pressed to make underwriting profitable, caught as they are between the Scylla of inflationary increases in claims and the Charybdis of regulation of rates by the state insurance commissioners; but at least they should be able to improve the return on capital employed and increase the contribution of their worldwide activities to Britain's invisible earnings.

NOTES

1 See *Britain's Invisible Earnings,* Report of Committee on Invisible Exports, p. 145.

2 In 1968 they were reduced to three by the merger between Commercial Union and Northern Employers.

3 These figures have been calculated from Spectators' Insurance Index.

4 Committee on Invisible Exports, op. cit., p. 147.

5 Committee on Invisible Exports, op. cit., pp. 147, 148.

6 *The Economist*, Insurance Supplement, July 1967, p. xv.

7 J. Plymen and S. Pullan, 'Insurance Profitability—Past, Present and Future', *Post Magazine and Insurance Monitor*, 3 October 1969, p. 1815.

8 The calculation of rates of return on capital employed is fraught with difficulties mainly because of the problem of valuing liabilities to arrive at net worth. Using various bases for calculating the rate of return for U.K. companies operating in the U.S.A. between 1959 and 1968 I arrived at an average figure for the whole period of between 5 and 7 per cent.

Chapter 17

PROSPECT AND RETROSPECT

'There are certain things and persons that look as if they could never die: things of such vigour and hardiness that they seem constituted for an interminable duration, a sort of immortality.'

Mary Russell Mitford

IF WE look back at the evolution of the British insurance industry over the centuries since its early origins, with true historical perspective, we must reach the verdict that it is a success story. The pioneers despite their inevitable mistakes gradually established the foundations for successful operations and in particular had the good sense to realise the vital importance of being able to meet their obligations even in times of catastrophic losses. It was this reputation for meeting large claims that above all else enabled the industry to achieve its international ascendancy and to ensure that London became the unchallenged centre of the world of insurance industry. Consequently, along with other financial institutions in the City of London, it has made, and is continuing to make, an important contribution to the nation's invisible earnings while at the same time it provides an essential service to domestic insurers.

Nevertheless, an honest and objective appraisal of its contemporary state suggests that its image is looking decidedly tarnished. During the decade which has just ended, while life business has continued its impressive and profitable growth, non-life business has been continually ailing. What is more, the position was worse at the end of the decade than at the beginning. In 1969 non-life underwriting inflicted heavier losses on insurance companies than ever before—even than in 1963 which, as we have already seen, was itself the worst year since the San Francisco earthquake.

The British Insurance Association has reported that its members' underwriting losses amounted to the staggering sum of £38·4 million on its world-wide operations; motor insurance alone contributed £39·7 million to this figure which was offset by a small profit of only £1·3 million on fire and accident business. Table 99 shows the results for the last three years .

While motor insurance has been unprofitable in almost all parts of the world, the major sources of the losses were the United Kingdom and the

U.S.A., for which the figures were £15·4 million and £14·5 million respectively. So far as this country is concerned a major factor has been the outbreak of fierce price competition which followed the breakdown of the tariff. In this sense the industry has contributed to its own difficulties but these have been intensified by the more intractable problem of accelerating inflation which has afflicted almost all the major industrial countries. However, the position is not uniformly gloomy for there is reason to believe that marine and aviation business has improved mainly as a result of rating increases. Since marine underwriting is written

Table 99

WORLD UNDERWRITING RESULTS 1967–69

	1967 Profit/Loss	*% of Premiums*	*1968 Profit/Loss*	*% of Premiums*	*1969 Profit/Loss*	*% of Premiums*
Fire and Accident	+13·1	+1·6	− 3·3	−0·3	+ 1·3	+0·1
Motor	marginal loss	—	− 9·6	−1·6	−39·7	−6·4
	+13·1	+1·0	−12·9	−0·8	−38·4	−2·3

Source: British Insurance Association.

on a three-year basis, we do not yet have the 1967 results. However, preliminary indications suggest that the delayed claims from 'Hurricane Betsy' have been digested and that the 1967 marine accounts will show a small profit. The aviation insurance market is expanding fast and in spite of the airlines' projected self-insurance scheme it has successfully coped with the problem of providing cover for the jumbo jets as they come into service.

Nevertheless, the overall condition of non-life business is very unhealthy and it is fortunate that B.I.A. members succeeded in earning £135 million from their short-term investments derived from fire, accident and marine business. It is only through the ability to fall back on the income from these reserves, which have been built up out of earlier periods of prosperity, that the companies have still managed to underwrite ever-increasing risks, such as jumbo jets, without being forced to raise fresh capital in most inauspicious circumstances. But the industry's condition is unstable. Without the prospect of medium-term viability the spectre of a future lack of capacity with all its consequences cannot be banished. The restoration of underwriting profitability is essential.

Before we consider possible remedies we have to diagnose the reasons for the decline in the fortunes of non-life business. While a variety of adverse factors have clearly coalesced to create an unfavourable environment, this would not necessarily have induced unprofitability, had the industry exhibited a greater ability to react to changing external circumstances. The insurance companies, like the commercial banks, the other major component of the London financial market, have to some extent been the victims of their own previous success which contributed so much to London's reputation as a financial centre. The respect with which they have been regarded, by the international financial community, has tended inevitably to breed complacency and conservatism. This would have been a threat to the industry's future at the best of times but the implications have been far more damaging for one reason above all else, namely the rapidity of technological change.

After centuries in which the conditions of underwriting have altered slowly and almost imperceptibly insurers have suddenly had to face a whole series of fundamental changes in the space of ten years or so, which have ranged from the launching of mammoth oil tankers to the more mundane consequences of the greater use of inflammable plastics in factories. It is suggested not that they have failed to respond to these challenges, but that they have been ill-equipped to respond quickly enough, either administratively or psychologically. Since at this point of time there is no reason to believe that the environment of the 1970s and 1980s will change more slowly, it is essential for the industry to learn from the errors of the 1960s, to make good the losses arising from those errors and to pursue policies which are sufficiently flexible to meet new challenges. Before considering in detail possible desirable measures for restoring the industry's health, it should be pointed out that many of them have already been discussed within the industry which is itself becoming increasingly conscious of the need for change.

Since in the previous chapters we have discussed at length the competitive situation and the performance of the industry, it would be superfluous to cover the same ground again. It will be recalled that we considered the performance of the life branch to be generally more satisfactory than that of the non-life branch and, not surprisingly, in the light of its persistent growth and high profitability the industry is less aware of the need for reform. Nevertheless there are weaknesses, of which the greatest are the defects in the competitive process and the speed of innovation, which are attributable in part to consumer ignorance and the working of the intermediary market. There is little doubt that if these defects were removed, the life branch would be more competitive, more efficient, and more capable of reaping the benefits which may well accrue from the swing to more selectivity in the provision of social security benefits by the state.

Since life assurance is a complicated product, it is difficult to take effective measures to reduce the existing discrepancies between the best and worst policies on offer at any time. As we have seen, the vast majority of life companies sell their policies through intermediaries, such as brokers and part-time agents, to whom they pay a commission. This is a thoroughly unsatisfactory system for the reason that the commission varies with the cost of premiums and with the type of policy. Furthermore, some companies pay less commission than others and a few, including those currently offering the most attractive policies, pay no commission at all. Given such a system, it would indeed be surprising if the individual policyholder, who approaches a broker or agent, were to receive objective and disinterested advice on such a technical subject.

It is tempting to reach the conclusion that the best and most beneficial solution for the policyholder would be the elimination of the commission payable to intermediaries. All insurers would then be in the position of the London Life and Equitable who market their products through their own staff and Press advertising. The objection to such a solution is that it would place the onus for comparing the merits and demerits of different policies on the individual policyholder who is ill-equipped for such a task. Even policyholders whose requirements are straightforward need expert advice from professionals who have an up-to-date knowledge of the bewildering variety of different products on the market. The important thing is that the remuneration of such advisers should be determined in such a way that they are given every incentive to provide the best disinterested advice for the client.

One possible solution would be for the broker to derive his income from two sources. First, the client could pay a small consultancy fee for professional advice and, secondly, the insurer could reimburse the broker according to a scale which would reflect the administrative costs incurred in preparing and processing the policy. Such a reform would go some way towards overcoming the problem of consumer ignorance but it would need to be reinforced by the work of such bodies as the Consumer Council and the Consumer's Association which could provide comprehensive comparative analyses of life insurance at frequent intervals. In a reformed market there would be scope both for selling directly to the customer and through the professional broker; but the part-time agent who is unable to provide the necessary expertise should be gradually eliminated. This is not a revolutionary suggestion for it has been accepted in the industry for some time that the introductory agent is paid excessively for his services.

Even if such measures enhance the consumers' ability to make meaningful comparisons between policies, it will be incumbent upon the insurers to be clear in their own minds about the nature of the various products which they are offering. In particular they need to emphasise that they are selling two separate categories of product, namely, life cover and investment expertise. 'These two things are tied together to form the life assurance policy—only because the life assurance tax relief makes it worth doing so. But the policyholder of tomorrow will increasingly demand that the prices of these two items should be shown separately in the bill.'[1] A move in this direction has already been made by some companies such as the Scottish Widows' with its 'Investor' policy. Under this scheme the investor's premiums are placed in a special fund on the principle of a unit trust with charges and deductions for life cover clearly indicated.

Finally, more market research should be undertaken into the needs of the policyholder in an era of rising prosperity. British insurers have been wise enough to appreciate that even with increased social security there is plenty of scope for profitable activity in the gap between the continuously rising floor of state provision and the continuously rising ceiling of what richer citizens want to spend privately or in groups. But they need to investigate more closely the emerging needs of policyholders in fields such as insurance against sickness, medical expenses and the resultant loss of earnings.

Provided that life insurers learn the major lessons from the recent experiences of the non-life branch, that adaptability and flexibility in response to the challenges of a changing economic and social environment are essential to ensure continued success, the prospect is encouraging. The figures published by the B.I.A. for 1969 show that life insurance premiums rose by 3 per cent overall, and a striking 17 per cent overseas, which is the highest rate of growth ever recorded. There is no reason why the next decade should not witness even more impressive results.

Non-life business presents a more intractable problem because unprofitability has been allowed to persist for so long that only far-reaching reforms will suffice. These are essential not only in the interests of policyholders and shareholders but of the community as a whole since insurance is a vital service. For too long the insurance industry has tended to regard its business as its own concern but nowadays it is rightly regarded as publicly accountable. If insurers fail to put their house in order, then inevitably the state will be forced to intervene more and more; and the unusual degree of freedom from official restriction which they enjoy, to the envy of the majority of their foreign counterparts, will be nothing more than a happy memory.

Earlier we noted that general insurers pursue a full cost pricing approach[2] whereby premiums are theoretically fixed in order to yield a surplus over and above claims, commission and expenses. The guiding principle for profitable operations should be to ensure that premium rates are always economic and that methods of rating, selling and administration are as scientific and efficient as possible. In recent years there have been manifest weaknesses in all three areas. Although there have been some improvements recently, premium rates in most branches of non-life insurance have not been determined in a way which is suited to mass-produced insurance. As we argued earlier,[3] accurate rate fixing is impossible unless adequate loss statistics for the whole industry are collected and made available to individual insurers. If this essential information is not available, insurers are inevitably tempted to charge just whatever rate produces an overall profit for each broad class of risk instead of attempting to discover what factors effect the size of particular risks.

The B.I.A. has commendably taken the initiative in improving statistics on the incidence and nature of claims in the motor business. For technical reasons its collection of data was initially confined to the largest companies but more and more of its members are being brought into the scheme. But the assembly of adequate loss statistics is only a preliminary step. They must be scientifically analysed and used for rate-fixing by the insurers, but there is little evidence that this has yet occurred. Otherwise it is difficult to explain why the motor underwriting results for the first year after the B.I.A. introduced its scheme should have been the worst ever recorded. As *The Economist* put it, 'the results were disastrous, not because marketing is a nonsense, nor because price competition is bad, but because the underwriting was all wrong'.[4] Nevertheless there is a prospect here of an improvement in the future; but in many other branches of non-life insurance not even this essential first step has been taken.

One of the strangest features of the British insurance industry is that, although it was a pioneer in the development of actuarial principles in life assurance, there has been a curious unwillingness to employ the same expertise in resolving rate-fixing problems in general insurance. There is an urgent need for a more scientific and theoretical approach. It is worth quoting *The Economist* at some length on this point:

'The latest motor insurance fiasco could have been avoided by proper thought and research in advance. What about those hurricanes in America which time and again have been used to justify bad American results, regular though their occurrence is, and even though the losses continue even when there are no hurricanes of note? Has anybody worked out at all scientifically the incidence of hurricanes and how much needs to be allowed for annually to meet costs over the long term? (To be fair, the catastrophe funds now set up by the Royal and the Commercial Union suggest that the first steps in this direction are being made.) And what about those rising injury awards, which are repeatedly throwing insurers' accident accounts into the red? Isn't it reasonable to assume that the rise will continue, and that further increases should be allowed for as premium rates are set? And what about that new and unexpected phenomenon, inflation? Can't this be allowed for too?'[5]

It would pay the British insurance industry to take a leaf out of the book of the only other foreign insurance industry which consistently earns foreign exchange, namely that of Switzerland, where it is not unknown for a company to employ whole departments of university graduates for the scientific calculation of risks.

In any consideration of the problem of rate-fixing the question inevitably arises as to whether investment income should be taken into account prior to the determination of the premiums or used afterwards as a useful means of keeping the business solvent despite underwriting losses. It can be argued that, since the prospect of earning interest on the funds is explicitly taken into account in determining life premiums, there is no obvious reason why the general insurers should not do the same. As we have observed[6] some insurance commissioners in the United States already have successfully demanded that income from investments, based upon unearned premium reserves for motor business, should be taken into account in rating calculations. The American Insurance Association has attempted to counter these demands by commissioning Arthur D. Little, Inc., to produce a report on the case for including investment income. The authors of the Report concluded that profit margins in American insurance were slimmer than in business generally and that there was no justification for any revision of the pricing mechanism which would lower them even further. Nevertheless, companies operating in some American states are still under pressure and have had to concede the point.

In order to solve this controversial problem it is convenient to distinguish between insurance funds, that is, unearned premiums and unexpired claims, and general funds. In our view there is little justification for taking the income from general funds into account in rate-fixing on the grounds that the companies concerned could continue to earn this income, even if they ceased underwriting completely and operated as investment trusts. Nevertheless, it can be argued that this income is relevant in assessing whether the overall rate of profit in the industry is reasonable or not. In this context it is important to distinguish between that portion of capital and reserves which is embodied in real assets used in the insurance business, and that portion which is retained in the form of financial assets. A reasonable rate of profit on general insurance may be defined as a normal rate of return on capital embodied in real assets plus a small margin to compensate for the relatively slight degree of risk and the few constraints on portfolio choice to which the investment managers of general funds are subject. Since income from the investment of insurance funds is an inevitable by-product of providing insurance services, it should in principle be taken into account.

But two points should be noted. The first is, that when allowance is made for delays in payments of outstanding balances by agents and others, the amount which can be considered as free for investment is considerably reduced. Secondly, this income is not relevant to the determination of relative rates for different classes and any attempt to allocate parts of it to given classes of business must be arbitrary and may well lead to undesirable forms of price discrimination. When these various considerations are taken into account, there is much to be said for continuing to calculate rates on the basis of the underwriting account alone; but to take account of the sums accruing from the investment of insurance funds by accepting underwriting profit margins a little lower than otherwise would be necessary if such income were not available.

Weaknesses in the selling and marketing of insurance also need attention. It has for long been accepted that selling expenses are unreasonably high and that there are absurdities in a system whereby large companies maintain branches all over the country and at the same time pay large commissions to agents who do little more than introduce business much of which would have accrued to one of the large companies in any case. Probably the greatest absurdity is that since commissions are determined on a cost-plus basis, brokers and others have every incentive to recommend the most expensive cover to the intending insurers. In recent years when insurers have been attempting to raise premiums to more economic levels, for example in fire insurance, they have watched with exasperation brokers earning higher commissions on these higher rates and, worse still, handing back part of these higher commissions to their customers. It is not surprising that several of the large companies have been exerting pressure in favour of reforming the methods for remunerating brokers and agents.

Two years ago the B.I.A. established a panel of experts from several insurance companies under the chairmanship of Mr. Eric Orbell of the Commercial Union to consider this problem. It is understood that in May 1969 the panel recommended privately that a system of net premiums should be adopted by the industry. Under this scheme, instead of the companies paying commission to the brokers who bring in the business, they would pay only a service charge based on the work which the broker actually performs. The client paying premiums of £1,000 or more would have the choice of a direct approach to the insurance company and paying a lower 'net of commission' premium, or of paying this net premium to the broker plus whatever fee the broker could persuade him to pay for his advice and other services. Rumours about the intention of the major insurance companies to eliminate the brokers became so widespread that the B.I.A. felt it necessary to issue a special announcement to the Press in June 1969 explaining that a majority of its members had decided to accept the recommendations of the Orbell panel merely as a basis for further discussion. It was emphasised that this move was intended to be no more than a first step in a dialogue which might lead to some review of the basis of remunerating intermediaries.

Since then, soothing noises have been made in the direction of the brokers including an acknowledgement of the importance of their role in the industry. It was also made clear that the proposals for net premiums did not apply to marine and life insurance nor to overseas business. But their fears were hardly set at rest when British Leyland and Tube Investments approached the Commercial Union directly for insurance cover and were granted it at a 'net of commission' premium. With the development of the practice whereby firms appoint their own insurance managers,[7] direct negotiations between the insured and the companies is likely to become more, rather than less, frequent. Given such pressures both from the insurers and their major customers, it is clear that the brokers will have to establish a new *modus vivendi* within the insurance market and that they have much to gain from taking part in discussions on possible reforms.

Whatever system emerges, it is essential that two conditions should be satisfied. First, remuneration should not simply be geared to the value of the premiums but to the value of the advisory services and the routine administrative work. Secondly, it should encourage the reduction of costs which are at present unduly inflated by unnecessary duplication of administrative work between insurance companies and brokers. If the latter were enabled to reduce their staffs substantially by moving from the conduct of large-scale clerical operations to the provision of highly skilled advice for their clients, there is every reason for believing that a switch to fees away from commissions would still provide them with a profitable livelihood.

On balance, the adoption of net premiums, at least for the larger risks, represents a move in the right direction towards a more rational system for remunerating intermediaries. The present tariff operated by the Fire Offices Committee would prevent members from quoting net rates but there is no reason, in principle, why it could not be modified to allow them to do so. No doubt the Monopolies Commission when it reports will have something to say on this question. It would, however, be difficult to extend the system to the smaller risk since there is such a variety of ways in which the companies acquire this category of business. But at the very least all intermediaries should be paid a sum which as far as possible reflects accurately the work actually undertaken for the insurer. For all but the very small policies it might be possible to adopt a system such as has been recommended for life insurance whereby the intermediary receives payment both from the insurer and the customer.

So far as the tariff system is concerned, reform is necessary because it has been found deficient in various respects, as we have already discussed.[8] First, and in particular, it has tended to make the rate structure rigid and inflexible; secondly, it has depressed rates below economic levels; thirdly, it has inhibited non-tariff companies from adopting more suitable rate structures; and, finally, it has discouraged individual tariff companies from initiating reforms and innovations independently. Even at its height the tariff system was never universally applied and its scope has in recent years been further reduced by the abandonment of the motor and household fire tariffs. But in view of its deficiencies we have to ask ourselves whether it should play any part in the determination of rates. The answer must surely be that *prima facie* it is not in the public interest that insurers should collectively fix rates save in the most exceptional circumstances. Any plea for exemption from this general rule should be justified by special application to the Monopolies Commission which in any case will shortly be reporting on the advantages and disadvantages of the major surviving tariff, that in fire insurance.

At first glance the severe losses experienced by motor insurers since the abandonment of the tariff would appear to provide useful ammunition for the advocates of the system. It is in the interests of nobody that general insurance should degenerate into violent price competition without regard to the underlying risks. Historically, this has usually led to insurers being driven out of business to the benefit of no one, least of all the consumers, and it was a recognition of this fact which provided the original stimulus for collective prevention of price wars. Since the abandonment of the motor tariff has clearly led to uneconomic price cutting, it could be argued that the correct policy would be to return to a less rigid form of collective tariff. But that would be a counsel of despair for, as we have already argued, the disastrous results of 1969 can be attributed mainly to inadequate and unscientific rate-fixing. Already there are signs that the insurers are taking vigorous action to remedy the situation and it is far too early to conclude that the only solution is a return to the old discredited system. Provided that some of the obvious deficiencies in insurers' business methods are remedied, there is no reason to believe that motor underwriting, especially in the light of the potential growth of the market, cannot once again be made profitable.

The fire tariff raises different issues. As we have noted, the Fire Offices Committee is already abandoning the household tariff as from the end of 1970. When due allowance is made for the differences in market conditions as compared with those existing in motor insurance prior to the collapse of the tariff, there do not appear to be strong reasons for expecting drastic price cutting. Whether the industrial and commercial fire tariff should also be dropped is a more open question. This sector of the market has certain distinctive features, including the size of risks and the difficulty of predicting the incidence of claims even if detailed statistics are readily available. In these circumstances it is only too easy for the less circumspect and reputable insurers consistently to undercut their more prudent rivals by taking the risk that they will not be faced with exceptional claims arising from catastrophic losses. Such is the nature of the market that initially they might have gamblers' luck and be able to survive for a considerable period before Nemesis overtook them. But in the meantime all insurers would have been prevented from building up reserves against catastrophic losses and the whole market seriously weakened. Consequently, there is a strong case for the retention of the tariff, suitably modified, for this class of risk and it will be surprising if the Monopolies Commission is not convinced of this.

Another major weakness is the size of the industry's administrative expenses which tend to be markedly higher than for the average American company.[9] This is partly attributable to the level of selling expenses which we have already suggested could be reduced in a variety of ways. But more needs to be done as two members of the industry, J. Plymen and S. Pullan, have argued in the highly critical paper presented to the 1968 Conference of the Chartered Insurance Institute to which we have already referred.[10] Their view, with which it is difficult to disagree, is that profitability can only be restored to the industry by a revolution in the principles of insurance management. 'Up till now it has been traditional to regard insurance as being quite different from other classes of business and consequently immune from the normal financial controls that are used throughout industry.'[11] Their basic point is that it is time that the industry applied modern techniques of scientific management and ceased to treat it as an arcane mystery which only insurance men can understand. *The Economist* has consistently over the years made a similar plea for a more genuine professional approach. 'But if professionalism is lacking where it is really needed, there is too much of a synthetic brand of it where it is not. The whole business of administering and selling insurance is permeated with mystique. Insurance know-how is too often a cover for an inability to cut free from a self-created web of routines and complications. Insurance is not as difficult as some insurance men think it is. This will be obvious to them when they can escape from the prison of their own procedures.'[12]

This is stringent criticism but it contains more than a kernel of truth. It is a curious paradox that in underwriting, the one branch of the industry which most requires a professional approach, it has been too amateurish. 'The new professionalism that is needed has two sides: to start regarding insurance as a business, to which normal commercial and managerial techniques are applicable and to stop regarding underwriting as a job for amateurs.'[13] In fairness it must be conceded that the companies have been paying increasing attention to these criticisms from inside and outside the industry and have overhauled their administrative practices and their organisational procedures.

Indeed, it would be wrong to paint a picture of a completely torpid and stagnating industry, for during the last fifteen years its structure has been radically altered as a result of the mergers which have occurred. Most of the leading dozen or so companies are the products of mergers between two or three companies which were separate entities in the middle 1950s and, although the benefits have not always been as great as anticipated, they have tried to streamline their organisations by closing branch offices and concentrating more of their work in their head offices. Furthermore, no one can fairly accuse them of being slow to recognise the opportunities offered by computers for the reduction of costs. The concrete results are already apparent in the reduction of the expense ratio of the nine leading composite offices from 38·5 per cent in 1960 to 35·2 per cent in 1969, although the process has slowed down in the last two years. Thus, the gravamen of the complaints against the industry is not that it has failed to adapt its organisational structure to meet the challenge of change but that it has failed to adapt it quickly enough.

Other examples of administrative shortcomings are to be found in manpower planning and recruitment and in the fostering of research. With regard to the former, insurers, because they found it so easy to engage intelligent staff in the inter-war period when conditions naturally encouraged people to put a premium on life-long security, have been lulled into a complacent attitude to the recruitment and retention of staff. It has been an industry in which traditionally the future general managers have entered at the bottom and with a blend of luck and skill, including a reputation for not making mistakes, have eventually emerged at the top. This policy has inevitably meant frustration for the unlucky ones. Nevertheless, in the inter-war period they tended to remain with their companies since there was a conspicuous lack of opportunities in other industries. But in the post-war period full employment and rising prosperity have meant increasing competition for able young men some of whom, seeing their prospects for promotion blocked, have 'voted with their feet' and resigned. This problem has recently become more serious with the rapid growth of the large firms of brokers which, given the relatively poor salary structure of the insurance companies, have found it all too easy to attract young insurance executives. The better companies have tried to meet this challenge of the erosion of talent by recruiting more university graduates, but have still run into difficulties because many graduates have been unwilling to endure the boredom of routine work while waiting for 'dead men's shoes'.

To be fair, other industries have encountered similar problems in their graduate training programmes but they have been intensified in insurance by the previously mentioned failure to modernise their pay structure. A new source of competition is the increasing tendency for industrial and commercial companies to appoint their own insurance managers. If the insurers and underwriters are to be able to negotiate as equals with these new breeds of professional brokers and insurance managers, they must develop personnel planning systems which will ensure that they have men with the expertise and ability to cope with this unfamiliar challenge. While the more enterprising are certainly alive to the problem, the industry as a whole has not yet proved sufficiently adaptable.

J. Plymen and S. Pullan have argued that the scope for profitable research in insurance is considerable and that the research and development budgets need to be greatly expanded.[14] They believe that there is need for investigation into a wide range of problems, particularly premium rating, claims statistics and proper estimation of reserves for unexpired risk, outstanding claims, and even incurred, but not reported, claims. They advocate the recruitment of an operational research team completely free from routine departmental responsibilities and available to try to solve such problems throughout the whole organisation. Once again it must be conceded that some companies have already become more alive to the benefits of research but the industry as a whole has been rather slow to respond.

Inevitably, it must appear to the reader that we have been regaling him with a long list of sins of omission committed by the industry. Evidence that this is not simply the outcome of a natural penchant for indulging in carping criticism may be adduced from the fact that the vast majority of these deficiencies were first brought to light by members of the industry itself. Nevertheless, it is a fact of life that the same criticisms emanating from outside rather than inside the industry are liable to cause more resentment and irritation among those against whom those criticisms are directed. But it is in the interests of the industry itself that it should examine these suggested reforms as objectively as possible, for in the last resort it is accountable not only to its shareholders and policyholders but to the community as a whole.

This brings us to the question of the best ways of safeguarding the public interest and in particular the role of the state which has been a recurring theme throughout this book. Despite our criticisms of the industry's performance it can be argued that the competitive pressures of the last fifteen years have produced a number of improvements judged from the standpoint of the public interest. First, insurers have become more conscious of the need to reduce costs in all branches of the business; for example, the industry has taken the initiative in establishing a motor repair research centre at Thatcham. Secondly, the need for better loss statistics and improved statistical analysis to detect, for example, loss trends is generally accepted and has been given concrete expression in the formation of the B.I.A.'s statistical bureau. Thirdly, all the large companies and many of the smaller ones have transferred many of their routine operations on to computers in order both to reduce costs and to improve the quality of the management tools at their disposal. Fourthly, the mergers of recent years should eventually benefit consumers through a reduction in costs although, as we have noted previously,[15] the effects have been slower to appear than had been hoped.

On the debit side, the most undesirable aspect has been the series of failures of new motor insurance companies during 1966 and 1967 when 11 companies were compulsorily wound up and 600,000 policyholders found themselves temporarily without cover. Another unwelcome development has been the influx of unqualified people who have foisted themselves on to a gullible public by using the title of insurance broker and obtained insurance cover from companies whose main attraction was the size of the commission and not the quality of the service offered to the clients.

The degree to which state intervention and control is held to be necessary largely depends on the extent to which competitive forces can be relied upon alone to ensure that premiums are fair and reasonable, that the industry is efficient, that profits offer a reasonable rate of return on capital employed after due allowance for risk, that there is adequate capacity to cover all risks and, finally, that the industry is progressive. Since a wide disparity of prices, such as exists in insurance, is a classic symptom of defective markets, we have to acknowledge that in recent years the impact of competitive forces has been somewhat blunted. However, if we are correct in our diagnosis that a major cause of this unsatisfactory situation has been consumer ignorance, reinforced by obvious deficiencies in the organisation and modes of operation in the intermediary market, the remedies which we have suggested should go some way towards ensuring a more competitive environment.

If this belief is justified, and if the B.I.A. can in future be relied upon to take such collective action as is necessary to improve the industry's performance, especially in the collection and analysis of statistics, the role of state supervision may be reasonably limited to that of protecting the public from unsound insurers. Until 1967 the Board of Trade was inadequately equipped for this task for, although for many years the insurance companies' annual accounts have had to include far more detailed information than was required of other companies, there were omissions which reduced the effectiveness of surveillance. But the provisions of the 1967 Act have plugged some gaps. For example, in the past it was impossible to check up on an individual company's reinsurance arrangements but now they can be scrutinised by the Board of Trade along with their investments. There still remains the problem of adequate identification of liabilities which is essential for deciding whether companies are complying with the more stringent minimum solvency requirements of the 1967 Act. For some years the Board of Trade has been investigating the possibility of developing a method of testing the adequacy of non-life insurance reserves, which could be shown to be more objective than the conventional methods, and which would take proper account of any special circumstances justifying standards for a particular portfolio of risks different from the general average. More recently the Board and representatives of the British insurance industry have been participating in a similar study which was initiated by the Organisation for Economic Co-operation and Development. The outcome has been the development of a method which has been tested on a limited scale for selected motor insurance companies in five Western European countries with reasonably encouraging results. If the Board of Trade can apply this method to the more detailed information about individual companies' transactions now available, and so take early action to prevent companies in danger of insolvency from continuing to sell policies, there is a good chance of preventing a recurrence of the disturbing crop of failures which occurred in the mid-1960s.

It still remains to be proved that reliance on statutory solvency requirements is a satisfactory method of supervision. If it is found wanting, it will be necessary to consider other alternatives. Two have been suggested. The first is that non-life insurers should be required to deposit with the Board of Trade securities which could be made available to meet the unsatisfied claims of policyholders in the event of an insurer's failure. The objection to this system is that it restricts companies operating on an international scale, as most British ones do, from transferring funds to wherever they may be required to meet an unexpected flood of claims. Thus, a scheme of compulsory deposits may impede the effective utilisation of reserves and increase the capital requirements of an international company.

The second scheme is the imposition of minimum rates for different classes of business to ensure that companies are prevented from selling policies at uneconomic premiums which are likely to lead to eventual failure. Variants of this method are commonly used in many foreign countries but, although they have succeeded in protecting policyholders more effectively than in the United Kingdom, they suffer from certain disadvantages. First, it is difficult to determine an adequate rate without erring so far on the side of caution, in order to allow for exceptional losses, that it becomes excessive. Secondly, there is the same objection to an officially imposed tariff structure as to a collectively agreed one, namely that it tends to be too rigid. Consequently, it inhibits innovation and by increasing the advantages possessed by well-established insurers lessens the competitive pressures on the less efficient members of the industry. In the United States there have been other undesirable consequences. Insurers' efforts to improve risk classification and reduce the tendency for good risks to subsidise the bad, combined with controls over premium levels, have produced their inevitable synthesis. The appropriate levels of premium for some risks are above the ceiling and the business is therefore unacceptable. Meanwhile competition for the better risks drives down rates to the limit of profitability and beyond.[16] Certainly, the experience of other countries suggests that more detailed forms of state intervention do not unambiguously promote the public interest.

There is, thus, much to be said for the policy of waiting to see how effectively the Board of Trade deploys the additional powers granted to it under the 1967 Act. But the industry should be under no illusion that this may well be its last chance to stave off the threat of greater state control. Meanwhile, it should take every possible step through the B.I.A. to reform its methods and to improve its image. It would be well advised to take the following advice of *The Economist* to heart, 'British insurers must be prepared to accept ever-increasing social responsibilities, to co-operate where this means lower working costs, or fairer rating, and to compete vigorously on price and service. The alternative is to degenerate into quasi-utilities like their American counterparts, regulated hand and foot.'[17]

In conclusion, the criticisms and strictures of this final chapter should not mislead us into an unjustifiable denigration of the industry's performance. Its achievements and successes in the 300 years since the Fire of

London cannot be gainsaid. Above all, through its reputation for probity and reliability, it has established for itself a unique position in the insurance markets of the world which it has managed to maintain in the face of many obstacles. If it has fallen below its own high standards in recent years, it can be said in its defence that it had the misfortune in its respectable middle-age to be faced with a totally unexpected acceleration in the pace of technical change. Provided that it can successfully blend a respect for its own traditions with a newly-found spirit of innovation, there is no reason to believe that it will not successfully meet the challenge which faces it.

NOTES

1 *The Economist*, Insurance Supplement, 1969, p. xiv.
2 Chapter 13, p. 262.
3 Chapter 14, p. 301.
4 *The Economist*, Insurance Supplement, 1970, p. xii.
5 Ibid.
6 Chapter 16, p. 340.
7 At the latest count the Association of Insurance Managers in Industry and Commerce had 400 members.
8 Chapter 13, p. 276.
9 See Chapter 16, p. 341.
10 Ibid.
11 Op. cit., p. 1444.
12 *The Economist*, Insurance Supplement, 1967, p. ix.
13 *The Economist*, Insurance Supplement, 1970, p. x.
14 Op. cit., p. 1452.
15 Chapter 11, p. 227.
16 For a full discussion see *The Economist*, Insurance Supplement, 1965, p. xv.
17 *The Economist*, Insurance Supplement, 1966, p. viii.

POSTSCRIPT ON THE LIQUIDATION OF THE VEHICLE AND GENERAL INSURANCE COMPANY

On March 1, 1971, while this book was at the final stage of proof reading, it was announced that the Vehicle and General Insurance Company was insolvent and had gone into liquidation with the exception of the two life offices in the group. This provided proof, if proof were needed, that all is still far from well with the motor insurance market for three reasons in particular. First, it was the largest motor insurer to become insolvent in the post-war period, leaving almost a million drivers without cover over night; secondly, it was a member of the British Insurance Association, unlike the other companies which have failed in recent years; thirdly, its failure occurred despite the strengthening of legislative control by the 1967 Companies Act.

On page 278 of this book attention was called to the suspicion that the breakdown of the motor tariff had led to a situation in which many insurers were attempting to market their products at uneconomic prices. Such a price war has inevitably claimed its sacrificial victim. While undoubtedly the managers of the Vehicle and General took unjustifiable risks in neglecting to build up adequate reserves, it is somewhat ironic that a company which had done a great deal to introduce a new approach to rate-fixing and to question the archaic practices of the tariff system should have been the first victim of the newly-found freedom exercised by the previous members of the tariff agreement. It will not have gone unnoticed that most of the survivors of the price war have decided to raise their rates by substantial amounts. In the short period the demise of the Vehicle and General has caused widespread inconvenience and anxiety for its policyholders but in the long period it may well prove to be the case that insurers as a whole, particularly those with good driving records, will have every reason to be grateful for the short-lived incursion of a brash innovator into the insurance market. There is at the moment a tendency to place excessive emphasis on the immediate consequences of the bankruptcy and to ignore the fact that, had the Vehicle and General never burst rudely upon the scene, the motor insurance market would be less flexible and sensitive to the needs of policyholders.

Not surprisingly, the collapse of a major company has raised once again the whole question of supervision and control. In the aftermath questions have inevitably been raised about the role of both the Department of Trade and Industry and the British Insurance Association. Earlier in the book we have noted that the Board of Trade had been criticised in the past for failing to act quickly enough when a company was known to be in difficulties. Since there was reason to believe that all was not well with the affairs of the Vehicle and General for a year before its collapse, the Department of Trade and Industry is still exposed to the same criticism. In its task of supervising the industry it suffers from the major disadvantages, first of not getting information about the danger of insolvency early enough and, secondly, of not having at hand a quick and ready formula for determining whether an insurer is solvent or not.

We have also suggested that one of the major tasks of the British Insurance Association should be to take such collective action as is necessary to improve the industry's performance and image. Unfortunately, in its anxiety to disabuse the public of any belief that policies issued by one of its members are guaranteed by fellow members, it at first gave the impression of being somewhat insensitive to the anxieties of the industry's customers. For it announced that, while the third-party liabilities of the Vehicle and General's policyholders would be met by the Motor Insurers' Bureau and injury to passengers covered by a Vehicle and General policy would be paid for by the other insurance company concerned only if responsibility for an accident was shared, in all other cases the unfortunate policyholder involved in an accident would have no more financial protection than an ordinary unsecured creditor.

However, the B.I.A. had second thoughts and, on March 24, 1971, it announced that it proposed to set up a special compensation fund to meet the liabilities of the Vehicle and General's policyholders who were suitably covered in respect of passengers. The Motor Insurers' Bureau will be given the responsibility of administering this fund. Undoubtedly, the major causes of this change of heart were, first, the fact that a Bill to make passenger as well as third party liability compulsory was almost through Parliament and, secondly, the realisation that the initial reaction of the B.I.A. has damaged its image.

But this step has not stilled all criticism for the question has been asked why the B.I.A. is not prepared to take over all the responsibilities of the Vehicle and General towards its policyholders. That body's answer appears to be that such a step would create a far-reaching precedent and reinforce the impression, which it is anxious to remove, that the policies of its members are guaranteed by one another. To the suggestion that the B.I.A. should set up a guarantee fund similar to that operated by Lloyd's, its answer is unambiguous. It is both undesirable in principle since this is not the function of a trade association and undesirable in practice since it is the Government which has the power and responsibility for keeping an eye on the solvency of insurance companies.

Such a response is most likely to satisfy the industry's critics and the demands for the establishment of a state motor insurance system will become more and more insistent. Moreover, such demands will become more and more difficult to resist unless, first, the Department of Trade and Industry can convincingly demonstrate that its new legislative powers are adequate for the effective discharge of its supervisory function and, secondly, the industry shows itself more willing to devise some form of adequate protection against failure.

BIBLIOGRAPHY

I *Books and Pamphlets*

Bailey, Francis, *Doctrines of Life Annuities*, 1813.

Balogh, T., *Studies in Financial Organisation*, N.I.E.S.R. (Cambridge U. Press) 1947.

Barbour, Violet, *Marine Risks and Insurance in the 17th Century*, Journal of Economics and Business History, Vol. I, 1928–9.

Best's *Insurance Guide* (published annually).

Beveridge, W. H., *Full Employment in a Free Society*, London (Allen & Unwin) 1944.

Blake, R., *Esto Perpetua*, The Norwich Union Life Assurance Society, 1808–1958.

Bretano, L., *History and Development of Gilds and the Origin of Trade Unions*, 1870.

Clayton, G., and Osborn, W. T., *Insurance Company Investment*, London (Allen & Unwin) 1965.

Cow, W., *Encyclopaedia Britannica*, 11th ed.

Deane, P., and Cole, N., *British Economic Growth, 1688–1959* (Cambridge U. Press) 2nd ed. 1967.

Defoe, Daniel, *Essays on Projects*, 1692—reprint 1887.

Dinsdale, W. A., *History of Accident Insurance in Great Britain* (Stone & Cox) 1954.

Dover, V., *A Handbook to Marine Insurance* (Witherby) 6th ed. 1962.

Eden, Sir Frederick, *Insurance Charters*, App. I.

Ellis, W. Arthur, *Economic Survey 1919–1939*, London (Allen & Unwin).

Fisher, H. A. L., *A History of Europe*, Vol. I (Fontana ed.).

Flinn, M. W., *Origins of Industrial Revolution*, London (Longmans) 1966.

Francis, E. V., *London and Lancashire History* (Newman Neame).

Francis, John, *Annals, Anecdotes and Legends: A Chronicle of Life Assurance*, 1853.

Gaius, *Roman Civil Law*, 1915 ed.

Garnett, R. G., *A Century of Co-operative Insurance*, London (Allen & Unwin) 1968.

George, M. Dorothy, *London Life in the XVIII Century*, London (Kegan Paul) 1925.

Gibb, D. E. W., *Lloyd's of London—A Study in Individualism*, London (Macmillan) 1957.

Gill, Conrad, *History of Birmingham*, Vol. I (Oxford U. Press) 1952.

Golding, C. E., *History of Reinsurance*, 2nd ed. (privately printed for the Sterling Offices Ltd) 1931.

Halley, Edmund, *Philosophical Transactions*, Vol. 17.

Hancock, W. K., and Gowing, M. M., *British War Economy*, London (H.M.S.O.) 1949.

Hatton, B., *New View of London*, 1708.

Hopkins, H., *The New Look: A Social History of the Forties and Fifties*, London (Secker & Warburg) 1963.

Institutes of Justinian, A.D. 533.

Johnston, J., and Murphy, G. W., *The Growth of Life Assurance in the U.K. since 1880*, Proceedings of the Manchester Statistical Soc., 1956–7.

King, Gregory, *On the Naval Trade of England*, 1688, reprinted 1936 (Johns Hopkins Press).

Lengyel, S. J., *Insurance Accounts: An Economic Interpretation and Analysis* (F. W. Cheshire, Ltd) 1947.

Lipton, M., *Assessing Economic Performance* (Staples Press) 1967.

Liveing, E., *A Century of Insurance: The Commercial Union Assurance Group, 1861–1961* (Witherby) 1962.

Marsden, R. G., *Select Pleas in the Court of the Admiralty, 1547–1602*, Selden Society Publications, Vol. II.

Marshall, J., *Law of Insurance*, 1842.

Martin, F., *A History of Lloyd's and Marine Insurance* (Macmillan) 1876.

Molloy, Charles, *De Jure Maritimo, 1676*, Quoted by Raynes, 1st ed.

Montgomerie, J. (Ed.) *Steven's Mercantile Law*, 13th ed.

Morgan, E. Victor, *The Stock Exchange*, London (Elek Books) 1962.

Mortimer, J., *Everyman his own Broker*, 13th ed.

Ogborn, M., *Equitable Assurances, The Story of Life Assurance in the Experience of the Equitable Life Assurance Society*, London (Allen & Unwin) 1962.

Pardessus, *Lois Maritimes*.

Park, J. A., *System of the Law of Marine Insurance*, 1842.

Pearson, Lester B., *et al.*, *Partners in Development, Report of the Commission on International Development*, London (Pall Mall Press) 1969.

Pirenne, H., *The Economic and Social History of Medieval Europe*, London (Kegan Paul) 1936.

Pollard, S., *The Development of the British Economy, 1914–1967*, 2nd ed. London (Arnold) 1969.

Postan, M. M., *An Economic History of Western Europe, 1945–64*, London (Methuen) 1967.

Price, Richard, *Observations on Reversionary Payments*, 3rd ed. (Cadell & Davies) 1812.

Raynes, H. E., *A History of British Insurance*, 1st ed. London (Pitman) 1948.

Raynes, H. E., *Principles of British Insurance*, London (Pitman) 1953.

Richmond, S. W., and Sherriff, F. H. (Eds.) *Pitman's Dictionary of Life Assurance*.

Robson, W. A. *Nationalised Industry and Public Ownership*, 2nd ed. London (Allen & Unwin) 1962.

Sayers, R. S., *Financial Policy (History of the Second World War 1939–45)* H.M.S.O., 1956.

Schooling, Sir William, *Alliance Assurance, 1824–1924*.

Tanner Manuscript Collection, No. 74–32, Oxford, Bodleian Library.

Thomson, Roland, *Richard Price, Philosopher and Apostle of Liberty*, 1924.

Thomson, William T., *Present Position of Life Assurance Interests of Great Britain* (Edinburgh) 1852.

Trenerry, C. F., *The Origins of Early History of Insurance* (P. S. King) 1926.

Walford, Cornelius, *The Insurance Cyclopaedia*, 5 vols (C. and E. Layton) 1873.

Wheeler, James, *Manchester, Its Political, Social and Commercial History*, 1836.

Wilson, Sir Arnold T., and Levy, H., *Workmen's Compensation*, London (Oxford U. Press) 1937.

Woods, E. A., *The Sociology of Life Insurance*, 1928.

Worswick, G. D. N., and Ady, P. M. (Eds.) *The British Economy, 1945–1950* (Chpt. by M. C. Kennedy on 'Monetary Policy'), Oxford (Clarendon Press) 1952.

Wright, C., and Fayle, C. E., *A History of Lloyds*, London (Macmillan) 1928.

Young, Michael, *The Future of Industrial Assurance: Labour's Proposals for National Ownership by the Policyholders*, Transport House, 1950.

Youngson, A. J., *Britain's Economic Growth, 1920–1966*, London (Allen & Unwin) 1967.

II *Articles*

Blease, J. G., 'Institutional Investors and the Stock Exchange', *District Bank Review*, September, 1964.

Brownlee, John, 'History of the Birth and Death Rates in England and Wales taken as a Whole from 1570 to the Present Time', *Public Health*, June and July, 1916.

Carter, R. L., 'The Insurance Practices of Local Authorities', *Local Government Chronicle*, August, 1965.

Cleirac, E., *Les Us et Coutumes de la Mer*, quoted by Hendricks in the *Journal of the Institute of Acturaries*, Vol. II.

Coppock, D. J., 'The Climacteric of the 1890s : A Critical Note', *Manchester School of Economic and Social Studies*, 1956 .

Gonner, E. C. K., 'Population of England in the 18th Century', *Journal of the Royal Statistical Society*, 1912–1913.

Godfrey, Ambrose, 'An account of the New Method of Extinguishing Fires by Explosion (1724)', quoted by P. G. M. Dickson, *The Sun Insurance Office, 1710–1960*, 1960.

Matthews, R. C. O., 'Why has Britain had Full Employment Since the War?', *Economic Journal*, Vol. LXXVIII, September, 1968.

Morgan, E. Victor, 'Personal Saving and the Capital Market', *District Bank Review*, September, 1967.

Noyes, A. F., 'British Insurance and World Economy', *Journal of Chartered Insurance Institute*, Vol. 50.

Plymen, J., and Pullen, S., 'Insurance Profitability: Past, Present and Future', *The Policyholder*, September, 1968.

Phelps, F. H., and Handfield-Jones, S. J., 'The Climacteric of the 1890s, A Study in the Expanding Economy', *Oxford Economic Papers*, 1952.

Temperley, H. W. V., Article in *Cambridge Modern History*, Vol. X, 1907.

III *Official Publications*

Beveridge Report, Social Insurance and Allied Services.
Central Statistical Office *(Annual Abstract of Statistics).*
Central Statistical Office *(National Income Blue Book).*
British Museum, 816m.
Industrialisation and Foreign Trade, League of Nations (1945).
Board of Inland Revenue Annual Reports.
Insurance Directory and Year Book.
Hansard, Vol. 15.
Life Insurance Fact Book, 1969 (Institute of Life Insurance).
Reports of Industrial Assurance Commissioner.
Reports of the Select Committee on Joint Stock Companies, 1841 .
Report of Committee on Invisible Exports, Britain's Invisible Earnings.
Statute Book, 50 George III.
Weekly Law Reports.

IV *Periodicals and Newspapers*

The Banker.
The Economist.
The Economist Insurance Supplement.
Insurance Mail.
Policyholder.
Post Magazine and Insurance Monitor.
Which
'Which' Supplement on Life Insurance.
Spectator's Insurance Index.

INDEX

T = Table on page indicated